THE OMBUDSMAN ENTERPRISE AND ADMINISTRATIVE JUSTICE

This important new book presents an overview of one of the key institutions of administrative justice: the ombudsman. It presents a well argued thesis based on a thorough review of the literature and some new empirical research concerning the changing role of, and future prospects for, ombudsmen. It makes excellent use of international comparisons with a particular emphasis on Commonwealth experience. It will be invaluable to academics and policy-makers working in the field whilst also being accessible to students.

Tom Mullen, University of Glasgow, UK

The Ombudsman Enterprise and Administrative Justice

TREVOR BUCK
De Montfort University, UK

RICHARD KIRKHAM
University of Sheffield, UK

BRIAN THOMPSON
University of Liverpool, UK

ASHGATE

Published by
Ashgate Publishing Limited
Wey Court East
Union Road
Farnham
Surrey, GU9 7PT
England

Ashgate Publishing Company
Suite 420
101 Cherry Street
Burlington
VT 05401-4405
USA

www.ashgate.com

British Library Cataloguing in Publication Data
Buck, Trevor, 1951-
The ombudsman enterprise and administrative justice.
1. Ombudspersons. 2. Complaints (Administrative procedure)
3. Administrative remedies.
I. Title II. Kirkham, Richard. III. Thompson, Brian, 1955-
352.8'8-dc22

ISBN-13: 9780754675563

Library of Congress Cataloging-in-Publication Data
Buck, Trevor, 1951-
The ombudsman enterprise and administrative justice / by Trevor Buck, Richard Kirkham and Brian Thompson.
p. cm.
Includes bibliographical references and index.
ISBN 978-0-7546-7556-3 (hardback) 1. Ombudspersons--Great Britain. I. Kirkham, Richard. II. Thompson, Brian, 1955- III. Title.

KD4900.B83 2010
352.8'80941--dc22

2010027679

ISBN 9780754675563 (hbk)
ISBN 9781409420156 (ebk)

MIX
Paper from responsible sources
FSC® C018575
FSC www.fsc.org

Printed and bound in Great Britain by the MPG Books Group, UK

Contents

List of Figures and Tables

Figures

Tables

List of Abbreviations

AJTC	Administrative Justice and Tribunals Council
ADR	Alternative Dispute Resolution
AOA	Asian Ombudsman Association
AONI	Assembly Ombudsman for Northern Ireland
ABCIFER	Association of British Civilian Internees Far East Region
ANZOA	Australian and New Zealand Ombudsman Association
BIOA	British and Irish Ombudsman Association
CQC	Care Quality Commission
CAROA	Caribbean Ombudsman Association
CTRL	Channel Tunnel Rail Link
CIPFA	Chartered Institute of Public Finance and Accountancy
CSA	Child Support Agency
CIC	Citizen Information Centre
CSCI	Commission for Social Care Inspection
CO	Commonwealth Ombudsman of Australia
DCA	Department for Constitutional Affairs
DWP	Department for Work and Pensions
ESRC	Economic and Social Research Council
EPA	Environmental Protection Agency
ECHR	European Convention on Human Rights
EU	European Union
FOS	Financial Ombudsman Service
FSO	Financial Services Ombudsman
FTT	First-tier Tribunal
FoCO	Forum of Canadian Ombudsmen
HSO	Health Service Ombudsman
HC	Healthcare Commission
HMRC	HM Revenue and Customs
HO	Housing Ombudsman
IDeA	Improvement and Development Agency
ICE	Independent Case Examiner
IPCC	Independent Police Complaints Commission
IOA	International Ombudsman Association
IOI	International Ombudsman Institute
LGO	Local Government Ombudsman
LCD	Lord Chancellor's Department
MOD	Ministry of Defence

NAO	National Audit Office
NPM	New Public Management
NSWO	New South Wales Ombudsman
NZO	New Zealand Ombudsman
NICC	Northern Ireland Commissioner for Complaints
NIO	Northern Ireland Ombudsman
NIPrO	Northern Ireland Prisoner Ombudsman
NTO	Northern Territory Ombudsman
Ofsted	Office of Standards in Education, Children's Services and Skills
ODPM	Office of the Deputy Prime Minister
OFMDFM	Office of the First Minister and Deputy First Minister
OBC	Ombudsman British Columbia
OPCAT	Optional Protocol to the Convention against Torture and other Cruel, Inhuman or Degrading Treatment or Punishment
OECD	Organisation for Economic Co-operation and Development
PHSO	Parliamentary and Health Service Ombudsman
PO	Parliamentary Ombudsman
PALS	Patient Advice and Liaison Services
PONI	Police Ombudsman for Northern Ireland
PPO	Prisons and Probation Ombudsman
PDR	Proportionate Dispute Resolution
PASC	Public Administration Select Committee
PSOW	Public Services Ombudsman for Wales
QMI	Queensland Mines Inspectorate
QO	Queensland Ombudsman
RRO	Regulatory Reform Order
SPSO	Scottish Public Services Ombudsman
SCC	Services Complaints Commissioner
SAO	Southern Australian Ombudsman
SORT	Special Ombudsman Response Team (Ontario)
TO	Tasmanian Ombudsman
TCEA	Tribunals, Courts and Enforcement Act 2007
UT	Upper Tribunal
VO	Victorian Ombudsman
WAO	Western Australian Ombudsman

Foreword

It is now over 40 years since Parliament agreed, with apprehension in some quarters, to the Wilson Government's modernising proposal to establish a Parliamentary Commissioner for Administration, as the Ombudsman was rather off-puttingly called. The apprehension centred on a belief that this new office was a dangerous constitutional departure, which threatened to subvert the traditional role of Parliament and its Members in the redress of grievances.

It was to allay fears of this kind that it was agreed that the services of the office could only be accessed through a Member of Parliament; and that the office itself would be anchored to Parliament through the oversight of a select committee. The former provision has so far survived all attempts to remove it, despite its obvious absurdity (as shown by the fact that it was not applied to the NHS role). The latter provision has proved to be more useful, and has helped to strengthen the effectiveness of the office.

It is only necessary to recall these origins to see at once how far the Ombudsman institution – or 'enterprise' as it is described here – has travelled. It is now ubiquitous, in all its various forms, around the world. Yet what is more interesting is the way in which it has come to be seen not as a singular constitutional and administrative innovation but as part of a network of accountability mechanisms that have developed in the modern democratic state. Far from subverting the constitution, it was in fact the harbinger of a whole array of watchdogs and scrutineers that together enlarge and deepen accountability.

It is the great merit of this book that this is the perspective adopted by the authors, which makes it a valuable contribution not just to Ombudsman studies but to this wider terrain. The Ombudsman is firmly situated within the larger arena of administrative justice, but also as a key ingredient of what the authors describe as the 'integrity branch of the constitution'.

I am sure this is the right approach, and enables much fruitful analysis both of developments around the world and of new thinking about administration, law and the constitution. In this way it admirably succeeds in its ambition to bring the Ombudsman – and Ombudsman studies – into the mainstream.

Tony Wright

Former Chair of the Public Administration Select Committee.
Currently Visiting Professor in Government and Public Policy, University College, London; and Professorial Fellow in Politics, Birkbeck College.

Preface

As a collective endeavour, the seeds of the idea for this book derived from a chance meeting at an academic conference in 2006, and was further inspired by a Nuffield Foundation sponsored seminar series on administrative justice. At the time of the meeting it was becoming clear that in their work a generation of ombudsmen in the UK and elsewhere were pursuing bolder strategies than their predecessors. This was a trend that we identified as requiring research. What we were also clear about was the need to locate any such study of the ombudsman community within developments in the wider administrative justice sector as a whole. Often academics have criticized governments in the past for the lack of rounded thinking, yet there has also been a tendency for academics to study the administrative system within institutional and disciplinary silos. It was this desire to establish a broader analysis of the ombudsman enterprise that led to the team approach in this project, which incorporated our respective expertise.

The core of the research was a series of interviews with leading ombudsmen (public and private sector) in the UK, Ireland, Australia and New Zealand, and we gratefully acknowledge the funding awarded by the Economic and Social Research Council (ESRC) (Thompson, Buck and Kirkham 2008: (Res-000-22-2133)). From the knowledge obtained we have presented and taken part in numerous presentations, lectures, seminars and discussion groups, which has included an engagement with the ombudsman community itself in an attempt to feedback our findings. Articles have been published jointly and individually. The authorship credit of this monograph is distributed Kirkham (50 per cent), Buck (35 per cent) and Thompson (15 per cent).

Fate does not respect publication schedules. Two significant developments occurred as we were correcting proofs in Autumn 2010. First, the Law Commission published a consultation paper, Public Services Ombudsmen (Law Com CP 197), which develops earlier proposals for the ombudsmen in England and Wales. Many of their proposals resonate with the arguments made in this monograph. But they generally represent a more modest housekeeping exercise than the wider 'Leggatt-type' review we propose (p. 232). One of their proposals goes further though than our defence of Bradley (216-19), that public authorities must provide satisfactory 'cogent reasons' in order to reject the findings of the ombudsman; it strikingly asserts that the Parliamentary Ombudsman's findings should be binding unless judicially overturned. We do not think that this is the right approach.

Second, there were leaks of the coalition government's intention to abolish the Administrative Justice and Tribunals Council. This proposal risks removing from the administrative justice system the capacity to provide an ongoing holistic overview of administrative justice and an approach that was sensitive to the complexities of devolution in this field. As some of our recommendations demonstrate, we are not against rationalisation, but whatever the outcome of the Coalition Government's programme of cuts we would strongly advise that some form of intellectual capacity is retained in the system to provide the holistic overview that we have argued for.

During the conduct of this research we have incurred a major debt of gratitude to all those who have happily given us their time, answered questions and follow-up questions, provided us with material and further contacts, and have been kind and thoughtful hosts to visitors. We thank everyone, in the list below, for their various contributions to our research endeavour.

Ann Abraham, Tawhida Ahmed, John Aquilina, Geoff Airo-Farulla, Simon Alston, Marie Anderson, Mark Aronson, Bruce Barbour, Jodi Berg, Bob Black, John Bourn, Ron Brent, Arlene Brock, George Brouwer, Alice Brown, Heather Brown, Tony Brown, David Bevan, Peter Cane, Suzanne Carman, Victoria Chico, Simon Cleary, Richard Collins, Eric Drake, Leo Donnelly, Chris Field, John Findlay, Tom Frawley, Peter Frost, Marcia Fry, Donal Galligan, Chris Gill, Matthew Groves, Carolyn Hirst, Fran Holbert, Paul Holloway, Susan Hudson, Rhoda James, Jeff King, Dimitrios Kyritsis, Quinell Kumalae, Chris Lambert, Trish Longdon, Paul Lynch, John MacQuarrie, Bill Magee, Zahida Manzoor, Fiona McLeod, John McMillan, David McGee, Diane McGiffen, Frank McGuinness, Dallas Mischkulnig, Derek Morgan, Colin Murphy, Simon Oakes, Nick O'Brien, Deirdre O'Donnell, Nuala O'Loan, Emily O'Reilly, Peter Patmore, Ian Pattison, Dennis Pearce, Adam Peat, Linda Pearson, Clare Petre, Tony Redmond, Carolyn Richards, Rafael Runco, Eve Samson, Anne Seex, Mary Seneviratne, Stephen Shaw, Lewis Shand Smith, Philippa Smith, Rick Snell, Bob Stensholt, Anita Stuhmcke, Georgia Symonds, John Taylor, Mark Taylor, Vivienne Thom, Phil Thomas, Peter Tyndall, Beverley Wakeham, Chris Wheeler, Pat Whelan, Nicola White, Jenny Whistler, Jerry White, Peter Wilkinson.

Richard Kirkham would like to thank the support and patience of his wife, Coralie, and two daughters who were born during the project. Trevor Buck would like to record his appreciation of the many ways his wife Barbara assisted him during the writing of this book.

Brian Thompson offers his views in this book in an individual capacity and not as a member of the Administrative Justice and Tribunals Council.

Trevor Buck
Richard Kirkham
Brian Thompson

PART I
Theory and Context

Chapter 1
The Ombudsman Enterprise: An Introduction

The Ombudsman Enterprise

In a relatively short space of time the ombudsman[1] has become one of the essential institutions that a constitution should possess. Few countries today operate without at least one ombudsman and the idea has also been experimented with at the global level within regional and international organizations (Reif 2004; French and Kirkham 2010). In some countries, such as the UK and Australia, the concept has been adopted wholeheartedly right across the public and private sector, with the result that for some forms of complaint the ombudsman has become the dispute resolution mechanism of first choice. This rapid evolution of the ombudsman enterprise means that the institution is deserving of reanalysis.

The use of the phrase 'ombudsman enterprise' in the title of our book is not accidental. Although the focus of this book is mainly the developing role and relationships of the UK ombudsman community, we also refer extensively to the ombudsmen bodies in other jurisdictions. According to the context of the discussion, therefore, the 'ombudsman enterprise' may refer to the UK situation or more broadly to the developing and active role of ombudsmen offices in other jurisdictions. In both cases, the word 'enterprise' reflects our general view that has arisen from this study – that the ombudsman community in the UK (and in some other jurisdictions) figures as a much more significant element in the delivery of public services and in our constitutional arrangements than has hitherto been recognized in academic literature. The word 'enterprise' has been used deliberatively to communicate this sense of a proactive approach adopted by ombudsman bodies, and that it is currently a 'work under construction'.[2] It is in this context that this book attempts to examine and analyse the ombudsman enterprise as constituted in the early twenty-first century.

---

1 There is some disagreement as to the correct term for the institution (Rowat 2007, 44-5). In different texts reference can be found to ombudsman, ombuds or ombudsperson. This book adopts the predominant term used in the UK, the ombudsman, which continues to be used despite a significant proportion of female British ombudsmen in recent years. The term ombudsman derives directly from Sweden where the first ombudsman was established, once described as 'the best known Scandinavian after Hammarskjold and Canute' (De Smith 1962, 9).

2 'Enterprise' is defined as 'a project or undertaking, especially a bold one' (*OED*).

Although this is a book about ombudsmen, it does not contain a detailed exposition of the various powers and remits of the various ombudsmen that exist in the UK or around the world.[3] Such detailed information can be found elsewhere in a number of commendable texts (Gregory and Giddings 2000; Seneviratne 2002; Kucsko-Stadlmayer 2008). Instead, what this book attempts is an analysis of the technique of ombudsmanry and an evaluation of its potential for growth. The prime reference point is the UK public sector ombudsman community, with the term 'ombudsman' being used to describe fully independent institutions only.[4] Yet the book is partially inspired and informed by developments in both the private sector and outside the UK, in particular in Australia, New Zealand and Ireland, where the ombudsmen operate within very similar legal systems to the UK (Thompson, Buck and Kirkham 2008). The hope is that because the book explores theory and methodology more than technical questions of jurisdiction, it should be useful to ombudsman communities around the world and across sectors.

An underlying argument of the book is that the ombudsman is now an established feature not just of systems of administrative and civil justice, but also of the constitution. In one respect, this is an uncontentious proposition. If the bigger constitutional picture is taken into account then the ombudsman is only one of a range of institutions that have been devised over the years to heighten the accountability of governments to their citizens and, latterly, private bodies to their customers. Where there is a difficulty, however, is in establishing the full strength of the ombudsman's constitutional worth. This difficulty is perhaps more pronounced in the UK than elsewhere, as administrative lawyers generally have struggled to convince the legal community of the importance of their work. Fortunately we have moved on from the 1930s when Lord Hewart, the Lord Chief Justice of England, described administrative law as 'continental jargon' (Hewart 1937, 96). Until recently, however, the subject remained the poor relation of the common law system and it was left to a relatively small cohort of academics to investigate the merits of dispute resolution procedures outside the courts.

The situation is much improved today, not least because there is now an assigned Administrative Court in England and Wales, and few would doubt the constitutional importance of judicial review. Yet amongst legal scholars there remains some division in understanding and appreciation of the role of the ombudsman institution within the wider 'administrative justice system'; the latter notion is itself a contested one (see Chapter 3). In much standard work on administrative law the predominant view of the ombudsman is that it represents an important variant form of dispute resolution. It is a lead example of what

3 Brief summaries can be found in Appendices 1-3.

4 For instance, full membership of the British and Irish Ombudsman Association (BIOA) is only open to those schemes that can demonstrate 'independence from those whom the Ombudsman has the power to investigate. The word "ombudsman" does not have to appear in the title of the scheme.' <http://www.bioa.org.uk/about.php> (accessed 16 February 2010).

has become termed 'alternative dispute resolution' (ADR), which in essence means dispute resolution outside of the courts. In private law too the work of the ombudsman has belatedly begun to gain recognition (James 1997; Gilad 2008), although probably not as much as is merited by the sheer volume of work carried out by the ombudsmen concerned. In political science and public administration circles there has also been much good work done on the ombudsman (Drewry 1997; Gregory and Giddings 2002). The work of a range of ombudsman advocates in the past, therefore, has been successful in raising awareness to the extent that dispute resolution is no longer considered solely in terms of judicial redress.

Although the ombudsman institution has received greater recognition in academic texts in recent years, there is still a tendency for it to appear as a marginal topic and an overwhelming sense that the ombudsman remains an institution inferior to the courts (Abraham 2008c, 541). Others are much more sceptical of the effectiveness of the institution. From the original inception of the ombudsman onwards, there have always been some who have not accepted the notion that a body, largely without enforcement powers, can effectively promote justice. Sceptics within the academic and professional legal communities tend to view with suspicion the inquisitorial method of the ombudsman, placing much greater faith in the more traditional adversarial safeguards adopted through the courts. Today the most vocal critics are dissatisfied users of the ombudsman service who congregate on the internet in organized discussion forums,[5] but in the past distinguished academics have also argued that the entire ombudsman enterprise is a distraction from where real reform should be introduced in the administrative justice system – the courts and the law (Mitchell 1965).

There are those, however, who have consistently presented a much more positive view of the institution. Thus the claim has been made separately that the ombudsman is 'the jurisprudential development' (Lewis 1993, 676) and 'the most valuable institution from the viewpoint of both citizen and bureaucrat that has evolved during' the twentieth century (Pearce 1993, 35). There have also been a considerable number of scholars who have devoted their energies to arguing the merits of the ombudsman institution (e.g. Caiden 1983; Rowat 1985). Others have chartered the extensive twentieth and twenty-first century move towards ever more

5 Take for instance the critique applied by the Local Government Ombudsman Watch organization. 'The objective of Local Government Ombudsman Watch is to motivate others into campaigning for the abolition of the LGO [local government ombudsman] or its replacement with a truly independent local government complaints commission, where no commissioner previously worked as a council Chief Executive Officer. One that doesn't bury complaints and maladministration for their friends and ex colleagues. For the first time, councils will have something to fear when citizens threaten to complain to the local government watchdog.' Available at: <http://www.ombudsmanwatch.org/> (accessed 8 March 2010). See also Local Government Ombudsman (LGO) Watcher [York Office], available at: <http://lgowatcher.blogspot.com/> (accessed 16 February 2010); and Public Service Ombudsman Watchers, available at: <http://www.psow.co.uk/> (accessed 16 February 2010).

sophisticated administrative justice systems composed of a variety of non-judicial modes of redress, including the ombudsman (e.g. Birkinshaw 2010; Mullen 2010). Meanwhile the ombudsmen themselves have worked hard to develop their own profile, as well as improve the ombudsman technique. Perhaps the best evidence of this process can be seen in the work of a series of regional and international ombudsman associations across the globe.[6]

In terms of the sheer number of ombudsman bodies now in operation and the workload that is currently undertaken by them, the argument appears to be moving in the direction of enhanced recognition for the institution. In the UK in 1993, when the British and Irish Ombudsman Association (BIOA) was first formed,[7] there were 14 voting members, three of whom were local government ombudsmen (LGOs). There were also 14 associate members, a category which included complaint-handling schemes, and 19 ordinary members. By 2010 the number had risen to 32 voting members (representing 28 member schemes). There is now also a corporate associate membership divided into the following categories: consumer and professional organizations (3); complaint-handling bodies – large (17); complaint-handling bodies – medium (9); complaint-handling bodies – small (14). There is also an individual associate membership (51).[8]

The expansion of ombudsman institutions has occurred both in the public and private sectors. These are, respectively, those concerned with the administration of government and the delivery of public services funded by the taxpayer, and those operating in the goods and services economy and funded by industry stakeholders (Brooker 2008, 3). Although, as stated above, the focus of attention in this book is the public sector, we agree with other commentators that drawing a categorical distinction between public and private sector ombudsmen is not a helpful approach, and ombudsmen themselves (e.g. O'Donnell 2007) emphasize the features of their offices which are shared rather than those which differ.

> It would be wrong to take too narrow a view of what constitutes the state. For example, the privatisation of a range of public utilities led to the establishment by Parliament of a range of regulatory bodies that may properly be regarded as emanations of the state. There are other regulatory bodies that have been established in such fields as charities, financial services or gambling to which the same applies. Furthermore, as more of central and local government business is

6 See for instance the work of the British and Irish Ombudsman Association (BIOA), the International Ombudsman Institute (IOI), the International Ombudsman Association (IOA), the Australian and New Zealand Ombudsman Association (ANZOA), the Forum of Canadian Ombudsmen (FoCO), the Caribbean Ombudsman Association (CAROA) and the Asian Ombudsman Association (AOA). All these associations maintain websites.

7 The association was initially called the United Kingdom Ombudsman Association but was later renamed to include ombudsmen from the Republic of Ireland in 1994.

8 We are grateful to Mr Ian Pattison (Secretary to BIOA) for supplying details about the membership of BIOA: personal communication 19 February 2010.

> privatised or contracted out to private agencies, a wider view must be taken of what constitutes administrative justice. (AJTC 2009, para. 14)

The expansion of private sector ombudsmen[9] in the past 30 years[10] has not, however, been uniform. Many markets attracting a high volume of complaints are not covered by an ombudsman scheme, for example, in house-building, home improvements, electrical appliances and second-hand cars (Doyle *et al* 2004). Nevertheless it is now recognized that within the genus of ombudsmen there are a variety of species ranging from the classic, statutory, public sector ombudsmen to non-statutory private ombudsmen, and '[b]etween the two ends of the spectrum there is a range of bodies dealing in different ways with complaints and disputes, either between citizen and state or between firms and individuals' (AJTC 2009, 16). Public law scholarship has also had to recognize that the traditional private/public divide is far less of a binary opposition than it used to be (Wade and Forsyth 2009, 566-81; Harlow and Rawlings 2009, 18-22). Moreover, including such private sector institutions within the landscape of administrative justice allows for a useful cross-fertilization of lessons from each sector to the other (Mullen 2009, para. 2.8). Consequently, in this book there are some references to the private sector ombudsmen, some of which, such as the Financial Ombudsman Service (FOS), regard themselves as part of the administrative justice system. In 2009-10, the FOS received 925,095 initial enquiries, resulting in 163,012 new cases, i.e. a caseload volume that is at least comparable to some of the regular work of the county courts (FOS 2010, 3).[11] In the administrative justice sector as well the impact of the ombudsmen is significant. Although the bulk of citizen complaints are processed by the Tribunals Service, the combined workload of the four leading ombudsmen in England and Wales – Parliamentary Ombudsman (PO), Health Services Ombudsman (HSO), Local Government Ombudsman (LGO) and Housing Ombudsman (HO) – amounted to at least three times the number of judicial review applications for permission in 2008-09.[12]

9 These include: Energy Supply Ombudsman, Ombudsman for Estate Agents, Financial Ombudsman Service, Housing Ombudsman Service, Legal Services Ombudsman, Pensions Ombudsman, Removals Industry Ombudsman Scheme, Surveyors' Ombudsman Service, Scottish Legal Services Ombudsman and Telecommunications Ombudsman.

10 The Insurance Ombudsman Bureau was founded in 1981.

11 For example, there were 46,519 'small claims' hearings in the county courts of England and Wales in 2008 (Ministry of Justice 2010, 72, Table 4.12).

12 In 2008-09 the Parliamentary Ombudsman's office received 6,749 complaints (in respect of the 'top five' government departments) (PHSO 2009, Fig. 12); the Health Services Ombudsman received 6,780 (PHSO 2009, Fig. 13); the Local Government Ombudsman received 8,163 complaints forwarded to an investigative team (LGO 2009, Table 1); the Housing Ombudsman dealt with 3,870 complaints (Housing Ombudsman 2009, 66). The figures given above are for formal complaints registered with each ombudsman service. The figues for enquiries received are much larger, for example, the Parliamentary Ombudsman received 16,317 enquiries in 2008-09; 49.3 per cent by telephone, 35.7 per cent written

Numbers alone, of course, cannot tell the whole story, but a similar pattern emerges from elsewhere in the world. In Australia, as in the UK, by far the largest contributor to the provision of administrative justice is the tribunal system. However, due to the wider remits often given to the ombudsmen there, the difference between the workload of the ombudsmen and the courts is even starker than in the UK. Meanwhile, the International Ombudsman Institute (IOI) currently records that ombudsmen operate in approximately 120 countries, with the growth in ombudsmen increasing exponentially over the last 50 years, and the last two decades in particular.[13] One leading authority on the ombudsman institution has written of the global take-up of the ombudsman idea:

> In every continent and from all shades of political opinion there are calls for an increasingly prominent role for the ombudsman and for it to be established where it does not yet exist. Both developed and developing countries have embraced the concept regardless of varying levels of socio-economic developments. (Ayeni 2000, 6)

Evidently, this growing faith in the utility of the institution of the ombudsman can be interpreted in a number of different ways. One factor behind this trend has been the move to cheaper forms of dispute resolution than the traditional court format, loaded as it is with procedural rigidity and expensive lawyers. Yet although cost-effectiveness, expedition and accessibility have been factors in the adoption of alternative redress schemes, it should not be concluded that the ombudsman institution is a form of 'cheap justice'. In many instances the claim can be made that the ombudsman can and does provide better justice than other more formal dispute resolution fora. Moreover, as was heralded in a recent UK government White Paper, the idea of 'Proportionate Dispute Resolution' (PDR), or 'fitting the forum to the fuss',[14] is a legitimate goal to pursue. In the public law context, there is also an underlying suspicion that the inquisitorial and principled methodology of the ombudsman is actually much better suited to adjudicating on disputes in the complex world of administration than the individualistic adversarial rights-based focus of the courts and the law (Verkuil 1975).

---

and 15.0 per cent by email (PHSO 2009: 2, Figure 1). A total of 7,169 applications for permission to apply for judicial review were received in the Administrative Court in 2008 (Ministry of Justice 2010, 16).

13 'By mid-1983, there were only about twenty-one countries with ombudsman offices at the national level and about six other countries with ombudsman offices at the provincial/state or regional levels.' (International Ombudsman Institute website. Available at: <http://www.law.ualberta.ca/centres/ioi/About-the-I.O.I./History-and-Development.php> (accessed 19 February 2010).

14 This evocative phrase was first used in Sander and Goldberg (1994) and often appears in the literature on ADR.

Whatever the true driving force behind the development of ombudsman regimes, the sheer scale of the impact of the ombudsman institution around the world rests uncomfortably with the relative neglect of the institution in mainstream legal and constitutional writing to date. Some ombudsman scholars, however, have long observed a general international acceptance of the role of ombudsmen in securing good governance (Reif 2004). The establishment of good governance clearly requires the adoption and balance of a range of institutions; the ombudsman model is often utilized because it is sufficiently flexible to find an appropriate location within the desired institutional matrix. The review of complaints about the quality of administrative practice represents the core of the ombudsman model, but in many countries the ombudsman has a much wider mandate, such as considering freedom of information disputes and corruption complaints. Even in the area of human rights, traditionally seen in many countries as a paradigm case for court-based adjudication, there are calls for the ombudsman to play a bigger part (O'Reilly 2007) – a call which reflects developments already taking place elsewhere in the ombudsman world.

In this context, a principal aim of this book is to place the ombudsman enterprise firmly within the overall constitutional map and to understand the institution as a core accountability institution. Another aim is to examine the relationships between the work of the ombudsman and other agents in the administrative justice system. In the UK, the current ability of the administrative justice system to work harmoniously and rationally in the delivery of administrative justice is hampered by its complexity and is a topic that has recently received renewed attention (e.g. PASC 2000; PASC 2003; NAO 2005; Crerar 2007). One part of that system, the tribunal service, is currently undergoing a process of reform instigated initially by the Leggatt Review (Leggatt 2001) and facilitated by the Tribunals, Courts and Enforcement Act 2007. As with the tribunals system, the remainder of the administrative justice system has developed on a largely *ad hoc* basis, with only infrequent attention given to the coordination and overview of the system as a whole. As we shall see (Chapter 3), the ombudsman sector too is not immune from criticisms of unnecessary complexity and overlap.

This book begins from the premise that, once it is understood that the ombudsman enterprise is a mainstream and central element within the administrative justice system and the constitution, there is a need to evaluate the role that the ombudsman enterprise can and does perform and the manner in which this role has evolved. This is the task which we have set ourselves in this book and it is delivered through both a theoretical analysis of the work of the ombudsmen and a review of the current techniques that the ombudsmen employ in the performance of their various functions.

Background and Context

The history of the ombudsman has been well chartered elsewhere (e.g. Seneviratne 2002, 31-8). It is sufficient to note here that although versions of the ombudsman technique can be found to have been in operation many centuries before now, the modern reincarnation of the idea is almost universally understood to be the Swedish *Justitieombudsman* (see generally, Anderman 1962), with thereafter the idea spreading first to other Nordic countries and then, from its initial appearance in New Zealand in 1962,[15] around the rest of the world.

The UK's first ombudsman was the Parliamentary Commissioner for Administration, established in 1967.[16] In keeping with developments that led to the introduction of ombudsmen around the rest of the world, the ombudsman idea was adopted following recognition of the shortcomings and lack of coverage of existing systems of redress and justice. In Eastern Europe, Spain, Portugal and much of South America and parts of Africa, for example, the shortcoming identified was the profound lack of respect for human rights. Largely for historical reasons, it was determined that the courts alone could not be relied upon to improve conditions in this area and a new institution was required to strengthen the existing legal order. In much of the remainder of Europe, the reason for the adoption of the ombudsman institution has been more prosaic and has been linked to the growth of the administrative sector (Heede 2000). Large-scale bureaucracies created new opportunities for both arbitrary and incompetent exercise of power and, as a consequence, a growth in citizen complaints against the various emanations of the state. The general conclusion in most countries has been that the complex challenges posed by the nature of modern relations between citizens and public bodies are not ones that can be easily overseen by the courts alone. This discovery has led to the search for alternative means by which disputes can be resolved.

The UK provides a typical example of this trend towards mainstreaming the ombudsman enterprise. The postwar period witnessed a steadily declining deference to the traditional Diceyan vision of the constitutional order (King 2007, ch.4) and a growing recognition of gaps in the system of redress then available for citizens by which they could pursue grievances against state administration. Although the ombudsman idea was originally resisted, by the mid-1960s a new government entered the scene with a manifesto promise to introduce a new form of dispute resolution, the ombudsman, specifically designed to address the shortfall in public law redress.

15 Special mention should also be given to the influence of the Danish ombudsman in spreading the idea following the incorporation of this institution in the Danish constitution in 1953; the first *ombudsmand* (the Danish term), Professor Stephan Hurwitz, was elected on 29 March 1955. West Germany was the first country to adopt the ombudsman outside the Nordic countries when it introduced an ombudsman for military affairs in 1954.

16 Parliamentary Commissioner Act 1967 (c. 13). For some years the title 'Parliamentary Ombudsman' has been used in almost all formal references to the office, including the publications of the House of Commons Public Administration Select Committee. Since 2004 the office has branded itself as the Parliamentary and Health Service Ombudsman out of recognition that the same person has always held both posts.

In the years since the introduction of the ombudsman concept to the UK the hopes originally invested in the idea have not always been met. But what is clearer today is that there is a significant area within the overall system of justice which the ombudsman institution is well equipped to fill. A succession of governments have invested in the ombudsman idea, even if there have been occasional proposals to curtail certain features of the ombudsman scheme in the UK.[17] This official faith in the ombudsman enterprise reflects a general trend towards finding ways to rationalize and focus the courts' role in the resolution of disputes. Over the last ten to 15 years there have been a number of developments that have demonstrated this tendency, with various reviews undertaken, proposals drawn up and reforms introduced. Thus in the UK, amongst other developments, there has been John Major's much heralded *Citizen's Charter* (Prime Minister 1991), Lord Woolf's influential *Access to Justice* report (LCD 1996), the less successful Cabinet Office *Review of Public Sector Ombudsmen in England* (Collcutt and Hourihan 2000), the Bowman Review of the Crown Office List (LCD 2000), the Leggatt Review of tribunals *Tribunals for Users – One System, One Service* (Leggatt 2001), the government's radical White Paper *Transforming Public Service: Complaints Redress and Tribunals* (DCA 2004) and the transformation of the Council on Tribunals into the Administrative Justice and Tribunals Council (AJTC) under the Tribunals, Courts and Enforcement Act 2007. Reform in this area continues with a number of legislative developments in the ombudsman field in recent years[18] and further changes to complaint-handling arrangements being recommended in other reports, such as *The Independent Review of Regulation, Audit, Inspection and Complaints Handling of Public Services in Scotland* (Crerar 2007). Recently, the Law Commission has added more ideas to the melting pot with the publication of a series of papers on administrative redress (Law Commission 2008; 2010).

Meanwhile, as already alluded to, alongside the courts, tribunals and ombudsmen a plethora of complaints systems have developed, in particular different forms of *internal* complaints procedures and quasi-autonomous complaint handlers. The result is a much more sophisticated administrative justice system today than there has ever been, one which loosely brings together the different channels of citizen redress. The UK is not alone in this trend towards establishing more diverse routes by which individuals can gain redress from public authorities where necessary. Nor have radical developments been confined to the ombudsman sector. For instance,

17 For example, a report by Sir Geoffrey Chipperfield in (DoE 1995) recommended the abolition of the Local Government Ombudsman, on the basis that it would not be able to handle effectively the increasing volume of local government complaints. The report recommended that all stages of a complaint, including external review, should be carried out locally, but it was not implemented by the government (*Hansard*, House of Commons, Written Answers, Mr Curry MP (12 February 1996), cols 402-3).

18 For example, changes introduced by the Employment Equality (Age) Regulations 2006/1031, the Regulatory Reform (Collaboration etc. between Ombudsmen) Order 2007/1889 and the Local Government and Public Involvement in Health Act 2007 (c. 28).

Australia's administrative law reforms in the 1970s have had a long-lasting effect and in some respects have gone further than equivalent developments in the UK (Creyke 2010).

Yet although current arrangements for administrative justice provide extensive opportunities for citizens to obtain redress, it is a system understood in full by very few people. As the National Audit Office (NAO) described, 'public sector redress systems have developed piecemeal over many years and in the past they have rarely been systematically thought about as a whole' (NAO 2005, 7). The administrative justice system is also one which, subject to a few notable exceptions (e.g. Harris and Partington 1999; Adler 2010), remains under-researched within academic literature.

Models of Ombudsman

Much has been written on the ombudsman institution in the past. Of the more recent publications there have been detailed comparative studies of the ombudsman across the globe (Gregory and Giddings 2002), in Europe (Heede 2000; Kucsko-Stadlmayer 2008), the Caribbean (Ayeni *et al* 2000); of ombudsman and ombudsman-like institutions with a human rights dimension in both national and international systems (Ayeni *et al* 2000; Reif 2004) and several country-specific (Seniveratne 2002; Hyson 2009) and sector-specific studies (Groves 2002; Gilad 2008). In amongst this research attempts have been made to describe the basic features of the ombudsman (Gottehrer and Hostina 1998) and measure the impact of the institution of the ombudsman (Passemiers *et al* 2009). Perhaps the most significant exposition of the potential power of the ombudsman institution and its place in the administrative justice system comes from Carol Harlow and Richard Rawlings (Harlow 1978; Harlow and Rawlings 1997). They have argued that ombudsmen should make more of their capacity to identify systemic failures within government, a function which they describe as 'fire-watching', rather than the 'fire-fighting' role in which disputes are resolved and redress provided (Harlow and Rawlings 2009). An updated model of this analysis is claimed by Rick Snell, who has identified an audit and inspection role as a key part of the modern ombudsman's arsenal, which in tribute to Harlow and Rawlings he labels as 'fire prevention' (Snell 2007). Anita Stuhmcke has also identified the trend towards audit and inspection in the ombudsman enterprise as a powerful development and adopts the pursuit of 'integrity' as the key thread running through the ombudsman's work and the measure by which it should be assessed (Stuhmcke 2008a). Others have argued powerfully that whatever the exact make-up of the ombudsman, their most important objective should be the promotion of human rights (Ayeni *et al* 2000; Hossain *et al* 2000). This latter point has increasingly been stressed in the speeches of ombudsmen from around the world (e.g. Rautio 2002).

A preliminary point to make about all previous work on the ombudsman is that no one claims that there is one model of ombudsman. Indeed, what is apparent from a global perspective is that a key feature of the ombudsman technique is its flexibility and adaptability to new circumstances. This single factor alone helps to explain the rapid growth of the ombudsman institution around the world over the last 50 years. The ability of the ombudsman institution to operate comfortably in a range of different legal regimes, and perform the very different roles and functions that it has been used to deliver, also lies behind the success of the institution. More than one ombudsman scholar in the past has provided considerable evidence of the chameleon-like tendency of the ombudsman by identifying a series of different models of ombudsman (Heede 2000; Reif 2004; Kucsko-Stadlmayer 2008). As might be expected, such diversity in models adopted often reflects the particular issues that underpinned their original introduction. It would be a mistake, however, to understand all ombudsman schemes as neatly fitting into any standard fixed and predictable model of ombudsmanry. Indeed, as will be demonstrated in this book, the dominant model of ombudsman that has been used in the common law world has tended to retain a high degree of versatility in the way it operates.

Public sector ombudsmen ordinarily derive their authority directly from statute, hence it might be supposed that the specific roles of the institution could be clearly ascertained and modes of operation fixed by legislation. Such a conclusion, however, ignores firstly the continuous evolution of many of the ombudsman schemes since they were first established and, secondly, the high degree of residual discretion which is retained within ombudsman schemes. Two examples of these points, which will be returned to throughout this book, are the New South Wales Ombudsman (NSWO) in Australia and the PO in the UK.

The NSWO was introduced in 1975[19] with the power to investigate complaints about certain public sector authorities. Since then it has been given a range of additional responsibilities, for example child protection, community services and police complaints. It is currently organized into four divisions:

- a police division for overseeing police complaints and reviewing certain legislation giving police officers new powers;
- a general division including reviewing legislative compliance and handling inquiries and complaints about a wide range of public sector agencies;
- a child protection division that handles notifications from organizations providing children's services about the conduct of their staff and related investigations;
- a community services division responsible for reviewing the delivery of community services.

A common theme with these additional responsibilities is that they have significantly extended both the jurisdiction and the expectations of the office of the NSWO.

By contrast, the legislative amendments to the jurisdiction of the PO have tended to be technical in nature and retain the same basic understanding of the

19 Established under the Ombudsman Act 1974 (NSW).

role of the office as outlined in the Parliamentary Commissioner Act 1967. Yet this stability in legislative design does not necessarily imply a more conservative model of ombudsmanry because, in saying so little on the role that the ombudsman is supposed to perform, the brevity of the 1967 Act confers considerable discretionary flexibility on the office-holder to direct the office in the manner that he or she thinks fit (Kirkham 2007, 6). Therefore, although the 1967 Act says nothing about the importance of the ombudsman promoting 'good administration'[20] for instance, since the Act was passed it has been understood that this is an important function which the ombudsman should fulfil. Even the mode of operation employed by the ombudsman during the course of an investigation is only restricted by the 1967 Act up to a point, once more leaving each individual office-holder with considerable latitude to employ a range of different strategies in performing the ombudsman's various roles. The evolution and change in these strategies from office-holder to office-holder has been a feature of more than one ombudsman scheme (e.g. Snell 2007).

One area of unanimity amongst ombudsman scholars is that it would be mistaken to conceive of the ombudsman as an institution with a limited remit only of real concern to administrative lawyers interested in dispute resolution. The practice of the ombudsman enterprise around the world speaks of a much more active institution capable of providing a constitutional service in the upholding of integrity in governance and administrative justice in a number of different ways. Further, although the emphasis on 'redress' (resolving disputes) and 'control' (promoting good administration) that has in the past been the dominant form of analysis employed to describe the work of the ombudsman is largely retained in this book, additional tangential aspects of the ombudsman's work need also to be highlighted, such as training and oversight.

A final preliminary point is worth making. If there are quasi-definitive common elements of the office they are the adoption of certain key institutional features, in particular independence and strong investigatory powers (Gottehrer and Hostina 1998). As will be argued, these features are integral to the ongoing effort to legitimate the authority of the ombudsman institution. Alongside these features, an almost universal attribute of the office is the overall difference in the ethos of dispute resolution that comes with the ombudsman technique when compared to the standard legal technique. Above all:

> The consensual resolution of public interest disputes requires a recognition by all major private and public interests that the best chance of achieving their individual objectives will occur through the enhancement rather than at the expense of apparently competing interests. This is a building process, not a destructive one. (Owen 1990, 683)

20 See further, Chapter 5.

It is this difference between the rules-based and predominantly adversarial approach of the courts and the equitable and inquisitorial method of the ombudsman that provides a real choice for complainants and different possibilities for all-round benefits to be secured from the process of dispute resolution.

The Ombudsman as a Constitutional Misfit

It can be claimed that the ombudsman provides an almost unique array of services. One of the arguments of this book though is that despite this impressive capacity the ombudsman model has never been properly understood in *constitutional* terms. This claim links to a broader critique of traditional constitutional theory and its obsessive focus on an outdated model of separation of powers.

A major problem in conceptualizing the role of the ombudsman in constitutional terms is that the dominant constitutional theories do not explicitly refer to such an institution (McMillan 2005, 11-13; Snell 2007). In describing the foundations of the liberal democratic constitution, most standard analyses still rely upon a separation of powers model within which power is distributed around the executive, the legislature and the judiciary. The British parliamentary version of the constitution is less easy to fit into this model but, through the twin constitutional principles of Parliamentary supremacy and the Rule of Law, achieves much the same result (Vile 1967). In other words, an executive is established under the direct supervision of Parliament and is required to operate within the law, as interpreted and applied by the courts. Crucially, both the standard separation of powers model of the constitution and the British variant satisfy key public law demands of a liberal democratic constitution. Thus these models establish a legitimate and workable basis for the exercise of public power, while facilitating democratic oversight and a legally defined system of control which allows for the redress of individual grievances. The analytical focus of these various constitutional models tends to be on maximizing the input of either the judicial or democratic branch of the constitution in considering the capacity of the constitutional system to control the work of the executive. This is perhaps unsurprising given the pivotal status granted to Parliament and the courts.

This book does not seek to challenge the basic wisdom that the executive government, Parliament and the courts should operate at the core of the liberal democratic constitution. Nevertheless, in advocating the constitutional role of the ombudsman the aim here is to avoid some of the weaknesses that derive from following a too rigid adherence to orthodox versions of the separation of powers theory derived from eighteenth-century theorizing of the likes of Baron Charles de Montesquieu (Cohler *et al* 1989) and Alexander Hamilton (Goldman 2008). As more than one eminent work has recently demonstrated, the dynamics of a twenty-first century system of government have called into question both the practicality and underlying coherence of the separation of powers doctrine (e.g. Vibert 2007; Carolan 2009). One difficulty that modern writers have to deal with is the mass growth in administrative bureaucracy that occurred throughout the twentieth century (Carolan, 2009); a more particular development is the steady introduction of a whole variety of autonomous regulatory, audit, inspectoral and other unelected professional bodies designed to call the exercise of public power to account (e.g. Gay and Winetrobe 2003; Vibert 2007; Harlow and Rawlings 2009).

When evaluating the continuing usefulness of the tripartite model of the constitution the ombudsman makes an interesting case study. The ombudsman is a form of unelected accountability institution, the existence of which has evolved into an increasingly permanent arrangement. Yet this permanence is not easily accounted for by the traditional tripartite constitutional design which leaves very little room for serious consideration of unelected accountability institutions, other than at an inferior level or as a subset of one of the three core branches of the state. This insight does not necessarily make separation of powers theories redundant, as unelected accountability institutions will generally be established by the legislature and possess reporting frameworks that can be traced back to either the legislature or the executive. But, at the very least, the complex impact of the various roles performed by unelected accountability institutions on processes of government and their standard mode of operation means that, by itself, the tripartite model no longer makes complete empirical sense as an adequate explanation of the 'modern administrative state' (Harlow and Rawlings 1997, 83).

Exactly where the ombudsman fits into the tripartite analysis is a difficult question to answer. Given that many ombudsmen are labelled as 'parliamentary ombudsmen' and ombudsman scholars themselves see the association between Parliament and the ombudsman as fundamental to the design of the office, locating ombudsmen within the parliamentary sphere would at first sight appear the obvious solution. The reporting arrangements of many ombudsmen are to democratic assemblies and where it works well this relationship is one of the greatest potential strengths of the office. But although it is the case that in some instances the support of Parliament is vital to the success of the ombudsman's work, this is only rarely a significant factor in the vast majority of ombudsman investigations. The reserve power to report to Parliament acts as a guarantor of their independence and funding arrangements (Giddings 2008, 102), but ordinarily they operate without any meaningful support or intervention from Parliament. Worryingly, in some instances the democratic assembly pays virtually no attention at all to the ombudsman. In these circumstances to label the ombudsman as a mere agent of Parliament is an over-simplistic analysis.

A further argument may be made that the ombudsman should belong to the executive branch of the constitution. This understanding lay behind the initial introduction of the Commonwealth Ombudsman in Australia (Kerr 1971; Bland 1973; Snell 2007, 102). Despite the ombudsman's role in resolving grievances against public authorities, it is dependent for its success on the executive's willingness to comply with the ombudsman's findings and recommendations and the general respect that the executive has for its work. Although the ombudsman does not implement any direct executive power, the ombudsman could be conceived as a form of control that has been internalized by the executive. This analysis though rather downplays the independence of the institution from any form of political intervention and its ability to report directly to Parliament. Furthermore, as we shall demonstrate in this book, positioning the ombudsman within the executive branch could not account for the very real autonomy that the ombudsman possesses in the performance of a number of different roles which, taken together, contribute to calling to account the exercise of power by the executive.

As the ombudsman resolves disputes, perhaps the best fit for the ombudsman in standard analysis is to bring it within the judicial branch of the state and treat it akin to a small-claims court (Craig 2008, 247-9). Indeed, some have concluded that the civil courts themselves might learn much from a more careful study of ombudsman processes and procedures (Merricks 2007, 142). But the ombudsmen are not set up like courts, or even quasi-judicial bodies, and adopt a very different methodology of dispute resolution. Nor do the ombudsmen ordinarily possess legal powers of enforcement when it comes to their findings and recommendations. This categorization of the ombudsman, therefore, is only possible if we adopt an extremely liberal interpretation of what the judicial branch of the constitution entails and ignore the numerous other attributes of the ombudsman. Furthermore, although the courts have claimed the right to judicially review the work of the ombudsman, the case law has generally been respectful of their discretionary authority.[21] This implies that the courts themselves have come to accept the ombudsman's autonomous status. Thus the ombudsman cuts right across separation of powers theory and 'is both alien and complementary to the Westminster tradition' (Stuhmcke 2008, 322).[22] In the words of the Supreme Court of Canada, '[t]he powers granted to the Ombudsman allow him to address administrative problems that the courts, the legislature and the executive cannot effectively resolve'.[23]

The work of the ombudsman and other institutions challenges orthodox versions of the constitution, a challenge that has yet to be coherently met in the UK (Gay and Winetrobe 2008). Such developments have led a number of writers to build more sophisticated theories of the constitution and accountability, theories which are potentially useful when attempting to provide a coherent description of the role of the ombudsman. A seminal piece in this regard is that of Bruce Ackerman, who has argued that the separation of powers model that lies at the heart of the US constitution is outdated as it inadequately takes into account the twentieth-century growth in bureaucracy and the need to control that bureaucracy (Ackerman 2000). His solution is to recognize and develop other branches of the

21 See further, Chapter 6.

22 Citing Goldring (1985), Stuhmcke was referring specifically to the Australian Commonwealth Ombudsman, but the point works well as a general anaysis of parliamentary ombudsmen.

23 *Re British Columbia Development Corp. v. Friedmann* (1984), 14 D.L.R. (4th) 129, at 139-40.

constitution. Likewise, in political science there are a number of commentators who have explored the impact of 'horizontal accountability' mechanisms that operate outside the political sphere in countries around the world (e.g. O'Donnell 1999; Sampford *et al* 2005). A theme that runs through this work is the extent to which healthy constitutions are reliant on horizontal accountability mechanisms based on professional oversight, in addition to the more familiar vertical accountability mechanisms founded on the democratic connection between the electorate and the state. Along the same lines, Vibert has gone as far as to conclude that the array of unelected institutions that exist in the UK today is best understood as a new version of the separation of powers doctrine (Vibert 2007). Public lawyers have also recognized that traditional models of accountability centred on Parliament and the courts have long since been bolstered by a sophisticated range of mutual and interdependent mechanisms and institutions (Harlow and Rawlings 1997; Scott 2000). With this understood, the emphasis has moved on to ensuring that this non-political regulatory regime is legitimate, accountable and efficient (e.g. Scott 2000; Crerar 2007; Black 2008). Even those who have focused on the strong links that many unelected accountability institutions have with Parliament (bodies frequently referred to as parliamentary 'watchdogs') will concede the difficulty that such bodies pose for standard parliamentary visions of the constitution (Winetrobe 2008; 2008a). These developments have also been receiving serious attention in several parliamentary reviews around the world, including that of the Public Administration Select Committee (PASC) in the UK.

> There is now an extensive network of bodies concerned with the regulation of standards of conduct in public life. These constitutional watchdogs have different functions, and are organised in a variety of different ways. They cover the essential ground and generally work well in safeguarding high standards of conduct; but they have often been set up in response to particular problems and insufficient attention has been paid to their design features and the need for coherence in the system as a whole. The time has come to recognise that the machinery of ethical regulation is now an integral and permanent part of the constitutional landscape. (PASC 2007, 4)

What these various works highlight is a complex network of checks and balances in the modern-day constitution, a network which can only be partially understood and imperfectly evaluated if viewed solely within the prism of the standard separation of powers theory. Perhaps an even more important message to come out of such work is the need for these additional institutions to exist. Their existence provides strong evidence that in the modern administrative state the core institutions of the traditional tripartite model, by themselves, are incapable of upholding the full range of values that underpin the constitution. If separation of powers theory retains continuing relevance as a constitutional theory it is because of the institutional values inherent within it, more than the institutional structure it has traditionally been associated with (Carolan 2009, 2). Inevitably, such a conclusion raises questions about what those values are, but it is the ombudsman's role in upholding some of the expectations of public authority that citizens have that explains the institution's constitutional importance.

Methodology and Outline

In analysing the ombudsman's ability to uphold certain public expectations as to how authority should be exercised, this book has been put together in three parts. Building on the background and themes developed in this chapter, Part I ('Theory and Context') is an examination of the theoretical context in which the ombudsman operates. In Chapter 2 the aim is to understand the underlying contribution of the ombudsman to the overall constitutional order, albeit as only one player within an increasingly complex network of accountability in the administrative justice system. The ombudsman's speciality is adjudicating on disputes surrounding failures in good administration; this is the core constitutional expectation that the ombudsman is required to uphold. However, given the inherent flexibility of the ombudsman model the work of the office need not stop there. Other constitutional values can also be addressed through the ombudsman model, such as human rights and the rule of law itself, and in addition the ombudsman can operate to provide forward-looking advice and guidance on systemic issues as well as retrospectively resolving individual disputes. This is a mighty set of roles for an unelected institution to perform, hence Chapter 2 concludes by noting that, as with all accountability institutions, there is an essential need to maintain legitimacy in the ombudsman office by ensuring that sufficient procedures are in place to verify its own performance.

Still at the theoretical stage, Chapter 3 focuses on the administrative justice system within which the ombudsman operates. This approach lays the foundation for a theme that will be pursued throughout the book, the idea that where there are flaws in modern-day ombudsmanry many of them relate directly to weaknesses and challenges experienced across the wider administrative justice system. The chapter analyses exactly what is meant by the term 'administrative justice system', current leading theories are analysed and the competing tensions identified. An overview of the policy developments in administrative justice is also given. What becomes clear from recent debates is that a more sophisticated concept of administrative justice has evolved and it is one that requires institutions within the administrative justice system to perform a role that goes further than resolving complaints and facilitating redress. Ideally, the administrative justice system should feedback information and best practice into the public sector. Seen in this light, the ombudsman appears as an extremely advanced component of the administrative justice system.

In analysing the concept of administrative justice, Chapter 3 lays out three key features that need to be addressed in the design and analysis of institutions within the administrative justice system, namely, 'getting it right', 'putting it right' and 'setting it right'. These features provide the framework for the rest of the book. In Part II ('The Ombudsman Technique') the manner in which ombudsman enterprise currently assists the goals of 'getting it right' and 'putting it right' is analysed.

The ability of ombudsmen to address the expectations of administrative justice, inadequately upheld elsewhere in the constitutional system, has long been recognized. What is new is the evolution of techniques within the ombudsman community to maximize the ombudsman's impact. Since the last substantial account of the ombudsman enterprise in the UK (Seneviratne 2002) there have been a number of significant developments in the field, both in the UK and elsewhere, with some ombudsmen demonstrating a hitherto rare willingness to experiment creatively with the powers of the office. Yet around the world there have only been a few substantial attempts to address the subject in academic works. The consequence is that outside the ombudsman community itself there remains too often a relatively conservative view of the work of the ombudsman. The developments that have occurred may be cyclical and due to personalities rather than evidence of long-term change, but they may also mark a maturing of the office of the ombudsman in jurisprudential terms. The argument developed in this book is that recent trends in the ombudsman enterprise have demonstrated the potential capacity of the office of the ombudsman to add value to the administrative justice system as a whole.

The evidence to support such claims derives from two main sources. In addition to the available scholarly literature, regular speeches and lectures have been given and a number of reports produced that have divulged the strategic thoughts and direction of the ombudsman community. Ombudsman associations[24] too have provided a forum in which ideas about the ombudsman enterprise can be debated and advanced. The second source that has been used to substantiate the views put forward in this book is a series of interviews conducted by the authors in 2007 and 2008 with ombudsmen and various stakeholders in the ombudsman community in the UK, Ireland, Australia and New Zealand, funded by the Economic and Social Research Council (Thompson, Buck and Kirkham 2008). What these interviews reveal is a much more activist and forward looking approach to the ombudsman enterprise than has hitherto been presented in the standard textbooks on administrative law.

Chapter 4 begins the process of detailing the modern ombudsman technique by exploring its complaint-handling function, the means by which the ombudsman helps to 'put things right'. One of the office's most important stakeholders is the complainant, yet if there has been one recurring criticism of the ombudsman in the past it is that the office has not always provided a prompt and relevant service that has suitably maintained the confidence of the complainant. Most recent ombudsmen appear to be wise to this issue and have made significant efforts to adapt their methods to improve the user experience. Whether they have yet been successful is one of the areas where future research will be necessary. This

24 See n.6 above.

chapter describes an evolution in attitudes towards customer service and identifies a number of problem areas that need resolution in the wider administrative justice system, as well as the ombudsman community. What this chapter also identifies is the extent to which ombudsmen have developed new techniques to enhance their capacity to provide an effective complaints service.

In Chapter 5 the focus moves on to the means by which ombudsmen contribute towards the 'getting it right' agenda of administrative justice. A key advancement in ombudsman practice that is explored here is the enhanced tendency to produce systemic reports and even pre-empt complaints on occasion by undertaking reviews akin to administrative audits. This practice illustrates another running theme of this book, which is the realization that ombudsmen operate with huge reserves of discretion and are therefore surprisingly free to adopt best practice and innovate where appropriate. The key is that this flexibility in operation is used wisely to retain the relevancy, efficiency and impact of the ombudsman institution. A number of ombudsman schemes have innovated in recent years, using this inherent discretion to promote good administration.

In Part III ('Setting it Right') of the book, the 'setting it right' component of the ombudsman's work is explored. Chapter 6 focuses on the fundamental issue of accountability. In today's constitution the ombudsman is one of a range of unelected institutions employed to provide assurance to Parliament and the wider population as to the efficacy of government. The interaction of these different bodies is important if the most effective form of accountability is to be achieved. The ombudsman is an institution endowed with remarkable power that itself needs to be called to account. Not only can an ombudsman fail due to error or incompetency, but an ombudsman can also fail through timidity. If ombudsmen are to achieve their potential then they need to be willing to be forward thinking and dynamic. This chapter explores the means by which the use of the ombudsman's powers and the suitability of methods deployed can be monitored. The chapter also evaluates the ability of the ombudsman to be independent and returns to the issue of the ombudsman's place in the constitution with an analysis of what is entailed by the label 'Parliamentary Ombudsman'.

Chapter 7 returns to a consideration of the bigger picture of administrative justice and the constitution. The operation of the overall landscape in which the ombudsman operates is analysed, together with the ways in which the ombudsmen have been able to integrate themselves into the wider administrative justice system. The ombudsman's characteristic lack of enforcement powers has, to an extent, incentivized their formation of strong relationships with the other players in the constitutional order. A particular concern is that the administrative justice system should be established to make the best use of the ombudsman's services. A key example is the ability of the ombudsman to promote good administration. At the same time, there are some major structural developments and proposals that will be considered at this point. In particular, 2007 saw the establishment of the AJTC to oversee the work of the entire sector.

Finally, in Chapter 8, some general observations are made about the state of the ombudsman enterprise in the early twenty-first century. There are many very positive signs and several ombudsman offices around the world have begun to demonstrate that the institution is capable of fulfilling the hopes and aspirations that have been invested in it. But there are problems as well and weak points within the structure of the concept, in particular much more work needs to be put into analysing the real impact of the institution. This chapter suggests some ideas as to the way forward and summarizes the overarching themes that have been uncovered during the course of writing the book.

Chapter 2
The Constitutional Role of the Ombudsman

Introduction

As befits the unwritten nature of the UK constitution, there is a lack of clarity surrounding the ombudsman's constitutional status and its exact role and purpose. This is unfortunate for, as an Australian commentator has observed, diminished returns may be received from the ombudsman concept where it is 'treated as an institutional treasure rather than a constitutional resource' (Snell 2000, 189). Such a description neatly encapsulates how the ombudsman has too often been perceived as a niche body with a limited statutory remit. It will be argued in this chapter, however, that the ombudsman enterprise has now developed to the point where its real constitutional potential ought to be re-evaluated.

Although there is currently a worrying deficit in *public* understanding about the role and work of ombudsmen in the UK, there is some evidence in recent years of a reawakening of *professional* attention, to administrative justice generally and ombudsmen in particular. The prevailing understanding of the judiciary towards the ombudsman enterprise has become much more one of positive engagement (e.g. LCD 1996). Ombudsmen are placed more at the centre of the administrative justice system in recent influential policy documents issued by the Department for Constitutional Affairs (DCA 2004) and the Law Commission (Law Commission 2008). A most encouraging sign has been the increasing attention paid by practising lawyers towards the benefits to be obtained from using the ombudsmen (Halford 2009), as highlighted in the work of the Public Law Project.[1]

Deficits in understanding still remain, however. With a few notable exceptions (e.g. IPPR 1991) debates about constitutional reform have tended to concentrate on maximizing legal and political control over the exercise of public authority, with comparably little consideration given to other techniques of accountability (Abraham 2008a; Kirkham, Thompson and Buck 2009). Likewise debates on human rights in the UK have tended to ignore altogether the input of the ombudsman.[2] In contrast to such conventional approaches, it is argued in this chapter that the

---

1 See the Public Law Project website at <http://www.publiclawproject.org.uk/> (accessed 22 February 2010).

2 By way of example, see the evidence to the Joint Committee on Human Rights (2008).

role of the developing ombudsman enterprise within the broader constitutional framework has become a central one.

To the extent that the ombudsman is already described in constitutional terms, it is ordinarily presented through a discussion of the ombudsman as an alternative dispute resolution (ADR) mechanism which upholds the individual citizen's right to redress. Another common constitutional strength of the institution that is often advocated is its capacity to promote 'good administration'. This chapter will consider, in addition to those roles, the preservation of such constitutional values as the rule of law, democracy and accountability in government. The chapter also considers briefly the accountability required to be applied to the ombudsman enterprise itself which is a necessary element of public assurance to legitimize the wide-ranging and powerful spectrum of tasks now managed by the ombudsman enterprise.

Fitting the Ombudsman Enterprise into the Constitution

It has already been argued in Chapter 1 that an attempt to explain the ombudsman's work by linking it directly to one of the three traditional core institutions of the state will fail to provide a complete and coherent explanation of the institution's contribution to the constitution. The ombudsman operates autonomously from executive government, Parliament and the courts. The executive can ignore the ombudsman's determinations but in practice does so very rarely, and is in any event legally obliged to comply with its investigatory requests; the legislature can scrutinize the work of the ombudsman and remove the office-holder, but does the first infrequently and the latter in extremis only; and the courts can determine the meaning of the ombudsman's legal powers but has largely declined to intervene in the discretionary judgment of the office.[3] Therefore, if the ombudsman is not a part of, or under the direct control of, the tripartite structure of the state how is one to understand the ombudsman's constitutional role?

It is argued here that a more profitable approach to understanding the ombudsman's contribution is to evaluate its role in the promotion of the *values* that underpin the constitutional order. In doing so, four interlinked propositions are made to explain why the ombudsman enterprise and a whole range of additional, expert, unelected institutions are required in modern constitutions. The first proposition is that it is incumbent upon public authorities not just to operate lawfully in their day-to-day activities but also to meet a range of other public expectations. These values could be referred to as components of a broad version of the 'rule of law' or of an additional constitutional standard, such as 'integrity'.

The second proposition is that there are certain constitutional values and public expectations that courts are ill-equipped to secure; the principle of good administration is a particularly apposite example of such a constitutional value

3 See Chapter 6, n.67.

as it requires public authorities to pursue 'proper conduct' as well as 'lawfulness' (Brenninkmeijer 2006).[4]

The third proposition is that there is a necessity to build integrity or accountability institutions in order to complement Parliament's imperfect supervision of the executive. It is often assumed that constitutional values that cannot easily be captured by the formal legal system must be inherently 'political' and therefore ultimately Parliament's responsibility. However, such a response fails to take into account the intellectual, practical and organizational limitations of Parliament. The fourth proposition is that there needs to be a procedure or a set of procedures in place by which legitimate grievances can be brought and upheld in order to meet the range of constitutional expectations of public authority (McMillan 2005, 3). The most obvious forum that meets this latter proposition is the court, but there is no reason to suppose that it should be the only such forum, or indeed the preferred forum, to which one should turn when looking to resolve public law disputes. Disputes that centre on failures in administration characteristically require oversight by more than one institution if they are to be comprehensively addressed.

Constitutional Values and the Rule of Law

In essence, a key justification for ombudsmen is the need to secure certain essential constitutional values that it would be much more difficult to secure in full without the existence of the ombudsman enterprise. The ombudsman enterprise may offer a number of practical advantages for the citizen in terms of, for example, providing an additional choice of remedy and investigative processes more suited to the dispute in question. But the underlying need to secure constitutional values that are imperfectly accommodated in our existing constitutional arrangements remains a driving force behind the construction of the ombudsman enterprise.

Conventional analyses of the British constitutional order largely confer on Parliament, not constitutional theory, the role of determining the values that are upheld within constitutional arrangements. Nevertheless, although it is recognized that constitutional theory is a much-contested subject, there are some common threads present in constitutional writing which provide a strong starting point for our argument that mainstreams the ombudsman enterprise within the UK constitutional order. Turpin and Tomkins, for example, claim that even in the absence of an agreed constitutional theory, in the UK we do possess 'a

4 'Proper conduct can be codified, pinned down, distilled into general principles of good administration and translated into written law. But it remains, inescapably, a non-legal category. I see proper conduct as a chiefly *ethical* category. What we are really talking about is the ethics of good administration. Those ethics can be to a greater or lesser extent translated into concrete legal norms but that doesn't eliminate the ethical aspect. Behind the codification of the general principles of proper administration in statute lurks the more shadowy category of proper conduct as an ethical standard' (Brenninkmeijer 2006, 3).

constitutional order which acknowledges the necessary power of government while placing conditions and limits on its exercise' (Turpin and Tomkins 2007, 34). Indeed, constitutional theories tend to work from the premise that the establishment and facilitation of public authority is an axiomatic and desirable feature of modern constitutions, one which is necessary for the interests of the wider public good. There is, of course, enormous debate as to the proper role and appropriate size of the state and the level and nature of the interaction between the public and private realms. But in any event public law systems are required to empower public authority, albeit conditionally (Loughlin 2003, 162). This raises the classic paradox of constitutional law that, once a system of public authority is established for the benefit of its constituents, concentrations of power emerge and threaten the very freedoms considered essential to the liberal democratic state. The pursuit of the best means to resolve this dilemma – the appropriate control of state power – lies at the heart of much discourse on public law. A significant purpose of constitution building, therefore, is to create systems and institutions that prevent and/or call to account the abuse, arbitrary, incompetent or lazy exercise of public power by public authorities. This is the 'special and distinctive task' of public law (Harlow and Rawlings 2009, 20). The goal is to organize 'society in such a way that the individual is normatively acknowledged, structurally advantaged, and institutionally protected' (Carolan 2009, 105). Where differences emerge between constitutional writers is in defining the exact remit and powers of the systems and institutions created to perform this role and, in the UK at least, the ultimate source of legal authority under which such institutions operate.

The underlying purpose of the control of power is not expressly detailed in the UK constitutional order as it has been in states emerging from revolutionary, civil war and/or colonial independence settlements, but the logic of control is implicit in its constitutional arrangements. The electoral control of Parliament and, indirectly, the executive is the major justification for the continuing strength of the doctrine of parliamentary supremacy (Ekins 2003). Further, the rule of law is granted such a pre-eminent place in the constitution precisely because it provides legitimacy and control to the exercise of public authority. As Jeremy Waldron has recently concluded, the rule of law requires 'that people in positions of authority should exercise their power within a constraining framework of public norms rather than on the basis of their own preferences, their own ideology, or their own individual sense of right and wrong' (Waldron 2008, 6). Moreover, it is always understood that the application of the rule of law impacts equally on us all (Dicey 1885, Pt 2, ch.4). In this sense, it 'is not a theory of law but a principle of institutional morality inherent in any constitutional democracy' (Jowell 2007, 5) which recognizes the equal value of all citizens. Even if we accept that the rule of law is otherwise a value-neutral concept, it is unquestionably designed to facilitate the constitutional control of public power through the prevention of the arbitrary exercise of that power.

If the control of public power is one of the fundamental themes in constitution building, there is much to be said in favour of including within the constitution a range of mechanisms to prevent arbitrary rule, including the ombudsman. But the work of the ombudsman does not fit neatly into standard constitutional theorizing, with its emphasis on democracy and the rule of law. Ombudsmen are not voted for by the electorate and it cannot be claimed that they directly express the electorate's constitutional values. As for the rule of law, although there is a lack of unanimity on what it means (Kairys 2003), central to the concept is the understanding that public authorities must operate within the legal powers granted them. As a consequence, the rule of law has ordinarily been associated almost exclusively with the operation of the law as 'publicly and prospectively promulgated and publicly administered in the courts' (Bingham 2007, 69). This has often led to an understanding of the rule of law as a constitutional principle which is focused on the judicial interpretation of legal doctrine, once again excluding the ombudsman from constitutional analysis.

Theoretically, a narrow interpretation of the rule of law based on judicial reasoning has the advantage of providing a neat fit for the concept into traditional understandings of the separation of powers model. Such an interpretation, however, does not appear to cater for a description of the ombudsman's work. Nevertheless, the aspiration of control which lies behind the rule of law is paralleled by the work of the ombudsman. This connection can be illustrated by two well-known limitations of a constitutional interpretation of the rule of law that focuses only on the judicial and legal input into its operation.

Firstly, the courts are not in practice the only institutions that enforce the law. To take but one example from the ombudsman community, in 2003 the Health Service Ombudsman (HSO) for England issued a report which found that a number of health authorities had acted with maladministration leading to injustice (HSO 2003). Central to the finding of maladministration was the failure of the health authorities concerned to apply the law as determined by the Court of Appeal judgment in the *Coughlan* case in 1999 (HSO 2003, 2).[5] The finding entailed, albeit indirectly, that in this instance it was the ombudsman that applied and upheld the law. This example illustrates a much bigger point – that the adoption of a range of regulatory, audit, quasi-judicial and inspectorate bodies within the modern constitution has resulted in institutions other than the courts ensuring that the rule of law is being followed and applied (McMillan 2005). In other countries, this aspect of the ombudsman's work is more explicit and can involve the interpretation of the law (Bonner 2003).

A second problem with restricting constitutional interpretations of the rule of law to the law as applied in the courts is that such an approach leaves open to debate the extent to which moral values and broader expectations of public authority can be included within the concept. The classic legal debate between positivism and natural law is a familiar one and will not be pursued here.[6] What is of interest here though is the extent to which constitutional values upheld by such

5 For an analysis, see Kirkham (2003).

6 See Hart (1958); Fuller (1958) and, generally, Cane (2010).

bodies as the ombudsman can be legitimately described as rule of law values. The history of the growth of additional accountability institutions implies that there are other mechanisms than the courts by which our liberty and our expectations of public authority can be upheld. Such bodies are generally established to promote and uphold particular constitutional values and are appointed with autonomous and specifically designed powers to operate outside the ordinary political and legal processes. Further legal strength is given to accountability institutions where they are granted powers by Parliament.[7] If the work performed by such bodies is not recognized through the adoption of a more nuanced approach being taken towards our constitutional understanding of the rule of law, then it is unclear where the values that additional accountability institutions uphold are detailed in constitutional theory.

The Integrity Branch of the Constitution

A narrow version of the rule of law doctrine, therefore, is unlikely to cover in full all constitutional values worthy of protection. The search for an alternative theoretical framework required to understand properly the constitutional input of bodies such as the ombudsman is much assisted by an examination of developments in Australia. As in the UK, over the last 20 years there has been a series of incidents and scandals in Australia that have brought to public attention the potential for abuse of power within government.[8] A feature of the Australian response has been an understanding that existing institutional mechanisms, such as Parliament and the courts, are insufficient to guarantee acceptable standards amongst those individuals and public authorities responsible for making decisions in the public name. This understanding led to new specialized institutions and practices being created to investigate breaches of public expectations and re-establish what has commonly been referred to as 'integrity' in government (Brown and Head 2005). The organized development of a 'national integrity system' in Australia, specifically designed to tackle the various forms of institutional variance from perceived standards, has led more than one writer to suggest that there is now an accepted constitutional understanding as to the importance of an 'integrity branch' of the constitution.

> Institutional integrity … requires a governmental instrumentality to be faithful to the public purposes for the pursuit of which a power was conferred or a duty imposed. Furthermore, its conduct must be in accordance with the values, including procedural values, which the institution is reasonably expected to obey by those who are affected by its conduct and decisions. In any stable polity there is a widely accepted concept of how governance should operate in practice. The

7 As Gay notes, many accountability, or as he terms 'watchdog', bodies are not confirmed in statute and are constitutionally weaker as a result (Gay 2008).

8 See, generally, Head *et al* (2008).

> role of integrity institutions is to ensure that that concept is realised. (Spigelman 2004, 724-5)

Integrity, therefore, is being posited as a fundamental and multifaceted constitutional value to be adhered to by government institutions in their relations with the governed. Arguably, the concept of integrity reflects a targeted variant of the more familiar notion of 'accountability'. But the pursuit of integrity in the exercise of public authority has obvious parallels with the underlying purpose of the rule of law, the prevention of arbitrary rule. Indeed, perhaps the better understanding is that the rule of law is a subset of the broader concept of integrity, with a significant feature of the concept of integrity being that it includes the rule of law but goes further than judicially developed principles alone. Acting lawfully is not enough for public authorities; other expectations of 'proper conduct'[9] must also be met.

Given the diversity of the concept, the need to secure institutional integrity is almost certainly best achieved through constitutional networks containing additional bodies working alongside the courts and Parliament, with different specialities and methods. Importantly, although the mode of operation of integrity institutions may not always rely upon traditional legal technique, because ordinarily they will have a parliamentary mandate for their work they will nevertheless be responsible for upholding an expectation of public service that has clear constitutional authority. As the next section demonstrates, the ombudsman's core role – to consider complaints about administrative conduct – provides a particularly good example of an aspect of the integrity branch of constitutional expectation that is inadequately accommodated within a narrow rule of law analysis.

Good Administration as a Constitutional Objective

Recognition of the weaknesses in the parliamentary and legal processes to secure full accountability of public authorities is evident in the evolution of most constitutions. The introduction of almost all ombudsman schemes, and indeed the wider administrative justice system, can be traced to the failure of existing mechanisms to provide sufficient confidence that one expectation of government or another was being properly upheld. Anita Stuhmcke has identified three key elements to institutional integrity which directly link to the roles performed by different bodies within the administrative justice system, including the ombudsman.

> Briefly, and of course very generally, judicial review as undertaken by courts ensure the first element, namely that decisions made by government agencies are authorised by law. Judicial review may also extend to the second element of 'ensuring that powers are exercised for the purpose, broadly understood, for

9 See Brenninkmeijer (2006) and n.4 above.

> which they were conferred'.[10] Tribunals are bodies that undertake merits review to ensure that both the correct and preferable decision is made in a particular case, thereby placing emphasis upon the first and second elements. While no doubt the third element of institutional values is infused to varying degrees within both the operation of judicial review and merits review, the mechanism of ombudsmen best reflects this element of review. It is in this manner that an ombudsman, by contributing to the values of which an institution must obey, provides integrity review. (Stuhmcke 2008a, 353)

It is the fundamental importance of this third element, with its emphasis on public authorities operating according to institutional values that are not necessarily defined in law, which provides the rationale for labelling the work of the ombudsman as constitutional. Stuhmcke's third element of institutional integrity resonates closely with current representations of the ombudsman's functions. For instance, the office of the UK's Parliamentary and Health Service Ombudsman (PHSO) defines its work as investigating to establish whether public bodies have 'acted properly or fairly or have provided a poor service' (PHSO 2009, 2). Likewise the Northern Ireland Ombudsman (NIO) represents its vision as 'to ensure that the people of Northern Ireland are served by a fair, effective and efficient public administration that is committed to accountability, openness, and quality of service' (NIO 2007, 4). This emphasis on the preferred conduct of public bodies in their decision-making, as opposed to the substance of the decisions made, is usually referred to as 'good administration' and is widely understood to be an important constitutional value.

The arguments in favour of a constitutional right to good administration are strong and gaining ground (Kirkham, Thompson and Buck 2009, 601). Relatively recent developments have produced a right to good administration in the European Union (EU), as derived from the European Court of Justice's caselaw and confirmed in the EU Charter of Fundamental Rights.[11] At much the same time, an associated European Code of Good Administrative Behaviour was adopted by the European

10 Quoting The Hon. J.J. Spigelman (Spigelman 2005).

11 '(1) Every person has the right to have his or her affairs handled impartially, fairly and within a reasonable time by the institutions and bodies of the Union.

(2) This right includes: the right of every person to be heard, before any individual measure which would affect him or her adversely is taken; the right of every person to have access to his or her file, while respecting the legitimate interests of confidentiality and of professional and business secrecy; the obligation of the administration to give reasons for its decisions.

(3) Every person has the right to have the Community make good any damage caused by its institutions or by its servants in the performance of their duties, in accordance with the general principles common to the laws of the Member States.

(4) [omitted].' (Article 41, Right to good administration, EU Charter of Fundamental Rights).

Commission in 2000.[12] The UK government has also expressed some interest in the possibilities for enacting a legal right to administrative justice within a proposed new Bill of Rights and Responsibilities (Ministry of Justice 2009, paras 3.39-3.47; Joint Committee on Human Rights 2008, para. 129).[13]

To date, however, constitutional architecture has not generally favoured a concretized legal 'right to good administration'.[14] Instead attempts to provide a more complete breakdown of the concept of good administration are generally undertaken through 'soft law' techniques. For example, government departments are reminded in a number of ways of the need to pursue good administrative practice and policy in order to withstand the threat of judicial review proceedings. The official advice to government departments (TSol 2006, 7) about judicial review proceedings declares at the outset that '[a]ll public bodies should aim to practise "good administration": they should aim to perform their public duties speedily, efficiently and fairly'. More details as to what this might entail can be found now in the publications of many ombudsmen offices, with the PHSO's *Principles of Good Administration* a good example of working up a template of 'good administration' as part of their 'improvement' work (PHSO, 2007a).[15] The *Principles* are intended as broad statements of the PHSO's perception of what public bodies (within its jurisdiction) ought to be doing to deliver good administration and customer service. As such, they are intended to clarify both the sorts of behaviour expected from public bodies and the tests to be applied in determining whether maladministration and service failure have occurred. The *Principles* provide six principles of good administration, each of which is given some further detail in the document. These are:

1. getting it right
2. being customer focused
3. being open and accountable
4. acting fairly and proportionately
5. putting things right
6. seeking continuous improvement.

---

12 The extent to which this code succeeds in explicating the content of the charter's right to good administration in Article 41 is contestable (Mendes 2009).

13 The right has also been referred to as the right to 'fair and just administrative action'. As this book was completed the Administrative Justice and Tribunals Council (AJTC) put out for consultation its draft principles of administrative justice.

14 Although see Article 33(1) of the Constitution of the Republic of South Africa, Act 108 of 1996, substituted by s.1 (1) of Act 5 of 2005): 'Everyone has the right to administrative action that is lawful, reasonable and procedurally fair' and Article 18 of the Namibia Constitution of 1990.

15 The PHSO has additionally published *The Principles for Remedy* in October 2007 and *The Principles of Good Complaint Handling* in November 2008. All three sets of *Principles* were reprinted with minor amendments on 10 February 2009. See further, Chapter 5, p. 142-3.

This approach to good administration contrasts with that taken in the law. Clearly some aspects of the concept of good administration can be enforced through the courts, as what it entails parallels so many of the standard values claimed of the rule of law. Leading textbook authors have even proclaimed that '[t]here can be little doubt that the central purpose of administrative law is to promote good administration' (Beatson *et al* 2005, 1). This claim is a strong one, despite the absence of a specific legal ground of good administration, because its achievement is implicit within a range of legal tests employed in judicial review. Much of administrative law is an exercise not only in achieving compliance with the rule of law by defining the limits of statutory powers, but also in the close scrutiny of the procedural aspects of decision-making (Harlow and Rawlings 2009, 618-21). This implies that the rule of law upholds a deeper range of constitutional values than the mere adjudication of powers, with such values touching on the conduct and decision-making processes of public authorities.

> The Rule of Law is not just about general rules; it is about their impartial administration. ... A procedural understanding of the Rule of Law requires not only that officials apply the rules as they are set out; it requires application of the rules with all the care and attention to fairness that is signaled by ideals such as 'natural justice' and 'procedural due process.' (Waldron 2008, 7-8)

In other words, there would be much reduced value in conferring on public authorities prescribed legal powers, even powers that minimized residuary discretion, if those powers were then implemented unfairly, unreasonably and inconsistently (Millett 2002, 310). Furthermore, unless there is good reason to operate otherwise, public authorities should be open and transparent and make available prospectively the rules and policies that they will apply in their decision-making. The central importance of such standards of administrative propriety in public decision-making is captured by the oft-repeated quote that '[the] history of liberty has largely been the history of the observance of procedural safeguards'.[16]

Despite this connection with the rule of law, however, good administration is a constitutional expectation that is not easily dealt with by the standard legal techniques as practised in the courts, even after the development of a series of principle-based tests (for example, 'reasonableness', 'legitimate expectation' and 'fairness') in English law (Harlow and Rawlings 2009, 95-105). This is largely because the concept of good administration goes much further than legal standards alone, a point aptly reflected in the slogan 'life beyond legality' deployed by the European Ombudsman (Diamandouros 2007) and others. Mirroring Stuhmcke's analysis of institutional integrity referred to earlier, Mendes has deconstructed the multifaceted concept of good administration into three layers – firstly, the procedural guarantees protecting substantive rights of persons dealing with

16 Frankfurter J. in *McNabb v United States* 318 US 332 (1943).

the administration; secondly, the legal rules structuring the exercise of the administrative functions and finally:

> Non-legal rules form the third layer of good administration. They define standards of conduct directed at ensuring the proper functioning of the administrative services delivered to the public, both ensuring and demonstrating their efficiency and quality. Naturally, this segment of good administration is mostly displayed by the Ombudsman's intervention. Indeed, [the European Ombudsman] has consistently held that 'principles of good administration [require] Community institutions and bodies not only to respect their legal obligations but also to be service-minded and ensure that members of the public are properly treated and enjoy their rights fully'. (Mendes 2009, 5)[17]

This multidimensional feature of good administration makes 'its meaning ... particularly amorphous and elusive' (Halliday 2004, 13). Take, for instance, the following attempt at defining the concept.

> [Public authorities] must be efficient, meet the expectations citizens have, act for the general good of the public as a whole, be consistent ... and do all this in the most expedient way. Other standards can be mentioned, but all basically derive from considerations of a common sense of fairness and justice and the expectations citizens are entitled to. (Heede 2000, 90)

This inclusion of a range of intangible, equitable and context-dependent criteria within the concept of good administration is extremely problematic for the legal technique and threatens to cross the legality/merits divide.

As a constitutional value, therefore, good administration raises some interesting questions as to how it should be enforced and its true importance. The uncertainty as to the degree to which the right to good administration can be explained and made legally enforceable largely explains the rarity in express reference to the right within constitutions. The difficulties are noted in the UK government's work on the point, including the dangers of introducing legalism in areas not yet so occupied (Ministry of Justice 2009a, paras 3.39-3.47). Indeed, it specifically rules out the PHSO's principle 2 (being customer focused) from being included in any statutory formulation of a right to good administration on the basis that this matter should not be justiciable through the courts. This approach, therefore, led the UK government to map out an approach that encompasses the notion of good administration that may go further than merely a concretization of exclusively legal rules.

> [T]here are a number of ways in which the principles of good administration might be framed in a Bill of Rights and Responsibilities, ranging from a general

17 See European Ombudsman (2008, 31; 2009, 29).

> statement of a right of individuals to decision-making which is lawful, rational and procedurally fair, to a more detailed statement of the principles drawn from the existing law and the values which underpin fair decision-making and good administration. (Ministry of Justice 2009a, para. 3.46)

It is the existence of the technical difficulties surrounding the idea of good administration that largely explains why constitutions around the world include a range of other mechanisms, in addition to the courts and the law, to deal with disputes on good administration.

Applying Good Administration Beyond the Reach of the Judiciary

The strengths of the courts are legion but it has often been observed that a court's ability to resolve disputes 'declines as the tasks it undertakes deviates from the triadic model' based on the judge and two opposing parties (Barber 2001, 76). In such circumstances, the courts are called upon to resolve a dispute with potentially wide boundaries, numerous unrepresented interests and without sufficient information. A key difficulty the courts face in understanding and defining good administration lies in both the political and practical dimension of implementing public policy and the 'polycentric' nature of much decision-making in the public sector, where the effects can impact on thousands and even millions of people whose interests cannot necessarily be represented in the court forum.[18] Public authorities often possess a considerable amount of discretion in how they undertake their powers and responsibilities and will operate within a variety of financial and logistical constraints. Some individual decisions will impact on only a few people and the consequences will be predictable. On other occasions, however, the knock-on effect of individual decisions will be huge and thoroughly unpredictable, or the financial consequences of certain decisions will have implications on entirely unrelated government activity and even overall fiscal policy. Sometimes decisions will have to be made in haste; in other circumstances there will be more time to consult and consider in depth a wide variety of options. Thus, given the potentially huge complexity of much government activity, the comparative lack of clear legal rights in many areas of administrative law, the implications for the public purse and the existence of large-scale numbers of third party interests, the task of adjudication in this area is extremely difficult.

To tackle this challenge the courts have evolved a range of legal tests, but it is not always clear that the grounds of administrative law facilitate consistent applicability. Halliday has claimed that '[a]dministrative law is riven by competing priorities and is essentially schizophrenic in character' (Halliday 2004, 112), whilst others have expressed concerns that some public law disputes invite the judiciary to settle cases according to heavily value-laden criteria. Examples include the resolution of human rights disputes (Waldron 2006, 1366-9) and the application

18 On polycentricity, see Fuller (1978), Allison (1994) and King (2008a).

of equitable standards such as fairness, substantive legitimate expectations and proportionality (Spigelman 2005). The end result is a concern that the law in this area is open to considerable differences in interpretation and is often unpredictable in application.[19]

In the UK, the ability of the Administrative Court in judicial review proceedings to interrogate comprehensively evidential matters is also limited in practice. The discovery of documents and cross-examination of witnesses is ordinarily not attempted within judicial review proceedings, meaning that the Administrative Court 'does not provide an obvious forum for the resolution of complex issues of fact' (Law Commission 2008, para. 4.20). The difficulty with this methodology is that in many disputes focusing on good administration issues it will not be possible to draw conclusions through an examination of just the final decision or action undertaken by an agency. The more detailed scrutiny required to assess good administration may well necessitate a critical examination of the conduct of the officials involved (Brenninkmeijer 2006).

An illustration of the difficulties facing the courts in this area can be ascertained from the *Association of British Civilian Internees: Far East Region* (*ABCIFER*) case.[20] In *ABCIFER* the Court of Appeal was called upon to evaluate the legality of the Ministry of Defence's (MOD) handling of an *ex gratia* compensation scheme. From the wording of the judgments in both the Administrative Court and the Court of Appeal it was clear that the judges involved had a low regard for the decisions made by the MOD. Yet no specific arguments were presented as to whether standards of good administration had been met and no detailed scrutiny of the inner workings of the MOD undertaken. The application of legal tests to the decisions made resulted in the court being unable to find any illegality in the MOD's actions.[21] By contrast, another failed applicant to the scheme took his complaint to the Parliamentary Ombudsman (PO). Whereas the court had explored a few narrow legal questions, the PO undertook a wide-ranging investigation of the operation of the *ex gratia* scheme and produced a comprehensive report, *A Debt of Honour* (PHSO 2005a). In the report, the PO made four findings of maladministration.

19 Although for a defence of the capacity of the court in this area, see Millet (2002) and King (2007, 2008a, 2008b).

20 *Association of British Civilian Internees: Far East Region v Secretary for Defence (ABCIFER)* [2002] EWHC 2119 (Admin); [2003] EWCA Civ 473; [2003] QB 1397.

21 In a later case, *R (on the application of Elias) v Secretary of State for Defence* [2006] EWCA Civ 1293 on the same *ex gratia* scheme the Court of Appeal did find against the MOD. In that the eligibility criteria did indirectly discriminate against the applicant on racial grounds, the criteria were not proportionate to the aim to be achieved and were not objectively justified, and were therefore unlawful. This eventual finding does not nullify the argument being made here, however, as the finding only affected a narrow aspect of the administrative error that was identified by the PO.

Perhaps the most illuminating finding was the PO's determination that the manner in which the scheme had been announced was misleading and lacked clarity, 'which represents such a significant departure from standards of good administration to the extent that it constitutes maladministration' (PHSO 2005a, para. 155). This finding of maladministration was made in the full knowledge and acceptance of the Court of Appeal's ruling in *ABCIFER*[22] that the same announcement had not given rise to a legitimate expectation in law. Thus, in circumstances where the court had found in favour of the MOD, the PO had established that standards of good administration had been breached. This comparison of the capacity of decision-making in the courts with the investigatory ombudsman inquiry has been replicated on other occasions[23] and demonstrates that there are real limitations in relying upon the legal technique alone as a safeguard of good administration standards.[24]

The argument being made here is that there exists a necessarily opaque division of labour between the ombudsman and the courts when it comes to resolving disputes on good administration. Sometimes the rationale for one institution being responsible for the dispute will be directly linked to the technical limitations of the other institution; on other occasions the primary reason(s) will be practical and based on the choice of the aggrieved citizen involved. Either way, for the standard of good administration to be enforced in full, the choice between the courts and the ombudsman is important and will in all probability also include the involvement of other institutions as well.

The Ombudsman and Good Administration

In the common law world the dominant focus for the ombudsman enterprise has been the investigation of failures of public authority to meet standards of good administration. The informality and breadth of investigatory techniques used to achieve this characterize the ombudsman endeavour in contrast to traditional adversarial techniques used in the courts. It could be said, however, that the ombudsman enterprise might suffer from the absence of court processes such as cross-examination of witnesses in court.[25]

Ultimately, the strength of claims in favour of the adversarial and facilitative techniques adopted in courts and tribunals, respectively, need to be balanced against the investigatory skill of the ombudsmen and a series of pragmatic considerations.

22 [2003] QB 1397, paras 55-75.

23 The overlap can work both ways.

24 The limits to the court's capacity are implicitly reflected by the amount of academic debate on the doctrine of deference and the ability of the courts to work out the limits of their legitimate competence: see King (2008b).

25 It should be noted that Article 6 of the European Convention on Human Rights requires the opportunity to cross-examine as an essential procedural safeguard in the determination of civil rights.

Even in the age of freedom of information legislation, and with the support of a legal team, it is not always clear that a claimant will have the ability, capacity or knowledge to uncover the required information to resolve the dispute. By contrast, the ombudsman is set up to investigate administrative practice across an extremely wide jurisdiction, possesses the requisite investigatory powers, is experienced in the art of uncovering the factual underpinning of a dispute and is skilled in evaluating issues of administrative process. Through these advantages, and being in control of the investigation, the ombudsman is also in a strong position to overcome 'any inequality of arms that might otherwise diminish the fairness of the process' (O'Brien 2009, 469).

In addition to the ombudsman's ability to uncover relevant information, the basic threshold test which enables an individual complainant to access the ombudsman's jurisdiction is an important tool in the ombudsman enterprise. The details of this test do of course vary from one scheme to another, but it is generally focused on the quality of administrative decision-making, captured rather inelegantly in UK terminology by the term 'maladministration'. The strength of this test is fourfold.

Firstly, maladministration, or its equivalent, allows the ombudsman to tackle issues where there is no obvious available legal test; for example, where administrations do not meet the standards of 'customer service' widely expected of modern administrative bodies, standards that are rarely detailed in legislation or considered in court, but have been central to policy developments in administrative justice.[26]

Secondly, the test is malleable. Ombudsmen are not bound by precedents or hampered by restrictive statutory definitions or even judicial efforts to refine the ombudsman's powers. Even in ombudsman schemes where the test is explained in more detail by legislation,[27] it has proved to be sufficiently flexible to allow the oversight of the full range of administrative malpractice. This allows for the evolution of principles and standards over time and for a different intensity of test to be applied in different situations. The imposition of fixed legal tests often does not mirror administrative practice or affect departmental incentives (Harlow and Rawlings 2009, 40; Stuhmcke 2008a). On the other hand, the ombudsman's flexibility and use of general principles is particularly appropriate for dealing with the murky and context-dependent concept of good administration and the complexity of administrative decision-making (Abraham 2008d, 687).

Thirdly, and linked to the previous point, the maladministration test should not be considered to deal solely with issues difficult to resolve through the law. It is firmly understood within the practice of the ombudsmen that breaching the law is not an example of good administration and can lay the grounds for a finding of maladministration.[28] Breaches of human rights, which many consider

26 See further Chapter 3, pp. 76-7.

27 See further Chapter 4, pp. 108-9.

28 For example, see PHSO (2007, 4) where the first principle of good administration is described as 'Getting it Right: Acting in accordance with the law and with due regard for

as 'fundamental to the concept of good public administration' (SPSO 2005, col. 2521), can, by using this logic, inform findings of maladministration where a public authority has failed to give due consideration to human rights legislation (O'Reilly 2007; Abraham 2008c; O'Brien 2009). Such innovative use of the law to base a finding of maladministration has its dangers. Indeed, although it is generally understood that it is not the role of the ombudsman to interpret the law,[29] it is highly probable that in many instances an ombudsman's findings will be indirectly informed by a judgment as to the legality of the investigated body's actions (O'Brien 2009). Where such a judgment is made explicitly, then an ombudsman is exposed to a judicial review challenge, for example, as in *Argyll and Bute Council, Re Judicial Review of a Decision of the Scottish Public Services Ombudsman.*[30] Despite the risks, however, the inherent flexibility of the maladministration concept does mean that the ombudsman can operate as a genuine alternative to the courts even where the underlying problem is the investigated body's non-adherence to the law.

Finally, the greater subtlety and persuasive nature of the ombudsman technique make it ideally placed to deal with disputes that touch upon the most sensitive areas of executive decision-making. A much-cited example of such an area is social and economic rights. Although jurisprudence and theoretical thinking is split on this point (Langford 2009), the orthodoxy is that such rights are not areas suitable for court-based adjudication.[31] Yet internationally agreed commitments to social and economic rights still remain, and citizens will regularly feel let down by the actions or lack of action by public authorities in areas such as the provision of social housing, health care, disability and social services. Precisely because ombudsmen already deal with complaints that touch upon dignity and rights in a range of public services, they are well placed to develop these themes as matters of good administrative standards, flexibly applied and improved upon over time, rather than enshrined in hard-edged legal standards (Abraham 2008c).

Good Administration and Politics

In contrast to the case made above in support of the suitability of the ombudsman enterprise to monitor good administration, traditional analyses of the 'law and

---

the rights of those concerned …'. See also HSO (2003, paras 20-27); Diamandouros (2005) and The Ombudsman Act 1976 (Cth), s.15.

29 However, the European Ombudsman appears increasingly to be developing an interpretational role: 'National and regional ombudsmen may ask the European Ombudsman for written answers to queries about EU law and its interpretation, including queries that arise in their handling of specific cases. The European Ombudsman either provides the answer directly or, if more appropriate, channels the query to another EU institution or body for response' (European Ombudsman 2009, 77). Some of the Nordic ombudsman schemes do allow for the ombudsman to develop legal principles and interpret the law (Bonner 2003).

30 [2007] CSOH 168. In this case, an incorrect interpretation of the law was the main reason why the Court of Session overturned a report of the ombudsman.

31 For example, see Straw (2009).

policy divide' indicate that such disputes are properly resolvable in the political arena. Where the executive is given legal authority to act, such analyses assume that only Parliament can override executive action; and the courts' powers to apply judicial review are, as we have seen above, limited in many respects. It should be remembered that the introduction of the UK's Parliamentary Commissioner for Administration in 1967 was met by strong objections based on the perception that such an office would undermine the principle of ministerial responsibility (Kirkham 2007, 5). But parliamentary oversight, on its own, is clearly limited by the volume and detail of the modern-day administrative state, and would also involve making a heroic assumption about the capacity of the UK's elected representatives to deliver.

To establish a proper system of control over executive decision-making, therefore, at the very least Parliament requires support. However, the introduction of new institutions such as ombudsman bodies required to investigate disputes about good administration will often involve strong quasi-political elements being considered that the courts will be reluctant to address (O'Brien 2009, 470). This in turn raises the problem that it may be difficult to maintain the legitimacy of the ombudsman office and there is a danger that the office itself can become politicized and prone to influence by external forces (Harlow and Rawlings 2009, 566). To combat these risks, the public sector ombudsman design ordinarily includes two important features. Firstly, effective reporting arrangements between Parliament and the ombudsman is established in order to subject the office to proper scrutiny.[32] Secondly, public sector ombudsmen do not, as a general rule, possess the power to enforce their recommendations.[33] It is this second design feature that provides the key justification for entrusting the ombudsman to investigate disputes that cross the law and policy divide.

Ombudsman recommendations are not binding on public authorities precisely because to make them binding would override the legal discretionary authority of a public body to act. The ombudsman's investigatory process allows an independent assessment of the efficacy of the public body's actions set against standards of good administration. Moreover, because most ombudsman schemes are capable of being backed up by supporting parliamentary processes of review and reflection, the findings of the ombudsman carry significant political impact. Even where that supporting parliamentary process is not utilized, the combination of independent expert review and the potential for parliamentary pressure has fostered an extremely effective model in which most ombudsman recommendations are implemented (Kirkham, Thompson and Buck 2009). Conversely though, the non-enforceability of ombudsman recommendations, coupled with the prospect of parliamentary review and reflection, acts as a safeguard against an overactive ombudsman. As O'Brien points out, '[t]he ombudsman's word carries weight, but

32 This subject will be returned to periodically in this book as it goes to the heart of the legitimacy of the ombudsman model. See further, Chapter 6, pp. 179-85.

33 See further, Chapter 7, pp. 210-19.

it is frequently far from the last word' (O'Brien 2009, 470). The ultimate power of the public body to reject the ombudsman's (non-binding) recommendations constitutes a strong safeguard against inappropriate ombudsman intervention in political decision-making. Even where an ombudsman's recommendations are rejected – on occasion precisely in those areas in which the ombudsman is touching on political sensitivities – the input of the ombudsman can be extremely positive, and can enrich the political debate. It can also help public authorities to engage publicly with citizens about the issues involved; a process that can be deemed a success in terms of promoting accountability (Kirkham 2009, 127-8). The tension that is created by the power to investigate quasi-political aspects of government administration, coupled with the non-enforceability of recommendations, is one that needs proper monitoring through suitable mechanisms of accountability, but it is one of the most important contributions of the ombudsman model.

Choosing Between Different Forms of Dispute Resolution

It is now widely accepted that the ombudsman represents a genuine alternative to the courts in tackling vexed questions of whether or not standards of good administration have been breached (Law Commission 2008). This book will not attempt to draw hard lines between those complaints that are better dealt with by the courts and those by the ombudsman, but it is possible to identify some additional practical reasons as to why the ombudsman may or may not be considered the preferable option.

Much has been made in recent public policy initiatives in the UK of the appropriateness of the ombudsman in dealing with many forms of administrative dispute (DCA 2004, 16-21), even those involving human rights.[34] Many of the arguments in favour of greater use of ombudsman services are those that are advocated in favour of non-curial, 'alternative dispute resolution' (ADR) generally; for example, informality, accessibility, flexibility, cost-effectiveness and the impact on enduring relationships between the parties to a dispute. As the ombudsman service is ordinarily free to the complainant and requires no attendance at a formal hearing, the burden and stress involved in this process is arguably significantly reduced, more proportionate to the scale of the dispute and better value for the public purse. This contrasts with the legal approach, complete with appearances in court and rigorous formality, which is often deemed disproportionate to the kind of complaint being brought and the potential remedy available.

Running ombudsman offices is not necessarily cheap, though it is difficult at present to compare the cost per complaint of resolving a dispute[35] across the

34 *Anufrijeva v Secretary of State for the Home Department* [2003] EWCA Civ 1406; [2004] QB 1124.

35 According to the NAO's report, the average cost of handling a single 'complaint' (defined in the report normally as 'any written or spoken expression of dissatisfaction with the service we provide') across central government is estimated at £155, though there is a wide range around this average across the different policy sectors. For example, costs of

Table 2.1 The overall scale of redress systems across central government in 2003-2004

Type of redress system	New cases annually (000s)	Total staff	Total costs (£ million)	Number of agencies involved
Appeals and tribunals	803	6,170	366	97
Complaints	543	2,170	59	230
Ombudsmen and mediators	42	985	73	11
Compensation	*na*	*na*	*12*	*12*
All types	**1,388**	**9,325**	**510**	**230**

Note: Compensation cases arise from complaints or appeals and so the number of cases and staff involved are not separately itemized here. National Health Service (NHS) compensation costs are not covered here.

Source: NAO (2005, 44).

range of remedial mechanisms in the administrative justice system. Calculations have been attempted, though there are considerable difficulties in working out the unit cost per ombudsman case, particularly where the ombudsman has embarked on a major inquiry that may affect thousands of individuals.[36] A National Audit Office (NAO) report in 2005 calculated that the absolute costs of 'ombudsman and mediator' cases appeared to be around one-fifth of those relating to 'appeals and tribunals'. The report attempted to cost the major generic forms of administrative redress as set out in Table 2.1.

A further consideration is the ability of different dispute resolution mechanisms to make a short- and long-term impact on administrative behaviour. This is the subject of much debate and difficult questions have been raised about the traditional legal technique's effectiveness in this regard (Hertogh and Halliday 2004). It is alleged that court and tribunal processes can encourage a defensive response from

complaints in defence are nearly 20 times the overall average but those in industry, commerce and science are under one-third of the average. The average cost of an appeal or tribunal case is around £455 across central government, though there are some relatively low-cost systems in transport and industry but high costs in environment and local government. The report does not offer a comparable unit cost per ombudsmen complaint on the basis that 'there is a wide variation in the nature of cases and how they are dealt with by different ombudsmen'. However, in 2003-04 the Pensions Ombudsman completed 2,880 cases at an estimated cost per case of £560. The Prisons and Probation Ombudsman provides 'a well-researched cost per case figure for a completed assessment (£134) and for a completed investigation (£1,189) in his Annual Report for 2003-04'. See NAO (2005, paras 2.14, 2.20 and 2.22 and Figures 11, 15 and 17a).

36 For example, the total cost of the ombudsman's investigation into the prudential regulation of the Equitable Life Assurance Society was £3.743 million (PHSO 2009, 39).

the respective sides, rather than a constructive engagement with the issues. Worse still, litigation can inappropriately distil argumentation into narrow points of law rather than addressing directly the underlying causes of the dispute. This leads to a further concern that, once disputes are resolved, the focus on legal points will do little to encourage the public body concerned to tackle any underlying problems. Finding ways to work around the law is unfortunately an alternative scenario (Canon 2004), or even ignoring the law, because judicial review does not impose sufficiently strong sanctions for subsequent breaches (Halliday 2004, 103-5; Richardson 2004, 119). Not all agree with this negative analysis. The research of Bondy and Sunkin (2009), for instance, indicates that commencing, or threatening to commence, judicial review proceedings tends to encourage negotiated out-of-court settlements by placing pressure on a public authority to take a complaint seriously.[37] Platt *et al* (2010) have also found evidence that judgments in judicial review cases do, on occasion, profoundly influence subsequent decision-making in the public sector. Such conflicting research, however, suggests that the legal technique will be more influential in certain circumstances than others (Halliday 2004).

The ombudsman technique operates on a different model to the courts, one which is built upon persuading both sides to understand their respective needs and viewpoints, i.e. 'interest-based resolution' – a classic ADR/mediation approach. Through actively working with the body under investigation, opportunities will arise to persuade the body to understand the need for resolution and voluntarily to promote solutions and remedies where appropriate. Arguably, therefore, such an approach creates a better learning environment for the public authority. Indeed, the fear of the ombudsman community is that their relationship with public authorities, and their ability to secure redress and change, would change detrimentally were the ombudsman process to take on a more legalized dimension, for instance through the addition of legal powers of enforcement.

Hertogh contends that the policy impact of the courts and ombudsman is directly related to their styles of control. He distinguishes two styles of control for analytical purposes: 'coercive control' based on the use of authority backed by sanctions, as commonly associated with the courts; and 'cooperative control', as adopted by the ombudsman (Hertogh 2001, 54). This 'cooperative' style of control involves greater flexibility to tailor the main remedy – a non-binding recommendation – to the circumstances of the complaint. An instance of this flexibility is the ability to recommend that a compensation payment be made – something that is extremely hard to obtain from the courts in public law (Law Commission 2008). Above all, and building on the previous point,

> [T]he ombudsman [can] take a more expansive adjudicative perspective … look to the underlying causes of citizen grievance and, over time, and by way of a

37 'We can estimate that for every ten threats of litigation, more than six are resolved without proceedings being commenced' (Bondy and Sunkin 2009, 244).

> cumulative and iterative process ... make recommendations that will remedy not just the plight of the individual complainant but others already, or yet to be, in the same or similar situation. (O'Brien 2009, 470)

For many complainants it is this acceptance of responsibility and recognition of the need to improve that they will most want to see from the responsible public body.

The arguments surrounding the ombudsman technique in dispute resolution are not all one way (King 2007a, 27-9). For instance, although the process is said to be comparatively stress-free for complainants, for many the fact that the ombudsman takes ownership of the complaint may be a disadvantage rather than a strength. At its worst complainants may feel they have lost control of a complaint and have virtually no knowledge of its progress until the final conclusion is reached. There may be a sense of a lost opportunity in being prevented from undertaking a cross-examination in open court.[38] Indeed, the standard lawyer's viewpoint would be to place more faith in their ability and motivation to develop a case than rely upon an investigatory body alone (Justice-All Souls 1988, 98). Moreover, once the investigation is completed there is no effective appeal mechanism, being replaced instead by the relatively weak power to judicially review the report of the ombudsman or internally complain to the ombudsman about how the complaint was handled.

There are also fundamental concerns about the opaque nature in which the ombudsmen go about their work. 'The values of openness, fairness and impartiality [are] hard to police given the extensive unrecorded discussions taking place between the ombudsman and parties at every stage' (King 2007, 28). Whilst ombudsmen can produce detailed reports outlining their reasoning and findings, this is no longer the norm. Even where it is, the process by which the investigation is undertaken is shrouded in a certain amount of mystery, leaving the suspicion that either disputes are negotiated to a conclusion without full appreciation of the interests of the complainant or, worse still, there is a bias in favour of the body under investigation. There is even a danger of a perception being created 'that the Ombudsman is a part of the Establishment and tends to sustain its activities' (Ranjan Jha 1990, 79). Finally, the very flexibility of the ombudsman powers offends a basic tenet of the rule of law – certainty. How, it can be argued, can the ombudsman contribute to improvements in good administration when it is unwilling to see the meaning of maladministration defined in detail and offer precedents as evidence of application?

Such allegations would, of course, be firmly rebutted by the ombudsmen. Objections to the ombudsman technique tend both to undervalue the fairness of the procedures open to the ombudsman and overplay the importance of the adversarial approach to justice. In the words of one judge, '[a] public hearing is not the only

---

38 See Chapter 4, pp. 102-6.

fair way of finding facts'.[39] One of the strengths of the ombudsman model is that the office is not restricted by the straitjacket of judicial procedures and has the flexibility to choose the method of investigation most appropriate to the case in hand. This can mean that, if the ombudsman deems it appropriate, a hearing is held at which both parties to a dispute are present and represented by lawyers.[40] Ordinarily though the inquisitorial approach is adopted, an approach which is backed up by wide-ranging powers of investigation with regard to documents and people.[41] Ombudsman legislation also 'provides for a substantial degree of due process'.[42] By law, the public body complained against is afforded 'an opportunity to comment on any allegations contained in the complaint'[43] and, by practice, the ombudsmen generally submit extracts of their draft reports to both the public body and the complainant for comment on the factual accuracy of the investigation.

The key to understanding the merits of the ombudsman process lies in the realization that it provides a different service that is, at the very least, a necessary option in the armoury of the administrative justice system. Thus the objective in promoting the benefits of the ombudsman technique is not to argue that the method is always superior to the alternatives, but rather to suggest that it represents a viable and extremely useful option which in some instances will be the better choice for the parties concerned. To require ombudsmen to conduct their activities in the full glare of the public eye, to allow for the parties to participate in oral hearings and to build into the system a fully fledged appeal process, would be to convert the ombudsman model into a judicial process and denude it of many of its most special features. In particular, there would be a danger that public authorities would start treating ombudsmen in the same manner as the legal process. For instance, public authorities would be more likely to employ lawyers in their dealings with the ombudsmen, would be less cooperative in the provision of information and much less open to admitting areas of fault and exploring with the ombudsman alternative solutions. In return, ombudsmen would be placed under pressure to reconsider their methods and adopt a more legalized methodology in order to defend the minutiae of their decision-making.

The ombudsman technique works optimally in an environment in which the bodies investigated can be encouraged to engage constructively in the process rather than in a fully defensive mode, a situation facilitated by the lack of

39 *Bradley and others v Secretary of State for Work and Pensions* [2007] EWHC 242 (Admin) at [58] (Bean J).

40 E.g. the HSO has conducted formal hearings in Case 483/1981-82, reported at pages 47-63 of Health Service Commissioner, Third Report (Session 1983/4), published on 13 December 1983; Case 309/1983-84, reported at pages 94-113 of Health Service Commissioner, First Report (Session 1984/5), published on 3 December 1984.

41 E.g. Parliamentary Commissioner Act 1967, ss.8 and 9; similar powers are possessed by the other ombudsmen.

42 *Bradley* [2007] EWHC 242 (Admin) at [58] (Bean J).

43 Parliamentary Commissioner Act 1967, s.7(1).

enforceability of findings and recommendations. Not only does this entail that bodies investigated can enter into the process in a slightly more relaxed fashion because they retain the option not to comply, but it also places a particularly strong onus on the ombudsman to explain and justify their conclusions and thereby persuade the body of the need to comply. The extent to which the ombudsman is required to enter into this process to defend their findings also provides a response to the common critique of the ombudsman's decision-making – that they are overly based on discretion and are lacking in predictability. In most complex cases detailed and explanatory evidence-based reports have to be produced to justify the ombudsman's conclusions. Furthermore, although the general rule is that the ombudsman does not follow precedent, most ombudsman schemes do offer guidance on the equitable principles that inform their determinations and publicize their previous findings.[44] Such case studies can, over the years, build up a picture of a consistent and coherent approach to some categories of complaint.

Questions of Accountability

The argument presented above has been that the ombudsman enterprise upholds and promotes standards of good administration, broadly understood. In doing so, alongside other institutions in the administrative justice system, the ombudsman's existence enhances the capacity of the constitution to provide for the redress of grievances. In addition, as will be expanded upon throughout this book, the ombudsman is well placed to offer positive, forward-thinking assistance to public bodies in improving administrative practice for the future. Taken together, these attributes mean that the ombudsman is best understood as one of a range of accountability institutions within the constitution, tasked with the role of upholding the rule of law, justice, democracy, human rights and, more generally, the integrity of public authority.[45] These are big claims which will be explored and defended throughout this book. Thus before looking at the practice of the ombudsman enterprise to test the effectiveness of the offices in meeting these claims, in this section the potential impact of the ombudsman's contribution will

44 For example, '[b]oth in cases that go to report and in those dealt with via the intervention method, a record is kept of the criteria applied and (where relevant) of the decision on the propriety or otherwise of the action under investigation. These records are an important aid to the annual analysis of the cases encountered by the National Ombudsman.' National Ombudsman for the Netherlands at: <http://www.ombudsman.nl/english/ombudsman/decision/decision_criteria.asp>.

45 This argument has been made in a series of articles by the current PHSO: see Abraham (2008; 2008a; 2008b; 2008c; 2008d). See also the lectures of the European Ombudsman, available at: <http://www.ombudsman.europa.eu/activities/speeches.faces;jsessionid=C9D667EE254564CD245B3BA77782D1D7> (accessed 8 March 2010), for example, Diamandouros (2005).

be summarized by way of comparison with current understandings of the concept of accountability. This concept, as it relates to the ombudsman enterprise, can be best understood in the bifurcated sense of i) the capacity of the ombudsman to promote the accountability of public authorities it has oversight of, and ii) the extent to which the ombudsman offices themselves are accountable bodies within the administrative justice system. These two aspects are dealt with in the sections below.

The Capacity of the Ombudsman to Promote Accountability

Accountability 'is one of those golden concepts that no one can be against' (Bovens *et al* 2008, 225), yet it can mean subtly different things to different people (Mulgan 2003). Over the years, the use of the concept has expanded in both political and legal literature. For the purposes of this work, three dominant perspectives on accountability that regularly appear within academic literature will be employed to demonstrate the ombudsman's contribution; these are the 'democratic', 'constitutional' and 'learning' perspectives (Bovens *et al* 2008, 223). These three versions of accountability theory cover a broad range of objectives. It is going to be rare for an accountability institution to deliver on all objectives at once given the tensions amongst them. The strength of the ombudsman institution, however, is that it is capable of promoting all three perspectives of accountability.

From a 'democratic perspective', '[a]ccountability controls and legitimizes government actions by linking them effectively to the "democratic chain of delegation"' (Bovens *et al* 2008, 231, Table 1). The input of the ombudsman into the democratic process is most evident where the ombudsman reports the results of its work to an elected assembly, which is frequently the case with public sector ombudsmen schemes. As already identified, the effectiveness of this arrangement will vary from scheme to scheme. It can no longer be argued that the current ombudsmen operate as subservient agents to the various democratic assemblies that they can report to. Indeed, as will be discussed in more detail later in the book,[46] there is a concern that most legislatures pay insufficient attention to and make inadequate use of the ombudsman as extensions of their own capacity to call the executive to account. Nevertheless, there is the potential for an extremely effective relationship between legislatures and ombudsmen in two main respects.

Firstly, complaints handling has always been closely linked to the democratic enterprise as practised in legislative assemblies. The Scottish Parliament, for instance, set up a petitions committee[47] when it first came into force, whilst Westminster Members of Parliament (MPs) have always jealously guarded

46 See further, Chapter 6, pp. 179-85.

47 'The ability of individuals, interest groups and others to petition the Scottish Parliament was a significant plank of the all-party Consultative Steering Group's vision of public access. The institution of a Public Petitions Committee (PPC) by the Parliament is intended to ensure that petitions are treated in a manner consistent with this vision.'

their right to pursue complaints on behalf of their constituents and the House of Commons has recently reviewed proposals for a petitions committee and e-petitions system (Maer 2009). Ombudsmen provide significant assistance to elected members in the performance of this aspect of their representative function. This enhancement of the work of Parliament was one of the most important motives for the establishment of the office of the PO (Whyatt 1961). Thus, even though it has been argued that MPs still deal with many more complaints than the PO (Rawlings 1990) the existence of the ombudsman remains important and frees up time for elected representatives. The relationship between MPs and the PO has 'changed radically' over the years and MPs appear to be better informed about the office and more willing to use the available machinery (Harlow and Rawlings 2009, 533). In particular, the ombudsman provides a specialized service capable of dealing with the more complex and difficult disputes which would probably be beyond the capacity of most elected representatives to pursue.

Secondly, a real strength of unelected institutions like the ombudsman lies in their ability to supplement parliamentary activity 'so that their technical scrutiny is used as the basis for holding ministers to account' (Hansard Society 2001, para. 1.25). Parliaments are generally overstretched and have insufficient time, capacity or arguably the expertise to undertake rigorous empirical investigation. A body such as the ombudsman, therefore, can make up for this shortfall by providing the independently verified information and analysis that is necessary to challenge the executive in the performance of its duties. Such work is of even greater public benefit where the ombudsman has utilized its capacity to broaden out its work from the investigation of individual complaints to a wider study where there is evidence of systemic faults within an administrative process.

From a 'constitutional perspective', the aim of accountability institutions should be to 'prevent or uncover abuses of public authority' (Bovens *et al* 2008, 225). This perspective maps very closely to the concept of securing institutional integrity referred to earlier in this chapter.[48] Clearly, uncovering abuses of power is central to the investigation of complaints and the provision of administrative justice. In turn, administrative justice systems support the work of democratic assemblies in the fundamental respect of retaining public trust in government.

That this trust is retained in government is vital for democracy, as for most citizens the most immediate form of interaction with public authority will be through their experience of public services (Committee on Standards in Public Life 2005, paras 1.20-1.25). If this experience is poor then the relationship between the citizen and the state becomes compromised, whatever the outcome of the various elections that the citizen can vote in (Abraham 2007). An important aspect, therefore, of securing trust in government is the provision of external

---

Scottish Parliament website, available at: <http://www.scottish.parliament.uk/vli/history/whisp/whisp-99/wh01-30.htm> (accessed 9 March 2010).

48 See pp. 28-30 above.

assurance of the services provided by government and allowing for redress where grievances arise.[49]

On a similar point, the European Ombudsman has argued in a series of lectures that the ombudsman institution has an important part to play around the world in upholding both the rule of law and democratic government (e.g. Diamandouros 2005; 2007). A key feature of the ombudsman's contribution is the ability of the office to promote transparency by uncovering and making public the inner processes of government decision-making. The ombudsman is perhaps better equipped to deliver this task than most other dispute resolution agents because of the powers and techniques it adopts. A key part of this process is not only the revelation of error where that has occurred, but also the activity of independently verifying the efficacy of the decision-making processes within government.

The ombudsman's ability to uncover abuses of power goes further than individual complaints. Ombudsmen around the world possess greater or lesser powers to expand their investigations so as to present in-depth reports on aspects of administrative activity which can affect a great number of persons. Such reports can secure redress for a significant number of individuals not involved in the original complaint, as well as enabling ombudsmen to intervene in areas where, for reasons such as the vulnerability of those affected, complaints have not been received or are surprisingly rare. The exploration of this facet of the ombudsman's work will be one of the focuses of this book. It may even be that the ombudsman's potential arsenal of investigatory tools could be expanded even further to increase the impact of the office in identifying systemic flaws in the administrative system. Several ombudsmen and academics already advocate that the future of the ombudsman institution lies in proactive audit and inspection, as much as it does in investigating complaints.

Much of the reason for this development is that ombudsmen also aspire to promote the 'learning perspective' of accountability, under which the objective is 'to make governments effective in delivering on their promises' (Bovens *et al* 2008, 225). Part of the natural workload of the ombudsman is the attempt to influence the development of administrative practice in the future by using the information found within investigations not just to resolve complaints, but to prevent reoccurrence. Although this objective is not unique to the office of the ombudsman, it is in many respects easier for the ombudsman to deliver than other dispute resolution bodies. The strength of the ombudsman lies in its investigatory technique, together with the autonomy and flexibility of the office's powers. The ombudsmen's control of the investigation puts them in a strong position to explore facts and events more broadly than might be strictly necessary to resolve the individual complaint. A further much cited advantage of the ombudsman model in promoting learning is the emphasis it places upon constructive engagement with the body under investigation (Hertogh 2001). The results can be profound. As

49 There is a debate to be had, however, as to whether the introduction of accountability institutions has promoted trust in public authority (Lapsley and Lonsdale 2010, 74-5).

the current Commonwealth Ombudsman has put it: '[A] single and well-written report can be more effective in triggering political and departmental change than a decade of oversight by courts, tribunals and investigation agencies' (McMillan 2005a, 5).

As will be described in Chapter 5, the capacity of the ombudsman to assist public authorities in learning lessons, and in so doing promoting good administration, stretches beyond investigations. Training events are staged by many ombudsman offices, advisory services offered and a whole variety of publications produced to highlight various aspects of good practice.[50] The aim of such activity is to collate the experiences gained through various investigations and feed that back to the public service bodies most likely to benefit from that wisdom. One of the challenges for the current generation of ombudsmen is to establish how far this area of work can be taken.

One important aspect of a good accountability institution is its ability to assist and empower individuals directly, not just through Parliament or the executive. This can be achieved through the provision of information and advice, and by encouraging the public bodies complained about to do the same. The achievement of this direct value to the public will strengthen claims that the ombudsman enterprise can justifiably lay claim to operate as an autonomous branch of the constitution, albeit intertwined with Parliament, the executive and even the courts.

Being Accountable: Upholding the Legitimacy of the Ombudsman

Ombudsmen, as with any accountability institution, are required to demonstrate that they achieve the goals claimed of them. In addition to promoting the accountability of the public authorities they have oversight of, discussed in the section above, ombudsman offices must also be held to account for their overall performance. Such a task inevitably also raises questions as to the legitimacy of the ombudsman to operate the public power it does, and is all the more necessary given concerns about the dangers of overburdening public authorities with excessive scrutiny requirements (Bovens *et al* 2008, 227-30; Crerar 2007, iv-v).

As with other unelected and predominantly professionally based accountability institutions, legitimacy is vital to the ombudsman if it is to influence the behaviour of citizens and public authorities. Yet lacking legal powers of enforcement as well as democratic validity, common problems that such institutions face include a lack of awareness and public support for their work. In order to be successful, therefore, ombudsmen are dependent on finding ways to ensure that their role and output is respected by those whose work they seek to influence.

> More particularly, institutional analyses of organizational legitimacy argue that there are three sets of reasons for social acceptance. Legitimacy may be pragmatically based: the person or social group perceives that the organization

50 See further, pp. 141-5.

> will pursue their interests directly or indirectly. It can be morally based: the person or social group perceives the goals and/or procedures of the organization to be morally appropriate. Finally, legitimacy can be cognitively based: the organization is accepted as necessary or inevitable … Research on what motivates compliance with legal and voluntary norms echoes this triptych. (Black 2008, 144)

An element of credibility derives from the longevity of the institution, its legal status, its connections to a democratic assembly (Giddings 2008, 97) and a realization that other options of administrative dispute resolution are frequently less attractive (Law Commission 2008). But the ombudsman is not always seen in such favourable light, either by the establishment[51] or by complainants;[52] hence ombudsmen are prompted to justify their work on an ongoing basis in order to preserve their claim to legitimacy.

A key battleground for the ombudsmen is one of explaining the intrinsic worth of the institution and persuading its stakeholders that the goals of the institution are appropriate and necessary. All the main ombudsman organizations put considerable energy into promoting their respective offices through lectures, articles and regular communication with public officials. Such public communication is backed up by the adoption of self-imposed organizational standards designed to supplement and comply with the rationale for the ombudsman. The formation of a collective professional grouping in the form of the British and Irish Ombudsman Association (BIOA) to establish and monitor such standards provides a benchmark of legitimacy. The BIOA has established four key criteria for schemes to meet before they can be considered full members. The 'Criteria for Recognition by BIOA' are 'independence of the Ombudsman from those whom the Ombudsman has the power to investigate; effectiveness; fairness and public accountability'.[53] Of these various standards the importance of independence goes to the core of any viable dispute resolution mechanism and implies that a number of subsidiary elements are present in ombudsman schemes – for example, an open and non-political appointments process, security of tenure or long fixed term of office, difficulty of removal, security and control of budget.[54] Likewise, ombudsmen strive to demonstrate fairness in their investigatory procedures which, given the nature of

51 See Chapter 1, p. 5.

52 See the various websites listed at Chapter 1, n.5.

53 See BIOA website at: <http://www.bioa.org.uk/criteria.php> (accessed 10 March 2010). See also the 'BIOA rules' at <http://www.bioa.org.uk/rules.php> (accessed 10 March 2010). More generally, there are also strong parallels here with regulation theory. Baldwin and Cave, for instance, identify five main sources of agency legitimacy: legislative mandate, expertise, efficiency, due process, accountability (Baldwin and Cave 1999, 77).

54 See 'Part B' of the 'Criteria for Recognition by BIOA' at: <http://www.bioa.org.uk/criteria.php> (accessed 10 March 2010).

their work, includes respecting the confidentiality of individuals involved in an investigation.

The other two core criteria for BIOA membership, demonstrating effectiveness and public accountability, go further than strengthening the constitutional argument for the ombudsman; they call for evidence to substantiate an argument that the institution fulfils the interests of the ombudsman's stakeholders, whether they are complainants, administrators, parliamentarians or general citizens. It is not our purpose to attempt to speak for such interests in this book. Instead, as a starting point, the approach taken in evaluating questions of effectiveness will be to assess the ability of existing ombudsmen to meet the various accountability claims that can be made of the ombudsman. Evidently, measuring the effectiveness of an accountability institution is fraught with difficulty and raises considerable methodological and theoretical problems. To begin with, any analysis needs to be wary of drawing snapshot conclusions, as it is likely that the extent to which the ombudsman achieves particular objectives will vary over time and will depend on the resources available and the specific strategies chosen in any given period of time. Snell (2007) suggests a model of ombudsmanry which analyses a range of ombudsman roles and predicts that over time the achievements of an ombudsman institution in delivering different roles will change according to perceived needs.

Attempts to evaluate the effectiveness of an ombudsman institution are further complicated by the recognition that the ombudsman invariably functions in a complex agency environment.[55] Some of the most famous ombudsman investigations – investigations that could be rightly claimed as successes – partly owed their outcomes to the contributions of Parliament, the media, lawyers, the courts and various inquiries and internal reviews. The extent to which the ombudsman institution can claim to have made a difference in such cases is almost impossible to quantify; equally it is usually difficult to ignore altogether the impact the ombudsman has made in changing the course of events.

Notwithstanding these and other analytical obstacles, an attempt will be made in this book to evaluate the extent to which ombudsmen achieve the potential that is inherent within the institution. This is a question, though, that needs to be addressed on an ongoing basis through the establishment of permanent satisfactory accountability arrangements for the ombudsman. This is a significant issue to be considered in relation to the modern, complex, administrative state, where unelected institutions perform profound accountability functions (Harlow and Rawlings 2009, 282-337; Gay and Winetrobe 2008). The ombudsmen themselves largely accept the need for strong accountability mechanisms in order that they can demonstrate their effectiveness and further strengthen their claims to legitimacy. As will be seen, there currently exist a number of different operating solutions; in particular, the relationship between Parliament and the ombudsman is usually understood as crucial (Gay and Winetrobe 2008). The extent to which

55 Much has been written recently on the problems posed by polycentric regulatory regimes: see Black (2008).

the arrangements to call the ombudsman to account are adequate is the focus of Chapter 6.

Conclusion

In the context of modern democratic constitutions, with their emphases on individual rights, accountable government and the rule of law, the services that the ombudsman can provide are of high constitutional value. These constitutional essentials are too important in value to be entrusted to the courts and Parliament alone, given the superiority in resources and information possessed by the modern executive. The challenge for the design of appropriate constitutional architecture is to find the best ways to make use of the alternative tools available. The ombudsman enterprise provides an extremely interesting example of such alternative methodology.

The ombudsman's core speciality is holding public authority to account against its adherence to understood standards of good administration. It achieves this most regularly in the investigation of complaints, but its mandate goes much further as the ombudsman is capable of actively improving administrative performance in a number of ways. The optimum focus for the ombudsman is inextricably linked to the wider functionality of the administrative justice system and the constitution. In this respect, one of the strengths of the modern ombudsman is its adaptability to meet new demands and respond to existing conditions. Due to this flexibility, there are many who think the institution is potentially one of the administrative justice system's strongest pillars. The following conclusion has been drawn from Australia, a country with a highly comparable legal system.

> Australian Ombudsmen, more than any other part of the New Administrative Law package introduced in the 1970s, have had the capacity to move beyond their originally conceived mandate, to attract new jurisdictions from governments and to constantly redevelop and refine their mission and purpose. Furthermore, of all the administrative law processes and institutions it is the Ombudsman that is best placed to respond to what have become central concerns of public law … (Snell 2007, 100-101)

To argue that the ombudsmen are capable of delivering a range of important constitutional services is an important step, but the question of whether or not ombudsmen do achieve their stated goals is another issue altogether. In the following chapters the extent to which the ombudsmen have developed techniques fit to perform their accountability role will be further explored and analysed. Before looking at the practice of the ombudsman enterprise in detail, however, further context-setting is appropriate, which is the task of Chapter 3.

Chapter 3
Concepts, Theories and Policies of Administrative Justice

Introduction

Although it was argued in Chapter 2 that the ombudsman enterprise operates within a wide-ranging and complex network of accountability institutions, insofar as the ombudsman's work can be compartmentalized it fits into a distinct subset of the constitution known as the 'administrative justice system'. Much of the later analysis in this book will demonstrate that maximizing the potential of the ombudsman enterprise will involve the proper and full integration of the ombudsman into the administrative justice system. The extent to which this system is coherently organized is the subject of much academic and political critique. Nevertheless, within recent policy developments and academic thinking there are signs of agreed thinking on the purposes of the administrative justice system. What is striking, although hardly surprising, is the degree of fit between these goals and the work of the ombudsmen. In particular, the emphasis in the administrative justice system has moved on from retrospectively resolving disputes to feeding back information into the administrations complained against in order to prevent mistakes recurring. In essence, this is exactly the duality of roles that the ombudsman is already so well designed to perform.

In order to understand the contextual developments within which the ombudsman operates, this chapter discusses the contested notions of 'administrative justice' and the 'administrative justice system', a field inhabited by public sector ombudsmen amongst others. Subsequent sections of the chapter review and discuss the principal theories of administrative justice and provide an outline of the developing policy context relating to the construction of a more coherent administrative justice system in the UK.

Concepts of 'Administrative Justice' and the 'Administrative Justice System'

The concepts of 'administrative justice' and the 'administrative justice system' are contestable and changing notions in public law, policy and scholarly discourse. As will be seen later in this chapter, the meaning of these concepts has been nuanced by policy developments that have generated a more expansive vision of both the concept of administrative justice and the range of territory occupied by the administrative justice system. There are some key features which develop our understanding of these concepts that can be noted.

Firstly, the concept of administrative justice tends to be used both *descriptively* to identify the decision-making interface between government agencies and citizens, and *normatively* to describe how such decision-making ought to be delivered. The task of mere description, at first sight, looks straightforward, but the public/private divide has become less clear and consequently has made this task more problematic. The Financial Services Ombudsman (FSO), for example, has jurisdiction over settling complaints between consumers and businesses providing financial services; this is notionally a private sector activity. This can be compared to the direct relationship that the Parliamentary and Health Services Ombudsman (PHSO) has in settling complaints between citizens and government departments; a thoroughly public sector activity. But where the provision of financial services raises significant issues of public interest and concern, for example, the mis-selling of mortgage endowment policies, the state's response, possibly in the form of increased regulation, may challenge one's conception of where the private/public divide lies (Merricks 2010; Oliver 2010). The task of posing a series of normative questions about how decision-making by government agencies *ought* to be organized and delivered is perhaps even more problematic; the various answers to this type of question will in turn depend on more fundamental political, social and cultural values. The plurality of normative models of justice is a theme which will be taken up in the section on theories and typologies below.

Secondly, it is only relatively recently that the idea of an administrative justice 'system' has appeared. Contemporary attempts to describe the administrative justice system inevitably involve consideration of whether such a system exists at all. As will be described later in this chapter, a more holistic, joined-up vision of administrative justice as a system has evolved, particularly since the appearance of the government's White Paper *Transforming Public Services* (DCA 2004). It is not only the systemic features of administrative justice that must be considered. The range of the administrative justice field has also widened. While earlier legal scholarship tended to focus almost exclusively on a pyramid of redress mechanisms – courts, tribunals and (sometimes) ombudsmen – more recent policy developments have emphasized the importance of the first-instance decision-making process, particularly from the users' perspective. Equally, earlier theoretical approaches (Mashaw 1983) tended to focus almost exclusively on the first-instance decision-making processes of government agencies without much account of how remedial mechanisms fitted into their visions of administrative justice. Furthermore, the field has widened in alignment with a general increase of state involvement across an increasing number of policy sectors. The field has also been further occupied by additional forms of remedial methods, such as internal review mechanisms, and a growing cluster of other complaint handlers and early dispute resolution methods.

The concepts of both administrative justice and administrative justice system can be deployed to suggest that there are underlying *principles* of administrative justice that set the boundary for defining the landscape and that regulate how any resulting 'system' should operate. The Nuffield Foundation in its work on the topic drew a clear distinction between 'administrative justice' and 'justice in administration'.

> We recognise that 'administrative justice' is a wide-ranging if rather imprecise concept. The Foundation's work will start on the basis of a distinction between 'justice in administration', where 'justice' may be in competition with other administrative criteria, and 'administrative justice', which we take to cover reactions to alleged deficiencies in first instance decision-making. 'Administrative justice' has at its core the administrative decisions by public authorities that affect individual citizens and the mechanisms available for the provision of redress. These latter include tribunals, ombudsmen, complaints handlers, internal review and other forms of early dispute resolution. (Nuffield Foundation 2008, para. 3)

By contrast, an Economic and Social Research Council (ESRC) sponsored seminar series on administrative justice refrained from providing any precise definition of these concepts, though it focused on, amongst other things, theoretical perspectives and the extent to which coordination could be achieved between various elements of the emerging 'system'.[1]

For most purposes, the current discourse about an administrative justice system is to be taken as a reference to a vision of reformed arrangements rather than existing ones. The use of the concept of administrative justice system often involves an implicit critique of the status quo. For example, the PHSO has stated: '[t]o speak of an administrative justice "system" is still a bit of a misnomer, since there is nothing very systematic about the current rather fragmented set-up' (Abraham 2009).

Academic and professional lawyers have frequently regarded administrative justice as inclusive only of judicial review by courts and statutory appeal to the tribunals; sometimes the list also includes complaints to the ombudsmen, though this is often considered an 'alternative' to the first two. Traditional legal scholarship has largely excluded consideration of first-instance decision-making, internal review and complaint mechanisms within public agencies. Ombudsmen have been generally marginalized to superficial treatment, if any, in law syllabuses and professional legal education.

This myopic tendency to focus on judicial review in administrative law remains strong (though not unchallenged) in contemporary legal culture in the UK. This was illustrated in the Law Commission's consultation paper on administrative redress (Law Commission 2008), which set out a disappointingly narrow agenda

1 The aims of this seminar series are set out in the *Adjust Newsletter*, April 2006. Available at: <http://www.council-on-tribunals.gov.uk/adjust/06_2.htm> (accessed 11 March 2010).

Table 3.1 The four pillars of administrative justice

Pillar 1	Pillar 2	Pillar 3	Pillar 4
Internal mechanisms for redress, such as formal complaint procedures	External, non-court avenues of redress, such as public inquiries and tribunals	Public sector ombudsmen	Remedies available in public and private law by way of a court action

Source: Law Commission (2008a, para. 1.8).

to strengthen mainly *court*-based remedies against public bodies. Its definition of the landscape of administrative justice, set out in Table 3.1, focused exclusively on remedial mechanisms and provides a four-way categorization. The categorization is successful in that it distinguishes pillar 4, the main subject of the Law Commission's attention, from other internal and external mechanisms of redress. Ombudsmen are awarded their own pillar (3), but in fact might have been more logically listed under pillar 2, that being a non-curial form of external redress. The typology also fails to identify the various levels or tiers of either internal complaint or external redress mechanisms.

However, the vision of administrative justice contained in *Transforming Public Services* (DCA 2004) did articulate a policy that focused specifically on administrative justice as a 'system'. This mirrors policy development later elsewhere, with the mainspring for government policy over at least the last decade being the pursuit of a 'customer-focused', 'user' or 'bottom-up' approach to any reform initiatives.

Towards a Definition of Administrative Justice

In the years since *Transforming Public Services*, a consensus has arguably emerged on how we might identify the subject matter of administrative justice. Any definition should be a broad one sufficient to capture a range of activities around the citizen–state interface that public bodies are tasked to deliver. Although for analytical purposes some commentators will want to use administrative justice in the more limited sense of a focus on government agency decision-making and a discussion of the normative models available (Halliday 2004, 114), in this book, the field of administrative justice can be taken to include the wider architecture of the administrative justice system. This will include not only the first-instance decision-making by government agencies, but also the full range of remedial mechanisms (including ombudsmen) and the accountability relationships surrounding both the agencies delivering first-instance decision-making and those delivering remedies. This bifurcated definition of administrative justice is, so far, consistent with a definition put forward by Mullen. He argues that 'the principal justification of adopting such a broad definition is that it delimits a coherent field of inquiry and enables discussion of administrative justice to respond to the full range of citizens' concerns about their interaction with public services' (Mullen 2009, 2).

The previous traditional focus of administrative law scholarship on exclusively court- and tribunal-based remedial mechanisms, therefore, has had to give way to the inclusion of initial decision-making. Equally, earlier theoretical perspectives, which have been limited to the examination of initial decision-making processes, have had to be widened in scope to include redress mechanisms (Adler 2010, 148).

Our working definition though adds a third dimension to this framework to include the governance and accountability arrangements that form a key part of the environment in which government agencies and institutions that deliver remedial mechanisms operate. The increasing implicit and explicit recognition of administrative justice as at least an emerging 'system' requires, in our view, consideration of the network of governance and accountability relationships surrounding the public agencies responsible for decisional and remedial processes. The inclusion of this third limb of accountability better enables us to locate administrative justice within the wider political and constitutional environments. We can now summarize our working definition of the administrative justice system as inclusive of the following:

1. all initial decision-making by public bodies impacting on citizens – this will include the relevant statutory regimes and the procedures used to make such decisions ('getting it right');
2. all redress mechanisms available in relation to the initial decision-making ('putting it right');
3. the network of governance and accountability relationships surrounding the public bodies tasked with decision-making impacting upon citizens and those tasked with providing remedies ('setting it right').

One can see that a 'user' policy perspective[2] leads inevitably to the acceptance of initial decision-making within our definition. After all, this is the first-line contact a citizen has with the state. From a user perspective, the ability of public bodies to get the decision right first time ('getting it right') is probably even *more* important, at least in the short term, than the prospect of having to challenge an adverse decision by resort to one or more redress routes ('putting it right'). There are of course real advantages in having successful remedial systems developed, as the considerable literature on the importance of justice in the democratic state attests to (Rawls 1999). From the state's perspective, remedies will enable corrections to be made where necessary to decisional processes to deliver intended policies accurately. They are also likely to provide a greater sense of public confidence and legitimacy in the processes at issue. From the user's perspective, they provide a supportive mechanism to assert rights and claims against the state, in addition to providing a participatory means to discharge social grievances within a structured and orderly framework.

2 See pp. 76-7 below.

But, as our working definition suggests, a study of administrative justice must also take into account the wider framework of democratic accountability in which the institutional arrangements to 'getting it right' and 'putting it right' are set. We have found, for example, in the course of our research on public sector ombudsmen, that it would be extremely difficult to understand fully and explain how the ombudsman agencies have developed and changed and how they might be usefully reformed in the future without some quite detailed consideration of their governance and accountability relationships. The policy developments in the UK prompt a holistic analysis, whereas the omission of this dimension would prevent necessary 'joined-up thinking'. For example, any assessment of the role of the PHSO would be incomplete without consideration of both the internal and external accountability controls applicable to this office. Chapters 6 and 7 discuss in some depth the accountability and assurance dimensions of ombudsman organizations. Likewise, ombudsmen do not operate in isolation even in dispute resolution terms, hence the importance of fitting the ombudsman enterprise appropriately within the wider administrative justice system, as will be analysed in Chapter 7. This element of our working definition we have designated, for ease of reference, as 'setting it right'.

Some commentators have used rather narrower definitional starting points to explain administrative justice. For example, in Mashaw's landmark work, *Bureaucratic Justice*, he defines administrative justice as 'the qualities of a decision process that provide arguments for the acceptability of its decisions' (Mashaw 1983, 24).[3] He had in mind not just any decisions within the field of public administration but those decisions that were directed specifically to implementing state-driven policies. His focus was very much on the *processes* designed to achieve those ends. The problem with Mashaw's definition, however, is that it would exclude consideration of rights of redress (the second limb of our working definition) or the regulation of public administration and issues relating to the public accountability that form the wider environment for such decision-making processes (the third limb of our definition).

Our working definition of the administrative justice system so far is largely descriptive of the extent of the terrain rather than its normative value. Some commentators would also want to define administrative justice to include 'the principles that may be used to evaluate the justice inherent in administrative decision-making' (Adler 2003, 323-4). As we have seen, the Nuffield Foundation was careful to isolate 'justice in administration' in their approach. Implicit in our working definition is the inclusion of normative debates about how institutional arrangements ought to be organized to make them 'right'. Consequently, there is a range of normative models of 'getting it *right*', 'putting it *right*' and 'setting it *right*'. Our notion of administrative justice encompasses the underlying principles that *ought* to be present in the system as a whole. The advantage of adding this important dimension to our definition is that it ensures that any consideration of

3 Adler (2003, 329) suggests, for clarification, that this should be read in effect as the qualities of a decision process that provide arguments for the *legitimacy* of its *outcomes*.

the administrative justice system considers not only outcomes and processes but also the more difficult qualities of fairness and legitimacy that we might expect to be present in the system. It enables us to see more clearly that there is often a competition between visions of administrative justice – a theme further explored by the theorists of administrative justice.[4] This approach also enables a more profound and critical examination of the *assumptions* underlying government policy and legislation rather than merely focusing on the more technical difficulties of *delivering* those policies and rules.

In summary, it is argued here that the tripartite focus on 'getting it right', 'putting it right' and 'setting it right' provides a more complete and coherent picture of the field of administrative justice and is one that fits the administrative justice system into the wider constitution. After all, while the provision of justice is an axiomatic feature of the administrative justice system, the system is also one that contributes to the accountability of governance and integrity in public authorities. In addition, the tripartite approach to administrative justice resonates with users' perceptions of dealing with government departments and other public authorities that are often experienced as a complex journey – sometimes a bumpy one – from one part of officialdom to another. The quality of that journey is sometimes lengthy, arduous, confusing and frustrating for some citizens. It is also implicit within this type of definition that both the substantive *law* and the *procedures* of each of the three elements can be critically examined. Consequently, our definition includes an underlying critique of the relevant principles of justice within the administrative justice system. This approach to defining the field, as Mullen (2009, 3) also notes, has the advantage that it reflects, or at least is not inconsistent with, the (only) statutory definition of 'administrative justice system' in the UK, to be found in the Tribunals, Courts and Enforcement Act (TCEA) 2007.

A Statutory Definition of 'Administrative Justice System'

It should be remembered that this legislative definition is, strictly speaking, only relevant to the functions of the newly constituted Administrative Justice and Tribunals Council (AJTC) as set out in paragraph 13(1)-(3), Schedule 7.

> In this paragraph 'the administrative justice system' means the overall system by which decisions of an administrative or executive nature are made in relation to particular persons, including –
> a. the procedures for making such decisions,
> b. the law under which such decisions are made, and
> c. the systems for resolving disputes and airing grievances in relation to such decisions.[5]

4 See further pp. 65-75 below.
5 Tribunals, Courts and Enforcement Act 2007, Sched 7, para. 13(4).

There are several comments that can be made about this definition. Firstly, and most significantly, the reference is to 'the overall system'. This reflects the holistic analysis of administrative justice undertaken in *Transforming Public Services* where the UK government expressly conceptualized the idea of administrative justice as a 'system', or, perhaps more accurately, that it *ought* to be developed into some kind of coherent system. It would be difficult to conceive of a 'system' without considering the fundamental accountability attributes inherent in 'setting it right'. Secondly, the 'decisions' affecting persons can be 'of an administrative or executive nature'. The use of both the words 'administrative' and 'executive' ensures that the landscape of decisions is sufficiently broad to encapsulate all decisions emanating from a direct government (executive) source as applied by the full range of public (administrative) bodies. Thirdly, sub-paras (a) and (b) make it clear that both the 'law' *and* 'procedure' relating to such decision-making (i.e. 'getting it right') are included within the contents of the definition. That the substantive 'law' is defined as falling within the content of administrative justice also opens up the possibility for critical examination of policy making lying behind the construction of the various legislative regimes that are administered for the public. Fourthly, sub-para (c) identifies 'systems' for i) resolving disputes and for ii) airing grievances – in essence, systems for 'putting it right'. These include the whole range of formal and informal mechanisms, from judicial review to statutory appeals in courts and tribunals to internal and external review processes and the various tiers of complaint-handling, including that conducted within the ombudsman enterprise.

Although the legislative definition is technically constrained to relate to the functions of the AJTC as described in the relevant Schedule to the TCEA, the broad remit of the AJTC is such that its appearance in the legislation is a very significant one, which needs further exploration to understand fully the 'wider system' of administrative justice.

Administrative Justice Theorists and Typologies

Before considering the response of government to shifting perceptions of what administrative justice entails, it is useful to consider the importance of appreciating the motivations that lie behind administrative decision-making. This is because dispute resolution mechanisms, and internal accountability institutions more broadly conceived, are less likely to be successful if they do not address such features.

The true power of the pioneering work of theorists in the administrative justice field is that they have exposed approaches to the subject which rely upon the imposition of legal values on administrative decision-makers. The primary targets of such critique are traditional studies of 'administrative law' which concern themselves with a focus on the way in which a (minimalist) state can control excess state power and subject it to legal control, characterized by

Harlow and Rawlings (2009, 22) as 'red light theory' or 'fire-fighting'. This approach puts the role of courts at the centre of the project to secure good administration; administrative law should operate to impact (retrospectively) on government as an external control to be invoked when power is abused. 'Green light theory' (Harlow and Rawlings 2009, 31) or 'fire-watching', on the other hand, places the courts' influence at the margins and the political process in the centre. This approach pursues a vision of administrative law as a more positive and collectivist facilitation of legitimate government action. It also focuses more on internal rather than external controls on the administration, for example, the doctrine of ministerial responsibility and techniques of internal administrative regulation. The emergence of the notion of 'administrative justice' over the past 20 years has, to an extent, been a result of the increasing influence of 'green light' over 'red light' theorizing, though of course the analysis of both external and internal controls is required for a comprehensive picture. As Adler (2010, 154) argues, an 'administrative justice' approach that combines the merits of both external redress mechanisms and other internal means to support the justice of administrative decision-making has much merit.

Most importantly, the growth of state intervention in every aspect of life has meant the generation of more institutions to deliver administration in the public sector, along with an increasingly sophisticated and complex framework of regulation, inspection and audit. The remedial mechanisms available have also proliferated since the foundation of the welfare state in the 1940s and 1950s. The terrain of administrative law and the normative concept of administrative justice could no longer justifiably concern merely court control through the evolving technique of judicial review challenge. As will be described shortly, such policy developments have led to significant changes to the culture of public administration which indicate a greater emphasis on the user focus and outcomes for the consumer of public services. This has resulted in the emergence of a more comprehensive and joined-up vision of administrative justice in the UK in the form of the tripartite definition of administrative justice ('getting it right', 'putting it right' and 'setting it right') explained above.[6]

Administrative justice theorizing helps explain the need for such developments, primarily because it purports to contain some kind of explanatory power to advance our understanding of the 'real world' administrative justice system. In doing so, however, it should be noted that the construction of theory itself is unlikely to be a neutral, objective activity. Our sense of what is an appropriate theory to adopt in this area is likely to be conditioned by an array of social, political, ethical and cultural values and viewpoints. The allocation, distribution and accountability of power within a society's administrative justice system is likely, indeed many would argue *ought*, to be a contested notion. It may be that the unstated assumptions and/or necessary conditions underpinning any particular theoretical approach may turn out to be more important than the

6 See pp. 56-9 above.

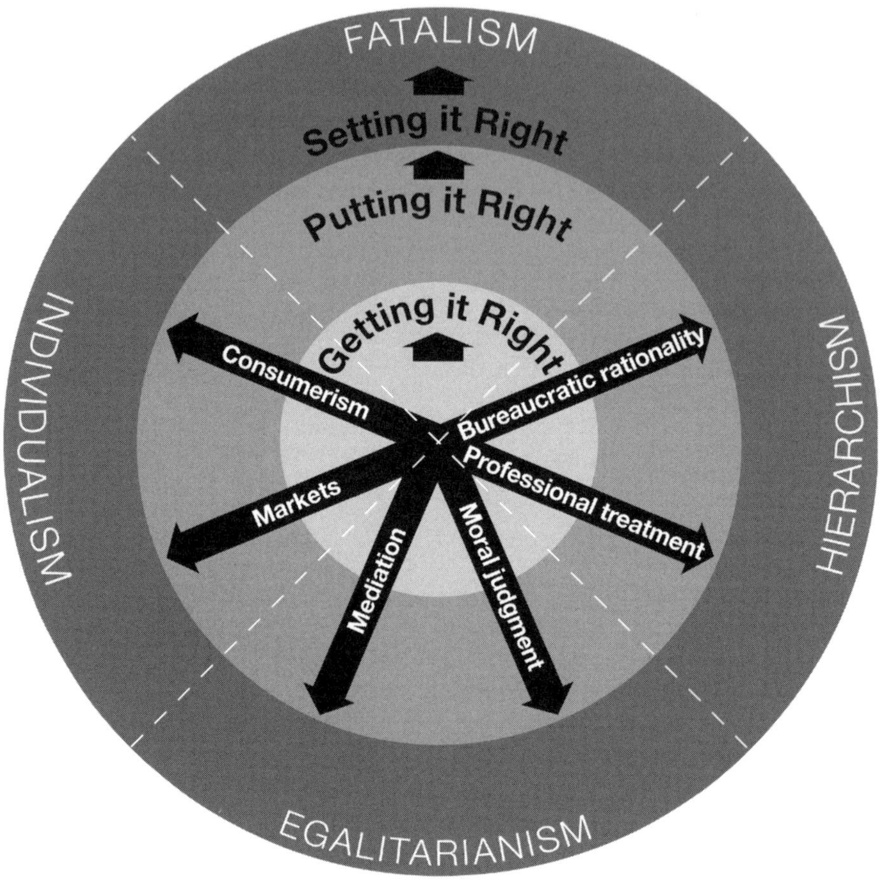

Figure 3.1 A typology of administrative justice
Source: The authors.

stated elements of the theory. In short, the theoretical perspectives discussed here may not always rigorously separate fundamental 'what is' from 'what ought' questions; engaging in theory building in this field is not a neutral activity (Jones 1999, 40).

The following section presents our own vision of administrative justice which has been built both from our respective research interests in this area and from our understanding of the theories and typologies proposed by other scholars in this field. We set out briefly our own vision and then explain in the subsequent sections how we have arrived at this understanding, with reference to the ground-breaking work of Mashaw (1983) followed by the extension and critique of his analysis by other scholars.

A Typology of Administrative Justice

Figure 3.1 illustrates our view of how administrative justice in a liberal democratic state such as the UK is structured. Our tripartite definition of administrative justice discussed above is represented by the three concentric rings. These three rings mark the functional landscape of administrative justice. The inner ring, 'getting it right', refers to the initial decision-making by public bodies, encompassing the relevant law and procedure. The middle ring, 'putting it right', refers to the whole range of redress mechanisms (including ombudsman offices) that are available in respect of the initial decision-making process. The outer ring, 'setting it right', refers to the network of governance and accountability relationships surrounding both the public bodies tasked with first-instance decision-making and those responsible for providing remedies, which we would argue better enables us to locate administrative justice within the wider political and constitutional environments. There is an understandable relationship between the concentric rings. One can easily visualize any first-instance administrative decision being made by a public service impacting on a member, or members, of the public. The public agency will want to get the decision right first time. But where there is something wrong with that decision it will enter the middle ring, where an external body – a court, tribunal, ombudsman or other independent complaint-handler – will attempt to provide some type of remedy for the flawed decision and 'put it right'. Finally, the overall context for all this activity is represented by the outer ring that represents the complex network of governance and accountability relationships; the mechanisms of 'getting it right' and 'putting it right' will not operate successfully unless such governance and accountability relationships are also established or 'set' appropriately. This 'setting it right' tier of administrative justice is further explored in Chapters 6 and 7.

These three rings reflect the core *functions* of the administrative justice system. They are also broadly parallel to some of the characteristic *institutions* of the administrative justice system. For example, returning to the ombudsman enterprise context: 'getting it right' refers to all those public authorities (within the statutory ambit of ombudsman investigation) that make millions of decisions every day affecting the citizen; 'putting it right' refers to all the ombudsman bodies receiving complaints and attempting to resolve them; 'setting it right' refers to the governance and accountability bodies that will ultimately impact on first-instance decision-making and remedial processes. The 'setting it right' function can be illustrated by the trajectory of a particular complaint, for example, about a decision from the Department for Work and Pensions (DWP) which, probably after an internal review by the DWP, is referred to the PHSO. As an exemplar of administrative justice, this complaint can be analysed with regard not only to the initial decision-making and remedial processes but also with regard to a number of accountability bodies and relationships relevant to both the DWP (for example, the Social Security Advisory Committee) and the PHSO (for example, the internal audit committee and the Public Administration Select Committee). In this way, our understanding of administrative justice can connect to the wider policy and constitutional environments.

Figure 3.1 also maps a number of theoretical dimensions onto our function-based tripartite definition. The six arrows (containing text) refer to the three well-known 'models of justice' as formulated by Mashaw (1983) ('bureaucratic rationality', 'professional treatment' and 'moral judgment'), two of the additional models provided by Adler (2003) (consumerism, markets)[7] and finally the 'negotiation/mediation' category identified by Kagan (2010) (indicated simply as 'mediation' in Figure 3.1). These models are further explained below, but in essence they represent the underlying drivers of administrative justice which are in competition with each other for dominance in any one scenario. For example, Adler's work on the assessment of special educational needs found that, in Scotland, 'professionalism, strongly supported by bureaucracy, was the dominant configuration' but in England 'the dominance of the professional model was more effectively challenged by the bureaucratic, legal,[8] and consumerist models' (Adler 2003, 341). Adler's analysis criticized the limited application of Mashaw to first-instance decisional processes (getting it right) and extended the application of Mashaw's analysis to remedial mechanisms (putting it right); consequently the text-bearing arrows extend to the outer edge of this middle ring. But it is unlikely that the Mashaw/Adler dimensions can be easily applied, if at all, to the activity described in our notion of setting it right, as there are qualitative differences in the nature and behaviour of the public bodies and relationships that occupy this territory. Our interest in them is not derived from their direct involvement in administrative decision-making and remedies from such decision-making. It is instead to be found in the way in which accountability, inspection and audit or 'integrity' institutions structure the constitutional and public management environment in which these core administrative activities take place. Put another way, one can see the setting it right element as referring to the way in which the constitutional template is framed and sets the boundaries (red light theory) and opportunities (green light theory) of the core activities within the administrative justice system.

The dotted lines mark out the four quadrants (hierarchism, egalitarianism, individualism and fatalism) familiar to those acquainted with 'grid-group' cultural theory. This approach is further explained below, but in short the idea represented here is that these four quite fundamental cultural biases found in social life can translate into competing visions of 'getting it right', 'putting it right' and 'setting it right'. Consequently the dotted lines delineating cultural biases reach into all three concentric rings. Furthermore, Figure 3.1 also suggests, following Halliday and Scott's (2010, 197) analysis, that the Mashaw/Adler/Kagan dimensions can

7 Adler's third extension, 'managerialism', has been dropped from our graphic illustration for the same reasons noted by Halliday, i.e. that this category is in reality an aspect of bureaucratic rationality (Halliday 2004, 123).

8 Adler relabelled Mashaw's 'moral judgment' model as 'legal', see p. 67 below.

be mapped into one of the quadrants of cultural bias. For example, bureaucratic rationality and professional treatment appear in the 'hierarchism' quadrant.

It is not suggested that Figure 3.1 represents any magic formula to unlock the working of administrative justice, but it does provide a framework that usefully combines the functional and institutional perspective of our tripartite definition of administrative justice with various strands of theoretical scholarship in this field, which can then be used to formulate critical interrogation and analysis of particular aspects of the administrative justice system. The typology presented thus enables a critical exposure of a number of interacting analytical layers at work in the administrative justice system. The sections below further explain the intellectual foundations of the various elements contained in Figure 3.1.

Mashaw and the First Tier of Administrative Justice: 'Getting it Right'

Modern thinking on administrative justice begins with Mashaw, whose early work focused very much on theorizing around *process values* within administrative law, grounded in the liberal-democratic tradition of American constitutionalism. He observed the importance of processes on participants in evaluating the legitimacy of public decision-making (Mashaw 1981, 886). In his ground-breaking work, *Bureaucratic Justice*, Mashaw acknowledged the relative marginality of statutes and other legal rules and procedures in comparison to the concrete experience of those within administrative agencies and observed that '[t]he law in action is, in Karl Llewellyn's famous line, developed by "people who have the doing in charge"' (Mashaw 1983, 11). Mashaw's definition of administrative justice was constrained to 'the qualities of a decision process that provide arguments for the acceptability of its decisions' (Mashaw 1983, 24). He was searching for a more instrumental vision of administrative justice from within the administration rather than an externally oriented administrative law conceived in terms of abstract ideals and external constraints, a distinction that maps quite well onto the comparison between Harlow and Rawlings's (2009) green light and red light theories respectively. Mashaw alighted on the adjudication of claims for social security benefits in the United States as an exemplar for analysis. He was concerned primarily with the 'system for managing routine administrative action by low-level administrators. For it is here that 100 percent of bureaucratic implementation begins, and most of it ends' (Mashaw 1983, 16).

Mashaw identified three types of critique of social security disability programmes which he argued produced three types of justice arguments:

1. that decisions should be accurate and efficient concrete realizations of the legislative will;
2. that decisions should provide appropriate support or therapy from the perspective of the relevant professional cultures;
3. that decisions should be fairly arrived at when assessed in the light of traditional processes for determining individual entitlements (Mashaw 1983, 25).

From this he produced three models of justice: *bureaucratic rationality*, *professional treatment* and *moral judgment*, as set out in Table 3.2 below. From the perspective of *bureaucratic rationality*, administrative justice requires pre-eminently processes that are suitably rationalized to take account of costs. The classic techniques of decision-making are information retrieval and processing. The model is legitimated on the basis that it seeks to implement accurately, within any one field, pre-established social goals, while efficiently conserving social resources for other programmes.

The primary goal of *professional treatment*, on the other hand, is to serve the client. An administrative system, therefore, to administer welfare benefits would be client oriented. Such services to the client would of course be constrained by cost considerations. In the professional treatment model 'the incompleteness of facts, the singularity of individual contexts, and the ultimately intuitive nature of judgment are recognized, if not exalted' (Mashaw 1983, 27). In an administrative justice system under this model, substantive and procedural rules, hierarchical controls and efficiency considerations 'would all be subordinated to the norms of the professional culture' (Mashaw 1983, 28).

Finally, the paradigm adjudicatory situations in *moral judgment* are viewed as those of the civil and criminal trial. On the surface it may seem that if this approach is mainly about getting the facts right so as to apply legal rules correctly it is little different to bureaucratic rationality. However, Mashaw states that the moral judgment perspective should be viewed as 'value defining'. 'The question is not just who did what, but who is to be preferred, all things considered, when interests and the values to which they can be relevantly connected conflict' (Mashaw 1983, 29-30). In short, the moral judgment model has the goal of awarding entitlements on the basis of a notion of the deservingness of the parties in the particular context, giving rise to a claim for a right. Mashaw argues that this model implies a just process of proof and decision.

For Mashaw, these three models appeared to offer an illuminating framework within which one could analyse perhaps all administrative programmes delivered

Table 3.2 Features of the three justice models (Mashaw)

Dimension/ Model	Legitimizing Value	Primary Goal	Structure or Organization	Cognitive Technique
Bureaucratic Rationality	Accuracy and Efficiency	Programme Implementation	Hierarchical	Information Processing
Professional Treatment	Service	Client Satisfaction	Interpersonal	Clinical Application of Knowledge
Moral Judgment	Fairness	Conflict Resolution	Independent	Contextual Interpretation

Source: Mashaw (1983, 31).

by government agencies. For example, all other things being equal, health services would probably need to contain a significant element of professional treatment, whereas large systems of mass welfare benefit distribution might require a significant bias towards the bureaucratic rationality model.[9] Mashaw's analysis was, and remains, a refreshing reminder that the internal dynamics of front-line public bodies can explain much about decision-making processes and styles. Indeed, his work also resonates with Lipsky's (1980) concept of 'street-level bureaucrats' and Lipsky's claim that the officials who actually implement policy not only exert a great influence over policy delivery but, in effect, over the whole policy-making process. Others have also pointed out that empirical studies suggest that street-level bureaucrats' own perceptions of law and justice 'play a significant role in administrative decision making' (Hertogh 2010, 204). These ideas are quite consistent with Mashaw's (1983, 213) view that the social security agency in the United States had generated its own '*internal* law of administration'.

Extending Mashaw and the Second Tier of Administrative Justice: 'Putting it Right'

Mashaw's work has triggered much subsequent analysis, in particular by Adler, who has undertaken successive reconfigurations[10] of Mashaw's models of justice, the latest of which is reproduced below in Table 3.3. Firstly, he relabels moral judgment as the 'legal' model and substitutes 'legality' for its legitimizing value of 'fairness'.[11] Secondly, Adler identifies the core contribution of Mashaw's analysis as the way in which it enables us to see that the models coexist alongside each other, each of them is associated with a different conception of administrative justice, and that trade-offs are made between the models and the possibility of different trade-offs being made in any particular case (Adler 2003, 331; 2006, 621; 2010, 149). Thirdly, he argues that Mashaw's approach can also be taken to apply to competing models of *policy* as well as competing models of administration (Adler 2010, 151). Finally, Adler adds in three further 'managerial', 'consumerist' and 'market' models. Adler states that not all of his models are at play in every administrative system, but (in contrast to Mashaw's approach) account can be taken of absolute and *relative* strength of the models. He argues that his approach is capable of taking in both procedural and substantive justice and their interaction,[12]

9 Galligan also concludes that 'bureaucratic administration' 'will be the natural and dominant model' (Galligan 1996, 240).

10 Adler (2003, 333, Table 3); Adler (2006, 622, Table 3).

11 His argument here is that there is otherwise an unfortunate association of 'fairness' with the moral judgment model, implying that the remaining two models are 'unfair' (Mashaw 2003, 329).

12 '… the approach can be applied to competing normative models of outcomes, that is, to substantive justice, as well as to competing normative models of process, that is, to procedural fairness, and used to analyze the interactions between them' (Adler

Table 3.3 Six normative models of administrative justice

Model	Mode of Decision Making	Legitimating Goal	Mode of Accountability	Mode of redress
Bureaucratic	Applying rules	Accuracy	Hierarchical	Administrative review
Professional	Applying knowledge	Public service	Interpersonal	Second opinion or complaint to a professional body
Legal	Asserting rights	Legality	Independent	Appeal to a court or tribunal (public law)
Managerial	Managerial autonomy	Improved performance	Performance indicators and audit	None, except adverse publicity or complaints that result in sanctions
Consumerist	Consumer participation	Consumer satisfaction	Consumer charters	'Voice' and/or compensation through consumer charters
Market	Matching supply and demand	Economic efficiency	Competition	'Exit' and/or court action (private law)

Source: Adler (2010, 149, Table 1) from *Administrative Justice in Context* (Hart Publishing).

thus providing a two-dimensional (policy/process) approach compared to Mashaw's one-dimensional (process) approach.[13]

Adler's three additional models were developed in response to the advent of the New Public Management (NPM) culture.[14] 'Managerialism' refers to the increasing use of key performance targets, audit and defined standards of service to demonstrate the autonomy of public service managers and their organization's efficiency. Comparable to bureaucratic rationality, this model tends to focus on the management of the administrative system as a whole and only indirectly on individual users. 'Consumerism' has similarly been a feature of public sector reform

2003, 332). His review of the relationship between procedural and substantive justice reassuringly concludes that '[p]rocedural fairness can contribute to substantive justice but is also important in its own right' (Adler 2010, 141).

13 Adler (2003, 336-44) applied his six-model approach in four empirical studies: the impact of computerization on social security in the UK; on decision-making in the Scottish prison system; on the assessment of special educational needs in England and Scotland; and on the computerization of social security in 13 countries.

14 See pp. 76-7 below for a discussion of the policy influence of NPM.

since the mid-1980s and has been visible in, for example, the *Citizen's Charter* and related initiatives (Prime Minister 1991; Page 1999; Drewry 2005).[15] By contrast with managerialism, consumerism places the individual's needs as the highest concern and therefore the focus is on giving attention to the individual's service experience and responding to any dissatisfaction. The distinction between managerialism and consumerism is that accountability in the former is frequently 'top-down', whereas with the latter it is 'bottom-up'. In other words the consumerism ideal type envisions complaint systems driven by consumers ('voice'), as key to guiding the organization's development. The 'market' ideal type has many of the characteristics of the managerial and consumer models (Adler 2003, 334). The administrative system here is driven by competitiveness and in effect regulated by the price mechanism; the citizen is viewed as making a rational choice between competing products in the supply/demand framework. The legitimating goal of the producer organization is economic efficiency. Here the administrative system is accountable to the market and is always subject to the possibility that the citizen chooses an alternative provider ('exit'). Adler (2003, 335) concludes that the market as a model of justice can only be fair where one is talking about market procedures (whereas market 'outcomes' are rarely just).

Adler's extension of Mashaw's typology is not without its critics (Halliday 2004, 121-3; Cane 2009, 216; Sainsbury 2008, 326-7) and in our typology we have adopted Halliday's argument that rather than being a distinct model, managerialism should more properly be regarded 'as being a contemporary gloss on Mashaw's bureaucratic rationality'. But where Adler certainly does represent an advance on Mashaw is in recognizing that the constraint of Mashaw's focus on the internal, decisional processes of front-line public agencies misses out any examination of all redress mechanisms available in relation to the initial decision-making. Certainly, externally imposed redress mechanisms can be backward-looking in the sense that they are primarily concerned with redressing past injustice, and the available evidence does not suggest that this approach is particularly effective on its own. By contrast, internal forms of accountability are more likely to be designed to be forward-looking in the sense that they are intended to promote justice in administration for all and prevent injustice from arising in the first place. As Adler has argued, however, the complementary influences of both *external* and *internal* forms of accountability on public bodies are to be preferred (Adler 2003, 330; 2006, 619). Sainsbury too has argued that 'the "acceptability of (front-line) decisions" is enhanced if a remedy exi[s]ts; in other words, having some form of redress mechanism would add to the justice argument for any particular decision process' (Sainsbury 2008, 326-7).

Thus for our purposes Adler's addition of a 'mode of accountability' and 'mode of redress' to his matrix ensures that the analysis accommodates the 'putting it right' element. But so far neither Mashaw's nor Adler's analysis encompasses

15 See further, pp. 76-7 below.

Table 3.4 The organization of decision-making authority in administrative agencies

DECISION-MAKING PROCEDURE	DEGREE OF LEGAL CONTROL INFORMAL ⟵ ⟶	FORMAL
HIERARCHY ↑	expert or political judgment	bureaucratic legalism
↓ PARTICIPATION	negotiation/ mediation	adversarial legalism

Source: Kagan (2010, 164, Figure 1) from Adler (2010), *Administrative Justice in Context* (Hart Publishing).

the web of governance and accountability relationships represented by the outer concentric ring ('setting it right') in our typology set out in Figure 3.1.

Kagan, Halliday and Scott and the Third Tier of Administrative Justice: 'Setting it Right'

Some aspects of Kagan's work, and the attempts to apply 'grid-group cultural theory' to administrative justice by Halliday and Scott, resonate with our conception of 'setting it right' and provide analyses that further contextualize and connect decisional processes and remedial mechanisms to the wider political and constitutional environments. Kagan (2010) proposes a typology which identifies the organization of both decisional and policy-implementing processes as varying along two distinct dimensions: a degree of legal control (formality/informality); and a decision-making procedure (hierarchical/participatory) as set out in Table 3.4 above.

He argues that the dimension of legal control requires an assessment of the extent to which substantive decisions and decision-making procedures are structured by written legal rules; the more detailed and specific the more such rules can be characterized as legalistic or 'formal'. By contrast, 'informal' processes allow decision-makers a greater measure of discretion. With regard to the decision-making procedure dimension, there is a similar sliding scale between *hierarchically* organized administrative systems and *participatory* processes. In the former, routine decision-making procedures are dominated by a relatively insulated agency official, whereas in the latter, individuals and/or organizations have considerable opportunity to influence agency officials. Kagan claims that his typology takes in both front-line agency decision-making and review or appeal processes, and these can be characterized 'in terms of an approximate location within the spaces in [Table 3.4 above]' (Kagan 2010, 165).

The upper-left quadrant ('expert or political judgment') of Table 3.4 arises where administrative processes are hierarchical in the sense that an official controls the process and standards for decision, yet informal in the sense that 'the decision's authoritativeness rests on the professional or political judgment of individual officials, not conformity with detailed legal rules' (Kagan 2010, 165). He concludes that the more purely expertise-driven such a system is, the more restricted is the role for legal argument and the less likely the officials' decisions are to be reversed by appeals to higher officials or to the courts. The upper-right quadrant ('bureaucratic legalism') represents an administrative decision-making process characterized by a high degree of hierarchical authority combined with legal formality. He states that this mode emphasizes 'the uniform implementation of centrally devised rules, vertical accountability, and official responsibility for fact finding' (Kagan 2010, 166). Again, where the system is more hierarchical, the role for legal representation and the influence of citizens and contending interests is more restricted. The lower-right quadrant ('adversarial legalism') refers to agency processes that are closely constrained by formal procedural rules, but where hierarchy is weak and opportunities for participation by private individuals and organizations are high. The result is often a judicialization of administrative decision-making. Finally, the lower-left quadrant ('negotiation/mediation') allows individuals or organizations opportunities to present and argue their cases in an informal manner and the process is non-legalistic.

Kagan's matrix reassuringly maps onto Mashaw's three models of bureaucratic rationality, professional treatment and moral judgment, with the addition of mediation/negotiation a further dimension to the theoretical framework not present in Mashaw's approach (Halliday and Scott 2010, 188). Kagan does not claim to offer a full-blown explanatory theory as to why any particular public agency resembles one of these types of organization. But he does indicate some causal factors derived from the socio-legal literature; for example, features of the agency's legal mandate and powers, the agency's task environment, the agency's political environment and the attitude of agency leaders (Kagan 2010, 168). Similarly, Halliday has provided an analytical framework that explores the conditions that must be satisfied which impact on the effectiveness of judicial review to secure compliance with administrative law. One of the five conditions he identifies is the 'decision-making environment', the main point being 'that government agencies do not operate in a social, political or economic vacuum' (Halliday 2004, 87).

Interestingly, from the perspective of our conception of 'setting it right', Kagan focuses on the role of 'political mistrust' of the agency 'in shaping the political and legal accountability mechanisms for, and hence the structure of, administrative decision-making systems' (Kagan 2010, 168). He points out those cross-national differences in administrative decision style are explained by significant differences in national political traditions and attitudes. He explains the mechanisms thus:

> In an atmosphere of mistrust of the agency's professionalism, adopting a legalistic style of rule-application provides bureaucratic officials a somewhat safe haven. A vicious circle ensues. In an atmosphere of mistrust of the agency's professionalism, legislatures are less likely to fund the agency adequately and more likely to constrain its decision-making with more detailed rules, empowering critics on both the left and the right to challenge agency decisions in court. All this, of course, increases the likelihood that the agency officials will act legalistically rather than thoughtfully, which increases the likelihood that it will be viewed as unprofessional and untrustworthy. (Kagan 2010, 179)

It is interesting to note that Kagan's survey of the possible reasons why administrative decision-making in one programme resembles one ideal type of institutional design rather than another implicates the underlying 'political and legal accountability mechanisms' that will structure such a system, in particular the role of political mistrust. This takes the conception of administrative justice further forward than either Mashaw or Alder and this finding reinforces our justification for the third element ('setting it right') in our tripartite description of administrative justice.[16]

Cultural Theory

The four quadrants marked off by dotted lines in Figure 3.1 above illustrate the four cultural biases produced by 'grid-group' cultural theory. The representation of cultural theory in our typology is best understood as a background pulse which pulls in the direction of a relevant cultural bias when applied to any particular part of the administrative justice system. Cultural theory was first developed by anthropologists and political scientists 40 years ago (e.g. Douglas 1970; Douglas 1982; Thomson *et al* 1990). Grid-group cultural theory has also been applied to public management by Hood (1998), who argued that each cultural bias produces a distinct and basic logic of good administration. Building on this work, Halliday and Scott (2010) have constructed a 'cultural typology of administrative justice' in which the typologies developed by Mashaw, Adler and Kagan can be located. In essence, their claim is that their typology offers a better understanding of the relationships between the existing models of administrative justice and reveals new conceptions (Halliday and Scott 2010, 184). It is also claimed that this comprises a complete family of forms of administrative justice. They suggest a cultural typology of administrative justice, as set out in Figure 3.2.

In essence, the theory claims that people derive many of their preferences, perceptions, opinions, values and norms from their adherence to fundamental ways of organizing social relations. The group dimension refers to the extent to which people's

16 Furthermore, his comments on the relationship of the 'culture of rule application' in a public agency (Kagan 2010, 171-3) to decision-making behaviour is also revealing of the classic dichotomy between rules and discretion in administrative systems (Titmuss 1971; Adler and Bradley 1975; Bull 1980; Hawkins 1995).

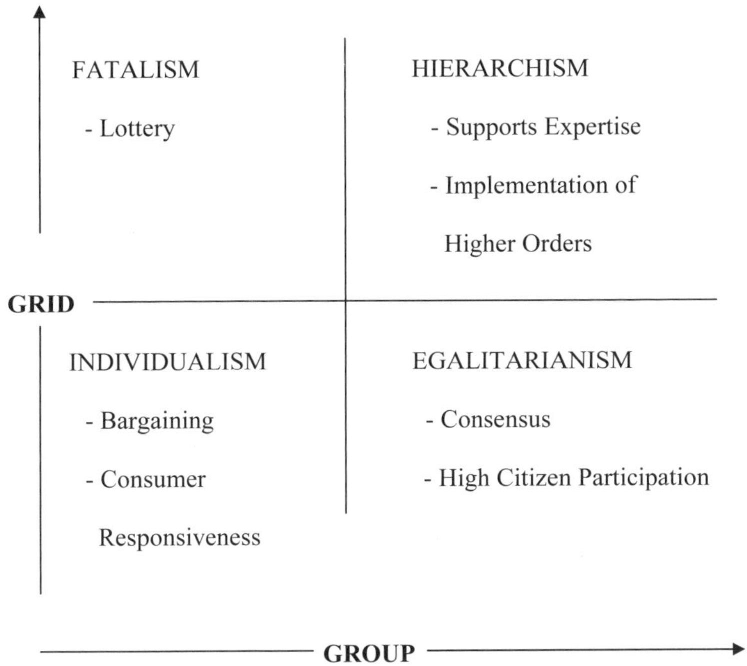

Figure 3.2 A cultural typology of administrative justice
Source: Halliday and Scott (2010, 192, Figure 2) from Adler (2010), *Administrative Justice in Context* (Hart Publishing).

lives are controlled by the group they live in. This varies in strength from intense to weak peer pressure. The grid dimension refers to the extent of structural constraints. This varies in strength from comprehensive regulation to where everything must be negotiated from scratch. Both dimensions produce four ideal types of cultural bias: 'individualism'; 'fatalism'; 'hierarchism'; and 'egalitarianism'.

The 'hierarchist' vision of administrative justice involves public officials exercising their expertise and judgment for the public benefit in a 'top-down' manner: '[d]ecision-making processes within hierarchism should support the exercise of expert judgment and/or the accurate and efficient implementation of higher orders' (Halliday and Scott 2010, 192). In contrast, the 'egalitarian' vision is sceptical and distrustful of government authority and expertise and favours decision-making by consensus – a 'bottom-up' approach – a position which translates, in the administrative justice context, to participating citizens and public officials being equal partners in decision-making processes. Halliday and Scott (2010, 193) suggest that the vertical dimension ('hierarchical/participatory') of Kagan's typology corresponds to the vertical ('grid') dimension of cultural theory. They also note that the continuum running between a hierarchic and egalitarian conception of administrative justice should be familiar to administrative lawyers: it is demonstrated in the flexible doctrine of procedural fairness[17] and the variable intensity of judicial review reflecting the competition between judicial control and agency autonomy. They conclude that '[w]e might frame the extent of citizen participation in decision processes as capturing the core element of grid-group cultural theory's application to administrative justice' (Halliday and Scott 2010, 193).

Following Hood's (1998) application of cultural theory to public management they associate individualism as producing self-interest and personal responsibility and for which the market is the appropriate model of social organization. The distinctive decision-making process associated with the individualistic cultural bias they identify as 'the characteristic mode of decision-making in market settings' (Halliday and Scott 2010, 194): in particular, it is a paradigm decision process involving 'bargaining' and 'consumer responsiveness'.

'Fatalistic' administrative justice, connoting a sense of powerlessness and exclusion, appears, at first blush, to reveal no positive vision of 'good administration'. Halliday and Scott (2010, 195) argue that the notion of a lottery is a paradigm decision-making process within this cultural bias and that the use of randomness in decision-making processes 'marks the abandonment of any faith in our ability to positively design just processes of administration'. Nevertheless, this more negative cultural bias can prompt positive strategies to improve administration, for example, via 'contrived randomness' (Hood 1998) and the imposition of unpredictable working conditions to avert anti-system conspiracies. The fatalist bias may be applied to deliberate randomness in some administrative systems, e.g. allocation of school places by lotteries.

It should be noted that our typology in Figure 3.1 follows Halliday and Scott's mapping of Mashaw and Adler's models of justice onto the four quadrants shown in Figure 3.2 above. Consequently, the text-bearing arrows in Figure 3.1 are mapped onto particular cultural bias quadrants. Mashaw's bureaucratic rationality and professional treatment models thus fall within the hicrarchist ideal type of administrative justice, with its emphasis on the accurate and efficient implementation of higher orders and its stress on the value of expertise. Mashaw's moral judgment, on the other hand, 'betrays an egalitarian stress on participative decision-making processes which aspire to consensus' (Halliday and Scott 2010, 197). Adler's (2003) additional prescription of 'consumerism' and 'market' fits very well within the 'individualist' vision.

Although, as already stated, Kagan's typology maps easily onto Mashaw's three models of justice, it is less clear where his category of 'negotiation/mediation' fits. Halliday and Scott argue that there are parallels with moral judgment in that this category requires decision-making sensitive to competing interests and that mediated solutions will reflect an egalitarian bias. It thus appears in our Figure 3.1 above as a distinct dimension appearing in the egalitarian quadrant.

17 Halliday and Scott (2010, 193) also point out that this parallels the continuum identified by Galligan (1996, 237-40) between 'bureaucratic administration' and 'fair treatment'.

As noted earlier, these cultural biases operate as an underlying influence in our typology of administrative justice and may add explanatory power to how particular elements of the administrative justice system operate. In particular, the 'setting it right' element is a representation of the complex relationships between, on the one hand, first-instance and remedial decision-making and, on the other, the wider constitutional and socio-political forces that shape such decision-making.

Applying the Typology of Administrative Justice

The combination of our tripartite definition of administrative justice with the existing theoretical perspectives discussed above highlights the extent to which those theoretical perspectives reach into the functions and institutions of 'getting it right', 'putting it right' and 'setting it right' respectively.

Having unpacked the contents of our typology of administrative justice, as represented in Figure 3.1 above, it may help to imagine how that illustration might look if applied to a specific administrative justice system. As we have seen in the preceding sections, the theorists are at least agreed that there is a characteristic element of competition for dominance of the underlying drivers of administrative justice when one considers particular systems. There is also some agreement that in many sectors of the administrative justice system it is likely that 'bureaucratic

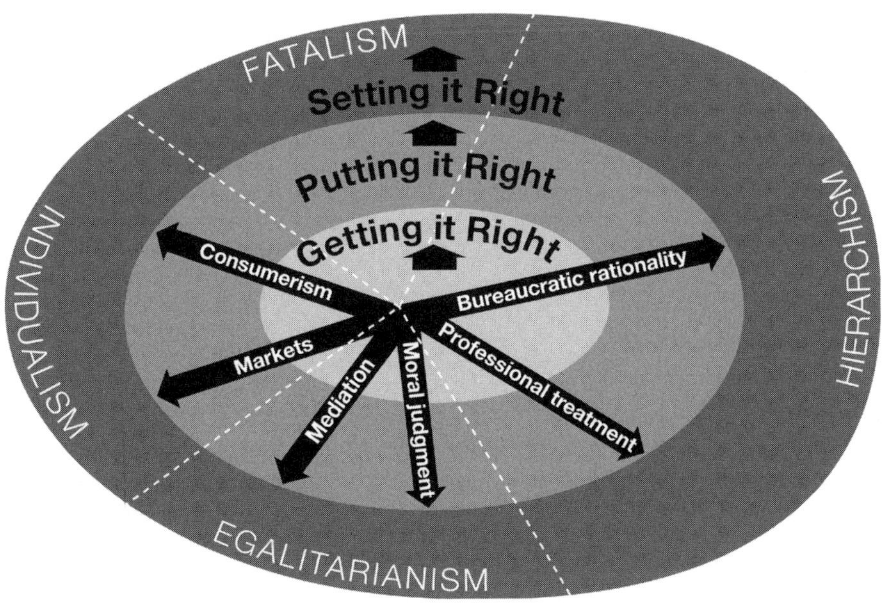

Figure 3.3 A typology of administrative justice: competition for dominance

Source: The authors.

rationality', which can be located within the cultural bias of 'hierarchism', will be the dominant element: see Figure 3.3 above.

The egg-shaped figure above is just one illustration of how our typology may be moulded by all the variables discussed to reflect the complex combination of models, roles and relationships within the administrative justice system. A range of distended versions of this figure could be posited to reflect a diverse family of particular administrative justice systems; but the central argument is that the underlying architecture of the typology remains the same.

The Administrative Justice System: Policy Development

New Public Management (NPM) and Citizen Charter Initiatives

Many of the intellectual developments in the idea of an administrative justice system identified in this chapter have been reflected in a series of policy developments in the UK which have led to the emergence of a distinct 'administrative justice system'. Perhaps the earliest evidence of the trend towards a wider conception of administrative justice was NPM,[18] which emerged in the 1970s and 1980s as a philosophy favoured by governments in developed countries to modernize public sector management. In the words of a leading commentator, it 'dominated the bureaucratic reform agenda in the OECD group of countries from the late 1970s' (Hood 1991, 3-4). The pervasive impact of NPM also formed an important part of Adler's rationale for adding 'managerialism', 'consumerism' and 'markets' to Mashaw's three models of justice. The underlying thrust of NPM is that a stronger market orientation applied to the public sector could lead to greater cost-effectiveness. Consequently, public services are increasingly managed, utilizing rigorous performance standards and monitoring – and recipients of public services have been reconstructed into 'customers'. Indeed, under this type of business modelling, the supply side of the market equation (the provision of public services) has to fit around the demand side (the messages that customers give about what they want). The NPM approach to public administration has not only permeated first-instance decision-making in the public sector ('getting it right'), but also the way in which the range of remedial mechanisms ('putting it right') have been delivered.[19]

18 'The term NPM was coined because some generic label seemed to be needed for a general, though certainly not universal, shift in public management styles. The term was intended to cut across the particular language of individual projects or countries (such as the French "Projet de Service", the British "Next Steps", the Canadian "Public Service 2000"). The analogy is with terms like new politics, new right, and new industrial state, which were invented for a similar reason.' (Hood 1995, 94).

19 A good example of the impact of NPM thinking on remedial systems is the way in which a 'culture of delay' in processing social security tribunal appeals was identified

However, the assumption that NPM was generating public managements converging to some sort of globalized uniform modernity is not without its challengers. Hood (1998), for example, argued that contrary to such widespread claims the constant shifting of styles and models of public management was unlikely to disappear. Indeed, public administration scholars are now turning to other doctrines of public management to explain better modern developments. Dunleavy *et al* (2006), for example, have argued that the wave of NPM, at least in 'leading-edge' countries, has now ebbed and that a range of linked and information technology-centred changes will be crucial in forming the next wave of change. They posit a new period of 'digital-era governance' in public management which should be capable of reducing the increased institutional and policy complexity engendered by NPM: see also Margetts and Partington (2010, 67).

Another key influence in policy development, related to NPM, was the *Citizen's Charter* initiative in the early 1990s (Prime Minister 1991). The emphasis of this initiative was on citizens as 'customers' of public services. The Citizen's Charter scheme had several elements, including the 'Charter Mark', to recognize excellence in the public sector. There were also individual charters for public services that set out the standards those services were expected to achieve. The scheme was not a uniform 'blueprint' for service provision, but a 'toolkit' to allow standards to be raised in each public service in the most appropriate way (Prime Minister 1991). The initiative gave rise to a multitude of customer charters and performance standard-setting and renewed the focus on accountability in public services. Some have questioned the legitimacy of the charter approach, particularly in the context of monopolistic, public services where there is no consumer 'choice' in reality (Drewry 2005). Nevertheless the charter initiatives, now subsumed less visibly within public management, have been a significant element in formulating the 'customer-focused' approach adopted in recent years. One commentator has concluded, for example, that the charter's greatest contribution was 'through highlighting the need for a more systemic approach to administrative justice' (Page 1999, 98).[20]

Tribunal Reforms and the White Paper of 2004

A key landmark in the policy development of administrative justice in the UK, since the Franks Committee (1957) report, has been the impetus provided by

by a Select Committee inquiry into the Social Security and Child Support Commissioners in 2000: see Buck, Bonner and Sainsbury (2005, 11-14). Similarly, a regime of 'customer service' was introduced into the Independent Review Service in the 1990s: see Buck (1998; 2001).

20 The introduction of the Citizen's Charter in the UK also assisted 'the reshaping of welfare services around consumer choice' (Adler 2003, 334).

the Leggatt Review of tribunals (Leggatt 2001).[21] This review has had a wider and more enduring impact on the development of the administrative justice landscape generally. The review provided the springboard for a comprehensive transformation of the tribunal system into a much more coherent judicial and administrative structure which was delivered by the enactment of the Tribunals, Courts and Enforcement Act (TCEA) 2007. The Leggatt Review (2001, Pt II) is also noteworthy for its reliance on examples of practice from Australasia as models for UK reform, and the focus it gave to utilizing tribunals not only to resolve individual disputes but also to provide 'feedback'[22] from their work to first-instance decision-makers.

Following the Leggatt proposals on tribunal reform, the government's responding White Paper, *Transforming Public Services* (DCA 2004), laid out a fully articulated official vision of administrative justice and how the administrative justice system should be developed. It provided a broad analysis of the need to consider the full range of the administrative justice landscape and how each element – the tribunals, courts, ombudsmen and other complaint-handlers – might work collaboratively and enable users to be signposted appropriately to the relevant agencies. The transformative quality of the policy framework advanced was reflected by the introduction of 'proportionate dispute resolution' (PDR), a key concept in this new vision of administrative justice.

> Our strategy turns on its head the Department's traditional emphasis first on courts, judges and court procedure, and second on legal aid to pay mainly for litigation lawyers. It starts instead with the real world problems people face. The aim is to develop a range of policies and services that, so far as possible, will help people to avoid problems and legal disputes in the first place; and where they cannot, provides tailored solutions to resolve the dispute as quickly and cost effectively as possible. It can be summed up as 'Proportionate Dispute Resolution'. (DCA 2004, para. 2.2)[23]

The advancement of this vision was also accompanied by a proposal to upgrade the Council on Tribunals' role and functions. The new Administrative Justice and Tribunals Council (AJTC) was proposed, retaining its traditional role to review a list of scheduled tribunals, but additionally taking on a wider remit to monitor the strategic direction of the 'administrative justice system'[24] as a whole. The

21 Another impact on these developments was an influential conference on administrative justice held in Bristol in November 1997 (Harris and Partington 1999, 537).

22 See Partington and Kirton-Darling (2006), which surveys feedback mechanisms relevant to tribunals and other parts of the administrative landscape.

23 This concept follows the well-established debates about ADR, or 'fitting the fuss to the forum' (Sander and Goldberg, 1994). See also Adler (2006a).

24 See the discussion above at pp. 59-60.

TCEA 2007, in addition to setting up the new two-tier tribunal system structure,[25] established the AJTC, a non-departmental public body, with this broader statutory remit compared to its predecessor body, the Council on Tribunals.

Law Commission and Other Reform Initiatives

Examples of the emerging vision of administrative justice can also be found in the activities of the Law Commission. It has considered wide-ranging reforms in the housing field based on PDR and has recommended 'triage plus' as an organizing principle for the proposed reforms (Law Commission 2008b). This is a system for allocating a priority level to cases to determine their order and manner of treatment.

The government's response in July 2009 (Ministry of Justice 2009b) indicated that it broadly accepted the Law Commission's recommendations on the provision of better housing advice and assistance via the triage plus method and reiterated its support for the promotion of mediation and ADR in the context of non-formal dispute resolution. Some further explanation of the concept of triage plus is given in Chapter 7.[26]

However, the Law Commission's proposals in their report on Administrative Redress (Law Commission 2008) were less compliant with the new vision of administrative justice and consequently drew a much less enthusiastic response from the government. As referred to earlier in this chapter,[27] this report closely examined the remedies available in both public and private law by way of court action to challenge administrative action, noting the limited prospects for monetary compensation in judicial review proceedings. It suggested that damages in judicial review should be more readily available subject to meeting certain tests.[28] In private law actions, it was proposed that certain activities, which met a new test of being 'truly public', could be placed in a specialized scheme in which the claimant would also have to satisfy the public law tests to establish liability. The government rejected outright the Law Commission's central proposals concerning the liability of public bodies in private and public law (Ministry of Justice 2009a). It expressed a number of concerns about the proposals, for example, that they would lead to 'defensive administration' and would increase litigation. But a fundamental basis of its concern was that proposals had failed to view the issues in the wider perspective of improving public services: '... the overarching purpose of redress policy is to ensure

---

25 The government's policy intention underlying Part 1 of TCEA 2007 was 'to create a new, simplified statutory framework for tribunals, bringing existing jurisdictions together and providing a structure for new jurisdictions and new appeal rights' (DCA 2007, para. 5). The Act established a 'First-tier Tribunal' (FTT) with rights of appeal to an 'Upper Tribunal' (UT) and onward appeal rights to the Court of Appeal: see Carnwath (2009).

26 See pp. 191-3.

27 See pp. 55-6.

28 The tests were 'conferral of benefit', 'serious fault' and 'causation' (Law Commission 2008).

that public bodies learn from their mistakes and provide a better and more consistent service, thus benefitting the public as a whole' (Ministry of Justice 2009a, para. 2). This underlying driver behind reform can also be seen in much Australian thinking on the subject (e.g. Creyke 2010) and in the AJTC's early work.

> [I]t is essential that organisations learn and apply lessons not only from redress mechanisms but also from other sorts of feedback, such as complaints. Good complaint handling and other responses to feedback need to be embedded in corporate governance systems, strategic and business plans, internal communications, staff training, and appraisal and reward of individuals. Moreover, a dynamic organisational model would require appropriate mechanisms for decision makers to comment on and contribute to the resolution of systemic issues as well as individual case points. (AJTC 2010, para. 32)

The modernization of public services undertaken by the New Labour regimes since 1997 has required high levels of investment. At present it is speculative as to how exactly the global economic recession that appeared in 2008 will impact on public services. However, it is interesting to note the last New Labour administration moving away from the lexicon of 'consumer choice' in its policy language, to providing individuals with specific 'entitlements' to public services reinforced by access to forms of quick redress (Prime Minister 2009, 64-5). There are several points to note about this shift in policy. Firstly, the government is careful to specify that the forms of redress envisaged are 'non-legal';[29] care will be taken to prevent drawn-out legal action in the courts. Secondly, amongst the envisaged forms of redress to be further relied upon is the existence of an 'independent ombudsman', though precisely what kind of ombudsman is not detailed. Finally, redress is seen as an engine for improvement of services not a threat to their sustainability. Whether these proposals survive the change in government following the May 2010 general election remains to be seen.

Public Sector Ombudsmen: Policy Development

The public sector ombudsmen clearly constitute a part of the second limb ('putting it right') of our tripartite definition of the administrative justice system, but through

29 'These guarantees, and others which we will set out, will be backed up by more responsive non-legal redress mechanisms, appropriately tailored to particular services. This will create a system which gives power to people to challenge organisations which are not delivering their entitlements on a personal level with minimal bureaucracy. In particular, where a service falls below an acceptable standard, we will seek to ensure there are alternatives open to patients and parents. Redress could take a number of forms, which might include giving users the power to seek alternative services, or offering people greater powers to complain and have their complaint heard by an independent ombudsman' (Prime Minister 2009, 64).

guidance and recommendations can assist public bodies in the first limb ('getting it right'). In addition, there are distinct governance and accountability relationships that apply to the public sector ombudsman offices, features which relate to the third limb of our definition ('setting it right'). These various relationships are dealt with in following chapters. This section sets the scene by introducing some recent developments and thinking that specifically relate to the ombudsman enterprise in the UK.

There have been a number of pressures for reform, some of which are pinpointed in a House of Commons Library paper in 2008 and will be returned to throughout this monograph.[30]

- The large volume of cases rejected as inappropriate for investigation indicating confusion about the role and remit of the PHSO.
- The MP filter reduces the volume of complaints received by the PHSO, which does not compare well with ombudsmen in other jurisdictions.
- There has been a proliferation of ombudsmen with separate jurisdictions.
- The proliferation of complaint systems within departments has added to the confusion about roles and avenues of redress.
- A number of findings of the PHSO have been rejected by government departments (e.g. mishandling of pension advice).
- The existing statutory bar preventing investigation where the complainant has recourse to the courts is in need of modification due to the growth in administrative law. (Gay 2008, 6-7).

Some of the key policy responses of government to date are picked up here.

To Rationalize or Not to Rationalize?

Developments in the ombudsman enterprise have proceeded on two contradictory paths in the UK. The devolution settlements in both Scotland and Wales have been accompanied by rationalizations of their respective ombudsman offices, whilst in Northern Ireland there is only one ombudsman office in practice. While the rationalization of ombudsmen has been the watchword in Scotland, Wales and Northern Ireland,[31] the proliferation of ombudsmen in England has not yet been accompanied by any comparable effort. As a result, the policy impetus provided by *Transforming Public Services* and the desire to have 'joined-up government'[32] has yet to achieve similar comprehensive structural reforms to the English ombudsmen to that in the tribunal sector. Reform in the form of harmonization of

30 Though this paper related exclusively to the PHSO office, similar themes have affected other offices.

31 See pp. 83-4 below.

32 That is, the better coordination of government departments and agencies in order to improve the quality of public services: see Prime Minister (1999) and NAO (2001).

several ombudsman schemes at one stage looked likely following a Cabinet Office review of public sector ombudsmen in England (the Collcutt Review) which was conducted in 2000 in response to a paper presented by the Parliamentary Ombudsman (PO) and Local Government Ombudsmen (LGOs) (Collcutt and Hourihan, 2000, Annex A). The key conclusions in the Collcutt Review were:

- The current legislative provision for the ombudsmen is restrictive and is distorting the service. It needs a radical overhaul.
- Proliferation of methods of public service delivery will continue. This means finding new ways to help complainants and enabling the ombudsman to work with others to provide an integrated service.
- Reshaping of the ombudsmen is needed to respond to reshaped government.
- The MP filter can no longer be sustained in an era of joined up government and we strongly recommend that it is abolished. (Collcutt and Hourihan 2000, paras 2.43 and 3.52).

The Collcutt recommendations were initially met with some enthusiasm, firstly by the Public Administration Select Committee (PASC 2000) and the government.[33] However, no legislation was forthcoming in the wake of the Collcutt Review and government lost this opportunity to provide some root-and-branch structural reform.

Shortly after her appointment as PO/HSO, Ann Abraham, in evidence to the Select Committee (Abraham 2003), took the view that the ombudsman reform agenda should be refocused away from the creation of a single institution in England by primary legislation. She argued that merging the offices of the PO/HSO and LGOs would not in itself produce the 'joined-up' ombudsman service required (Abraham 2003, paras 7-9) and in any event devolution had undermined the original proposals.[34] The government appeared to think along similar lines and instead of a fully fledged attempt to produce new primary legislation to take forward the Collcutt Review recommendations, opted to achieve more modest improvements by means of a regulatory reform order (RRO), the Regulatory Reform (Collaboration etc Between Ombudsmen) Order 2007.[35]

The purpose of the RRO is to enable more collaborative working between ombudsmen (Cabinet Office 2005, para. 27) where there is an overlap in their respective jurisdictions. Under the RRO the ombudsmen are enabled to consult each other, share information and work together on cases relevant to more than one of their

33 *Hansard*, HC vol. 372, cols 464W-465W (20 July 2001), Cabinet Office Minister, Mr Christopher Leslie MP.

34 She pointed to the jurisdictional complications arising from the dissonance between her UK-wide jurisdiction and the Scottish, Welsh and Northern Ireland ombudsman offices – a problem that would not be solved by the creation of a single 'English' ombudsman office.

35 SI 1889/2007. The order came into effect on 1 August 2007.

jurisdictions and delegate their functions to each other's staff.[36] Whilst a beneficial step that has been welcomed by the ombudsmen in England, it is disappointing that the attempt to rationalize the organizations of ombudsmen in England has finished, for now at least, with a relatively modest set of reforms. The limited nature of progress on this front is also apparent when one examines the extent to which the RRO has been deployed since it came into force in August 2007.[37] However, the RRO does firmly establish a principle of joint investigation and reporting and some of the cases that will be dealt with under the RRO are likely to have wider implications in practice than merely resolving individual grievances.[38]

The approach to rationalization of the ombudsman community in England stands in stark contrast to that adopted elsewhere in the UK. The situation is complicated by the retention by the PO of 'reserved' matters in relation to the devolved territories; otherwise there has been a wholehearted integration of ombudsman services. In Scotland, following the Scottish Public Services Ombudsman Act, the SPSO took over the functions previously exercised by the PO/HSO (within devolved areas), the Commission for Local Administration and the Housing Association Ombudsman for Scotland. The future role of the SPSO has since been examined as part of a number of reviews, with emphasis being placed on further rationalizing the complaints handling network. Notwithstanding the introduction of the SPSO, the Crerar Review found that there were more than 20 external scrutiny bodies that handled complaints; but the various arrangements were diverse, complex and there was an inconsistent use of complaint outcomes to provide assurance and drive improvement. Subsequent proposals have accordingly recommended transferring additional responsibilities to the SPSO and making it the norm that when new complaints mechanisms become necessary they are brought within the jurisdiction of the SPSO (Sinclair 2008, para 74).

Rationalization along the 'one-stop shop' lines has occurred in Wales too following the Public Services Ombudsman (Wales) Act 2005 (PSOW). This legislation merged four ombudsman services: the Welsh Administration Ombudsman,[39] the Local Government Ombudsman for Wales, the Health Service

36 A good example of where the PO and LGO had to conduct parallel investigations and publish separate reports was the complaint made by Mr and Mrs Balchin (PHSO 2005b). The complaint was against the Department of Transport and Norfolk County Council in relation to the council's refusal to purchase the complainants' former home in advance of an intended road bypass scheme.

37 The volume of cases has fallen short of even the expected 50 cases per annum predicted in the pilot project conducted by the HSO and LGO pilot. The PHSO's annual report for 2007-08 notes only ten joint investigation cases in hand (PHSO 2008, 52) and for 2008-09 the PHSO records only 15 joint investigations (PHSO 2009, 38).

38 For example, in March 2009 the PHSO and LGO published an influential report concerning six investigations about the provision of public services to people with learning disabilities, three of which were investigated jointly (HSO and LGO 2009).

39 Government of Wales Act 1998, s.111 and Sched. 9.

Ombudsman for Wales and the Social Housing Ombudsman. The PSOW also enforces a code of conduct for local councillors in Wales.

In Northern Ireland, there are separate offices of the Northern Ireland Commissioner for Complaints and the Assembly Ombudsman for Northern Ireland, but in fact both offices operate as a single complaints service under the title Northern Ireland Ombudsman (NIO), an office originally established in 1969.[40] The pace of reform has been much affected by the imposition of direct rule by Westminster in 2002 and the return to devolved government to Northern Ireland on 8 May 2007. The NIO, Tom Frawley, has repeatedly noted his disappointment in particular at the delay in implementing the recommendations contained in the review of his office undertaken in 2004 (COFMDFM 2010, 2-3). This set out a vision of a new combined Office of Northern Ireland Public Services Ombudsman for public bodies, with a single point of entry and consistent remedies and a focus on the business of investigating complaints.

The reforms in Scotland and Wales do appear to capture the 'integrated ombudsmanry' concept favoured by Collcutt and other commentators (Seneviratne 2000, Thompson 2001). Elliot (2006) concluded that a 'two-ombudsman model' was implicated, i.e. an integrated 'local' ombudsman service existing alongside a UK-wide ombudsman for complaints over non-devolved matters. This model is harder to apply in England, because it has no devolved legislature of its own. Nevertheless, as Elliot points out, a two-ombudsman approach could still be applied in England, with local ombudsmanry responsible for such matters as local government, health, social housing and general England-only administration (Elliot 2006, 98). As in Scotland and Wales, reserved UK issues would be left to the PO, thus avoiding the difficulties inherent in the Collcutt Review.

Modernizing Ombudsman Legislation

As will be seen in the following chapters, the ombudsmen themselves have been at the forefront of adapting their working practices to enhance their capacity to act. Some positive developments though have been supported by legislative reform. The RRO, for instance, confers a permissive power on ombudsmen to 'appoint and pay a mediator or other appropriate person to assist him in the conduct of an investigation of a complaint under [the three Acts]'.[41] The SPSO Act facilitates greater accessibility to the SPSO, including provision for a representative to

---

40 The current provisions are contained in the Ombudsman (Northern Ireland) Order 1996 and the Commissioner for Complaints (Northern Ireland) Order 1996. On 1 December 1997 these were extended, by the Commissioner for Complaints (Amendment) (Northern Ireland) Order 1997, to include complaints about doctors, dentists, pharmacists and optometrists (ophthalmic opticians) providing family health services and by other health care professionals in health and personal social services.

41 See RRO 2007, Articles 12, 13 and 14. This is a more specific power than that set out in the Public Services Ombudsman (Wales) Act 2005.

complain on their behalf and allowing oral complaints in certain circumstances; the publication of all investigation reports; and publicity of cases where an injustice has not been remedied. Both the SPSO and PSOW Acts, along with recent amendments to the LGO Act, add to the usual formula of injustice caused by 'maladministration' by providing that complaints may be made where injustice is caused by a service failure.[42] Meanwhile a more radical reform initiative still has been recommended in Northern Ireland, with a government report proposing that the ombudsman should have authority to undertake systemic reviews flowing from individual complaints and following consultation and agreement with the Comptroller and Auditor-General (OFMDFM 2004, para. 7.2.8).

Improving Access to the Ombudsman and Links between Complaints Mechanisms

One set of reforms debated by the Law Commission should be noted. The Law Commission's consultation paper on administrative redress, discussed above,[43] suggested specifically four reforms to improve access to the ombudsman system (Law Commission 2008, paras 5.31-5.88). These have all been supported in subsequent reports which have additionally called for a wider consideration of the Public Service Ombudsmen (Law Commission 2010; 2010a). Firstly, it suggested that the courts should have a specific power to stay proceedings when a case would be more appropriately dealt with by an ombudsman's investigation. Secondly, it suggested that direct access for complainants to the PO should be allowed; albeit MPs would also be able to refer claims arising from their constituency business (the 'dual track' option).[44] Thirdly, it suggested the repeal of the current statutory bars which qualify the jurisdiction of the ombudsman to accept complaints that could be pursued in the courts. It proposed that the ombudsmen should be able to conduct an investigation where, in all the circumstances of the case, it was in the 'interests of justice' to investigate the claim. Fourthly, it proposed that the ombudsmen be given the power to refer questions of law to a court, a power previously supported by Lord Wolf (LCD 1995, ch.18, para. 18) and one which the AJTC was willing to back (Law Commission 2010, para. 5.30).

All of these proposals will be returned to in this monograph as they remain valid. The government's response to the ombudsmen-related proposals from the Law Commission was less critical than their response to the main proposals concerning liability in public and private law, but the New Labour administration which fell in May 2010 did not fully endorse these proposals. At the time of writing the Law Commission, building on its earlier work, produced a consultation paper that

---

42 See Scottish Public Services Ombudsman Act 2002, s.5(2); Public Services Ombudsman (Wales) Act 2005, s.7; Local Government Act 1974, s.26(1).

43 See pp. 55-6 above.

44 Of 32 consultees, all bar one were in favour of abolishing the 'MP filter' in its present form and 16 favoured the dual track option (Law Commission 2010, paras 5.34, 5.38).

specifically addresses public services ombudsmen. In addition to the four issues referred to above, it has also made suggestions relating to the appointment of the Parliamentary Ombudsman, the rationalisation of ombudsman reports, the resolution of complaints and the possibility of reports being laid before Parliament by the Local Government and Housing Ombudsmen (Law Commission 2010a).

The Ombudsman's Constitutional Role

The theme of the ombudsmen's location within the UK constitutional structure is commented upon in some detail in Chapter 2. However, here it is worth noting that developments in the practice of ombudsmen around the world have increasingly brought their work into closer focus with the wider policy-making community and the courts. In the 40 years since the PO was introduced, the UK constitutional and administrative justice landscape has changed, requiring a reappraisal of the ombudsmen's relationships with the legislative, executive and judicial elements of the constitution, and, we would argue, an appraisal of its role within the 'integrity' dimension of constitutional arrangements.[45] We have argued elsewhere that whereas the focus of most constitutional reform agendas is on the political system and the establishment of legal rights, it is equally important to pay attention to the role undertaken by unelected accountability and integrity mechanisms in providing systemic overviews of the performance of governance. We see around the world 'models of ombudsmanry that set out a much more important place within the constitution for the office than has been occupied in the past' (Kirkham, Thompson and Buck 2009, 615).

One continuing theme of this monograph is that the time is now right to mainstream the important functions that are performed by the public sector ombudsmen within existing and future constitutional arrangements. Certainly, the frequent publication of guidance on generic and systemic issues such as good administration marks a shift in the perception of the ombudsman office-holders themselves of their role from the traditional focus on resolving individual grievances to an additional concern about generic administrative failure (Gay 2008, 9), a point that will be returned to in Chapter 5.

The increasing 'improvement' role of the PHSO,[46] for example, has a possible constitutional implication, as Ann Abraham, the current PHSO office-holder, has consistently advocated.[47] The few, but notable, stand-offs between the PHSO and

45 See further, Chapter 2, pp. 24-9.

46 See further, Chapter 5, pp. 125-41.

47 'It is certainly not the place of the Ombudsman to usurp the function of the legislature and the Executive. It is however very much the role of the Ombudsman, as the purveyor of public benefit, to invite further reflection on the empirical evidence disclosed by complaints that these unintended but nevertheless adverse consequences continue to occur and must be recognised in future policy development' (Abraham 2008a, 212-13).

the executive over individual departments' refusal to accept recommendations are also alive with constitutional implications.[48] Indeed, the PHSO has actively considered the matter at least since the appearance of the government's publication of its Green Paper, *Governance of Britain* (Ministry of Justice 2007).[49] The *Bradley* case in the Court of Appeal in February 2008[50] has been seen in the ombudsman community as a welcome reinforcement of the ombudsman's constitutional position. It is also likely that the ombudsman enterprise generally in the UK will increasingly contribute towards the resolution of human rights issues in public administration, both in conducting investigatory work and in the office's relations with other bodies. Some ombudsmen are starting to see the potential of their office to promote the 'incremental emergence of a human rights culture' in public services (O'Reilly 2007). Indeed Ann Abraham has put it thus:

> If a human rights culture is to be realised on the ground, public servants can reasonably expect to be judged against standards that expressly acknowledge the place that human rights principles should play in public administration. Good administration will invariably show signs of a human rights culture. For the Ombudsman, as protector on behalf of Parliament of those features of good administration, the task of making findings of maladministration is unavoidably implicated with human rights considerations, and in a way that is far less feasible for the High Court, which will find many of the relevant disputes well beneath its elevated horizon. (Abraham 2008b, 377-8)

The changing constitutional landscape will inevitably raise questions about the future relationship of the ombudsmen with the courts and tribunals.

Conclusion

Developments in the ombudsman enterprise have been influenced by, and been the catalyst for, wider movements within the administrative justice system. This is unsurprising and how it should be. Understanding the interrelationships between the concepts, theories and policies of administrative justice is essential for an appreciation of how the ombudsman enterprise has been constructed and

---

48 For example, *Rochester Way, Barlow Clowes, Channel Tunnel, Debt of Honour* and, in particular, the *Occupational Pensions* report and the *Bradley* case. These notable cases are detailed further in Chapter 7.

49 Ann Abraham has emphasized that the office was not merely an alternative to the civil justice system (in the courts) but a way of ensuring that 'that Parliament could guarantee an independent and authoritative voice for aggrieved citizens' (PHSO 2008, 4).

50 *R (on the application of Bradley and others) v Secretary of State for Work and Pensions* [2008] EWCA Civ 36, [2008] 3 All ER 1116. A further explanation of this case is given in Chapter 7, pp. 216-19.

is likely to develop in the future. In the following chapters the contribution of the ombudsman enterprise towards satisfying the three key aspects of administrative justice identified in this chapter will be explored in detail.

PART II
The Ombudsman Technique

Chapter 4
Putting it Right: Resolving Complaints and Assisting Citizens

Introduction

As previous chapters have established, the ombudsman enterprise has a clear dual focus within the wider constitutional and administrative justice networks ('setting it right'): to resolve individual disputes with the view to 'putting it right' where failures in administration have been identified, and to contribute to the process of 'getting it right' first time around by feeding back to public authorities knowledge and advice on good administration. This chapter will focus on the first of those roles. In doing so it will pick up from the last chapter, which described how the key changes in public management and the deliberate customer focus in policy making have focused attention on a bottom-up appraisal of users of the administrative justice system. This approach is consistent with the messages arising from the theorists of administrative justice, some of whom have proposed a 'consumerist' model of justice.[1] The combined effect of these developments is that the constitutional contribution of the ombudsman enterprise should now be understood to go further than simply investigating complaints. Accordingly, it is the general service provided to complainants by ombudsmen, inclusive of advisory and quasi-counselling work as well as the investigation of individual complaints, which will be analysed in this chapter.

The Central Importance of Complaint-Handling

The complaint-handling role of the ombudsman is specified in all ombudsman legislation[2] and in many circumstances the ombudsman will be the only viable redress mechanism left through which a citizen can pursue their grievance against a public body. There is, nevertheless, an ongoing debate about the appropriate balance to be struck between the roles of individual complaint-handling and systemic investigations designed to identify widespread maladministration (Harlow 1978; Marin 2009). Some have even suggested that the complaint-handling role should be removed from the ombudsman altogether (Crerar 2007, para. 11.18(g)

---

1 See Chapter 3, pp. 60-87 for the theory and policy developments respectively.

2 For example, Parliamentary Commissioner Act 1967, s.5 and the Local Government Act 1974, ss.24A and 26.

and (h)). The merits of the ombudsman conducting systemic investigations and the importance of this work will be discussed further in Chapter 5, but the proposals to downgrade the complaint-handling role has found little favour in the ombudsman community, a point supported by the interviews conducted by the authors in research for this book (Thompson, Buck and Kirkham 2009). There is some evidence of a shift in some ombudsman schemes towards systemic work and a rationalization of the complaints that the ombudsmen accept (Stuhmcke 2008; Jones 2009, ch.4)[3] but the complaint-handling role remains a central feature of the ombudsman enterprise, setting it apart from other accountability institutions. Other aspects of the ombudsman's work revolve around and are informed by the core task of complaint-handling. The information provided by complaint-handling allows ombudsmen to direct their efforts to promote good administration, even on occasion acting as an early warning system of serious underlying problems with the inner workings of public bodies. Complaint-handling also provides the basic experience and immediate contact with administrative activity that the ombudsman requires in order to lay claim to being an expert in the field of good administration (e.g. SPSO 2007a, paras 3.11-3.20). Finally, and perhaps most idealistically, complainants are important because the ombudsman enterprise is located within democratic constitutional arrangements intended to reflect the interests of individual citizens and legitimize public authority.

The combined weight of these various motivations is revealed in the strategy documents, annual reports and speeches of ombudsmen around the world which today make clear that a key aspiration of the office is to provide a quality complaints service to the complainant. There is a growing trend within the ombudsman enterprise to analyse in more detail what such a service might entail, with some schemes developing Client Service Charters.[4] The New South Wales Ombudsman (NSWO) for example, as well as describing one of its values as to 'provide the same high quality service that we encourage other organisations to offer' (NSWO 2009, 1), makes the following 'guarantee of service':

> We will:
> ›› consider each matter promptly and fairly, and provide clear reasons for our decisions

---

3 See also Ann Abrahams, the Parliamentary and Health Service Ombudsman (PHSO), in evidence to PASC (2009, Ev.14).

4 For good examples see the websites of the Irish Ombudsman: <http://www.ombudsman.gov.ie/en/AboutUs/ClientServiceCharter/>; the Commonwealth Ombudsman <http://www.ombudsman.gov.au/pages/about-us/our-office/service-charter.php>; the Queensland Ombudsman <http://www.ombudsman.qld.gov.au/AboutUs/OurPolicies/ClientServiceCharter/tabid/70/Default.aspx>: and the Northern Territory Ombudsman <http://www.ombudsman.nt.gov.au/about-us/service-standards/our-commitment/> (accessed 12 April 2010).

›› where we are unable to deal with a matter ourselves, explain why, and identify any other appropriate organisation where we can

›› help those people who need assistance to make a complaint to the Ombudsman

›› add value through our work. (NSWO 2009, 17)

Likewise, the PHSO considers complaints about the service against its own *Principles of Good Administration*.[5] Such approaches provide some important clues as to how the ombudsman enterprise has had to raise its game. In the UK, the early generations of ombudsmen were alleged to offer a high-standard but long-winded, inflexible and cold form of complaints service. One consequence was that investigation times spiralled and dissatisfaction with the office became pronounced (e.g. Select Committee on PCA 1986). Today difficulties remain in processing complaints promptly, but an equally pressing problem now is the risk of complainants getting lost and dejected in the maze of the administrative justice system with insufficient support made available. This places an additional burden on their offices to ensure that their own complaint-handling attains the same or better administrative standards which they seek to secure in the wider public sector. The challenge to the ombudsman enterprise to maintain and advance customer care in a changing public services culture goes to the core of its own credibility and legitimacy.

Most guidance on complaint-handling makes clear that putting in place a cultural expectation as to the importance of complaint-handling is essential to the achievement of a good service (CO 2009a, 5-8). Hence the existence within ombudsman schemes of numerous corporate plans and mission statements detailing the ombudsman's responsibility to the complainant is a welcome first step. But to be meaningful, aspirations need to be backed up by deeds. In this respect there is evidence of a number of developments in recent years which represent a serious effort on the part of ombudsman offices to improve the quality of service they provide.

Making Contact with the Ombudsman

At the forefront of the core values espoused by the ombudsman enterprise is the acknowledgement that they provide a complaints service for all citizens. This is not a niche service and, with complaints being free to the complainant, it is not accompanied by a de facto income-related bar. Further, public statements of purpose made by ombudsmen match the widely made claim that the ombudsman represents a comparatively stress-free route towards redress for the average citizen. If this claim is to succeed, however, then it is incumbent upon the ombudsman institution

5 See <http://www.ombudsman.org.uk/make-a-complaint/unhappy-with-our-service> (accessed 28 August 2010).

to live up to it in a number of respects. Making contact with the ombudsman is dependent on whether people are aware of the appropriate routes for complaint and the level of accessibility. These issues, along with questions relating to the use of evidence and statistics, are discussed in the three sections below.

Awareness

The general public's awareness of the work of the ombudsman is a perennial concern for most offices around the world. The few awareness surveys that have been commissioned in the UK and elsewhere suggest that the ombudsman institution is not well known by the general public. A survey commissioned by the Commonwealth Ombudsman of Australia (CO), for example, found that people's 'unprompted' awareness of the office was only 33 per cent (CO 2007, 45), while in the UK the last major survey rated awareness levels at between 37 and 45 per cent depending on the ombudsman concerned (MORI 2003, 25-7).[6] Another common observation that comes out of these surveys is that complaints to the ombudsman are disproportionately made by people from older, white, middle-class backgrounds rather than from the poor, young or ethnic minorities (Van Roosbroek and Van de Walle 2008, 293).

The poor record of public awareness of the ombudsman enterprise ought, however, to be viewed in the context of the public's relatively low awareness of comparable institutions such as courts and tribunals. Indeed, the survey work undertaken for a National Audit Office report (NAO 2005, 61) on citizen redress in the UK found that, although nine out of ten people were confident that they would be able to complain or appeal, when asked in the abstract what they might do if they experienced something going wrong in their dealings with a government department or agency only three-quarters of them could provide a useful suggestion as to what they might do to put things right. Nevertheless, in the same survey few people mentioned the ombudsman.[7] To address this problem, each ombudsman office has to make some difficult strategic choices within the confines of limited budgets. For instance, operating a range of regional offices around the jurisdiction of an ombudsman scheme or going on tours around the country are two ways of ensuring that the regions of a nation have good access and knowledge of the ombudsman, but these options may be expensive and have uncertain outcomes.[8] Associated with the risks of wasting public resources, there is also a risk that

6 By contrast, two separate surveys conducted in Australia have claimed a 73 per cent awareness of the ombudsman – see the 2002 Queensland Householders Survey conducted by the Office of Economic and Social Research (QO 2003, 36) and Ombudsman Victoria's Annual Report (OV 2008, 88). In the private sector, the Financial Ombudsman Service claims a public awareness rate of 74 per cent (FOS 2009, 74).

7 'Only one respondent in 14 mentioned any kind of ombudsman unprompted in our national survey, a disappointing level of salience' (NAO 2005, 64).

8 For example, the Northern Territory Ombudsman was forced by budget constraints to close its Alice Springs office (NTO 2009, 8).

awareness strategies may achieve undesirable results. Any awareness campaign must consider carefully the quality of knowledge that is aimed for. Inflated claims may encourage unrealistic public expectations, in particular where the campaign projects an image of the office as the citizen's advocate rather than maintaining a position of neutrality between citizen and state. An increased volume in complaint enquiries, therefore, may simply reflect a flawed and misdirected awareness campaign that has undermined rather than enhanced the public's confidence in the ombudsman enterprise.

The issue of the public's awareness of the ombudsman enterprise needs also to be viewed in the light of the policy developments already discussed[9] whereby, increasingly in the UK and elsewhere, the ombudsman operates as a second-tier complaint mechanism following an internal review by the public body or agency complained against. There may also be parallel routes of redress to a court, tribunal or another independent complaint-handler. Consequently, a more cogent analysis of awareness issues might be available by examining the various pathways to complaints landing at the ombudsman's office. The lack of awareness of the ombudsman might be a factor, but so too might be the failure of the internal complaints mechanism to make the citizen aware of the option to complain further.[10] In short, it is likely that citizens' awareness of their option to complain specifically to an ombudsman is inextricably linked to the bigger picture of the administrative justice system. From the complainant's perspective it can be difficult to identify the correct body to which to complain. Indeed, there is some evidence that most people have a very vague idea of the distinction between appeals and complaints (NAO 2005, 68). The Kafkaesque prospect for complainants is dramatically illustrated by the analysis for an HM Treasury review in 2006 by British Telecom Directory Enquiries that found 'over 4,000 published numbers for HMRC [Her Majesty's Revenue and Customs], DWP [Department for Work and Pensions] and Home Office alone and over 50,000 published numbers in the public sector' (Varney 2006, 60). The UK ombudsman sector provides a prime example of the problems facing the complainant, despite the harmonization of ombudsman schemes in Scotland and Wales.[11] In the UK, there are several top-tier public sector ombudsman offices: the Parliamentary Ombudsman (PO), the Health Services Ombudsman (HSO), the Local Government Ombudsman (LGO), the Public Services Ombudsman for Wales (PSOW), the Scottish Public Services Ombudsman (SPSO), the Northern Ireland Ombudsman[12] (NIO) and the Housing

9 See Chapter 3, pp. 81-7.

10 One survey found that of those people who made an internal complaint, 48 per cent were dissatisfied with the final outcome, yet only 2 per cent had subsequently contacted an ombudsman (MORI 2003, 21-2).

11 See Chapter 3, pp. 81-4.

12 Strictly speaking this encompasses two separate offices: the Northern Ireland Commissioner for Complaints (NICC) and the Assembly Ombudsman for Northern Ireland (AONI).

Ombudsman (HO),[13] with the jurisdictions of some overlapping with regard to the nature of government services provided, the classic example being medical and social care.

Various outreach strategies have been developed to raise awareness of the ombudsman enterprise. A key focus is obtaining media coverage (O'Reilly 2009), as evidenced by the efforts put in by some ombudsman schemes to track how often the media have covered the office in their stories (e.g. Brown 2009, 212). A rare example of using the media is the regular Saturday evening slot on the Austrian public broadcasting company ORF given over to the Austrian Ombudsman to explain some of the leading cases that the office has dealt with.[14] Such coverage is unlikely to be obtainable by most ombudsman schemes, but some do have a strong media-friendly approach. The Police Ombudsman for Northern Ireland (PONI), who features in the press on an almost daily basis, has become embedded in the process of resolving sectarian disputes in the province. Such is the impact of PONI that it is one of the few ombudsman offices that can boast 80 per cent plus ratings in awareness terms (PONI 2009, 12-16).[15] Although not in quite the same league, other ombudsmen also have relatively easy opportunities with which to sell their product. The PHSO, the CO and the Ontario Ombudsman all provide good examples, albeit in very different ways, of using high-profile investigation to access the media for more general purposes (e.g. Jones 2009, ch. 11). However, as the Irish Ombudsman has pointed out, the media is not a risk-free route to improving public awareness of the ombudsman; coverage of the office will not always be favourable (O'Reilly 2009).

Other ombudsmen pursue alternative strategies, sometimes ones that are targeted to specific communities. To give only a few examples: the Tasmanian Ombudsman operates a stall at one of the largest festivals in the state (TO 2009, 13); the Gibraltar Ombudsman makes himself available to hear complaints in the market square every Saturday; the Prisons and Probation Ombudsman once produced an award-winning video describing his work;[16] the Northern Territory Ombudsman has an advert available on YouTube (NTO 2009, 7-8); the NSWO has a poster campaign targeted at young people (NSWO 2006, 29); the South Australian Ombudsman, through its 'Justice Access Referral Programme', appointed a series of volunteers

13 This list does not include the police and armed forces sectors.

14 'Each week particularly striking cases are presented to an average audience of 320,000 viewers. The programme has reached an average market share of 29 per cent and is thus one of the most frequently viewed ORF programmes on Saturdays' (Austrian Ombudsman Board 2008, 6). For programme summaries, see: <http://www.volksanw.gv.at/en>. A similar programme on the ombudsman has been aired in Canada on CBC Tc since 1974 (Hyson 2009, 7).

15 Coincidentally, PONI is the only office covered in this research that monitors awareness levels on an annual basis.

16 See *On The Case*, issue no. 7, Autumn 2002, available at: <http://www.ppo.gov.uk/docs/on-the-case-autumn-02.pdf> (accessed 14 April 2010). A more recent report has reviewed the need for their publicity materials to be updated and improved (PPO 2008).

to inform local citizens and assist in the submission of complaints (SAO 2002, 195-199);[17] the Western Australia Ombudsman has a scheduled 'Ask the Ombudsman' slot on a radio Nightline programme four times a year (WAO 2008, 6); the New Zealand Ombudsman each year stages a series of 'clinics' around the country to inform local organizations of the office's services and to receive complaints (NZO 2009, 37);[18] the Irish Ombudsman facilitates the submission of complaints at Citizen Information Centres (CICs) around Ireland through both ombudsman staff attending regular sessions and by training CIC staff to receive complaints themselves (IO 2008, 42). Together with these examples, most ombudsmen will make public speeches and attend a range of public fora. Considerable emphasis is also placed on designing user-friendly websites and making available informative literature on the ombudsman in a range of languages.

Perhaps the most important focus of the ombudsman's energies in this area, however, is the targeting of those complainants most likely to complain (MORI 2003, 14). This is achieved largely by working with first-instance complaint-handlers to encourage them to make their complainants aware of their rights to complain to the ombudsman, and with those citizen advice organizations that are most likely to first meet aggrieved citizens (PO 2004, 4; LGO 2008, 20). This approach may seem to be passing on the responsibility, but it goes to the heart of the problem of directly connecting the ombudsman into a systematic overarching administrative justice network. The general public does not necessarily need to know about the ombudsman, but the citizen that has experienced a grievance does. In this sense it is reasonable to assume that the most obvious place for the citizen to complain to in the first instance is the organization that the citizen blames for the maladministration. It is therefore unsurprising that most ombudsman institutions focus a lot of their training efforts, as well as their awareness efforts, on working with service providers to improve their complaint-handling procedures. Inclusive within good complaints systems should be clear information which makes the complainant aware of the opportunity to pursue their complaint further, should they feel it necessary, with an ombudsman.[19] A good model here is the Public Services Ombudsman Act (Wales) 2005 under which public bodies within the

17 The South Australian Ombudsman has also recently commented on the need for his office to comply with the Commonwealth government's new access to justice strategy involving a triage approach to signposting complainants (Bingham 2009).

18 See also the Western Australia Ombudsman's Regional Awareness and Accessibility Program, available at: <http://www.ombudsman.wa.gov.au/CPS_Info/RAAP.htm> (accessed 14 April 2010) and the regional awareness and communication work of the Queensland Ombudsman (QO 2009, 61-4).

19 A survey conducted for the SPSO found that the most frequent source of referral to the SPSO was from the organizations that they were complaining about (ORC International 2008, 9).

jurisdiction of the ombudsman are under a legal duty to take reasonable steps to inform members of the public of their right to complain to the ombudsman.[20]

Access

Assuming a potential complainant is aware of an appropriate ombudsman body then gaining access to the ombudsman should not be difficult, albeit localized problems, such as inattentive staff or unhelpful literature, will occasionally still occur (e.g. ORC International 2008, ch.6). Ombudsman schemes today aid the process of applying by making available information and application forms on the internet and offering a degree of assistance on the phone, with phone calls occasionally made available free of charge (e.g. SPSO and QO).[21] It has also become the norm for information on ombudsmen to be made available in a range of languages.

Some UK ombudsman schemes remain slightly harder to access than their counterparts elsewhere given that they still require a complaint to be made in writing (e.g. PO, HSO). This requirement does appear to discourage some applicants from complaining by adding a degree of inconvenience and hassle to the process (MORI 2003, 52). In response to such concerns, the newer ombudsman schemes grant the ombudsman discretion to accept complaints orally and earlier schemes have often been amended along these lines; this approach has been long established in Australia and New Zealand.[22] Both the CO and the Northern Territory Ombudsman, for instance, regularly report that 70-80 per cent of complaints are now submitted either over the phone or in person. Noticeably, no major problems have been recorded as a result.[23]

The one major anomaly that remains in the ombudsman system in the area of access is the Member of Parliament (MP) filter that applies to the PO, and its equivalent for the Assembly Ombudsman in Northern Ireland.[24] It is extraordinary that in the twenty-first century this provision, which was originally envisaged as a temporary measure designed to protect the PO from being swamped in its early days, still operates as a requirement for complainants. The MP filter places one more obstacle between the complainant and what they perceive as justice, even

20 Section 33. In the UK internal complaints mechanisms have developed more as a matter of good practice reflecting New Public Management (NPM) culture rather than legislative duty. Elsewhere, an example of a legal duty to establish internal complaints mechanisms is the Local Government Act 1993 (South Australia), s.270.

21 For a more critical viewpoint, see Dunleavy *et al* (2010, 442-4).

22 See SPSO Act 2002, s.10(3); PSOW Act 2005, s.2(4) and Local Government Act 1974, s.26B(3). See also, Ombudsman Act 1976 (Cth), s.7(1).

23 One possible downside is that inviting telephone applications may expose the ombudsman office to more unreasonable and vexatious complainants (NSWO 2009d, 13).

24 To the authors' knowledge, the French *Médiateur de la République* is the only other ombudsman to possess an equivalent provision, and at the time of writing its abolition was under consideration.

though the ombudsman's office will ordinarily help to redirect a complainant to a suitably amenable MP (PASC 2007, q.47; NIO 2007, 2). This problem was one of the reasons why it was felt necessary to set up a separate prisons ombudsman scheme to encourage prisoners to complain (Seneviratne 2002, 94). It is also anomalous that complainants have no one to whom they can submit their complaints during the period of time before a general election is held and after the Queen has dissolved Parliament (PASC 2009, Ev.12).

Insofar as the MP filter is defensible, it has almost certainly played a lead role in cementing Parliament's respect for the institution of the ombudsman (Giddings 2008, 96). Given the importance of a supportive Parliament to the success of the PO, the existence of a strong parliamentarian/PO bond is an asset. Whether the MP filter is still necessary to retain this strong bond is extremely doubtful however, particular as it misleadingly portrays the office as a servant of Parliament. There are other means by which the PO can promote its work in Parliament, in particular through the submission of reports. Nor would the MP's ability to refer complaints to the PO be prevented by removing the filter. Importantly, the most recent poll of MPs on the matter suggests that they no longer feel particularly sensitive about the issue, with 66 per cent advocating the filter's removal (Regulatory Reform Committee 2007, 24). The government has also periodically supported the idea (Collcutt and Hourihan, para. 3.19) and the current PO has expressed the view that the office need not fear being swamped should it be removed (PASC 2005, q.6). There are few advocates of the arrangement left and its retention is probably only explicable by a combination of deep-rooted conservatism within the civil service, coupled with the lack of parliamentary time and opportunity to introduce an amendment, which the government argues could not be made by way of a regulatory reform order (Cabinet Office 2005, para. 31).

In order to retain the best features of the MP filter, there is a middle ground that could be introduced: an amendment to the Parliamentary Commissioner Act 1967 that would allow complaints to the PO to be made either direct to the office or via an MP (OFMDFM 2004, 33). This reference in itself would make it clear in the legislation that the role of the MP is linked to the office. The Law Commission has also proposed that the maintenance of such a link could be supported by a regular reporting of constituent complaints to MPs by the PO's office (Law Commission 2008, para. 5.86). Its recent report suggests that a 'dual track' option should be seriously considered in the future (Law Commission 2010, paras 5.34-5.43).

Evidence and Statistics

A common question asked of the ombudsmen is whether they deal with a sufficient number of complaints. To measure the success of the ombudsmen in making themselves known and available to potential complainants, it is useful to consider the statistical evidence about workloads and other matters contained in a variety of forms within their annual reports. But such official statistics have to be examined with care. Changing methodologies and definitions deployed for collecting data can make comparisons from one year to the next and between schemes problematic.[25]

One reason why understanding data on the numbers of complaints is difficult is that ombudsmen also undertake an important signposting function of transferring grievances to other more appropriate bodies, with these contacts commonly recorded as 'enquiries'. In addition, the interpretation of complaint statistics is challenging as it is dependent in part on a number of assumptions about the nature and purpose of the particular ombudsman scheme and its relationship to the wider administrative justice system. There may be alternative potential redress opportunities available to a complainant. There may be different policies governing the appropriate balance to be struck between informal resolution and formal investigation, as well as the extent to which complaints should be referred back to a lower tier of complaint-handling.

The statistical evidence in relation to some complaints also belies the real significance of complaint-handling activity. For example, the HSO only investigated formally 13 complaints in relation to its report on the funding arrangements for long-term care patients (HSO 2003, 1), but the office subsequently received 4,000 more complaints, which were ordinarily passed on to National Health Service (NHS) health authorities to resolve on the basis of the HSO's earlier report. As a result of the HSO's findings, NHS health authorities agreed to reconsider the manner in which they handled thousands of equivalent cases even where a complaint had not been received (HSO 2004, 1). The full extent of the HSO's impact in this affair, therefore, was never fully accounted for in the complaints figures.

Notwithstanding the difficulties, some commentators have made unflattering comparisons between the workloads of the ombudsmen and other dispute resolution mechanisms, including cost comparisons (e.g. NAO 2005; Endicott 2009, 431; Dunleavy *et al* 2010). Although it is entirely legitimate to ask whether ombudsmen should be doing more,[26] without proper perspective and interpretation such comparisons can be dangerously misleading.[27]

Figure 4.1 sets out the headline complaint/enquiry figures for the major ombudsman offices in the UK for 2008-09. The figures for enquiries/complaints that travel along informal and formal investigative routes to formal reports tend

25 See PHSO (2005), the SPSO at <http://www.spso.org.uk/statistics/changes-recording> and the LGO at <http://www.lgo.org.uk/publications/annual-report/note-interpretation-statistics/> (accessed 21 May 2010).

26 The PO has often been criticized for handling insufficient numbers of complaints: see Buckley (2002, q.60). Australian ombudsmen tend to process many more complaints per population than UK ombudsmen, but these schemes usually possess a wider range of responsibilities than the UK ombudsmen.

27 See further, Stuhmcke (2008).

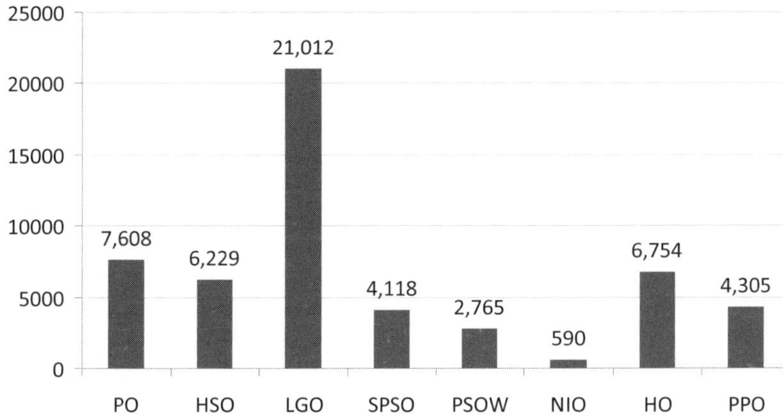

Figure 4.1 Number of enquiries/complaints received by principal UK public sector ombudsman services, 2008-2009

Notes: It should be noted that in the private sector the Financial Ombudsman Service handled 925,095 initial enquiries and complaints from consumers in 2009-10 (FOS 2010, 1).

Sources: PHSO (2009, 5 and 30); LGO (2009, 16); SPSO (2009, 8); PSOW (2009, 3); NIO (2009, 11); Housing Ombudsman (2009, 6); PPO (2009, 49).

to diminish to much smaller figures not shown in Table 4.1.[28] However, the global complaint/enquiry figures provide a reasonable proxy to identify an overview of the levels of activity within each office. There are of course a number of factors which go to explain the variations year on year within each individual ombudsman office, in addition to the inherent (and often unpredictable) levels of maladministration in public authorities; for example, changes in an ombudsman scheme's jurisdiction, publicity and media coverage. But one broad conclusion that can be safely drawn is that for most ombudsman schemes the number of complaints received has increased significantly since the office(s) were first introduced. Nor is there much evidence from the UK, Ireland, Australia and New Zealand that the use of ombudsman schemes is declining.[29] In any event, although other branches of the administrative justice system may receive a greater volume of complaints, the

28 For example, the numbers of formal reports issued by the PO and HSO in 2008-09 were 187 and 507 respectively (PHSO 2009, 30).

29 Complaints to the Western Australian Ombudsman have declined since 2000, although this was partly attributable to the establishment of the Corruption and Crime Commission on 1 January 2004 to deal with complaints about the police (WAO 2005, 8). In other schemes, such as the PSOW, the number of complaints/enquiries received is still increasing, whilst in others the numbers have stabilized, e.g. LGO and NIO.

significance and impact of the caseload processed by the ombudsman enterprise needs to be assessed more fully by measures other than mere volume.

Customer Service

Advising and Working with Complainants

As has already been alluded to,[30] the focus on customer service in public management, including the ombudsman enterprise, has become more pronounced over recent years. The CO, for instance, states as one of its key measures of success '[t]he quality and timeliness of services of the office will improve through better front line service, clearer policies, more consistent processes, improved recording and better utilisation of staff skills' (PB Statement 2009, 238). Consistent with this aim, the CO has established a Public Contact Team to receive and assess all telephone approaches to the office (CO 2006, 10) and opened a shop front located on the ground floor of its offices in Canberra (CO 2004, 3). Likewise, in the UK both the PHSO and the LGO have moved towards emphasizing up-front customer communication through the establishment of a Customer Service Unit for the PHSO (PHSO 2007, 49-55) and a centralized Advice Team for the LGO (LGO 2009, 5). The New Zealand Ombudsman has also established a call centre to improve its service and streamline operations (NZO 2005, 40) and other ombudsman schemes have rationalized their organization to process initial complaints and enquiries more effectively (QO 2005, 10). Such developments are not necessarily particularly innovative or novel, but they do represent a demonstration of intent that was not always there in previous generations.

Technical advances have also played a part in the provision of a better service, with computer databases now regularly employed to track and inform the progress of complaints and to make links between investigations where possible. Websites for most ombudsmen have been revamped in recent years and are generally much more helpful and informative than they once were. To maintain improvements most ombudsmen schemes now conduct regular consumer satisfaction surveys and on occasion employ management consultants to provide an externally generated overview and new outlooks.

For all these advances, the ombudsmen are faced with a series of fundamental challenges in managing their relationship with complainants. An early task for the ombudsman is to deal with those contacts with the office which involve complaints that have either been submitted to the ombudsman prematurely or incorrectly.[31] Some of the ombudsmen's jurisdictions are very dense, with annexes to ombudsman statutes listing in detail the bodies within jurisdiction. To complicate the matter

30 See Chapter 3, pp. 76-7.

31 E.g., there were 2,830 enquiries outside of remit and 2,681 made prematurely (PHSO 2009, 9).

further some bodies will be within jurisdiction for some functions and excluded for others.[32] In order to provide quality customer service, therefore, there is a real need for ombudsmen and their staff to understand not only their jurisdiction and the functions of the bodies they can investigate, but also to have a grasp of other relevant remedies and redress mechanisms that may be available. In the absence of a centrally coordinated forum for advising complainants and/or submitting complaints into the administrative justice system, increasingly this is a role that the ombudsmen are being called upon to undertake (PASC 2008a, q.32-3). This has led some ombudsman schemes to target guidance at potential complainants to assist them in submitting effective complaints, not just to the ombudsman but also to the first-instance complaint-handler (NSWO 2009a).

When complainants have contacted the ombudsman incorrectly, the general onus in ombudsman schemes now is to do what they can to redirect the complainant to the appropriate body and provide tailored procedural advice where appropriate (SPSO 2007, 44). This may even include identifying a particular person who should be contacted and undertaking to contact that individual and forwarding any relevant papers (PHSO 2009, 7). With premature complaints, a similar process applies, although here a complainant should be reassured that they can return to the ombudsman if they are dissatisfied with the lower level handling of the complaint, ideally without requiring the complainant to repeat the details of their complaint (CO 2004, 74-5).

Even where an ombudsman can deal with a complaint, many complainants will not appreciate the difference between the various appeals and complaints processes available to them and will be more interested in the decision or action they are complaining against being overturned than anything else. Faced with this degree of expectation of the ombudsman office, it is unsurprising that complainants can become disillusioned with the process, as reconsidering the merits of a public authority decision is not what ombudsmen are designed to undertake. In this regard, understanding the subtleties of a complaints process based on the search for maladministration, as opposed to an appeal process, might be a cause of bewilderment and frustration for many complainants. But encouraging realistic expectations amongst complainants and explaining from the outset the limitations of the ombudsman procedure, as well as its strengths, is a priority for the ombudsman enterprise. There is some evidence to support the idea that where clear guidance is given early in a complainant's contact with the ombudsman office, their subsequent experience of the office will be more favourable (e.g. Ipsos MORI 2007, 20-24). This is an issue in which more than one ombudsman office is currently investing much time and effort (CLA 2009).

Together with a lack of full awareness of the nuances of the ombudsman scheme, a citizen who complains to an ombudsman office may well be suffering from a degree of complainant fatigue. By the time that complainants come to the ombudsman, many will have already experienced two or more negative rejections

32 For example, see Local Government Act 1974, Sched. 5, para. 5 (as amended).

from the overall complaints and public sector decision-making process. In addition, some complainants will just be perplexed having been bounced around the administrative justice system, often finding it difficult to find the appropriate body that is willing to take on board their complaint. The existence of the problems caused by the complexity of the administrative justice system is widely recognized (e.g. Mullen 2009, para. 7.117). In this context, complainants' previous experience of the administrative justice system as a whole may well mediate their relationship with ombudsman offices. Last-resort complaints directed at the ombudsman system itself, therefore, may reflect dissatisfaction with the wider administrative justice system. This feature of the ombudsman's work draws attention to the need for good communication with the complainant and the need to explain from the outset the remit of the office. Helping dissatisfied complainants come to terms with this fact is also going to be one of the jobs for the ombudsman office.

In response to the above challenges it is often argued that one of the key purported strengths of the ombudsman is its capacity to reduce the stress and cost of complaining. It does this largely because, once the complaint has been submitted, it operates in an investigatory capacity and is thereafter not reliant upon the continued input of the complainant. Frequently the complainant is no longer involved at all until the ombudsman arrives at a conclusion. The ombudsman's investigatory technique in effect means that once a complaint has been submitted, the ombudsman takes ownership of it and the complainant tends to lose control over the process (NSWO 2009d, 21). The danger with this arrangement is that it can create a sense of disenfranchisement for a complainant, which can become a source of considerable frustration. Accordingly, a further challenge for ombudsman offices is to keep complainants informed throughout the process.

The removal of control of the complaint from the complainant and the ombudsman's investigatory technique in general can be defended, and has been in other parts of this book.[33] Nevertheless, the onus is on the office to confront the customer service issues it faces. Alongside the establishment of user-friendly call centres aimed at providing better advice to complainants and communication during the course of an investigation, ombudsmen attempt to learn from regularly commissioned customer satisfaction surveys.[34] Care must be taken in interpreting the results of these surveys because of the 'outcome effect'; those who obtain a satisfactory outcome to their complaint are more likely to express satisfaction with the process. For example, the Ipsos MORI (2007, 4) survey of LGO customers found that 'of those with a positive outcome, 76 per cent are satisfied with the way in which their complaint was handled, while of those who did not receive a positive outcome only 41 per cent are satisfied'.

33 See Chapter 2, p. 34-45.

34 See PHSO (2009, 19); LGO (2009, 26); SPSO (2009, 12) for the common sources of complaint, such as delay. The LGO responded to the Ipsos MORI survey in 2007 by setting up an advice team and a first contact centre with a 'signposting' facility (LGO 2009, 5 and 26).

The delays experienced by complainants in the processing of their complaints have in the past also proved to be a real problem. For example, in 1997-98 the average time for an investigation in the PO's office was 100 weeks (PO 1998, para. 1.10). Difficulties in this area can indicate problems in obtaining evidence from public authorities. In recent years there have been significant efforts made to improve timeliness, although performance can fluctuate, and delays in complaint processing still appear in recent satisfaction survey results.[35] Most ombudsman schemes, in keeping with NPM culture, have now established a series of targets to meet and report annually on their performance. As a minimum, schemes will commonly record the percentage of complaints dealt with in a relatively short period of time and the corresponding figure for a more substantial period of time.[36] By such measures internal and external pressures are placed upon ombudsman schemes to provide a prompt service. Enormous quantities of contacts to ombudsman offices are dealt with quickly and efficiently. Yet the complexity of some complaints handled by the ombudsman enterprise has increased and such cases will often take a considerable period of time to resolve. To address the subsequent problem of delay the ombudsman technique has had to evolve, as will be described shortly.

Customer Service – Realistic Expectations

In response to the challenge of providing a quality complaints service, the majority of ombudsman schemes considered in the research for this book have invested heavily in improved 'front-of-house' arrangements and become more aware of the importance of ongoing communication with complainants. Further, most ombudsman schemes now report annually on their performance against stated business goals; for example, the LGO's business goals in 2008-09 included the following aspirations:

1. To make decisions that are sound and justified.
2. To provide customers with a service that meets their needs and reasonable expectations.
3. To promote awareness, understanding and use of our services.
4. To influence the improvement of local government through guidance and advice.
5. To increase our efficient use of resources. (LGO 2009, 22)

All the goals are backed up by various measureable indicators. Despite all this effort, however, there is every likelihood that the bid to achieve full customer

35 For example, PHSO (2009, 19) and SPSO (2009, 12).

36 For example, the LGO has three time-band targets: to clear 50 per cent of all complaints within 13 weeks; 80 per cent within 26 weeks; and 96 per cent within 52 weeks. See LGO (2009, Table 8).

satisfaction, whether by enhanced service or procedures, will always reach a natural glass ceiling.

> The correlation between satisfaction and a complaint being upheld and dissatisfaction with a complaint not being upheld [is] evident, as is the case in public sector ombudsman surveys generally. This of course holds some very real challenges for ombudsmen – their purpose is to rule fairly and objectively on the complaints brought to them; there is no capacity to boost satisfaction levels by adjusting the fundamental principles and laws under which such organisations operate. (Craigforth 2009, 2)

Inevitably the 'outcome effect' referred to earlier will continue to make it very difficult to distil genuine and objectively justifiable complainant dissatisfaction with the performance of an ombudsman from a straightforward unwillingness to accept the failure of their complaint. Although the outcome effect must be part of the explanation for the existence of a vociferous, user-based critique of the ombudsman service,[37] it would be a mistake to conclude that dissatisfied complainants continue to feel a grievance purely because they have misunderstood the nature of the ombudsman's power or are incapable of accepting their discretionary judgment. Ombudsmen themselves have been known to concede serious flaws;[38] judgments in judicial review cases have occasionally been critical,[39] as have Parliamentary Select Committee reports. As will be analysed in Chapter 6, the only solution to this risk is to put in place suitable accountability arrangements to verify the quality of the ombudsman's output.

The Ombudsman's Use of Discretion

The ombudsman enterprise is facilitated by a series of discretionary powers which have been well documented in standard public law texts. But the use of these powers by the ombudsmen has evolved over time, reflecting the full flexibility of the discretion built into most ombudsman legislation. The vital importance of the ombudsman's extensive powers of investigation to the ombudsman enterprise have already been described in Chapter 2 and the full capacity of the ombudsman to use those powers will be analysed in Chapter 5. In this section, the manner in which the ombudsmen have interpreted their powers will be explored.

37 See Chapter 1, n.5.

38 'I conclude that the SPSO's handling of the complaint was characterized by very considerable delay and confusion. Bluntly, it is the worst case of complaint handling by an Ombudsman's office that I have seen.' LGO Jerry White (SPSO 2009a), annex 1, para. 5.

39 See *R (on the Application Balchin) v Parliamentary Commissioner for Administration* [2002] EWHC (Admin) 1876, para. 48.

The Decision to Accept a Complaint

Once a complaint is submitted, all ombudsman schemes have a range of legislatively prescribed tests which they apply to ascertain whether it should be accepted for further investigation. Failure to accept a complaint is one of the most common grounds for pursuing judicial review against the ombudsman. Inevitably, this has led to much legal discourse in the past on the jurisdiction of the ombudsman.[40]

Typically complaints will be tested to see whether they have been made within time; are within the office's jurisdiction; the public body involved has been given an opportunity to respond to the complaint; there exists a more suitable alternative remedy, such as a tribunal or court which has or has not been pursued;[41] there is prima facie evidence of a justifiable complaint to which the ombudsman can potentially contribute towards resolving; and that the complainant has potentially suffered an injustice. Given this breadth of discretion involved in deciding whether or not to accept a complaint, there must be organizational pressures to use this power to ration complaints according to the available resources.

In terms of the law, aside from ensuring that an ombudsman's jurisdiction is kept up to date so that new public bodies are placed within its remit,[42] the powers of the ombudsman are well settled. Ombudsmen are excluded from investigating certain matters, with commentators in the past frequently criticizing the common exclusion of the power to investigate contractual[43] and personnel issues[44] (e.g. Seneviratne 2002, 106-9). Even here, though, there is some evidence that the ombudsman can adopt a liberal approach towards the exclusion of contractual issues so as to facilitate investigation (*ibid.*).

One issue of particular relevance to developments in modern government is the capacity of the ombudsman to investigate complaints against private agencies performing public functions. As is widely understood, this development raises the question of the extent to which public law protections, including the ombudsman, are, or should be, available against bodies in the private sector (e.g. Oliver 2010). The law on this issue differs from scheme to scheme. In New Zealand, for instance, the ombudsman appears to be precluded from investigating the work of private bodies (Cameron 2001).[45] Similarly, the Public Services

40 For a detailed analysis of the jurisdiction of the UK ombudsmen, see Seneviratne (2002).

41 This issue will be returned to in Chapter 7.

42 This is usually done by continual amendments to a legislative list. A presumption that all public bodies were within jurisidiction subject to listed exceptions would be simpler (Beatson *et al* 2005, 722).

43 Although this exclusion is not included in either the PSOW or NICC schemes.

44 The major exception is the NICC.

45 See The Ombudsman Act 1975 (NZ), s.13.

Ombudsman (Wales) Act requires that the bodies investigated must be listed under the Act, subject to limited exceptions,[46] which makes it less likely that private bodies will be considered within jurisdiction. It is submitted here that the better position is that detailed in the Parliamentary Commissioner Act 1967 and most other UK and Irish ombudsman schemes, which empowers the ombudsman to 'investigate any action taken by or on behalf of a government department'.[47] Quite how far this provision can be pushed has never been tested in the courts and it is probable that this power applies for investigative purposes only and the remedy would remain with the public body that had employed the private body concerned. To clarify the legal position in particular areas where such activity is most common, good practice is to specify the ombudsman's jurisdiction in private sector work more clearly, as in the legislation that affects the work of the LGO on adult funded social care.[48] In the UK at least, therefore, the current state of the law suggests that most of the ombudsmen are well placed to deal with the practice of transferring public functions to the private sector.

The Ombudsman's Powers of Investigation: Maladministration and Human Rights

In the UK the key common test upon which investigations are based is maladministration that leads to an injustice. Absent any detailed definition in UK legislation or case law, this test has received much scrutiny over the years and arguments have been put forward that it should be replaced by something stronger and more meaningful for both complainant and public authority (e.g. Justice 1977; Lewis and James 2000, 116-17).[49] Certainly around the world there are plenty of alternative models that could be used. In Ireland, for instance, the ombudsman investigates actions to establish whether they have been:

i. taken without proper authority
ii. taken on irrelevant grounds
iii. the result of negligence or carelessness
iv. based on erroneous or incomplete information
v. improperly discriminatory
vi. based on an undesirable administrative practice, or
vii. otherwise contrary to fair or sound administration.[50]

46 Section 7.

47 Section 5(1). This approach contrasts with the leading UK administrative law case on the issue, *YL v Birmingham City Counci*l [2007] UKHL 27; [2008] 1 A.C. 95.

48 Under s.35 and Sch 5 of the Health Act 2009 the LGO is given 'powers to investigate complaints about privately arranged or funded adult social care'.

49 Although, as Seneviratne notes (2002, 46-8), JUSTICE later withdrew the proposal (Justice-All Souls 1988, 138).

50 Ombudsman Act 1980 (Ireland), section 4(2)(b).

The legislation in New South Wales on the same point is slightly different. Here the questions that the ombudsman is asking of public body actions includes whether they have been:

a. contrary to law
b. unreasonable, unjust, oppressive or improperly discriminatory
c. in accordance with any law or established practice but the law or practice is, or may be, unreasonable, unjust, oppressive or improperly discriminatory
d. based wholly or partly on improper motives, irrelevant grounds or irrelevant consideration
e. based wholly or partly on a mistake of law or fact
f. conduct for which reasons should be given but are not given
g. otherwise wrong ...[51]

Yet although both pieces of legislation provide some helpful substance on the ombudsman's role and there are significant similarities, neither can be said to provide a definitive explanation and the subtle differences between the two highlight the diverse complexity of the concept of maladministration. In particular, the reference in the respective Acts to actions that are 'otherwise contrary to fair or sound administration' and 'otherwise wrong' does not suggest that these Acts provide full certainty. As discussed in Chapter 2, this result is hardly surprising given the inherent indeterminacy of the goal of good administration which the ombudsman is most commonly designed to tackle.

Nor is it clear that providing a fuller legislative definition of maladministration would better inform complainants and public bodies as to the purpose of the ombudsman's work. The ombudsman would still retain full discretion as to any test's meaning and application, as it relates to individual complaints and more generally. Indeed, in the interests of transparency, it is arguable that as a matter of obligation it should be the ombudsman's duty to provide more detailed public, non-statutory guidance as to what it believes maladministration – or its opposite, good administration – amounts to. Belatedly, this is the route that most ombudsman schemes have gone down in developing various codes, guidance and sets of principles detailing what amounts to good administration.[52] Further, more user-friendly guidance is generally provided to complainants on the websites of the ombudsmen. Such an approach is arguably more effective than attempting to list the ombudsman's powers in more detail within legislation, an approach which risks placing unwanted boundaries on the office and adding an unwanted legalism to the process.

In any event, it is no longer evident that the maladministration test restricts the ombudsman's operations as it was once alleged to do. Of the various elements identified in the Irish and New South Wales legislation above, all can be found

51 Ombudsman Act 1974 (NSW), s.26.
52 See Chapter 5, pp. 141-4.

within the decision-making of the ombudsmen in the UK. Consider the following examples, taken from ombudsman reports in the UK, where maladministration was found:

- *Taken without proper authority/contrary to law* – failure to abide by a Court of Appeal decision (HSO 2003).
- *Taken on irrelevant grounds/considerations* – in disposing of the property of a homeless complainant, failure to take into consideration law and council's own guidance.[53]
- *The result of negligence or carelessness* – the failure to record an interview and the loss of correspondence.[54]
- *Based on erroneous or incomplete information* – where information provided by the government on occupational pensions had been misleading (PHSO 2006a).
- *Unreasonable, unjust, oppressive or improperly discriminatory* – where a decision had been made on the basis of impartial evidence unsupported by alternative evidence.[55]
- *Based on an undesirable administrative practice* – poor case-handling, deficient customer care and delay (PHSO 2010a, 13-15).
- *Conduct for which reasons should be given but are not given* – where a medical examination had been required in conjunction with a claim for disability living allowance and a full explanation had not been given as to how the subsequent medical report would be used.[56]
- *Otherwise contrary to fair or sound administration or wrong* – where a decision 'flew in the face of the facts' and 'was therefore perverse'.[57]

The flexibility of the ombudsman's use of the maladministration test is perfectly illustrated by the issue of human rights. Nowhere in the UK's human rights legislation is the ombudsman referred to as a potential remedial mechanism, but quietly in recent years the ombudsmen have been raising human rights issues within their reports (O'Brien 2009). In the *Six Lives* report for instance, the HSO and LGO referred specifically to the culture of human rights that informed understandings of appropriate standards of care for people with learning difficulties (HSO and LGO 2009). Although the subsequent findings of maladministration could have been made without reference to the Human Rights Act 1998 (HRA), the ombudsmen made clear the direct connection between their findings and the upholding of human rights standards (PHSO 2009, 20-21). In *Injustice in Residential Care*,

53 Taken from a case example given by former LGO, Jerry White (2007, 82).

54 C.434/03 – cited in PO (2004, 9-10).

55 Case 200700991– Vale of Glamorgan Council; available on the PSOW website.

56 C.1905/02 – cited in PO (2004, 13).

57 LGO Report of an Investigation into Complaints 00/A/0713; 00/A/08675; and 00/A/10234 against the London Borough of Lambeth. Cited by Seneviratne (2002, 46).

another report issued jointly by the HSO and LGO, the ombudsmen demonstrated even more clearly the degree of fit between human rights standards and the test of maladministration. Here the ombudsmen found that both the local authority and health trust concerned had failed to address sufficiently the article 3, 8 and 14 implications when putting in place care arrangements for the complainant. It was this failure to demonstrate that human rights standards had been followed that grounded the finding of maladministration (HSO and LGO 2008, paras 81-2). The connection between the work of the ombudsman and the promotion of human rights has been adopted by other ombudsman schemes, noticeably by the Irish Ombudsman (O'Reilly 2007).[58] This is a focus of work for the ombudsman that also fits into the vision of human rights dispute resolution developed by the Commissioner for Human Rights[59] and has been approved by the Council of Europe.[60] There is also at least one court ruling in the UK that encourages the ombudsman's work in this area.[61]

One thing that comes out of an analysis of maladministration is the clear crossover between so much of the ombudsman's work and the grounds of administrative law (Halford 2009, 84-8). This is inevitable as the underlying purpose of administrative law is essentially the same as the maladministration test, namely to apply appropriate standards of good administration. The difference is in the methodology applied and there is much evidence now that the technique applied by the ombudsman allows for complaints to be resolved on grounds that would be less likely to be successful in the courts (Kirkham 2006, 817), as for instance in dealing with complaints about delay (McCurtie 1997).

As with the grounds of administrative law applied in judicial review, the common legislative stipulation is that the ombudsman must not evaluate the 'merits of a decision taken without maladministration'.[62] This has led to a further point of concern with the maladministration test that it restricts the ombudsman to an examination of the manner in which a decision is made rather than 'with the nature, quality or reasonableness of the decision itself'.[63] This critique is supported by Merricks, who has pointed out that it is an 'unrealistic … fiction to suppose that the claimant is interested only in the process and not in the outcome' (2010, 261). However, it is unclear in theory on what grounds an ombudsman could criticize

---

58 See also Local Government Ombudsman, Report on an investigation into complaint no. 06/A/10428 against the London Borough of Havering, 31 October 2007.

59 10th Round Table of European Ombudsmen and the Council of Europe Commissioner for Human Rights, Athens, 12-13 April 2007. See <http://www.commissioner.coe.int> (accessed 18 May 2009).

60 Assembly of the Council of Europe, Recommendation 1615 (2003) on the Institution of the Ombudsman.

61 *Anufrijeva v Southwark LBC* [2003] EWCA Civ 1406; [2004] Q.B. 1124.

62 E.g. Parliamentary Commissioner Act 1967, s.12(3).

63 *R v Local Commissioners for Administration ex parte Eastleigh Borough Council* [1988] QB 855 at 863 (per Lord Donaldson MR).

the merits of a public authority decision. Moreover, a decision so bad that the ombudsman might regard it as maladministrative on that basis will ordinarily have been arrived at precisely because of a series of fundamental administrative failings. Accordingly, it is telling that in most ombudsman reports the ombudsman can take great care to avoid the policy behind the administrative process because it does not have the need to address it. A case in point is the *Debt of Honour* report in which the fairness of the criteria chosen by the Ministry of Defence in establishing an *ex gratia* compensation scheme was at issue. While expressing reservations as to the criteria chosen, the PO based her subsequent findings of maladministration on other grounds (PHSO 2005a, paras. 160-64).

The test of maladministration is not limitless, however, and in one respect it has been found necessary to expand ombudsmen's competence specifically through amendments to legislation. Thus in several ombudsman schemes now the office has the power to investigate 'an alleged failure in service' or 'to provide a service'.[64] This addition to the ombudsman's powers requires the ombudsman to make more direct judgments of the exercise of public authority. For instance, as a result of this provision much of the HSO's work involves investigating the clinical judgment of practitioners in the health service (Seneviratne 2002, 162-9). Here one of the biggest limiting factors on the ombudsman's work is the extent to which such investigations overlap into the law of negligence. However, to date the courts have appeared to support the ombudsman's approach in this area.[65]

Early Redress and the Decline of Reports

For all the fine intentions, ombudsman schemes are restricted in their resources. Governments increasingly exercised by tightening public finances have put pressure on a number of ombudsman schemes to demonstrate their continuing relevancy and effectiveness; on occasion some schemes have been threatened with closure[66] while others have been roundly criticized for their inefficiency (e.g. Select Committee on PCA 1986, 93-4). The ability to process complaints within reasonable time remains one of the major challenges for complaint-handlers (e.g. NZO 2002, 10-11; CO 2008, 2; PASC 2008, 1-22) and can lead to the efficacy of the organization being called into question.

Great effort has been put into streamlining the complaint-handling process in most ombudsman schemes (e.g. Harlow and Rawlings 2009, 543-9). An almost uniform response of the ombudsman enterprise has been a significant trend towards

64 E.g. National Health Service Reorganisation Act 1973, s.115/Health Service Commissioners Act 1993, s.3; Public Services Ombudsman (Wales) Act 2005, s.7 Public Services Ombudsman (Wales) Act 2005, s.7; Scottish Public Services Ombudsman Act 2002, s.5; Local Government Act 1974, s.26(1), as amended.

65 *R (Attwood) v Health Service Commissioner* [2008] EWHC 2315 (Admin).

66 It appeared that the Ontario Ombudsman office was being prepared for closure in 2005 (Marin 2009, para. 9), as was the LGO at one point (see Chapter 1, n.17).

expedition by lower level complaint mechanisms of simpler complaints, leaving the top-tier ombudsman offices greater capacity to devote to the more difficult and time-consuming cases and/or promoting good administration (Stuhmcke 2008). This has been achieved by re-emphasizing the legislative requirement for public bodies to be given the opportunity to consider a complaint before the ombudsman investigates, subject to exceptional circumstances.[67] The end result is that a significant number of complaints to the ombudsman are referred back to the public body complained against for detailed consideration. This is advantageous as internal complaints mechanisms will be closer to the source of the problem and ordinarily cheaper to operate. However, there are remaining concerns about this approach. The quality of internal complaints mechanisms vary considerably (PASC 2008; Gulland 2010) and an initial refusal to accept a complaint can discourage complainants from returning to the ombudsman at a later stage.[68]

Alongside the heightened emphasis on internal complaints mechanisms there has also been a move towards the consensual resolution of disputes, often described as early redress/intervention or local settlement/resolution, which can mean settlement arrived at through a simple telephone conversation. This technique is consistent with the general policy development in the UK to encourage 'proportionate dispute resolution' (PDR).[69] It also fits with the overall informal technique associated with the ombudsman enterprise and operates where a more detailed investigation is not needed to uncover the key facts underpinning the dispute. Despite the benefits of this approach, formerly there was a concern that the ombudsman's legal powers did not cater satisfactorily for the informal conclusion of complaints,[70] and subsequently some of the UK legislation has been amended to reflect this evolution of the ombudsman technique. Perhaps the most forthright recognition of this practice comes from the Public Services Ombudsman (Wales) Act 2005.

> (1) The Ombudsman may take any action he thinks appropriate with a view to resolving a complaint which he has power to investigate … .
> (2) The Ombudsman may take action under this section in addition to or instead of conducting an investigation into the complaint.
> (3) Any action under this section must be taken in private.[71]

---

67 For example, in Queensland 49 per cent of complaints were declined 'because the complainant had not tried to resolve their complaint with the agency concerned' (QO 2009, 21).

68 Research conducted by the SPSO found that 'of the 65 per cent of complainants who went back to the body after receiving our letter stating that they needed to complete the complaints process, 91 per cent were dissatisfied with the outcome (but did not come back to the SPSO)' (SPSO 2007, 43).

69 See Chapter 3, pp. 77-9.

70 But see *R (Mahnui) v Commissioner for Local Administration for England* [2002] EWCA Civ 973 [2003] BLGR 113, which ruled this practice legal.

71 Section 3.

The trend away from formal investigation and greater reliance on early redress though does raise some concerns about the transparency of this form of dispute resolution and the lack of subsequent publicity given to any identified maladministration. This is partially compensated for in the LGO scheme, in which if the ombudsman decides a report is not necessary he can issue a 'statement of reasons' for this decision.[72] The emphasis on PDR also creates increasing pressure to verify the efficacy of internal complaints procedures. One response, in Australia at least, is that ombudsmen are increasingly taking on an oversight role of internal complaint mechanisms.[73] Finally, the deliberate reduction in first-instance complaint-handling by the ombudsmen and the use of early redress risks the office losing out on significant information. Although a risk, the increased level of systemic investigatory activity that is currently being conducted by the ombudsmen suggests that this has not proved a significant problem to date.[74]

Obtaining a Remedy

One of the strongest distinguishing characteristics of public sector ombudsman schemes is that although they are established to facilitate redress, they rarely[75] possess the legal power to enforce a remedy. This lack of enforcement powers means that there are certain remedies that can only be provided for in a court of law, such as the securing of an immediate injunction against a public body or a declarative interpretation of the law. But as ombudsmen operate with a wide discretion, there are remedies that the ombudsman can and does facilitate that are not readily available through the standard legal process. From the complainant's point of view, therefore, there are sometimes distinct advantages in using the ombudsman.

The beneficial feature of ombudsman recommendations is that they often include very practical suggestions which can be flexibly and innovatively applied to meet the particular needs of the complainant and the injustice experienced. Sometimes such recommendations might be procedural in nature, such as recommending that a new hearing is convened or an appeal allowed so that the original decision can

72 Local Government Act 1974, s.30(1B), as amended by the Local Government and Public Involvement in Health Act 2007, s.175.

73 See Chapter 5, pp. 114-5.

74 See Chapter 5, pp. 133-6.

75 The exception is contained in The Commissioner for Complaints (Northern Ireland) Order 1996, SI 1996 No. 1297 (N.I. 7), article 16(1) and 17(1). This enables a 'person aggrieved' who has sustained injustice in consequence of maladministration to apply to the county court for damages against the body complained against; and the Commissioner can apply to the High Court where a body has 'engaged in conduct which was of the same kind as, or of a similar kind to, that which amounted to such maladministration' and the conduct is likely to be repeated. This power has not been used since 1985 (White 1994). See also Kirkham, Thompson and Buck (2008, 521, n.63).

be reconsidered. On other occasions ombudsman recommendations will go to the substance of the decision itself, for instance recommending that an offer of a particular service is made or there is an agreement to undertake a certain action. Some recommendations may also be regarded as actions to improve administration, such as changing a practice or procedure, the provision of training, the revision of information or guidance.[76] Two examples of remedies frequently offered which demonstrate the flexible nature of the ombudsman's work are the apology and the provision of financial compensation.

Apologies and Compensation

As a remedy the apology is rarely given much attention in most legal texts or referred to in court cases, yet promoting apologies where appropriate is integral to the ombudsman technique of dispute resolution. There are a number of underlying rationales that underpin the importance of apologizing (OBC 2006). With many complaints the most important response that a complainant wants is a positive recognition of the hurt suffered, together with an acknowledgement of responsibility. Furthermore, even where eventual resolution will involve more tangible remedial offers, once an apology is offered the way is then opened for a quicker and more amicable resolution of disputes. Apologizing can also help to facilitate just the sort of considered response to the errors that have occurred that the ombudsman specializes in encouraging public authorities to undertake. In addition, an approach to dispute resolution which encourages apologies is arguably more satisfactory for complainants because it avoids the delay, expense and stress of a legal action.

In the public sector scenario, apologizing will not always be appropriate, particularly in those situations in which the public authority is genuinely confident of the righteousness of their actions, there is a significant legal argument at stake or there will be profound knock-on implications for the public purse. Yet from the public authority perspective, despite the usual fear of floodgates that early apologies may generate, an open approach which acknowledges responsibility for errors made early on can be ultimately more cost-effective than resisting marginal complaints. At the same time, such an approach helps in retaining public confidence in the service being provided.

Most ombudsman schemes promote the apology as a remedy without any specific legislative direction or support for such an approach. However, around the world fears have been expressed that the law discourages the making of apologies within both the public and private law context because apologies can be interpreted as recognition of legal liability, thereby exposing the apologizing party to subsequent legal action (e.g. Cohen 2002; NSWO 2001, 115). Given their reliance on apologizing and the wider benefits of encouraging non-judicial forms

76 For an excellent analysis of the redress offered by the ombudsman, see Halford (2009, 91-8).

of dispute resolution, a number of ombudsmen schemes have led a debate on the issue and advocated apology legislation which allows for apologies to be made without prejudice to later legal actions (e.g. NSWO 2002, 139; OBC 2006; SPSO 2005, 7; NZO 2007, 10). In some jurisdictions such pressure has led to apology legislation being introduced.[77]

Given the short period of time within which most apology legislation has been in place it is too early to ascertain its effectiveness or its impact on ombudsman schemes. Not only is it unclear, therefore, as to whether or not such legislation is helpful, but it is highly likely that different forms of apology legislation will have different impacts. For instance, in terms of encouraging apologies, the effectiveness in England and Wales of a provision of the Compensation Act 2006[78] has been questioned because it fails to define whether the Act protects genuine admissions of responsibility, as opposed to mere 'expressions of regret' (Vines 2008, 203). The distinction is important, as there is research to suggest that it is the former type of apology that really makes a difference in terms of promoting resolution and avoiding litigation (Robbennolt 2006; Lazare 2004).[79] Regardless of whether or not apology legislation is helpful and the form in which it should be introduced, an important focus of attention for ombudsmen is addressing the culture of dispute resolution within the organizations that they investigate. In health care, for instance, the PHSO still notes that too often providers and practitioners remain reluctant to apologize when something goes wrong (PHSO 2008, 45). To address this issue, many ombudsman schemes already produce detailed guidance on making an apology and promote its merits in their work (NSWO 2009b; SPSO 2006).

Ombudsman recommendations ordinarily come in a package, with recommendations of an apology often accompanied by a recommendation that financial compensation should be made available. Standard legal texts assume that financial redress obtainable through the ombudsman will be small as compared to that obtained in the courts (Law Commission 2008, para. 3.76). Such an analysis though does not fully factor in the difficulty in securing damages in public law, even post-HRA. Thus the ombudsman provides the potential for financial compensation in an array of matters, in many of which the chances of obtaining a financial settlement in law will be negligible (Halford 2009, 81-2). Despite efforts

---

77 For a useful table of global legislation in this area, see Vines (2008, 224-30).

78 'An apology, an offer of treatment or other redress, shall not of itself amount to an admission of negligence or breach of statutory duty' (Compensation Act 2006, s.2).

79 See generally, Vines (2008). Arguably, apology legislation that only protects 'expressions of regret' may actually make the situation worse by encouraging 'phoney' apologies. The legislation in British Columbia (Apology Act 2006, in particular ss.1 and 2) and New South Wales (Civil Liability Act 2002, ss.68 and 69) provide good examples of full apology legislation; see also the Australian Capital Territory (Civil Law (Wrongs) Act 2002), Saskatchewan (The Evidence Act), Manitoba (The Apology Act 2007), Alberta (Alberta Evidence Act) and Nova Scotia (Apology Act 2008).

to promote the provision of damages in the courts (Fordham 2009), following the government's rejection of the Law Commission's consultation paper on the matter this situation does not look like changing in the near future.[80]

Guidance on the principles the ombudsmen apply in calculating recommendations for compensation is publicly available for most schemes (e.g. LGO 2005; PHSO 2007). In practice, the scale of financial compensation recommended by the ombudsman varies enormously. Sometimes compensation is used as a consolation to recognize the distress and/or inconvenience of having to bring a complaint.[81] Often, however, the provision of a financial payment is aimed at restoring the complainant to the position prior to the injustice or hardship and could include reimbursement of expenditure incurred as a consequence of the injustice. In such circumstances payouts can reach high levels.[82] The most heavy-hitting ombudsman investigations on the public purse are those that are selected because they represent good examples of a systemic problem within a public organization involving many hundreds, even thousands of people. Hence, in the HSO's investigation of long-term care referred to earlier,[83] the eventual sum of money made available for redress was £180 million (HSO 2004, 15). A more substantial compensatory package still has been put together in response to the *Occupational Pensions* report by the PO.[84]

Implementing Ombudsman Recommendations

Where remedies are recommended by the ombudsman it is for the public authority concerned to provide the remedy, and ultimately it is at their discretion whether or not the remedy is provided and in what form. The fact that the ombudsman enterprise can help facilitate apologies and financial compensation without enforcement powers demonstrates well the efficacy of this form of dispute resolution.

The main responsibility for pursuing the implementation of recommendations lies with the ombudsman. This task is carried out primarily by way of persuasion and relying upon the goodwill that the office has built up over the years. Should this tactic fail then, to varying degrees, ombudsman schemes contain a formal means by which their recommendations can be given extra attention in the

80 See Chapter 3, pp. 79-80 for discussion of the Law Commission's proposals.

81 In one investigation by the LGO the remedies to complaining parents included payments of £350 each as well as the setting up of new appeals (LGO 2008, 11).

82 In the *Balchin* report, a payout of £200,000 was made largely out of recognition of the loss of value to the complainant's property as a result of public authority maladministration (PHSO 2005b, 26 and 45).

83 See p. 100 above.

84 See DWP News Release, 17 December 2007, which contained the announcement of a 'substantial package of help for up to 140,000 people' who had lost their savings following the collapse of employer-sponsored pension schemes. Available at: <http://webarchive.nationalarchives.gov.uk/20091222172119/http:/dwp.gov.uk/newsroom/press-releases/2007/december-2007/pens51-171207.shtml> (accessed 31August 2010).

political arena. Thus most, although not all,[85] schemes create a procedure by which the relevant legislature can be notified when a public authority refuses to implement an ombudsman's recommendations. The special procedure by which this takes place will be analysed in Chapter 7. The key point here though is that this approach to dispute resolution highlights the constitutional choice to make the issue of finalizing an ombudsman recommendation a political matter rather than a legal one.[86]

The nature of the ombudsman's peculiar enforcement process has been defended in Chapter 2;[87] here it is necessary to explore the impact of this arrangement. In terms of results, the ombudsman's lack of enforcement powers rarely leads to any disadvantage for the complainant, as for most ombudsman schemes virtually all recommendations are implemented (Kirkham, Thompson and Buck 2008, 512). Admittedly, public authorities sometimes delay any positive response to ombudsmen's reports for significant periods of time. On occasion this has been because the provision of a remedy has also been affected by corresponding proceedings in Parliament and/or the courts. Of most concern, sometimes the remedy finally made available has differed considerably from that which the ombudsman originally recommended. Even so, outright rejections of ombudsman reports are extremely rare. To take the UK ombudsmen for example, leaving aside those ombudsman reports that have been quashed by the courts, the PO has an almost perfect record of implementation;[88] neither the SPSO nor the PSOW has yet to record a single instance of a recommendation of the office remaining unimplemented;[89] the more recently established Assembly Ombudsman for Northern Ireland and its predecessor, the Northern Ireland Parliamentary Commissioner for Administration, in a period of almost 40 years, have also recorded very few occasions when recommendations have not been implemented; likewise with the HSO for England, and formerly Scotland and Wales, the number of recommendations that remain unimplemented is minimal and almost invariably

85 The LGO is the main exception. LGOs have the power to issue a further report which is required to be considered by a full sitting of a local authority's elected council, and if that fails to secure implementation, the LGO can require that an advert is secured in a local newspaper in which the local authority is called upon to detail the ombudsman's findings and explain their reasons for rejecting the ombudsman's recommendations (Local Government Act 1974, ss.30, 31, 31A and 31B).

86 Subject to the exception of the NICC to apply to the High Court for relief in certain cases: see n.75 above.

87 See pp. 39-40 above.

88 Arguably the only outstanding exception is the *Court Line* report (1974-75). With *Court Line*, although for political reasons the government rejected the PO's report following a vote on the floor of the House of Commons, it did subsequently make a remedy available to the affected individuals, albeit not entirely in line with the PO's recommendations; see Fifth Report of the PCA (HC 498 of 1974-75, para. 92).

89 But see the special report issued by the PSOW (2006a).

minor in impact.[90] Only with the LGO for England has there been significant numbers of unimplemented recommendations, but even here the success rate today is commonly cited as over 99 per cent.[91] Elsewhere in the world, the non-implementation of ombudsman recommendations is also not a phenomenon that occurs very often, albeit bruising battles with public authorities have been reported (e.g. IO 2009, 10).

Despite the apparent success of existing enforcement arrangements, this feature of the ombudsman design has been subject to criticism over the years and has meant that some ombudsman reports have remained unimplemented by public authorities.[92] When ombudsman reports are left unimplemented, complainants are left without full redress in circumstances in which the ombudsman has found their grievance to be fully justified. Inevitably, this is a source of discontent and critique of the ombudsman model. Not only does this mean that some complaints remain unremedied, there is also a danger that the lack of enforcement power adds to the overall perception of the ombudsman as a weaker institution when compared to the courts.

The credibility of the ombudsman model, therefore, depends upon a judgment that such disadvantages are outweighed by the greater flexibility and operational capacity that this feature of the ombudsman scheme brings to the process. The nature of the ombudsman design, including the non-enforceability of the institution's recommendations, makes it easier for the ombudsman to take on complaints that raise issues that overlap into political decision-making and which the courts would be unlikely to resolve. Maladministration remains a significant source of grievance regardless of the level of political controversy surrounding the matter. If the overarching constitutional goal is to heighten the accountability of political decision-makers, then the ombudsman technique contributes to this process by throwing light on decisions in an informative manner that other institutions find more difficult to address. Precisely because the ombudsman lacks powers of enforcement, this contribution can create or add to a dynamic dialogue between several core institutions of the constitution that tests government decision-making to the full.

---

90 E.g. the HSO reported that a GP had failed to apologize following one of her recommendations (PHSO 2006, 36).

91 See also Law Commission (2010, para. 5.86 and n.3). Unfortunately, 2006-07 is the last year when these figures are easily ascertainable. The LGO listed 12 reports which resulted in an unsatisfactory outcome out of 1,531 reports issued over the previous ten years (LGO 2007a, 9, Table 9). For 2008-09 the LGO listed six investigations as requiring further reports; for 2007-08 only two special reports were issued, but one had proceeded to the stage of being published in the press: see LGO website.

92 An example from the LGO is the complaint of a woman with special needs whom the ombudsman found had been let down in a number of respects by Trafford Borough Council. The LGO had offered £100,000 compensation but the LGO was only prepared to offer £10,000: see Kirkham (2008, 253-4).

Taking the Complaint to the Public and the Courts

The frustration caused by public authorities refusing to implement ombudsman recommendations has led to complainants searching for additional routes by which to continue their complaint. Some of the more high-profile ombudsman investigations have been accompanied by well-organized publicity campaigns before, during and after ombudsman investigations. Two high-profile examples were the *Occupational Pensions* (PHSO 2006a) and *Equitable Life* (PHSO 2008a; 2009b) cases where a series of media stunts to maintain public profile and active lobbying of MPs were undertaken to support the complaints. Given the inherent political nature of the resolution process in the ombudsman design, this is an inevitable aspect of the ombudsman's work requiring good judgment in handling the media.

Judicial review of an ombudsman's report will be looked at in Chapter 6. In recent years, however, it has become clear that there is another route by which an ombudsman decision can become the focus of legal proceedings. When an ombudsman issues a report which finds that there has been maladministration that has resulted in an injustice to the complainant, there is a public law obligation on the public authority involved to respond to the report. At this point it is possible that the public authority could reject both the findings and recommendations made in the report. If it does so, however, that decision can become the subject of a judicial review application. The lead case on this form of legal action is *Bradley*,[93] a case which has been the subject of much academic comment. This possibility will be returned to in Chapter 6. Given the costs and risks attached to pursuing judicial review, however, it is unlikely to become a common form of remedy of much utility to the majority of complainants.

Achieving Closure

A review of the work of ombudsman schemes reveals that another feature of their work, and that of other complaint-handlers, is worthy of a mention.

> In our work at Ombudsman offices over the years, we have noticed an increase in complainants whose behaviour is frequently challenging in a number of ways: they tend to be very angry, aggressive and abusive to our staff; they often threaten harm; they can be dishonest or intentionally misleading in presenting the facts, or deliberately withhold relevant information; our offices are frequently flooded with unnecessary telephone calls, emails and large amounts of irrelevant printed material. These complainants tend to insist on outcomes that are clearly not possible or appropriate, or demand things they are not entitled to. At the end of the process they are often unwilling to accept our decisions and continue to

93 *Bradley v Secretary of State for Work and Pensions* [2007] EWHC 242; [2007] Pens. L.R. 87, partially upheld in the Court of Appeal [2008] EWCA Civ 36.

> demand that we take further action on their complaint. Frequently, they also take their complaint to other agencies, Ministers, or courts of law where they start up the complaint cycle again. Even though the percentage of complainants who behave in this way is quite small, they nevertheless demand a disproportionate amount of our time and resources, and cause serious stress to staff and indeed themselves. (NSWO 2009c, 1)

Within ombudsman schemes a threefold strategy has evolved to close complaints that are not upheld. Firstly, legislation tends to require the provision of reasons when ombudsmen make decisions, even for those complaints that are never accepted.[94] Secondly, internal review procedures have been established to allow for the reconsideration of certain issues regarding a complaint.[95] Finally, policies have been put in place to deal with the complainant who remains unpersuaded by either of the previous two options, focusing in particular on the unreasonable complainant (e.g. NSWO 2009d; SPSO (2009b); LGO 2007b).

There is not the room here to discuss the issue of unreasonable complainants in more depth, but it does illustrate another outcome of dispute resolution that is not frequently touched upon in administrative justice literature and is a key role that the ombudsman must perform: namely, assisting complainants in coming to terms with the rejection of their complaint. As we have seen earlier,[96] the 'outcome effect' ensures that it is often difficult for some customers, whose complaints have not been supported by the ombudsman, to maintain a beneficent view of the ombudsman process. The latter operates with significant attention given to the provision of customer service. One consequence of this is that the option of dismissing complainants through appeal mechanisms and highly procedural filter mechanisms, as in judicial review, is less readily available to ombudsmen. The ombudsman enterprise entails that more attention needs to be given to the public service of helping complainants achieve closure in their grievance claim.

Conclusion

Measuring the effectiveness of the ombudsman system in delivering a quality complaints service or the expectations of complainants is a task beyond the scope of this monograph. Much more independent research needs to be undertaken on this matter. Yet some tentative conclusions can be drawn on the evolving nature of the ombudsman technique in this area and the challenges currently facing the office.

---

94 E.g. Parliamentary Commissioner Act 1967, s.10(1); Public Services Ombudsman (Wales) Act 2005, s.12(2).

95 See pp. 170-72.

96 See p. 104 above.

The ombudsman model has proved to be incredibly durable in the face of developments within governance. In particular, the discretionary powers of the ombudsman have proved sufficiently flexible to enable them to address new legal issues, heightened citizen expectations and increases in workload. There have also been significant experiments to improve the complainant experience. Whereas previously the ombudsman was typecast as a slow-moving and rather formal institution, the modern ombudsman office is much more likely to provide a professional, telephone and internet-based, consumer-focused service.

At the same time, however, the demands coming from the complainant, supplemented by the internet, appear to be increasing. These developments mean that in addition to the complaint-handler function, there are several subsidiary roles that have become essential features of the ombudsman's work, such as being a receptacle for complaints generally, an adviser, a regulator of lower level complaints systems, and one of the endpoints in the administrative justice system that enforces the collective need for public decision-making to be respected once grievance mechanisms have been exhausted. In performing these various roles difficult choices have to be made; in particular most ombudsman schemes have a considerable amount of discretion available to enable individuals to access and progress through the complaint process. Ombudsmen frequently have a reasonable breadth of discretion in the interpretation of their legal powers. It would be naive to think that these forms of discretion are not unaffected by the resource capacity available to ombudsman offices and the changing culture of public management which may raise expectations as to the standards and timeliness of service delivery.

Out of this analysis, three themes in particular deserve further attention and will be returned to in later chapters. Firstly, the capacity of the ombudsman to deliver a first-class service to complainants is dependent, to a high degree, on the effectiveness and design of the overall administrative justice system. This implies that the ombudsman service cannot be evaluated in isolation from the institutions that operate in parallel to it. If customer care is to be taken seriously, there need to be well-known access points to the administrative justice system, appropriately designed links between the different aspects of the system, clear demarcations of responsibility and effective procedures for transferring complaints from one branch of the system to another. Overall, a more coordinated approach towards customer care, in particular at the very beginning of the process, should reduce the potential for the complainant leaving the system embittered and fatigued by the experience. However good the assistance given to the complainant, there will always be some whose complaints will be rejected; but the appropriate channelling of complainants at an early stage and a measure of proactive assistance should go a long way towards mitigating the degree of grievance and dissatisfaction felt. In this respect, there are a number of ideas and experiments in operation already that offer the potential for improvements in this area. The potential to improve the educative capacity of the system, establishing suitable advisory services and the concept of triage plus will be further explored in Chapter 7. It has been argued elsewhere with regard to the CO, however, that ombudsmen themselves have already chosen to take on board a triage-type control of complaints (Stuhmcke 2008, 334-5). Thus while the ombudsman retains the power and capacity to investigate, individual complaints are managed as the office deems appropriate. This development in itself represents a radical change in the role of the office as originally envisaged and could have unfortunate side-effects if adequate compensating arrangements within the wider administrative justice system are not in place.

Secondly, a connected theme that could be drawn from the current performance of the ombudsmen is that where dissatisfaction with the ombudsman enterprise is registered this may also tell us something about the overall balance of the administrative justice system and the suitability of the various redress mechanisms within it. The most common reason for an ombudsman rejecting a complaint is that it falls outside jurisdiction. This could indicate a problem either of connecting complaints to the right complaint-handler or the absence of an appropriate dispute resolution body to deal with the complaint.[97]

A third theme is the importance of accountability. Ombudsmen do possess a significant amount of discretionary authority and there are a series of pinch points within the ombudsman process that will always be the focus of scrutiny. Ironically one of the potential strengths of the ombudsman technique – the use of confidential procedures to foster positive engagement on the part of the bodies investigated – exposes it to the critique that it lacks transparency. Thus the argument that is being presented in this book is that to ensure the legitimacy of ombudsman schemes there must be appropriate procedures in place to call to account the exercise of ombudsman discretion. This issue will be taken up in Chapter 6.

97 Gulland (2010, 467) provides the example in her work of social care complaints in which many complainants would want the substantive elements of their grievance dealt with by way of an appeal.

Chapter 5
Promoting Good Administration and Helping to Get it Right

Introduction

In Chapter 2 the extent of the constitutional service provided by the ombudsman was identified, and it was emphasized that the ombudsman enterprise is capable of much more than complaint-handling alone.[1] This understanding is supported by the current emphasis within the administrative justice system on feeding back knowledge from complaints systems into administrative practice and decision-making in order to inform and prevent subsequent errors being made (Partington and Kirton-Darling 2006).[2] The key argument here is that preventing administrative errors happening in the first place is a more effective and efficient use of resources than purely providing a complaint-handling service.

The extent to which all parts of the administrative justice system can succeed in the objective of helping public authorities to 'get it right' first time around is open to question, but it has long been understood that the ombudsman can and does perform this role, and that it is well equipped to do so. This chapter offers an account of the various means by which this service is performed and charts an increased trend towards more ambitious efforts by various ombudsmen to maximize this aspect of the ombudsman's work. This tendency has led to the adoption of a number of novel techniques that have taken the office into areas akin to administrative audit. However, although the arguments in favour of the advisory and assistance role of the ombudsman are strong, careful consideration needs to be given as to how far this work can and should be developed. Attention also needs to be applied to the question of whether the performance of the ombudsman in this regard matches the aspiration.

Passing on the Lessons Learnt from Investigations

The method by which ombudsmen promote good administration that most directly links to their complaint-handling function is to submit recommendations that follow and directly relate to an investigation of a complaint. This is an extremely common tactic in all ombudsman schemes and flows from the nature of the

1 See pp. 46-9.

2 See pp. 77-9.

investigatory process adopted by ombudsmen and the wide discretionary powers to make recommendations.

The Power of Investigations

It is the potential depth and quality of the ombudsman's investigatory powers that legitimates and lends impact to the administrative and long-term recommendations that an ombudsman can make. Reference throughout this book has already been made to the scale of the ombudsman's investigatory powers in terms of obtaining documents and access to witnesses.[3] With the extent of these powers well established, ombudsman staff rarely need to threaten their use let alone enforce them in court.[4] In any event, most cases do not require such in-depth investigation. Likewise, an ombudsman does not generally choose to formalize the process by involving lawyers or requesting evidence under oath as this goes against the standard methodology of the office.[5] Indeed, one of the strengths of the ombudsman technique is that investigations can be speeded up through not being bogged down in procedural formalities (Marin 2009, para. 24).

In terms of uncovering faults within administrative organizations and processes, a further strength of the ombudsman technique is that they are free to pursue their own lines of enquiry provided that they come within the ambit of the complaint. Ombudsmen are not restricted to the arguments presented by the respective parties, a freedom that can facilitate a more rational line of enquiry. The full extent to which this grants the ombudsman in the UK latitude to pursue tangential issues is though currently limited by the interpretation applied to the ombudsman's remit to investigate in *Cavanagh*.[6] This ruling implies that the ombudsman can only investigate the strict terms of the complaint itself, which contrasts sharply with the situation in most other countries in which the ombudsman can initiate investigations without the need for a complaint.[7] In the UK, following a recent amendment to its powers, a sensible solution is provided for in the Local Government Ombudsman (LGO) scheme in which the ombudsman can investigate a matter that comes 'to his attention during the course of an investigation' if it appears that an injustice may have occurred.[8]

---

3 See Chapter 2, p. 36-7. This power is subject to a few qualifications, but these rarely impact on an ombudsman's work; e.g. see Parliamentary Commissioner Act 1967, s.8.

4 E.g. *Subpoena* (Adoption: Commissioner for Local Administration) (1996) 8 Admin. L.R. 577; *The Times*, 4 April 1996 (QBD).

5 The Financial Services Ombudsman (FSO) does not have formal powers to compel the attendance of witnesses, take evidence on oath or test evidence by cross-examination, but it utilizes 'hearings' in limited circumstances: see FOS (2010). In some of the Australian jurisdictions, especially where criminal prosecutions may follow, the added formality sometimes becomes necessary: see VO (2009).

6 *Cavanagh and Others v Health Services Commissioner* [2005] EWCA Civ 1578.

7 See below, pp. 137-8.

8 Local Government Act 1974, ss.24A(5) and 26D. See also the Scottish Public Services Ombudsman Act 2002, s.9, which allows a complaint to be made by a public authority on behalf of an aggrieved person.

Even without the flexibility provided by the power of own-initiative investigation, ombudsman investigations frequently uncover sufficient information to substantiate broader conclusions about the administrative processes being investigated. Unsurprisingly, the now considerable experience that has built up within the ombudsman community has led to ever more sophisticated and challenging techniques being employed by ombudsman offices in the course of more complex investigations. An illustration of the approach of ombudsmen towards investigations can be garnered from this description of an investigation plan drawn up by the Queensland Ombudsman (QO) in response to a prisoner's complaint (Box 5.1).

Box 5.1 Developing an investigative plan

Step 1: the allegations

Identify the conduct/event being investigated.
For example:

> *'Prisoner A claims he has been unfairly refused entry to a program for behaviour modification, which is a prerequisite for progression to a lower security classification.'*

Step 2: issues for investigation

Issue 1: Is the prisoner's allegation true?
Issue 2: If the prisoner raised the complaint with the DCS [Department of Corrective Services], did the department respond appropriately?
Issue 3: Does the department have a fair process for admitting prisoners to programs?

Step 3: benchmarking

This step relates to identifying the criteria against which issues are to be assessed:

- Relevant corrections legislation
- Department's policies and practice
- Fair and reasonable decision-making

In other cases, you will need to consider an agency's Code of Conduct and best practice.

Step 4: identify facts in issue

What facts need to be established to determine if the allegation is true or false?

- Was prisoner eligible to enter program?
- Did he follow the proper procedure for admission?
- What were reasons for not admitting him?

Step 5: possible avenues of inquiry

- What sources may be available to provide relevant evidence e.g. potential witnesses, records, site inspection?
- What are the advantages and disadvantages of different methods of gathering evidence?

Step 6: other tips

- Investigations rarely proceed as planned
- Be prepared to revise the plan – always follow the facts rather than trying to make the facts fit into the plan
- Obtain appropriate authorisation for amendments to the plan
- Keep referring back to the plan

Source: Bevan (2007, 1-2).

The New South Wales Ombudsman's *Investigating Complaints* guide (NSWO 2004, 26) incorporates a similar approach and uses the different stages of investigation to establish targets and a means of monitoring the investigation by the investigator and a supervisor. These planning tools make clear some of the factors which might direct an investigation. Further evidence of the refinement of the ombudsman investigative technique can be seen in Jones (2009), who has integrated skills into ombudsmanry more akin to those employed by the police or prosecuting authorities. Such approaches will not always be appropriate for all ombudsmen, as they will conflict with the traditional conciliatory model. But it may be that the traditional conciliatory model is in need of revision if it means that ombudsmen are forced to concentrate only on small investigations in order to retain good relations with the administrative bodies they investigate (Marin 2009, para. 14). Indeed, it has been argued by one commentator that for the ombudsman enterprise to address effectively the complexity of the issues generated by modern governance arrangements, ombudsmen will be required to reduce their reliance on soft negotiations with administrations and be more willing to take a harder line.

> This entails the ombuds becoming less passive and more active, more of an *animateur* than a moderator, a master of critical thinking, yearning to smoke out the symptoms of dysfunction and capable of tracking down their sources in a confrontational way if necessary. The core concern of ombuds should be to force both the plaintiff and the organization to face assumptions they may not be aware they are making, to contribute, through the ombudsing process, to the emergence of a *super-vision* (Innerarity, 2006: 194) that defines and clarifies the nature of the problem in a manner that makes all parties see things that they could or would not be able to see themselves. (Paquet 2009, 13)

The expansion of the investigatory skill set of the ombudsman, therefore, aids the growing vision of the model as an extremely flexible institution capable of taking on a wide range of investigations, including ones that touch upon large-scale and controversial issues. In many of the Australian offices this learning process has been aided by the diversity of the jurisdiction that they have been required to investigate.

Evidently, and quite correctly, there are some restrictions on what ombudsmen can do during the course of their investigations. In particular, ombudsmen have to bear in mind that without legal powers of enforcement the strength of their reports is dependent on the quality of the evidence provided and the cogency of the subsequent arguments made. It is entirely appropriate, therefore, that one element of procedural fairness that is demanded in ombudsman statutes is that the agency investigated is given the opportunity to comment on the complaint and a draft of any report to be issued. This process provides assurance of the details contained in the report; albeit care needs to be taken that the process remains a form of 'reality-testing' of any proposed findings and recommendations, rather than a negotiation on the ombudsman's conclusions. Although not required by legislation, as a matter of good practice pre-publication comment should also be offered to the complainant where appropriate.[9]

Administrative Recommendations

Just as the report of an investigation can include recommendations for redress for the injustice caused to the complainant, it can also contain recommendations which seek to prevent recurrence of that particular maladministration. The ombudsman's recommendations can go into detail about a particular action that should be taken or, more commonly, it may be that a procedure or process should be reviewed.

Some of these recommendations will be specific and localized to the administrative body under review. In other instances, however, the nature of the recommendations made will be much more wide ranging and challenging. For instance, following an investigation by the Tasmanian Ombudsman (TO) of the licensing process administered by the Poppy Advisory Control Board, the ombudsman concluded that the licensing system was not sufficiently flexible to cope with the prevalent practices in the industry. This finding came close to stating that the administrative process involved was systemically flawed. Hence the ombudsman went on to make wide-ranging recommendations that the scheme be redesigned, that the background legislation be amended to enable this, that the Control Board be put on a statutory footing and that a separate stand-alone legislative regime be considered for regulating an industry which had become important to the economy of Tasmania (TO 2008, 45-6).

Similarly challenging administrative recommendations can be found in the ombudsman reports of all the schemes researched for this monograph. An example comes from the Health Service Ombudsman's *Long-Term Care* report referred to

9 In *R v Parliamentary Commissioner for Administration, ex p Dyer* [1994] 1 WLR 621 it was ruled that such a practice was not necessary to comply with standards of natural justice.

in previous chapters, which investigated the processes by which decisions about charging for residential care were decided (HSO 2003). Within this report, not only did the HSO recommend redress to the individual complainants, but the report also recommended that health authorities throughout the UK and the Department for Health embark upon a process of review of thousands of other similar cases and review the guidance and procedures that underpinned decision-making in this area (HSO 2003, 8-9).

Within such reports, and many others, we see considerable evidence of ombudsmen attempting to make broader constructive comments about the quality of the administrative processes they investigate. The clear aspiration is to improve the quality of decision-making to prevent, or at least minimize the prospect of, future repeat flaws occurring in administrative systems. This approach is neatly summarized by the title of a recent Parliamentary and Health Service Ombudsman annual report: *Bringing Wider Public Benefit From Individual Complaints* (PHSO 2008). In this aspiration the ombudsman model has a number of significant advantages over other forms of dispute resolution, in particular the degree of accurate and relevant knowledge that it can obtain due to its powers and close interaction with the investigated body (Hertogh 2001, 56-7). At the same time, the methodology allows the ombudsman to engage and energize the investigated body in such a way that it actively inputs into the process of making improvements and identifying flaws. Ideally, the investigated authority can be encouraged to take control of the search for improvements, as for instance in the *Debt of Honour* report (PHSO 2005a) referred to in Chapter 2.[10] After much delay, the Ministry of Defence accepted the Parliamentary Ombudsman's (PO) report and then initiated an internal review which yielded additional important insights (Watkins 2006; Lunn 2009). Further, some of the issues explored in the *Debt of Honour* report were returned to in a subsequent investigation, the *'Cod Wars' Trawlermen's Compensation Scheme* (PHSO 2007c), which described an investigation into another *ex gratia* compensation scheme. One of the results of this later report was a wholesale review of the way that government departments administer *ex gratia* compensation schemes, the results of which have led to revised Treasury guidance on such compensation schemes.[11]

The nature of the administrative recommendations that an ombudsman will make will vary considerably and will be dependent on the administrative scheme in question and the problems identified, but the recommendations can reach a long way into the exercise of administration. In the UK, from the very beginning of the ombudsman experience there has been a debate about whether or not the ombudsman can determine that 'rules' are maladministrative, as opposed to procedures or individual actions (Select Committee on PCA 1968). The debate here is closely aligned to a parallel issue concerning the extent to which the ombudsman can question the policy decisions that underpin administrative activity. Here we

10 See pp. 35-6.

11 See PHSO press release 01/07 (22 February 2007).

see the perennial grey line between issues of procedures and legal requirements, and matters of policy. But despite the law in most ombudsman legislation stating that ombudsmen are not to question the merits of public decision-making, this has not prevented the ombudsmen from recommending that legislation itself or various forms of quasi-legislation be reviewed on the basis that it is the law/rule that is causing subsequent acts of maladministration to occur within the administrative process.

Another example from the PO's caseload that illustrates the point is the *Tax Credits* report which was written in response to numerous complaints about errors, delay and overpayment in the tax credits system. In the report, the PO found widespread evidence of maladministration and made several recommendations (PHSO 2005c, 8-9). Amongst these recommendations, and those of a later further report on tax credits (PHSO 2007d), it seems clear that the overall design of the tax credit system was both a source of complaint in its own right and a target for criticism by the ombudsman.

Publicizing Investigations

A key challenge for the ombudsman is to give their reports an impact within the public sector that goes beyond the public body reported against. To do this, for years ombudsmen have published documents containing investigated reports which provide digests of the most common forms of maladministration identified. At present, one of the best examples of this approach is the production of monthly case digests by the Scottish Public Services Ombudsman (SPSO).[12] Such documents continue to be produced, but today ombudsmen usually attempt to present a synthesis of the learning that can be derived from all these individual investigation reports.[13] The LGO, for instance, produces annual digests of investigations reports grouped according to subject matter, for example, planning, housing, social services and education.[14] Many annual reports are also partly designed with a view to publicizing important examples of maladministration and passing on lessons learnt. The difficulty with such approaches is that they risk being too overloaded with disparate examples to provide any real focused administrative advice, or they are too particular to the facts of an individual complaint to be easily applicable to other administrative schemes. Hence, whilst important productions for a range of reasons, ombudsmen have for a long time pursued other more targeted methods of promoting good administration.

---

12 Searchable summaries are available from 2002 to the present. Available at: <http://www.spso.org.uk/reports/search> (accessed 23 May 2010).

13 For example, the SPSO also produces 'monthly commentaries': see <http://www.spso.org.uk/reports> (accessed 23 May 2010).

14 Available at: <http://www.lgo.org.uk/publications/digest-of-cases/> (accessed 23 May 2010).

Identifying Themes

Most complaints to, and any ensuing investigation by, the ombudsman will be about a particular episode in which a complainant was aggrieved at the action or inaction of an agency. Within such investigations, where fault is found it will often be at least partly attributable to the circumstances surrounding an individual case and the manner in which it has been handled by individual officials. On many other occasions, however, investigations will have the potential to go beyond the particular to the systemic in identifying 'deficiencies in an agency's administrative processes that may be leading to actions/decisions that are unlawful, unfair or otherwise wrong' (Bevan 2008). On the basis of a single investigation, extrapolating broader conclusions about a public body's practices will often be difficult, but when two or more investigations are brought together then the ombudsman can begin to draw out deeper issues requiring attention within an organization. On the tax credits investigation referred to above, for example, the many complaints that the PO received, backed up by the few that she investigated in detail, revealed a consistently recurring theme in the maladministration.

In this regard the UK experience reveals two approaches that the ombudsmen have adopted to pass on messages about identified or potential systemic problems within an organization: publishing combined reports and conducting systemic investigations. The first method is essentially retrospective. A report is produced which links together the experience of the office acquired through investigation reports, albeit such reports can be supplemented by further work. The second method though is more proactive and involves the ombudsman recognizing a theme within the complaints it receives and making an early choice to conduct a joint systemic investigation.

There are plenty of examples of ombudsmen publishing reports of the retrospective kind to draw attention to common difficulties.[15] To take two from the HSO's collection: in the first, the HSO published a report on a complaint about treatment received from a doctor working for a general medical practitioner deputizing service. Given that the HSO had received a number of similar complaints he felt it necessary to draw wider attention to this issue and the way he dealt with such complaints (HSO 1999). Likewise, in a report on the National Health Service (NHS) complaints procedure, the HSO submitted a report dealing with two cases, but again made it clear that these had a connection to many other complaints that he dealt with and consequently broader relevance to people working in this field (HSO 1999a).

Some of the best work in this area has been conducted by the LGO, which in recent years has demonstrated how a retrospective reflection of similar investigations can provide constructive advice as to how a particular administrative

15 For a fuller list see n.25 below.

problem can be better handled.[16] The positive nature of this enterprise has been made clear by a former LGO.

> We are focusing more and more on feeding back to local authorities the wider lessons we derive from our work. One way of doing this is by pulling together the knowledge gleaned from a number of individual investigations on a particular subject, and distilling that knowledge into a single document for the benefit of all who may encounter similar cases … They are … a preventative measure, to help authorities pre-empt similar problems arising in the first place. (White 2005, 14)

This form of reporting goes well beyond the description of examples of maladministration and concentrates far more on the recommendations of good practice. The end result is akin to a handbook on best practice in the areas chosen for study, including pulling together advice from other regulators where appropriate.

Systemic Investigations

The pursuit of deep systemic understanding of an organization and the problems that may be occurring is aided by the capacity of the ombudsman, prior to the investigation, to conjoin similar complaints into one piece of work. This can be done because on occasion ombudsmen will note a trend of complaints in a particular area and choose a few of those complaints for more detailed investigation, on the basis that they are sufficiently representative of the whole. Such conjoined investigations deepen the information pool available to an ombudsman and provide a much firmer basis from which wider conclusions about the operation of an administrative process can legitimately be inferred. Once such a body of information is built up and consistently occurring maladministration identified, then the analysis of how errors could be avoided is a logical next step. Given that many of the decision-making procedures that the ombudsman looks at are likely to be employed again in the future, often many times, this iterative process of reflection and recommendation can be extremely useful. At the same time, because of the similarities between the chosen complaints and the general mass of complaints that an office is receiving, this practice avoids the need to repeat many tens, hundreds or even thousands of investigations on the same issue and basic fact pattern (Jones 2009, 2).

Many of the examples used in this book already are derived from conjoined systemic investigations, for example, the tax credits investigation referred to above.[17] This is unsurprising as most of the more forthright and wide-ranging ombudsman reports, reports which best demonstrate the full potential of the office,

---

16 See n.25 below.

17 For an analysis of the PHSO's approach in this area, see Harlow and Rawlings (2009, 549-51).

are those where two or more similar complaints have been conjoined in a wider investigatory process.[18] Such investigations will often have more bite precisely because significant numbers of citizens have been affected. Where ombudsmen receive multiple complaints about an organization, this can act as an early warning sign that there are faults in an administrative process. When repeat errors occur, it provides a clear indication that the rise in complaints is unlikely to be attributable to human error or special circumstances alone.

Needless to say, there are other ways by which such systemic errors within an administrative process can be uncovered, such as an organization's internal governance arrangements and external audit, along with political oversight or any other regulatory system of inspection. In addition to all these accountability agents, however, there is now considerable evidence from around the world of the part that ombudsmen can play in highlighting systemic faults (e.g. Marin 2009). Moreover, given that the ombudsman can claim to have a thorough working knowledge of matters of good administrative practice, their opinions as to suitable corrective measures cannot be taken lightly. Finally, lest it be argued that this activity encourages ombudsmen to go beyond their legitimate mandate, it should be recalled that their recommendations do not have binding effect. They are informative, and although the ombudsman has the capacity to pursue the matter in political and public circles, the public body retains full choice as to whether to heed the administrative advice or pursue alternative methods to address the faults that the ombudsman has identified.

The Increased Use of Systemic Reporting

As with the discussion of the complaint-handling work of the ombudsman, care needs to be taken in coming to conclusions based on statistics alone. Nevertheless, there is some evidence to suggest that over the last ten years there has been an increase in the use of systemic reports in the UK and probably systemic investigations as well (Kirkham 2005a).[19]

Most ombudsman schemes tend to publish their systemic findings at a more transparent level than ordinary reports, and have the statutory power to do this by submitting reports to Parliament in order to highlight matters of particular public concern. For example, the PHSO's power to submit a special report is contingent

---

18 Notwithstanding the difficulties, one complaint can be sufficient to inform a systemic investigation, e.g. *Debt of Honour* (PHSO 2005a), although note that in this instance the existence of thousands of other affected and aggrieved individuals was well known.

19 Note that because the Australasian and Irish Ombudsman schemes can also publish the results of their own-initiative investigations this way they are not included in this analysis. But judging from the language of the public pronouncements of the Australian Ombudsman, systemic work remains an increasing priority for them (e.g. McMillan 2009, 3).

on the identified injustice not having been, or unlikely to be, remedied,[20] and they have a further discretionary power to lay reports before Parliament as they 'think fit'.[21] Similarly, the Commonwealth Ombudsman of Australia (CO) has powers to refer a report to the Prime Minister's office and thereafter to Parliament where appropriate action has not been taken following an investigation,[22] and there is a comparable power to submit additional reports as a matter of discretion.[23] There are a number of other legislative formulations[24] (see Appendix 4). Such reports tend to be, although not exclusively so, reports that highlight underlying administrative deficiencies that deserve the attention of a wider audience.

The LGO's work in this area is illustrative of the trend towards placing more focus on their work on publicly identifying systemic findings and associated forward-looking recommendations and guidance. This change of focus has led to eight themed reports being produced since 2003 whereas previously there had been none.[25]

The HSO has published a variety of reports identifying systemic issues since the first was published in 1994 (HSO 1994).[26] Although neither the Northern Ireland Ombudsman (NIO) nor the SPSO has published a systemic report, the Public Services Ombudsman for Wales (PSOW) has produced two such reports, one in partnership with the LGO (PSOW 2006b; PSOW and LGO 2006). Most noticeably of all, however, the PO has undertaken systemic reporting ever since it was first introduced (PO 1967; 1967a), but there has been a significant increase in such activity since 1993 (Kirkham 2005a, 743-5).[27]

---

20 Parliamentary Commissioner Act 1967, s.10(3); Health Services Commissioners Act 1993, s.14(3).

21 Parliamentary Commissioner Act 1967, s.10(4). Health Services Commissioners Act 1993, s.14(4).

22 Ombudsman Act (Cth) 1976, ss.15-16.

23 *Ibid*, s.19(2)(b).

24 For example, Ombudsman Act 1974 (NSW), ss.31 gives the NSWO a wide discretion to send a special report to the Presiding Officer of each House of Parliament along with a recommendation it be 'made public forthwith'.

25 *Local partnerships and citizen redress* (July 2007); *Telecommunications masts: problems with 'prior approval' applications* (June 2007); *Memorial safety in local authority cemeteries* (March 2006); *Neighbour nuisance and anti-social behaviour* (February 2005); *Parking enforcement by local authorities* (December 2004); *Advice and guidance on school admissions and appeals* (March 2004); *Advice and guidance on arrangements for forwarding housing benefit appeals to the Appeals Service* (February 2004); *Advice and guidance on the funding of aftercare under section 117 of the Mental Health Act 1983* (July 2003).

26 We have idenitifed 11 such reports: (1995-96 HC429; HC504); (1998-99 HC341; HC410; HC496); (2002-03 HC399); (2004-05 HC144; HC413); (2006-07 HC386); (2007-08 HC632); (2008-09 HC203).

27 Since 1993 we have idenitifed 24 such reports: (1992-93 HC519); (1994-95 HC135; HC193); (1995-96 HC20); (1999-2000 HC305; HC635); (2000-01 HC271); (2002-

This move towards deepening the impact of the ombudsman office through systemic reports is backed up by various public statements by the ombudsmen themselves. For example, in a speech in 2009 the PHSO stated,

> The need is clear enough: to provide effective dispute resolution to aggrieved citizens yet at the same time to identify patterns of failure and opportunities for systemic improvement. It is in this latter regard that ombudsmen are especially well placed to take up the challenge. Less shackled than other parts of the justice system by a constraining common-law mentality, the ombudsman is relatively free to roam, to take an inquisitorial approach, to remain flexible and responsive, with an eye to the bigger picture and to the bigger ambition of bringing about coherent, systematic change. (PHSO 2009b)

Underpinning this view of the ombudsman enterprise is the understanding that to confine the ombudsman to the complaint-handling role alone is to waste an opportunity to take advantage of the information gathered in its complaint-handling capacity and the cumulative knowledge held within the office. The trend fits into a wider initiative to demonstrate the relevancy and utility of the office of the ombudsman, and to advertise the services that are offered within the ombudsman community. In this respect, systemic reports are one of the ombudsman's best ways of gaining parliamentary and media attention. Such work, therefore, also helps raise the profile and public awareness of the ombudsman.

Follow-up Reports

In a regulatory process that is not supported by powers of compulsion, there will inevitably be concerns that any recommendations made for long-term change will not be taken seriously and will remain largely unimplemented. Furthermore, given that the ombudsman process encourages and builds upon cooperative engagement with the investigated body, there is a risk of the ombudsman's findings and recommendations being captured by the input of the investigated body. Neither risk can be completely combated, though there are a few examples of ombudsmen reacting to clear evidence that previous reports had failed to resolve problems in a particular administrative scheme. The HSO's report into long-term care referred to earlier is one such example, which in fact represented a midway point in a long-running series of ombudsman investigations into the Department of Health's handling of what was undoubtedly an extremely difficult administrative and political issue (HSO 2003; 2004). Noticeably though, the reports do build upon one another and demonstrate an intent on the part of the HSO to monitor compliance with previous recommendations, albeit that such reports were largely

---

03 HC12; HC633; HC809); (2004-05 HC455); (2005-06 HC124; HC324; HC984); (2006-07 HC313; HC1010); (2007-08 HC615; HC815); (2008-09 HC367; HC435; HC367); (2009-10 HC181; HC329; HC448).

triggered by renewed complaints. Likewise, the issue of tax credits has been one that has challenged the PO's office on more than one occasion and has led the PO to undertake more than one further report (PHSO 2005c; 2007d) and comment upon in annual reports and evidence to PASC (2005). Ideally, ombudsman legislation would assist the process of closing ombudsman investigations by requiring public bodies to provide the ombudsman with evidence that their recommendations had been implemented or an explanation as to why they had not been met. A good example of the way forward is provided in a report of the Victorian Ombudsman (VO) submitted to Parliament. This report lists for a two-year period all the recommendations made by the office, the agency response and subsequent action, together with the ombudsman's view as to whether or not further implementation is required (VO 2010).

Returning to an investigation at a later date to verify whether or not real changes have been made is a tactic available to the ombudsmen and follow-up reports are not uncommon. The provision of a critical narrative relating to public issues that additionally carries with it (unlike the arrival and departures of governments) the continuity of these offices lends a real opportunity for the ombudsman enterprise to make a more fully-fledged 'integrity' contribution to the overall constitutional order. It would appear, however, that there is room for much further structuring and development of the ombudsmen's efforts to demonstrate more specifically the impact of their recommendations.

Own-Initiative Investigations

The increased use of themed reports and systemic investigation in several ombudsman schemes presents one of the clearest signs of the evolution of the ombudsman model from conservative portrayals of the office so frequently detailed in standard public law and administrative justice literature. Significant questions remain about the efficacy and effectiveness of this form of work, but from the research conducted for this monograph it is clear that virtually all the ombudsmen interviewed perceived the reporting of systemic maladministration and the passing on of lessons learnt as key parts of their work.

But how far should this technique be pursued? The systemic investigations hitherto cited were triggered by complaints. Thus there was a direct and relatively uncontroversial link between the complaint-handling exercise and the larger overarching systemic report that has derived from the investigation. It is clear, however, from a number of ombudsman schemes that there are several other viable triggers for systemic investigations. Some ombudsman schemes allow for the commencement of an investigation following the reference to the ombudsman by another agency or regulator,[28] Parliament,[29] or even the public body itself

28 For example, Ombudsman Act 1974 (NSW), s.42 (referral of complaints between relevant agencies).

29 For example, Ombudsman Act 2001 (Qld), s.19.

that is to be investigated.[30] More radically still, in other parts of the world, it is common for ombudsmen to possess an own-initiative power without the need to trigger this with an individual complaint. Such investigations could be prompted by the ombudsman's perception of public concern, or as a direct result of their own research on an issue. One example taken from a Queensland Ombudsman (QO) report[31] to Parliament reviewing the Queensland Mines Inspectorate (QMI) illustrates this point.

> While I had not received any complaints about the QMI, media and academic sources in Queensland and elsewhere have alleged in recent years that the QMI may not be adequately fulfilling its compliance roles under the [relevant legislation], and that mine safety standards may be falling as a result. (QO 2008a, x)

One of the allegations made was that the QMI was understaffed and had a high staff turnover which impaired its work. It was also alleged that the QMI failed to take enforcement action where there had been clear breaches of mine safety legislation and that it announced its mine inspections in advance, thus losing the element of surprise. Further, there were perceptions that the QMI had been 'captured' by the industry it regulated. This background was sufficient to persuade the QO to embark upon an own-initiative investigation.[32]

A more characteristic trigger of the own-initiative power is information derived from the ombudsman's individual complaint work. There may also be good reasons why the investigation of specific complaints will not suffice. In another QO investigation, this time into the Environmental Protection Agency (EPA), there had been complaints to the ombudsman about the lack of prosecution action by the EPA and its lack of cooperation with other bodies. The ombudsman had determined, however, that in individual cases there would be difficulties with ordinary investigations as they would cover events which had occurred a few years previously and so substantiation would be difficult (QO 2007, 34). It therefore appeared that a thorough administrative review of the EPA would be appropriate as it would allow the ombudsman to concentrate on alternative sources of information.[33]

---

30 Scottish Public Services Ombudsman Act 2002, s.9.

31 Made under an own-initiative power of investigation in Ombudsman Act 2001 (Qld), s.52.

32 See also BCO (2007) on the British Columbia Lottery Corporation prize payout procedures. This investigation was initiated following media stories and the failure of the Corporation following a freedom of information request to provide evidence to explain the apparent bias in its payout process.

33 Similarily, one of the reasons given by the Bermuda Ombudsman for conducting the *Atlantica Unlocked* own-initiative investigation was that the original '[c]omplainants

In this respect, therefore, the difference between an own-initiative investigation and more conventional systemic investigations is the ability of the ombudsman to pursue the investigation in a more targeted and proactive manner and detached from any particular complaints. To facilitate such work, more than one ombudsman organization has now established a dedicated team within their organization to focus on the pursuit of systemic investigations. The Ombudsman of Ontario, for example, has instituted a Special Ombudsman Response Team (SORT) to manage major high-profile and systemic investigations.

> These investigations generally involve probing the root causes of a complaint – or a group of complaints – to resolve significant underlying issues and prevent similar issues from arising in the future. SORT investigations are methodically planned and executed by a team of investigators according to strict timelines. They can involve interviewing hundreds of witnesses and reviewing thousands of pages of documents, as well as examining government policies and practices in other jurisdictions. SORT investigations usually result in the Ombudsman publishing a report and making recommendations that have a high public interest component. The vast majority of recommendations stemming from SORT investigations have been accepted and implemented by the government, resulting in real systemic improvements for Ontarians. (Ontario Ombudsman 2009, 33)[34]

This sort of activity has led a leading writer in Australia to come to the following conclusion: 'Previously the handling of systemic activity … was ad hoc, built upon complaint intelligence and generally once off. Now the role is more likely to be scheduled, derived from a multitude of sources and repeated on a frequent basis' (Snell 2007, 111). Here we see the seeds of the idea that the ombudsman is capable of being viewed as an agent of administrative audit and oversight, in addition to its other roles.

Widening the Scope of Ombudsman Investigations

A feature of the ombudsman practice of systemic investigation in Australia which appears to go further than some of the limitations in the UK jurisdictions would allow,[35] and which follows from the freedom granted to the ombudsman by not being tied to a specific complaint, is the ability to widen the tools of the

---

had expressed varying degrees of apprehension that, by being frank, they may put their own research and therefore careers at risk' (Ombudsman for Bermuda 2009, 20).

34 Other offices have specialized units to identify themes that might require further exploration, e.g. the Administrative Improvement Team introduced by the Western Australia Ombudsman (WAO 2009, 6).

35 E.g. see *Cavanagh and Others v Health Services Commissioner* [2005] EWCA Civ 1578.

investigation itself. By way of example, take the two QO investigations referred to above. In the first, the investigation included audits of the QMI complaints and investigation files, visits to four regional offices, joining two normal inspections; interviews with QMI senior management, inspectors and also with stakeholders in the mining industry association, trade unions, academics and a barrister who assisted in conducting coroner inquests into death in mines (QO 2008a). In the second, the focus from the outset was targeted on the appropriateness of regulatory procedures, especially for approving prosecutions; the adequacy of the supervision of compliance activity was supervised; whether the best compliance options were selected; the adequacy of record-keeping and the training of officers; and whether there were systems to cope with duplication of effort where other bodies had overlapping responsibilities with the EPA. The investigation involved research into various regulatory models, the preparation of audit checklists based on agencies' policies and procedures and good regulatory practice, which were used to audit a sample of 200 cases. Workshops were conducted with a range of officers to discuss their use of various compliance options, and interviews were carried out with senior officers to clarify practices and procedures (QO 2007, 34).

A paradigm systemic investigation of the CO which continues to have wide-ranging impact is the investigation(s) into immigration cases. This issue was precipitated by the discovery that one Australian citizen, Cornelia Rau, had been unlawfully detained for a considerable period of time, and another Australian citizen, Vivian Alvarez, had been unlawfully removed from Australia. In 2005 and 2006 the Australian government, following two earlier reports,[36] asked the CO to investigate 247 immigration detention cases. Eight published reports of the CO contained the results of those investigations. A further report published in 2007 drew together ten lessons for public administration (CO 2007a) from those reports. The core issue in each investigation had been whether the person's detention was unlawful or wrongful. The errors made in many of those cases 'pointed to systemic failures in immigration administration' and '[a]dministrative, legislative, policy and system-based changes that were recommended in the reports were accepted by DIAC [Department of Immigration and Citizenship] and addressed in a significant reform program that commenced in 2005' (CO 2007a, 2). This own-initiative investigation was preceded by many previous efforts by detainees to pursue redress, which included regular litigation in the courts and a number of inquiries and Parliamentary reports, none of which had fully succeeded in uncovering the long-lasting, rampant maladministration within the immigration services.

36 *Report of Inquiry into the Circumstances of the Immigration Detention of Cornelia Rau*, Report by Mr Mick Palmer AO APM, July 2005; and Commonwealth Ombudsman, *Report of Inquiry into the Circumstances of the Vivian Alvarez Matter*, Report No. 03/2005.

Use of the Own-Initiative Power

Clearly the use of this power varies from one ombudsman's office to another and will also reflect the resources and size of each scheme. The jurisdictions of the Australian and Irish ombudsman schemes, for example, vary considerably and often take the ombudsman into areas which would not be comparable to UK schemes. Nevertheless, it is apparent that the power of own-initiative investigation has proved to be a very useful feature of the ombudsman enterprise. Presuming that the bulk of recommendations made are acted upon, as with the CO's immigration cases discussed above, each own-initiative investigation will likely impact on the way in which considerable numbers of administrative decisions are made in the future. Given this potential for increasing the reach, and arguably the effectiveness, of the ombudsman, it is unsurprising that so many ombudsman schemes around the world, including for instance the European Union (EU) Ombudsman, include this power.[37] The power has not always been widely used, as for instance in Ireland and New Zealand, and has often been considered to be a reserve power only required for special situations. It is one area, however, which has so far been excluded from the jurisdictions of the UK ombudsmen.

Promoting Good Administration Outside Investigations

In both the UK and elsewhere the ombudsman enterprise does more than react to complaints received. To a greater or lesser extent, therefore, ombudsman offices will have some form of research base or office knowledge management system to identify trends and gaps in its work.[38] Ombudsman offices look to distil the information they uncover and pass on the lessons to a wider audience by a variety of different means. In addition to those methods looked at already – e.g. digests, themed reports and systemic investigations, this section looks at the various non-investigatory techniques currently in operation within ombudsman schemes.

Guidance

Given their position within the administrative state, ombudsmen are well placed to produce general good practice guides and provide various explanatory notes. Some of the Australian ombudsmen have taken this role very seriously and provide a wide

37 *Decision of the European Parliament on the regulations and general conditions governing the performance of the Ombudsman's duties*, Adopted by Parliament on 9 March 1994 (OJ L 113, 4.5.1994, p. 15) and amended by its decisions of 14 March 2002 (OJ L 92, 9.4.2002, p. 13) and 18 June 2008 (OJ L 189, 17.7.2008, p. 25), article 3(1).

38 For example, the role of the 'cross-agency team' in the NSWO is 'to strengthen communication and collaboration between our specialist areas and strategically target systemic issues involving one or more of our jurisdictions' (NSWO 2008, 15).

range of guidance material. The NSWO, for instance, has a series of factsheets for agencies which includes advice on topics such as apologies, conflicts of interest, reasons and quality customer service.[39] The QO has produced a guide, *Tips and Traps for Regulators*, which links advice on good regulatory practice with illustrations from anonymized investigations (QO 2009a). The practice of providing guidance is recognized in some UK ombudsman legislation, although not all, and has not generally been adopted to quite the same extent as in Australia, a result only partly attributable to the respective jurisdictions.[40] The LGO was probably the first to pioneer the publication of a range of guidance in the UK,[41] initially to address the general absence of internal complaints systems within local government. In contrast to the LGO, the PHSO has yet to be granted a specific power and duty to produce guidance. The Regulatory Reform Order (RRO) of 2007[42] had omitted the suggested inclusion of an express power to issue advice and guidance on good administrative practice, ostensibly on the basis of a lack of *vires*.[43] But this has not prevented the office from moving into this field of work.

The PHSO is one of the many ombudsman offices to have produced guidance on the content of good administration (e.g. PHSO 2007a).[44] Revealingly, the PHSO's reasons for producing such guidance reveal a double-edged motivation. At one level, the *Principles of Good Administration* provide the ombudsman with a partial defence against the criticism that the office's powers are wholly uncertain and unpredictable in application; at another they are aimed at assisting public authorities in their work. The two ideas are linked by the understanding that to find fault in an administrative action on the basis of 'maladministration' can also be regarded as the mirror image of 'good administration'. If the *Principles* are successful, therefore, they offer an objective framework within which public authorities should seek to work, and they help to clarify the expectations against which the PHSO's office will make an assessment of a complaint, a point made in a speech by the PHSO.

---

39 See the NSWO website at: <http://www.ombo.nsw.gov.au/guideorganisations/index.html> (accessed 23 May 2010).

40 E.g. Local Government Act 1974, s.12A; Public Services Ombudsman (Wales) Act, s.31.

41 At the time of writing, there were three key guidance documents available on the LGO website: *Running a complaints system* (LGO 2009a); *Good administrative practice* (LGO 2001); and *Remedies* (LGO 2005). Available at: <http://www.lgo.org.uk/publications/guidance-notes/> (accessed 23 May 2010).

42 SI 1889/2007. See Chapter 3, pp. 82-3.

43 See Select Committee on Regulatory Reform, *Second Report of Session 2006-07*, HC 383, para. 43.

44 By way of example, see also the European Ombudsman, *The European Code of Good Administrative Behaviour*, (2005); Office of the Ombudsman (Ireland), *The Ombudsman's Guide to Standards of Best Practice for Public Servants*, latest edition (2002).

> If I am to make authoritative findings of maladministration, I regard it as incumbent upon me to explain transparently what I consider to be the hallmarks of good administration. At the same time, if I am serious about asking public bodies to learn the larger lessons yielded by complaints and so incorporate those lessons into their future administrative practice, I see it as part of my job to distil for them the key elements of good practice and to hold up to them for future evaluation a picture of good administration against which they can judge themselves and be judged by the public and by me. That is what, in both aspects, my Principles of Good Administration set out to achieve. (Abraham 2007a, 5)

The *Principles* are intended to provide a framework for public bodies, and are 'not a checklist to be applied mechanically' (PHSO 2007a, 3). The overriding decision-making principle, therefore, remains one based in equitable factors, such as the need to produce reasonable, fair and proportionate results in the circumstances. The early evidence is that they have been well received and have proved constructive in administrative circles.[45] Expanding this approach, the PHSO has additionally published *The Principles for Remedy*[46] in October 2007 and *The Principles of Good Complaint Handling* in November 2008.[47] Similarly, other offices have produced guidance on the importance of apologizing (e.g. SPSO 2006; NSWO 2009b).[48]

On occasion, ombudsmen are capable of providing more focused advice about a particular aspect of the public sector's work, by pooling the observations they have gained through their work. The Australian Commonwealth Ombudsman's *Automated Assistance in Administrative Decision-Making: Better Practice Guide* (CO 2007b) and the HSO's *Consent in Cardiac Surgery: A Good Practice Guide to Agreeing and Recording Consent* (HSO 2005) provide good examples. The latter is particularly interesting because it was produced in partnership with the medical profession.

As described above, some of the best long-term guidance comes out of the systemic investigations already referred to. But another approach to pooling lessons together involves focusing less on a particular subject matter and more on an individual body. Adopting this approach the LGO publishes an 'Annual Letter' for each individual council it investigates.[49] Effectively this letter is a report which deals with all of the complaints received in the year, summarizing the manner

45 At the time of writing the Department for Work and Pensions had adopted the PHSO's *Principles* for their internal processes and complaints handling.

46 Harlow (2010) has argued that this is one area where the PHSO could go further, implying the CO's guidance on remedies represents a more useful approach.

47 The *Principles of Good Administration*, along with *The Principles for Remedy* and *The Principles of Good Complaint Handling*, were reprinted with minor amendments on 10 February 2009. Again, other offices have produced similar guidance.

48 See Chapter 4, pp. 116-17.

49 See the LGO's website at: <http://www.lgo.org.uk/CouncilsPerformance/> (accessed 23 May 2010).

in which the ombudsman has dealt with them and comparing the results with previous years. In doing this the commentary provided may also seek to identify trends, lessons and issues concerning the relationship between the council and the LGO's staff, such as the length of time it takes the council to respond to LGO requests. What the annual letter seeks to do, therefore, is offer an opinion on a council's handling of complaints (LGO 2009, 29) and encourage it to integrate its finding into the council's own management information which it uses to measure and then analyse its performance.

A further development in the period 2007-08 has been for the Queensland, Western Australian, Victorian and Commonwealth ombudsmen to produce regular bulletins which can be emailed to subscribers as well as being posted on their websites. These allow them to highlight some issues of concern arising from recent investigations.

Submissions

Most ombudsmen go out of their way to promote their work through lectures, meetings and the publication of various articles. Indeed, many such pieces have been cited in this book. In itself, these dissemination activities can contain important messages on good administration. More targeted efforts at influencing the development of policy of an administrative practice, however, are the submissions that the ombudsmen make to consultations and inquiries (Stuhmcke 2006, 40).[50] Such invitation for ideas are now common in the public sector and may be conducted by government, Parliament and other influential agents, such as the Law Commission and the Administrative Justice and Tribunals Council (AJTC).[51] The importance of this form of work is illustrated by the CO's inclusion of this function in his list of core systemic functions of the office (CO 2004, 4).

Training

Another sign of the positive input that ombudsmen are seeking to add to the process of promoting good administration is the willingness to organize and run training events to pass on the learning they have gathered in the course of their work. An obvious area of specialized competence possessed by the ombudsmen is complaint-handling, a function which in the modern administrative justice system is jointly delivered by public authorities and the ombudsmen. As already described in this monograph,[52] the emphasis on proportionate dispute resolution implies the need to ensure that the public authorities within the ombudsmen's jurisdiction

50 Stuhmcke in her work also identifies the meetings that ombudsmen stage with various government agencies as a driver of systemic change (2006, 39-40).

51 The PHSO and the CO have further advantages in this regards as they are both *ex officio* members of respectively the AJTC and the Administrative Review Council.

52 See Chapter 3, pp. 76-9.

have robust internal complaints mechanisms. This allows the ombudsmen to target their resources better on complaints that cannot be appropriately resolved by such mechanisms.

Many ombudsman schemes have taken on the challenge. For example, the LGO delivered 128 training workshops in 2008-09 for all levels of local authority staff, against a target of 120 for the year (LGO 2009, 29, Table 11). In Scotland the SPSO has cooperated with a higher education institution to provide accredited complaints training for staff in public sector agencies, and this institution is now providing accredited training to staff in British and Irish Ombudsman Association (BIOA) members' offices. In Australia, complaint-handling training is widely offered, with the QO also providing training in good decision-making. The training is aimed at compliance officers, complaint-handlers and their supervisors and managers. It seeks to provide an understanding of, for example, the principles of natural justice and good record-keeping within a context of the ombudsman's responsibilities and assisting them to assess the vulnerability of their office to maladministration. It also provides a self-audit toolkit for public authorities to evaluate their complaints systems (QO 2009, 56), including a checklist which could reduce the likelihood that their decisions would be challenged.

In this area of complaint-handling, however, pressure has been put on the ombudsmen to evolve their role still further. Most noticeably in Scotland and Wales there is a move towards using the ombudsman as a 'design authority' to oversee a standardized complaints procedure throughout public services. The Sinclair Review in Scotland specifically recommended that the SPSO be given a role to oversee a new 'fit for purpose complaints system' involving sectoral approval of standardized complaint-handling systems, the coordination of training, reporting and follow-up protocols, and the allocation of responsibility to service providers or scrutiny bodies on individual complaints to eliminate duplication of effort (Sinclair 2008, 4). In Wales, the ombudsman has engaged with a range of public service bodies in order to bring greater consistency to the management of complaints.[53]

Again, there is some precedent for this development from the QO scheme in Australia. Here the QO is responsible for auditing for compliance with the Public Service Commissioner's directive on complaints handling procedures (QO 2009, 6). This latter development has much to commend it, but there are risks attached. One of those risks is that it moves the role of the ombudsman distinctly beyond the relatively safe territory of investigation into administrative audit. Some ombudsman schemes have already gone a significant distance down this road.

53 See Mr Andrew Davies (Minister for Finance and Public Service Delivery), *Record of Proceedings*, The Public Services Ombudsman for Wales's Annual Report 2008/09. National Assembly for Wales, 1 November 2009.

Audit, Inspection and Monitoring

'Compliance auditing' is a role which most Australasian ombudsmen carry out. In considering this comparison though it needs to be understood that the jurisdiction of the Australasian ombudsmen tends to be more wide ranging than their UK equivalents; and it is in these additional areas the audit function is ordinarily applied.[54] The most common type of ombudsman audit relates to the police and other criminal justice agencies and the interception of telecommunications. The usual arrangement is for the ombudsman to make a biannual audit of the agencies' records, checking for conformity with the legal requirements on issue and execution of authorizations and destruction of intercepted material. The detailed report of the audit is ordinarily submitted to a minister or Attorney General and/or Parliament.

Other types of audit or monitoring include the oversight of the conduct of complaints against the police by the police (e.g. in the Northern Territory[55]) or complaints in prisons. A variation on audit is the power to conduct reviews. The New Zealand Ombudsman (NZO) has been made the 'National Protective Mechanism' under the Optional Protocol to the Convention against Torture and other Cruel, Inhuman or Degrading Treatment or Punishment (OPCAT).[56] OPCAT provides for visits by international and national bodies to places of detention in order to examine and monitor the conditions of detention and treatment of detainees. This role has been passed on to the NZO (NZO 2008, 32). Other ombudsman schemes elsewhere in the world have similar powers, as with the Danish Ombudsman, albeit again the focus of inspections is largely on places where individual liberty is restricted (Skinner and Hyman 2006, 106-8).[57]

Further extensions of the monitoring role of ombudsman can be found in the NSWO's powers of legislative review of a whole series of criminal justice powers (NSWO 2009, 138). Notwithstanding the debates about the role actually performed by the ombudsman in conducting this audit function, the enhanced expectation placed upon the office has led it to develop new techniques of investigation. By way of example, the NSWO has experimented since 1998 with conducting 'mystery shopper' audits of the various agencies within its jurisdiction to establish the quality of their customer service provision (NSWO 2009, 90).

---

54 There has been a steady increase in the compliance auditing work of the CO. In 2008-09, there were '30 inspections of the records of law enforcement and other agencies to ensure strict compliance with laws regulating telecommunications interception, electronic surveillance, controlled operations and access to stored communications' (CO 2009, vii). For a discussion, see McMillan (2005, 6-8).

55 See the case studies in NTO (2009, 39 *et seq*).

56 OPCAT enters into force for the United Kingdom of Great Britain and Northern Ireland on 1 November 2010.

57 In the same article it is suggested that most Canadian ombudsman schemes also possess the power to conduct inspections, albeit it is rarely used (Skinner and Hyman 2006, 108-10).

Evaluation

Out of this overview of current practice in the ombudsman community, two key questions need further analysis: how far can the ombudsman model be developed in order to promote good administration and how effective is this form of work?

The Evolving Ombudsman Model

The evidence is now strong that the residuary role of the ombudsman to promote good administration has been given increased priority in a number of ombudsman schemes around the world. At the forefront of this process has been the willingness of ombudsmen to investigate evidence of systemic maladministration.

> Systemic investigations are … the cutting edge of oversight. … They tackle root causes. Done properly, they can result in improved public policy, galvanize a bureaucracy and resolve hundreds of thousands, of existing and potential complaints in one fell swoop. They can save the taxpayer millions of dollars by crafting solutions to issues that are headed inexorably for the courts. Marketed well, they can demonstrate, often via the media, the value of an investigative agency to its immediate stakeholders and the public at large. … They can be challenging and they may require reallocating resources but the pay-offs can be huge. (Jones 2009, 2)

The extent to which some ombudsman schemes have taken on the challenge of promoting good administration has led Snell to opine that there has been a significant evolution in the ombudsman model beyond the traditionally understood redress (fire-fighting) and control (fire-watching) roles.

> Fire-prevention can be described as that area of activity where the Ombudsman uses own motion powers, systemic approaches, reporting and a continuing monitoring of departmental activities in a way that is not based solely or primarily on intelligence gained from previous complainants. Other activities in this area would include production of improved decision-making guides, provision of training courses and performance evaluations. (Snell 2007, 104)

Snell's analysis is largely dependent upon his research of the Commonwealth and New South Wales Ombudsman schemes, but our research has identified elements of this trend in other schemes as well. Support for the view that ombudsmen in Australia in particular have carved out a new distinct function of ombudsman technique can also be seen in the work of Stuhmcke, another keen observer of Australian ombudsmanry (Stuhmcke 2006; 2008a).

In terms of what is being aimed at there is nothing radically different in the ombudsman's ventures into audit, inspection, training or even legislative review. As with more familiar efforts at using techniques beyond complaint-handling, these are exercises aimed at promoting good administration and enhancing accountability. They also connect directly to the constitutional demand for promoting integrity in governance (Stuhmcke 2008a). The big argument in favour of moving in the direction of more proactive techniques which are not reliant on complaints is that it creates the opportunity to identify maladministration that occurs to people unwilling or unable to complain. Better still, such an approach enhances the chances of identifying maladministration before it gives rise to a complaint.

Alongside the benefits to individual users of services, two further more challenging rationales can also be put forward in favour of maximizing the potential of an ombudsman to promote good administration. Firstly, the systemic advice offered by the ombudsman can be potentially sold to investigated bodies as being cost-effective. In a public management culture where complaints are seen as an important opportunity to increase the organization's learning and efficacy, good systemic investigation and analysis is likely to support organizational efficiencies (Marin 2009).

Secondly, the accumulation of the ombudsman's various discretionary powers sets the ombudsman enterprise apart from other bodies within the administrative justice system. This combination allows the ombudsman to enter, with some considerable independent authority, areas of administrative activity that have a strong political dimension and that need quick investigation and resolution. If, for instance, it becomes clear from the media that a government department has lost considerable personal data through internal maladministration, and parliamentary interest in the matter demonstrates the degree of public concern raised, why should the ombudsman wait potentially weeks for a complaint to be received before investigating?[58]

The dangers of inviting the ombudsman to delve into investigations that touch upon issues of profound political sensitivity causes some observers considerable alarm (Harlow and Rawlings 2009, 566). But one more example, this time from one of the newest ombudsman offices in the world, demonstrates an added potential for accountability inherent in the ombudsman enterprise. The report (Ombudsman for Bermuda 2007) covered alleged discrimination involving medical professionals at a hospital in Bermuda. The issues involved were extremely sensitive in the context of the politics of Bermuda, yet the ombudsman was prepared to deliver difficult recommendations in a subject matter that challenged even the highest levels of government. The impact of the report was verified by the subsequent full or partial implementation of all of those recommendations (Ombudsman for Bermuda 2008, 28-31).

Other constitutional institutions, such as public inquiries, can be established which are capable of delivering a similarly comprehensive and authoritative analysis of the facts together with concluding recommendations; but the strength of the ombudsman institution is that it sits within the constitution on a permanent

58 An example taken from a PASC meeting, see PASC (2006, Ev.1, Q3-6).

basis. In so doing, the ombudsman builds up a pool of wisdom and eminence that grants its reports an added degree of authority. This makes it a particularly appropriate institution to be called upon to tackle large-scale examples of administrative wrongdoing, even where there is a quasi-political dimension to the affair.

Nevertheless, however strong the arguments for an active ombudsman, some of the more recent innovations in the ombudsman technique do involve the office operating in a judgmental fashion in the absence of specific complaints. To the extent that this may represent a new role, or at least an evolution of the existing role, ombudsmen may be reluctant to take on such work for fear that it compromises their more basic functions. It could do this in a number of ways.

Firstly, the ombudsman technique is built upon a model of cooperative engagement between the ombudsman and public bodies (or indeed private bodies) concerned. To aid this relationship, the input of the ombudsman generally occurs only in well-defined circumstances where there has been a complaint. This concept has been criticized both by lawyers, who would prefer greater procedural safeguards, and those who would rather the ombudsmen took a more forthright approach in their dealings with public bodies (Paquet 2009). Nevertheless, unlike the legal technique practised in the courts, the investigatory process conducted by ombudsmen is not set up as a battle, even though at some point ombudsmen are required to make a critical report. The danger is that this ideal is damaged by granting the ombudsman the additional power either to commence an investigation of its own accord or conduct intrusive audits or inspections of a public body's operations. By such a process the ombudsman could be viewed more as an active threat to a public body, leading to a reduction in the degree of positive cooperation made available, which in turn would compromise its ability to function.

Secondly, and building on the previous point, once the ombudsman is perceived to have the power and indeed the duty to investigate and audit public bodies in a wider range of circumstances than those triggered by an individual complaint, the office could become exposed to additional external pressures. This wider brief exposes the ombudsman to being invited and pressurized into investigating issues by a variety of interested groups and the media, whether politically motivated or otherwise. In short, there is a risk that the ombudsman can get drawn into the political domain and be seen to be acting in the interests of certain lobbies, an activity that could once more threaten the basic cooperative model that lies at the heart of the ombudsman enterprise.

Thirdly, ombudsmen who verify procedures through audit and inspection work are put in an awkward position should that procedure later be the cause of maladministration. At worst, the ombudsman could be seen to be complicit in the failure. Constitutionally there is also the concern that ombudsmen may be used to audit a function at the expense of more traditional mechanisms of political or judicial accountability (Stuhmcke 2008a, 375).

Fourthly, ombudsmen possess limited resources. Thus, where a power exists to pursue audits, for instance, then the ombudsman may feel obliged or tempted to invest significant resources in this function to the detriment of the core complaint-handling role. To take the argument further, the grandiose headline systemic piece of work may have an attraction and media-grabbing glamour to it that standard complaint-handling does not. Far from improving the situation though, investing too much energy on the 'fire-prevention' model might leave many grievances uninvestigated and leave complainants experiencing a much poorer service. The danger of this occurring though is less now that systems of internal complaint mechanisms are so extensive.

None of the arguments against the fire-prevention role of the ombudsman laid out above conclusively rule out any expansion in the ombudsman model, but they do suggest that caution should be exercised. Against such analysis, however, the expanded ombudsman model does appear to operate successfully in many countries. Evaluating the effectiveness of this improvement capacity of the ombudsman therefore is one of the key questions that the ombudsman currently faces.

The Problem of Evaluation

Although the claim in this monograph is that there has been a move in the direction of promoting good administration in many offices around the world, it is not being claimed the role itself is a new discovery. Ombudsman literature is full of arguments that the ombudsman should promote good administration and can and does succeed in securing long-term administrative improvements. Despite this widespread belief in the ombudsman model, however, what is lacking, to an alarming degree, is objective empirical evidence that this form of ombudsman work produces results (Stuhmcke 2006).[59]

To be fair to ombudsman scholars, a similar critique can be levelled at administrative law generally, despite some innovative research in recent years (e.g. Hertogh and Halliday 2004). But it is a serious charge and carries with it the risk that there is no strong evidence that ombudsmen do succeed in promoting long-term changes for the better in administrative practice. Certainly, amongst the few studies in the area question marks have been raised about the input of the ombudsman. The Chipperfield Commission (DoE 1995) in its review of the LGO in England found little evidence that the good practice guides provided by the LGO were given much attention in government circles. In a 2001 study of the HSO's oversight capacity of the National Health Service in the UK, Kerrison and Pollock (2001, 128) found that 'the Ombudsman's influence and persuasion have had little effect on bringing the NHS to account'.

Stuhmcke in her work though has demonstrated that there are many different aspects to the ombudsman's efforts to promote systemic change, ranging from 'thick' policy changing influences to 'thin' procedural changes (Stuhmcke 2006,

59 Our thanks also to Chris Gill for allowing us to read his Masters dissertation on this very point.

32-4). Measuring these various affects is a complex task and it will be difficult to make objective comparisons between the ultimate weight that should be attached to various claims to impact or perceived failures to facilitate real change.

Whether or not ombudsmen do succeed in their objectives, either in the complaint-handling or promoting good administration capacity, is a serious issue that ombudsmen need to be aware of, and address, in order to maintain the legitimacy of their work. There are some signs of progress and academics have started to produce some good work in this area (Hertogh 2001; Stuhmcke 2006; Passemiers *et al* 2009). There is a possibility that in the not too distant future there will be a body of evidence available that will be capable of forming the basis from which to evaluate the effectiveness of the ombudsman across a whole spectrum of ombudsman functions. Of equal importance, ombudsmen themselves are beginning to turn their attention to the issue (IFF Research 2010). Moreover, if the trend towards increased use of systemic reporting continues, inclusive within which will be systemic recommendations, at least some aspects of the ombudsman's impact should be measurable: namely whether or not recommendations have been implemented. At present, it is not always clear from the ombudsman's reporting that the office returns to its previous work to verify publicly whether or not these systemic recommendations have been implemented or have yielded results, but certainly some ombudsmen have seen an opportunity to demonstrate their worth by doing just this (Marin 2009). We would argue that this trend should be supported through Parliaments taking their oversight role more seriously and demanding that both ombudsmen and public bodies provide demonstrable evidence of the responses provided to ombudsman recommendations, both positive and negative.

This latter conclusion indicates our belief that, for all the statistical analysis that can be undertaken in this area, ultimately the answer to the question of the ombudsman's legitimacy lies in the provision of adequate accountability arrangements. This topic will be returned to in Chapter 6.

Conclusion

In Queensland, Australia, the second object of the ombudsman is 'to improve the quality of decision-making and administrative practice in agencies'.[60] Not all ombudsman legislation is so explicit about this role, but it has virtually universal support in the ombudsman community (Thompson, Buck and Kirkham 2008). Office-holders who pay less attention to this side of the ombudsman enterprise are less likely to maximize the returns from their labour.

What this chapter has identified is that the ombudsmen have developed a range of methods to deliver this service. There is still much more to do to demonstrate the effectiveness of this side of the ombudsman's work but, as our later recommendations will demonstrate, we believe that on a piecemeal basis the

60 Ombudsman Act 2001 (Qld), s.5(b).

full range of methods should be experimented with more than they have hitherto. Evidently, pursuing long-term administrative reform is a form of work which will draw the ombudsman into awkward and possibly controversial disputes with the public bodies being investigated. Here too though, around the world public administrators have come to accept the positive impact of the ombudsman's work, even if this acceptance has sometimes taken time and considerable persuasion to secure. In wonderfully provocative style, the Secretary to the Department of the Australian Prime Minister and Cabinet has written:

> … the Ombudsman is a pain in the bum. … I have a strong sense that I'm so busy being audited, evaluated, reviewed, monitored and investigated that I've got very little time left to wield covert influence for the benefit of the nation! Which, to put it another way, is to say that the system is working … (Shergold 2007)

One should not get complacent about the potential of the ombudsman enterprise and there is always the danger of over-scrutiny of the public sector, or at least inefficient scrutiny; but as the Secretary concluded:

> The pain in my bum is a small price to pay for identifying and remedying defective administration. It might even increase the trust which citizens need to have in their governments, parliaments and public services. (*Ibid.*)

PART III
Setting it Right

Chapter 6
Independence and Accountability: Legitimizing the Ombudsman

Introduction

For all the many good reasons that exist to explain and justify the role, technique and work of the ombudsman enterprise, its pre-eminent status within the constitution and general legitimacy cannot be taken for granted. As with other similarly established bodies, the long-term legitimacy of an ombudsman scheme depends upon stakeholders being able to retain confidence in the operation of the office and the determinations that the ombudsman makes. Without adequate arrangements in place to guarantee the ombudsman model, ombudsmen are exposed to the criticism of arbitrary decision-making, ironically the very objective that the institution is designed to contribute towards preventing. To secure confidence in its work, classically, alongside its claims to expertise and the fairness of its procedures, ombudsmen rely upon three key institutional features: statutory and frequently parliamentary support, independence and accountability. Properly addressing these three institutional features in the design and management of an ombudsman scheme is key to securing the ombudsman's effectiveness. This chapter analyses the manner in which current ombudsmen systems deal with each of these issues.

Understanding the Parliamentary Link

The principal public services ombudsmen are regarded as significant public officers whose role is enshrined in statute and possibly even formally recognized in the constitution.[1] This level of recognition chimes with the claim made in the first two chapters of this book that the ombudsman is best viewed as an autonomous constitutional body that interlinks with other institutions in a variety of ways. Conversely, a constitutional analysis which views the ombudsman as either a

---

1 This is common in European countries, but does also occur in common law countries and states, e.g. Constitution Act 1975 (Victoria), s.94E; Bermuda Constitution, s.93A. See also the report of the Constitution Review Group in Ireland (CRG 1996, 393-5), which recommended that the office of the ombudsman should be included within the Irish Constitution.

part, or simply an agent, of one of the three core institutions of the traditional constitution inadequately describes the real operation of the office.[2]

Nevertheless, the linkage between ombudsman schemes and the relevant legislature is important. In some schemes there is a deliberate linkage in the statutory design of the office.[3] Not all schemes are established with such clarity but, even where the title of 'officer of Parliament' or its equivalent is not formally created, a strong relationship is normally put in place. For instance, the UK's Parliamentary Ombudsman (PO) is not by statute an officer of the House of Commons but is accorded the privileges of such an officer (Gay and Winetrobe 2003, 16 and n.20). Moreover, most ombudsman schemes place a statutory duty on the ombudsman to report to Parliament.[4] Similar arrangements exist in Canada,[5] and throughout Europe the Parliamentary Ombudsman model is dominant, including the European Union (EU) Ombudsman. The Commonwealth Ombudsman (CO) in Australia could be considered an exception to the general rule, as a deliberate choice was made in the 'New Administrative Law' reforms of the mid-1970s to place it in the 'legal review category' alongside tribunals and the Federal Court,[6] though it is under a statutory duty to report to Parliament.[7] Likewise, although the Local Government Ombudsman (LGO) in England is not a Parliamentary Ombudsman, it does now submit its annual report to Parliament[8] and has sought enhanced links.

Thus although not all public sector ombudsman schemes are labelled as 'parliamentary' ombudsman, the vast majority will have a strong connection to Parliament, in terms of accountability and reporting arrangements. Unsurprisingly, therefore, many ombudsman schemes are considered lead examples of a constitutional model now widespread in the common law world, the 'officer of Parliament' model. The term itself is a loose one but refers to those accountability institutions that are set up as statutory officers, require independence from the

2 See further, Chapter 2, pp. 23-52.

3 A typical example is the New Zealand Ombudsman, created as a parliamentary officer; Ombudsmen Act 1975, s.3(1). The Scottish Public Services Ombudsman (SPSO) can be regarded as a 'parliamentary officer' (Gay and Winetrobe 2003, 50). The Victoria Ombudsman has been converted into an officer of Parliament: see the Constitution (Parliamentary Reform) Act 2003 (Victoria), s.19).

4 For example, Parliamentary Commissioner Act 1967, s.10(4) (annual report), s.10(3) (special report); Ombudsman Act 1980 (Ireland), s.6(7). However, the New South Wales ombudsman scheme was originally set-up outside the parliamentary sphere in 1990, but the legislation was later amended to create a reporting arrangement to Parliament and a select committee to oversee the work of the office: see Ombudsman Act 1974, (New South Wales), Part 4A.

5 E.g. Ombudsman Act, R.S.O. 1990, s.11 (Ontario).

6 See Pearce (1998, 67-8), a former Commonwealth Ombudsman, for criticism of this placement.

7 Ombudsman Act 1976 (Cth), ss.17 (special reports).

8 Local Government Act 1974, s.23A(3A), as amended by Local Government and Public Involvement in Health Act 2007, s.170.

executive, and which have a special relationship with Parliament (PAEC 2006, 24). This model has received considerable attention in both academic and parliamentary circles around the world, reflecting a belated attempt to come to terms with the implications of establishing autonomous accountability institutions (Gay and Winetrobe 2003; Griffith 2005; PASC 2007; Gay and Winetrobe 2008;). Such studies have established that current arrangements vary considerably between countries and accountability institutions, probably necessarily so (PASC 2007a, para. 47). There is no simple overarching model of the typical officer of Parliament, but there are some commonly acknowledged attributes which explain why the design is frequently adopted. In particular, these attributes facilitate the establishment of an institution that is legitimate and effective.

Firstly, given the novelty of the ombudsman idea in most legal systems when first introduced, there was a need to provide the ombudsman with a strong status within the constitutional order. The need for parliamentary support remains important today, primarily because ombudsmen ordinarily lack enforcement powers, whereas in democracies the electoral system grants the legislature a high degree of authority and legitimacy. By associating the ombudsman with Parliament, the comparative weakness of the ombudsman is mitigated. There is no better evidence of this process in action than the capacity in many schemes to call upon the support of the legislature when a public body refuses to accept significant features of an ombudsman's report.

Secondly, the work of the ombudsman parallels and complements the traditional work of Parliament, both in terms of resolving grievances and scrutinizing the executive. The similarities in these roles, and a growing recognition of the inadequacies of Parliament to perform them alone, were key reasons for building into ombudsman schemes a strong connection to Parliament in the first place. Thus Parliament may possess an interest in and capacity to deliver such functions as auditing and complaint-handling, but in practice these and other services are much better handled elsewhere. As with other accountability institutions, ombudsmen were introduced in part to assist Parliament in delivering its core functions (Hansard Society 2001, xi).

Thirdly, a strength of the officer of Parliament model is that it can secure the independence of the ombudsman from the executive (Harden 2000, 202), which is widely understood to be an essential component of successful ombudsman schemes (see further below). Given that the feature of independence is a fundamental requirement of an ombudsman scheme it follows that such sensitive issues as the appointment, budgeting arrangements and dismissal of the ombudsman should involve Parliament's participation.

Finally, as will be discussed later in this chapter, the officer of Parliament model also has the distinct advantage of building into an ombudsman scheme the natural division of labour required to deliver external oversight of the ombudsman offices. But there are some contradictions within the model which could undermine the ombudsman's effectiveness. Parliament is required to be both sufficiently involved in the work of the ombudsman to undertake proper scrutiny of the office and sufficiently distant in order to respect the ombudsman's discretion to direct the office as they see fit (Winetrobe 2008). A further tension which applies is that generally Parliaments are also expected to provide an ombudsman with support in its dealings with the executive, particularly where the latter has rejected the ombudsman's recommendations. Parliament has the required political clout to apply pressure against the executive where appropriate, especially if there exists an engaged Select Committee willing to take on these challenges. This format allows for a degree of cross-examination that most ministers would not appreciate in circumstances in which their department's decision-making is on shaky territory. The prospects of ministerial attendance at Select Committee sessions can have a profound influence on government.[9]

Fulfilling this combination of roles – guaranteeing independence, scrutinizing and supporting – is a delicate balancing act for a Parliament to attempt, as demonstrated during the early years of the Scottish Parliament. In Scotland, a strong version of the officer of Parliament model was introduced through the establishment of a number of parliamentary commissioners, but events proved that the relationship between the commissioners and Parliament had not been fully thought through. In particular, procedures for scrutinizing the commissioners were weak. Partly as a result, this led to extra focus being placed on the financial decisions of parliamentary commissioners, which in turn came close to undermining the autonomy of those offices (Winetrobe 2008, 49).

The Scottish experience demonstrates that the officer of Parliament model is a potentially unstable one that requires careful management. The tension that exists in officer of Parliament schemes weakens the argument that the legislature is the best vehicle through which to secure the ombudsman's independence. It would be naive to describe Parliament as truly neutral as it is loaded with vested interests, some derived from its members' political affiliations, others from its duty to call the executive to account. Either way, Parliament's stance towards its officers of Parliament is bound to be influenced by the nature of the ongoing relationship the officer has with the executive. The choice of Parliament to operate as the ombudsman's constitutional guardian is unavoidably flawed. To compensate for the inherent weaknesses in the officer of Parliament model, various practical solutions and conventions are required to make it work. Some of these solutions will be explored in the following sections on independence and accountability.

Yet the officer of Parliament model can work extremely well; the mutual benefits flowing from the relationship between the parliamentary officer and

9 'It was perhaps not fully appreciated when the [Parliamentary Ombudsman] Office was set up that the effect of a report to Parliament of unremedied maladministration by a government department was a potential depth-charge. The Commissioner's report had no party implications; the House tended to be united in demanding explanations from the department in a highly public manner. The relevant Secretary of State had to stand and deliver these. No sensible civil servant wants to put his minister in this situation' (Clothier 1996, 388).

Parliament have been referred to as 'interdependence' (Buchanan 2008, 88-90). Parliament can be much empowered by the input of accountability institutions, while accountability institutions are significantly weaker bodies if not supported by the aura that comes with being closely associated to Parliament. A consequence of this relationship is that an element of the accountability institution's autonomy is necessarily sacrificed, albeit for sound constitutional reasons.

> An officer of parliament ... is dependent on the parliament for resources. While the funding procedure must recognise its operational independence and minimise (and, ideally, eliminate) the potential for political interference in the selection of work priorities and the exercise of discretion and judgment, an officer does not have an unfettered right to resources and should be prepared to listen to any views that the parliament may express about how its resources should best be applied in the interests of the public. Having done so, the officer must be prepared to give a reasonable account of the office's overall performance applying the funding it has been given. (Buchanan 2008, 89)

Clearly, if the ombudsman had to act under instruction from Parliament the rationale for the office would be severely undermined, but this does not preclude some intervention by Parliament. As will be described later, ombudsmen are subject to direction over the information they must present and are required to respond to interrogation regarding the general management and strategy of their office. More controversially, such interrogation may even include reviews of individual investigations, a practice prohibited in some ombudsman schemes on the basis that it would be detrimental to their autonomy.[10] Yet the concern is arguably overstated. Where parliamentary reviews of investigations are undertaken they usually occur in a narrowly defined scenario. Parliamentary reviews are initiated by the ombudsman office itself in circumstances in which a public body has refused to implement the ombudsman's recommendations. In theory this review process could result in Parliament choosing not to support the ombudsman's findings (Kirkham 2006, 815-16). Given the potential fallibility of the office and Parliament's need to arrive at a balance between supporting the ombudsman and calling it to account, this flexibility in action is entirely appropriate; otherwise Parliament's scrutiny role would be compromised. Moreover, where a Parliament chooses to support the ombudsman, this is all the more convincing because it has properly tested the ombudsman's findings.

Further evidence of the potential for parliamentary input can be seen in those instances when Parliament offers a view as to the inquiries or investigations which the ombudsmen should undertake. An example of this came with the *Equitable Life* investigation carried out by the PO, which was partially prompted by

10 For example, the Ombudsman Act 1972 (South Australia), s.31; Ombudsman Act 1974 (New South Wales), s.31B(2).

significant pressure from parliamentarians.[11] More formal arrangements exist in several Australian ombudsman schemes for Parliament to refer a matter to the ombudsman for review,[12] albeit this power does not appear to have been used (Pearce 2005, 128). Yet possessing the power and duty to oversee, ask questions, advise, refer complaints or even refuse to support the ombudsman is a very different thing from actively controlling or being responsible for the ombudsman. The risk of this occurring cannot be ignored but at present there is little evidence of ombudsman schemes being hampered inappropriately by Parliament. Instead, it is widely accepted that for the autonomy of the office to be meaningful, ultimately the discretion to act must be the ombudsman's alone and Parliament must not have the power to direct the ombudsman as to how to act. This understanding is implicit within the statutes that establish ombudsman schemes, with some even explicitly referring to the ombudsman's autonomy to act.[13] It is in this sense that the view of the ombudsman as a mere agent or servant of Parliament is misconceived.

The Parliamentary Ombudsman model, therefore, is a complex innovation in constitutional practice.[14] To get the best out of the ombudsman, Parliament is required both actively to support the office whilst at the same time scrutinizing its work. Despite the difficulty of this challenge the role of Parliament should remain central to the success of public sector ombudsmen, including those schemes that do not label the ombudsman as a parliamentary officer within the relevant legislation.

Independence

The Importance of Independent Tenure

The best evidence of the autonomy of ombudsman schemes is the degree of importance that is ordinarily attached to the independence of the office-holder. Securing the independence of the office is a design feature that has always been considered to be an imperative for ombudsman schemes. Not only is it important

---

11 The PHSO received 898 complaints referred by MPs in respect of 1,008 people. She received 1,309 direct representations from a further 1,480 individuals (PHSO 2008a, para. 3.2). The MP filter in the PO and NIO ombudsman schemes also suggests that Parliament can control the workload of the ombudsman.

12 For example, Ombudsman Act 2001 (Queensland), s.19.

13 For example, Ombudsman Act 2001 (Queensland), s.13; Ombudsman Act 1980 (Ireland), s.4(1); Scottish Public Services Ombudsman Act 2002, Sch.2, s.2. However, the argument that the PO would not be subject to the court's supervisory jurisdiction in the UK on the basis that Parliament supervised this body via its Select Committee system was rejected in *R v Parliamentary Commissioner for Administration ex parte Dyer* [1994] 1 WLR 621, at 625.

14 J. Sedley referred to the PO as occupying 'a unique constitutional place'; *R v Parliamentary Commissioner for Administration, ex p Balchin* [1997] JPL 917 at 924.

to the ombudsman to avoid being seen as an internal form of control within the executive, but also ombudsmen cannot afford to be viewed as a partisan citizens' advocate. Instead, the complaint-handling role of the office makes it essential that it is, and is perceived to be, independent and impartial. Recognition of the importance attached to the issue of independence within the ombudsman community can be seen in the membership rules of ombudsman associations in the UK and Ireland, as well as in Australasia. The British and Irish Ombudsman Association (BIOA) has tiers of membership, with full membership reserved only for those schemes that demonstrate the highest standards of independence.[15] The Australian and New Zealand Ombudsman Association (ANZOA), by contrast, only has members that can meet requisite standards of independence (ANZOA 2010).[16] Within this standard an extremely important claim for authority and legitimacy is being made, upon which, in the eyes of both the complainant and public bodies, rests much of the authority that the ombudsman exercises.

The argument for independence, however, does not necessarily imply that initial complaint-handling should always be undertaken by a fully autonomous body, or that quasi-autonomous complaint-handlers (also known as 'executive ombudsmen') should not be used. But the full ombudsman standard of independence does represent the dividing line between those ombudsmen at the top of the complaints pyramid and those at the lower level. The justification for this division of seniority lies in the basic requirement that for complainants to be fully satisfied that their grievance has been handled properly, they are ultimately entitled to have access to a body that is not connected to the public body being complained against. Such an independent appeal process should be available to verify and legitimate the overall complaint-handling system. At this higher level, a complaint-handling body that is funded, appointed by or in any other way reliant upon the support of the administrative body that it is duty-bound to investigate cannot be considered to possess the requisite degree of independence, even if operationally such offices do achieve practical autonomy. The perception of agency control of the watchdog is the insurmountable obstacle here, which in turn gives the impression that the provision of complaint-handling services is a means to appease complainants rather than handle them seriously. This issue of independence can still be controversial,

15 See further, Chapter 1, pp. 4-5, 15-16.

16 See also the Canadian Council of Parliamentary Ombudsman. Not all ombudsman associations have stayed loyal to this demand for the independence of its members, a concession that has drawn significant criticism (Rowat 2007). The lead exception is the United States Ombudsman Association, which in 2000 allowed many executive ombudsmen, formerly registered as associate members, to become full members, complete with full voting rights. See also the so-called International Ombudsman Association based in the US and mainly made up of private sector ombudsmen.

as demonstrated in more than one recent attempt to place the Prisons and Probation Ombudsman (PPO) in England on a statutory footing.[17]

Establishing suitable arrangements to secure the independence of ombudsmen, therefore, is a vital component of ombudsman schemes. To clarify the importance of non-judicial complaints mechanisms, whilst at the same time recognizing the role and validity of quasi-autonomous complaints mechanisms, it has often been argued that only complaint-handlers that can demonstrate full independence should be entitled to carry the name 'ombudsman' (Rowat 2007). Unfortunately, the *ad hoc* manner in which the non-judicial complaints arena has developed has prevented such a neat solution being entrenched in law in most jurisdictions.[18]

Appointment

In general, the essential nature of independence to the legitimacy of ombudsman schemes is recognized around the world, although a weakness in some schemes is that this point is not specified in legislation. A major indicator of the ombudsman's status is that formal appointment is ordinarily granted by the head of state or a representative. Thus, for instance, this role is performed in the UK by the Queen, in Ireland by the President and in New Zealand by the Governor-General.[19]

Using a neutral figure to appoint the ombudsman grants the process a degree of independence, but the openness, transparency and independence of the appointment process itself is a more important test. This can be a problematic issue because the executive is generally speaking the institution best placed to organize such appointments. Yet there are ways to minimize the dangers inherent in an arrangement whereby a public body is strongly involved in organizing the recruitment procedure for a watchdog assigned to oversee its operations.

---

17 The PPO was established in 1994 on the recommendation of the Woolf inquiry into the riots at Strangeways and other prisons in 1990. In 2004 the PPO was given responsibility for investigating deaths in prison custody. There has been a commitment by the Home Office since 1998 to put the PPO on a statutory footing. During the course of the Criminal Justice and Immigration Bill in 2008, the government announced that the proposals to place the Prisons and Probation Ombudsman for England and Wales and the Prisoner Ombudsman for Northern Ireland on a statutory footing (Parts 4 and 5 of the Bill) would be withdrawn: '... it is evident from public statements made by the current ombudsmen and by the Parliamentary Ombudsman that there is significant concern about the provisions. All three ombudsmen have argued for a different model that provides for direct accountability to Parliament.' (Lord Hunt, Parliamentary Under-Secretary of State, Ministry of Justice, *Hansard*, HL debs, Second reading (22 January 2008), col. 128).

18 An exception is New Zealand, where the consent of the New Zealand Parliamentary Ombudsman is required before another complaint-handler can be granted the title ombudsman (Ombudsmen Act 1975 (New Zealand), s.28A).

19 Respectively, Parliamentary Commissioner Act 1967, s.1(2); Ombudsman Act 1980 (Ireland), s.2; and the Ombudsmen Act 1975 (New Zealand), s.3(2).

The most obvious solution is to involve Parliament in the process. For instance, although the PHSO is recommended by the Prime Minister, the final decision is made following consultation with the Leader of the Opposition and chair of the Public Administration Select Committee (PASC), with the latter attending the interview of candidates for the post (Giddings 2008, 93).[20] Ideally, such practices should be detailed in statute. In Queensland, the Law, Justice and Safety Committee must be consulted about both the selection process and the appointee;[21] in Victoria the ombudsman is appointed by the 'Governor in Council';[22] and in Wales the Assembly must be consulted.[23] The safeguard is even stronger in New South Wales, as the proposed appointee may be subject to veto by the Joint Ombudsman and Police Integrity Commission Committee.[24] More powerfully still, in Ireland and Scotland the final nomination for the appointment is made by the respective democratic chamber,[25] and the European Ombudsman must be appointed by the European Parliament after each election.[26]

Statutory arrangements which require nomination by Parliament allow for a solution to be adopted which removes the executive almost entirely from the appointments process, for example in New Zealand where an Officer of Parliament Committee has been established to deal with the sponsoring aspect of three parliamentary officer schemes, including the ombudsman. Amongst other things, the committee's remit includes: determining the budgets for each officer of Parliament; appointing auditors to undertake audits of the agencies of the officers of Parliament; recommending to the House of Representatives on the appointment of officers of Parliament; and considering the officers of Parliament operating intentions (Beattie 2006). Noticeably, what this list does not include is any extensive scrutiny of the operational performance of officers of Parliament or any duty to support the ombudsman in its dealings with the executive. This is because the model adopted in New Zealand makes a clear distinction between the *sponsoring* (determining of budget, resources and appointment) and *scrutiny* (dealing with reports, considering policies and administration of

20 '... and the panel has an external assessor from the Public Appointment Commissioner's office to ensure that the appointment is made fairly according to the Commissioner's Code of Practice' (Gay 2008, 2).

21 Ombudsman Act 2001 (Queensland), s.59.

22 Ombudsman Act 1973 (Victoria), s.3. The Governor must exercise the power of appointment in accordance with the advice of the Victorian Executive Council, which consists of at least two and normally four ministers who meet with the Governor and represent the government.

23 Public Services Ombudsman (Wales) Act 2005, Sched.1, s.1(2).

24 Ombudsman Act 1974 (New South Wales), s.31BA.

25 Ombudsman Act 1980, (Ireland), s.2(2); Scottish Public Services Ombudsman Act 2002, s.1(1).

26 Decision of the European Parliament on the regulations and general conditions governing the performance of the Ombudsman's duties, Adopted by Parliament on 9 March 1994 (OJ L 113, 4.5.1994, p. 15) as amended, article 6.

the government) functions of Parliament, with the latter undertaken by a separate committee. The strength of this two-committee model is that it enables the New Zealand Parliament to isolate practical issues of operational independence, such as appointment and budget, and deal with them in as non-partisan fashion as possible. Thus the Officers of Parliament Committee is chaired by the Speaker of the House and does not have a government majority. In making appointments the committee conducts the appointment process following a procedure which involves it setting the selection criteria and interviewing shortlisted applicants (OPC 2002). The committee invites ministerial participation and seeks to have unanimity amongst its members over the candidate who is chosen. The successful recommendation for appointment is then proposed to the House of Representatives in a motion in the name of the Leader of the House.[27]

The New Zealand approach to appointment is generally cited as a model of good practice. A further refinement to the New Zealand approach might be to require the successful appointment to attend a public pre-appointment hearing before the post was confirmed, thereby enhancing the transparency of the process of appointment. This process is becoming increasingly common in Westminster (Ministry of Justice 2007, paras.76-9; Liaison Committee 2008; PASC 2008c).[28] Yet the parliamentary solution to appointment is also problematic. The danger is that in passing the responsibility for appointment to Parliament the potential for the executive appointing a 'safe pair of hands' could be replaced by the risk of the appointment process being disproportionately affected by political horse-trading within Parliament. As one commentator has put it, 'the process involving endorsement by political caucuses (as a prelude to a unanimous resolution of the House recommending appointment) lacks transparency and brings an element of political acceptability, rather than merit, to the appointment' (Buchanan 2008, 86). A similar set of issues could be said to surround the appointment of the European Ombudsman.[29]

In an attempt to prevent inappropriate executive dominance of the appointment process and the imposition of unhelpful parliamentary compromises, PASC has explored the idea of establishing a separate autonomous committee with its own statutory authority – a Public Standards Commission – 'at arm's length from both government and Parliament (though it could have members from, or acting on behalf of, both)' (PASC 2007a, para. 108). Whilst such a solution would create

27 Ombudsmen Act 1975 (New Zealand), s.3(2).

28 'The House of Commons should also have a bigger role in the selection of key public officials. I propose, as a first step, pre-appointment hearings for public officials whose role it is to protect the public's rights and interests, and for whom there is not currently independent scrutiny. That includes … the local government ombudsman.' (Gordon Brown, Prime Minister, *Hansard*, HC Debs, 3 July 2007, col. 816).

29 P. Nikiforos Diamandouros was chosen by MEPs on 20 January 2010 to serve another term as European Ombudsman (Diamandouros, 340 votes; Monette, 289 votes and Bottoli, 19 votes). He has held the position since 1 April 2003.

an additional problem as to how such a sponsoring body would be appointed and held to account, it would have the benefit of freeing Parliament to concentrate on the role of scrutinizing the work of the ombudsman and supporting the office where necessary. This remaining duality of roles would still be difficult to manage, but delegating primary responsibility for the appointment of the ombudsman to an autonomous body would provide the most likely scenario in which such appointments could be made on the sole grounds of their capacity to do the job. Certainly in the larger jurisdictions, given the range of accountability institutions currently in operation and their constitutional importance, the establishment of such a body would be justifiable.

A compromise solution would be for a parliamentary committee to retain formal control but to contract out various aspects of its sponsoring role (Gay and Winetrobe 2003, 8), with such a duty possibly being confirmed in statute. By way of example, in its 2008 appointment of the Chairman of the Electoral Commission, the Speaker's Committee, which operates on a similar basis to the New Zealand Officers of Parliament Committee, employed a panel of five, including only one MP, to make a recommendation to the post. This recommendation was subsequently approved by the committee (Speaker's Committee 2008, 4-5).

Dismissal and Tenure

Once appointed, to preserve the autonomy of the office it is essential that the ombudsman is hard to remove given the risks attached where there is an ongoing fear of dismissal on quasi-political grounds. Here the strongest solution is the full security of tenure model, as traditionally applied to the judiciary.[30] However, in the UK concerns about age discrimination has led to a move away from fixing the end point of tenure at a specific age and to the adoption of fixed terms of office instead.[31] Fixed terms are used quite frequently in various public appointments in the UK and in ombudsman schemes around the world (Buchanan 2008, 86). Longer, fixed-term appointments can be sufficient to allow an individual to gain real command of the office and implement change where necessary. They can also allow the office to overlap terms of office of government and Parliament, adding to the sense of the autonomy of the office. Fixed terms for a period of somewhere between seven and ten years is the most common solution and also mirrors the experience of most ombudsman schemes in which very few ombudsmen have stayed in office for longer than ten years.[32] A bigger concern is the issue of reappointment, which is allowed for in a number of ombudsman

30 For example, Ombudsman Act 1972 (South Australia), s.10(1).

31 Employment Equality (Age) Regulations 2006, S.I. No. 1031, Sched. 8, Part 1 – although the current NIO legislation remains unchanged.

32 There are a few examples of periods of tenure for longer than ten years. For instance, Eugene Biganovsky was the South Australia Ombudsman for 22 years, Jerry

schemes.[33] The difficulty in this arrangement is that it allows for reappointment to be made based on a measure of the performance of the ombudsman in the first period of office. Ombudsmen certainly should be exposed to scrutiny and evaluation, but there is a danger that governments could see the reappointment process as a political opportunity to remove an ombudsman who is viewed as over-interfering.[34] Incumbent ombudsmen also might become over-cautious in the run-up to reappointment.

The common template for suspension and removal is that the appointing authority is vested with that power. Removal ordinarily follows an address or resolution approved by the relevant legislature, with the requirement being that the ombudsman is unfit to continue in office by reason of incapacity or incompetence, misconduct or becoming bankrupt. Some schemes safeguard the process further by specifying the majority needed to remove the ombudsman, as with the Scottish Public Services Ombudsman (SPSO), in which two-thirds of the total chamber must vote for removal.[35] By contrast, the LGO in England can be removed by the Queen for incapacity or misbehaviour without parliamentary approval.[36] This solution was presumably chosen because it was not felt appropriate for Parliament to be involved with an ombudsman scheme that is dealing with complaints about elected local government. More importantly, because the government minister who advises the Queen is never subject to investigation by the LGO, the autonomy of the LGO is not threatened improperly by this arrangement.

Independence is also strengthened by building into the appointment process suitably impressive and protected remuneration packages (Gottehrer and Hostina 1998, 3). Often, for instance, links are made explicitly in legislation between the salary of an ombudsman and the salary of a senior judicial rank or civil servant.[37] In other schemes, the ombudsman's pay is safeguarded through a combination of the use of autonomous agencies responsible for recommending pay levels, backed up by mechanisms for obtaining parliamentary approval of those recommendations.[38] Again, a feature of this arrangement is that a process is

---

White was a local government ombudsman in England for over 14 years, while in Norway Arne Fliflet is still in office as this book is written and has been so for 20 years.

33 See the ombudsman schemes in New South Wales, Australian Capital Territory, Queensland, Tasmania, Ireland, New Zealand, Scotland, and the Australian Commonwealth Ombudsman.

34 A New Zealand Ombudsman was not reappointed because the executive disagreed with some of her recommendations (Buchanan 2008, 84). Similar allegations have been made with regard to the Chair of the Committee for Standards in Public Life in the UK in 2007 (PASC 2007, para. 81).

35 Scottish Public Services Ombudsman Act 2002, Sched.1 s.4(1)(d).

36 Local Government Act 1974, s.23(6).

37 For example, the Ombudsman Act 1980, (Ireland), s.3.

38 An example here is the New Zealand Ombudsman, whose pay is recommended by the Remuneration Authority, with the Officers of the Parliament Committee responsible for approving the recommendation: Ombudsmen Act 1975 (New Zealand), s.9(1).

put in place to neutralize the potential for the executive and Parliament itself to put indirect and inappropriate pressure on the ombudsman. Another fundamental requirement is that the ombudsman has the freedom to appoint staff.[39]

Ombudsman Backgrounds

There have been very few significant allegations of bias made against members of the ombudsman community. By contrast, occasional concern has been expressed as to the *type* of office-holder that has been chosen, particularly where the ombudsman is appointed from the ranks of the bureaucracy that they are required to investigate. As a former insider, the ex-administrator has the requisite experience of the underlying issues of administrative practice being scrutinized. At the same time, this leaves the ombudsman vulnerable to the perception that they are inappropriately sympathetic to the administration's bureaucratic culture.

To support such a concern there is some evidence, albeit extremely subjective, that past employment may have an impact on the approach taken to the task of ombudsmanry. By way of example, most of the former PHSOs have been ex-civil servants[40] and in hindsight largely avoided pushing the boundaries of the office's potential.[41] The current incumbent, Ann Abraham (2002-present), however, comes from a non-civil service background, with experience as the Chief Executive of the National Association of Citizens Advice Bureaux, an organization more aligned to the complainant community than administration. Whether by coincidence or not, it is noticeable that her tenure has been marked by a series of high-profile investigations and a shift in the approach of the office. The tenure of office-holders such as Professor John McMillan (the Australian Commonwealth Ombudsman, former academic), Bruce Barbour (NSWO, former member of the Commonwealth Administrative Appeals Tribunal) and André Marin (Ontario Ombudsman, Canada, former Assistant Crown Attorney) also provides tentative evidence for the proposition that appointments from outside the administrative system under review bring a very different style to the post of ombudsman. All have been identified as having radically changed the approach of the ombudsman office (Snell 2007; Jones 2009).

This variety of appointments has contributed to the growth and development of the ombudsman model without any obvious detrimental side effects. No ombudsman scheme provides restrictions on appointment in terms of previous experience. Arguably, where ombudsmen act within a collegiate arrangement

39 For example, Public Services Ombudsman (Wales) Act, 2005, Sched. 1, para. 11.

40 Sir Edmund Compton (1967-71), Sir Alan Marre (1971-76), Sir Idwal Pugh (1976-78), Sir William Reid (1990-96) and Sir Michael Buckley (1997-2002). Sir Cecil Clothier (1979-84) and Sir Anthony Barrowclough (1985-90) were lawyers.

41 For a full analysis of the work of the first 33 years of the PHSO, see Gregory and Giddings (2002a).

there may be a case for such restrictions, for example, the Commission for Local Administration for England. The commission is made up of three separate ombudsmen, responsible for separate geographical locations.[42] Between 2005 and 2009 all three ombudsmen[43] were former chief executives of local authorities in England. This situation helped encourage the perception of bias in the office, even in the absence of any evidence to support such an allegation. The production of a robust appointment process, as discussed above, would appear to be the way forward to address this type of difficulty.

Budgetary Process

There are more subtle means than making partisan appointments with which to reduce the effectiveness of a watchdog body (CAIPE 2005). The capacity of the ombudsman office will be affected by the scale of its budget, as with other public organizations. Given the dangers of executive control via the resource allocation process,[44] at the very least there should be transparent procedures to verify the budgets supplied to ombudsmen. One Canadian select committee has laid out the following guidelines for its officers of Parliament.

> Primarily, the budget determination process must be removed from the exclusive domain of the executive; while at the same time, an appropriate performance review, budgetary challenge, and accountability mechanism must be maintained. Parliament must play a … critical role in the budget determination process, and resource-allocation decision-making must be based on objective and expert analysis. The process should be practical, transparent, simple, and expeditious. (CAIPE 2005, 21)

The standard safeguard against the executive placing exccssive financial constraints on an ombudsman office is for the budget to be tabled separately within a Consolidated Fund approved by Parliament.[45] In practice, however, the degree to which the ombudsman's budget is fully scrutinized by Parliament varies

42 The commission also includes the Parliamentary Ombudsman as an *ex officio* member and the Secretary of State must appoint two of the local commissioners as chairman and vice-chairman respectively: see Local Government Act 1974, s.23(2) and (7).

43 Tony Redmond (chairman), Jerry White (vice-chairman) and Ann Seex. Jerry White was replaced by Dr Jane Martin from January 2010 and she has been appointed vice-chairman.

44 PASC found evidence in its review that it was much easier to restrict the funding of accountability institutions where they were accountable to the executive rather than Parliament (PASC 2007, paras. 77-9).

45 See for instance Tasmania, where until recently the budget for the Tasmanian Ombudsman was submitted to Parliament within the overall budget for the Justice Ministry. From 2007-08, the ombudsman is separately listed in the Consolidated Fund (TO 2007, 1).

considerably. In particular, unless Parliament is granted by way of statute a role in agreeing the ombudsman budget, there is little evidence that it adds scrutiny or transparency to the process. The lack of scrutiny may be proportional given the size of the ombudsman budget; but what is important is that Parliament is able to intervene should the ombudsman's budget be unreasonably cut.[46]

The exclusive stewardship of public funds by the executive raises obvious concerns about an arrangement whereby a body that could be investigated by the ombudsman has responsibility for its funding; and it is inconsistent with the officer of Parliament model. The potential damage to perceptions of the independence of the office has in the past been recognized by the UK Parliament. A former select committee recommended that the PO be funded by the same system as the Comptroller and Auditor-General, namely through the control of a Parliamentary Select Committee,[47] a proposal which was accepted but never implemented by the government of the day (Select Committee on PCA 1993, para. 32). The New Zealand scheme already adopts much the same approach. Here the Officers of Parliament Committee examines the draft annual estimates of the ombudsman and then reports to Parliament which may, but usually does not, reject them. Parliament then recommends the appropriations to the Governor, which the government subsequently includes in the Appropriation Bill. Strong parliamentary procedures for scrutinizing ombudsman budgets also exist in other schemes. Under the Standing Orders of the Welsh Assembly the Public Services Ombudsman for Wales's (PSOW) budget estimates are considered by the Assembly's Finance Committee, which may modify it having consulted and taken into account representations, including holding a hearing with the PSOW. The estimates are then included as a specified item in the annual budget motion.[48]

An alternative model is currently under review in Canada, whereby an *ad hoc* cross-party committee has been established to consider funding requests from officers of Parliament and thereafter make recommendations to the Treasury (CAIPE 2005, 21; Hurtubise-Loranger 2008, 76-7). The advantage of this approach is that it gives expression to all the legitimate interests, though it is a weaker safeguard of independence than the New Zealand solution, as the executive retains ultimate control of the budget of parliamentary officers. Nevertheless, the Canadian solution does achieve transparency and gives the work of accountability

---

46 During the 1980s the Irish Ombudsman was forced to submit a special report to the Oireachtas (the Irish Parliament) after the government had proposed to halve the office's budget, amidst allegations that the then Taoiseach, Charles Haughey, was hostile to the concept of an Ombudsman's office. The support of the Oireachtas successfully helped to secure a much improved budget (O'Reilly 2009a).

47 For the Comptroller and Auditor-General this is the Public Accounts Commission. See also the Speaker's Commission and its oversight of the Electoral Commissioners.

48 See Welsh Assembly Standing Order 14.1 and Standing Order 27.15 to 17. These Standing Orders are available in National Assembly for Wales (2010).

institutions the serious attention they merit through the establishment of a separate non-partisan select committee.

Accountability

Establishing the ombudsman enterprise on a sound constitutional and autonomous footing is an essential starting point in securing its long-term legitimacy. Maintaining and demonstrating the ombudsman's status, however, also requires a process of adequate external oversight to provide transparent assurance of the effectiveness of the office.

Strong accountability mechanisms are vital to the ombudsman enterprise, all the more so if the theoretical claims made in this book as to the ability of the ombudsman to deliver important constitutional objectives are correct. With the ombudsman positioned at the top of the complaints ladder and with a wider role in promoting good administration, this raises the classic question – *Quis custodiet ipsos custodes?* (Who watches the watchmen?). The ombudsmen possess considerable discretionary powers,[49] the impact of which can be profound for both complainants and administration. Thus there is a need for the wider public and the ombudsman's more immediate stakeholders to be assured that these powers are being wielded appropriately, competently and with sufficient vigour. This can only be achieved if the ongoing performance of the ombudsman's work is properly evaluated by an effective system of regular oversight that garners an appropriate quality of legitimacy.

In conventional constitutional terms, the more powerful and direct forms of accountability – namely judicial correction of erroneous decisions and political removal from office – are, quite correctly, only available to a limited extent with regard to the ombudsman. Judicial review in the courts will focus primarily on procedural matters rather than the merits of decision-making; and powers of removal can only be used in exceptional circumstances where political considerations are removed from the process as far as possible. In practice, ombudsman schemes are kept in check by a variety of less direct scrutiny devices. These methods are not formally linked in any way and often operate in an irregular fashion, which makes it all the more difficult to quantify the effectiveness of the overall accountability arrangement.

Internal Reviews

Given the various points in the ombudsman complaint process where judgment and discretion are required,[50] it is unsurprising that many ombudsman schemes

49 See Chapter 4, pp. 106-9 and below, pp. 176-7.

50 For example, such as whether or not to accept the complaint for investigation, to close or continue the investigation early, to pursue an early settlement or to conclude the

have developed internal review procedures to meet complainants' needs for accountability of the ombudsman's handling of their complaints. Consistent with the goal of 'proportionate dispute resolution' (PDR), the first option for the complainant to pursue might well be a request for an internal review by the ombudsman's office.[51] This approach is consistent with the user-focused customer service strategies increasingly deployed in public management discussed in Chapter 3. The ombudsman enterprise has responded by increasing the transparency and accessibility of their internal review processes. For analytical purposes it is convenient to consider two categories of internal review: firstly, reviews of customer complaints relating to the *decision* made by the ombudsman; and secondly, those relating to the ombudsman *service* provided.[52] Such reviews are ordinarily conducted by a senior officer but the extent of that review will vary from scheme to scheme. For instance, the Northern Ireland Ombudsman (NIO) limits reviews to the service provided during the original investigation and the process adopted.[53] The SPSO, by contrast, will review the decision itself if the complainant can argue that it was 'based on important evidence which contains facts that were not accurate' or 'there is new and relevant information that was not previously available'.[54] Other ombudsman schemes are more opaque about the criteria to be considered but will review the merits of the original officer's conclusions and their explanation of that decision.[55] The potential outcomes from the review may include changing the original decision, an improved explanation of the decision or a reopening of the investigation. Unless the investigation has had to be reopened or there are exceptional circumstances, such as new evidence, ombudsman schemes generally only allow for one review of a decision.

An internal review will be restricted in its ability to satisfy fully the complainant[56] because it is not an independent process; but it does provide a measure of scrutiny

---

investigation with a full report.

51 See Chapter 3, pp. 78-9 for discussion of internal review mechanisms and PDR within the administrative justice system as a whole.

52 This bifurcation of customer reviews is sometimes, but not invariably, reflected in particular ombudsman schemes. For example, the SPSO website carries advice for decision and service complaints at <http://www.spso.org.uk/how-complain/complaining-about-spso/challenges-casework-decisions> and <http://www.spso.org.uk/how-complain/complaining-about-spso> respectively (accessed 4 May 2010).

53 See <http://www.ni-ombudsman.org.uk/geninfo.htm> (accessed 22 May 2010).

54 See <http://www.spso.org.uk/how-complain/complaining-about-spso/challenges-casework-decisions> (accessed 22 May 2010).

55 For example, see the Commonwealth Ombudsman's arrangements, <http://www.ombudsman.gov.au/pages/making-a-complaint/review-of-our-decisions/> or the Local Government Ombudsmen's arrangements in the UK, <http://www.lgo.org.uk/making-a-complaint/complaints-about-us/> (accessed 4 May 2010).

56 The LGO, for example, recorded that in 2008-09 it dealt with a total of 1,322 customer complaints, of which 1,242 were review requests, and of these 1,108 decisions (i.e. 89 per cent) were confirmed (LGO 2009, 23 and Table 4).

which is generally not required by legislation. The strength of the internal review process is that it can allow for a review of the merits of the decisions originally made by the ombudsman. A further benefit is that the process will be valuable in terms of verifying the quality of the investigatory processes applied by the ombudsman. However, for all of these beneficial contributions, internal appeals will always have reduced value purely because the process does not provide *external* assurance of the work being undertaken by the ombudsman.

External Reviews

The potential for a more robust review procedure by which complaints can be handled is provided by arrangements in the Financial Ombudsman Service (FOS). Within this ombudsman scheme the job of reviewing decisions is contracted out to an external, independent assessor, which adds to the perception of fair process.[57] The inclusion of this added process does have cost implications which are more easily assimilated by the FOS than most ombudsman schemes because of its resources and the scale of its operation.[58] But there are signs that the model might transplant into the public sector. The SPSO has recently engaged an Independent Service Delivery Reviewer to consider complaints about the service provided by the ombudsman that the office has not been able to resolve itself.

The model of an external reviewer is an interesting innovation, but its use so far has been limited to reviews of the *service* provided and not the substantive *decision* made by the ombudsman. Nevertheless, the value of the independent, external review as an accountability mechanism remains strong. Indeed, the rather exceptional independent review commissioned by the SPSO in 2009 may provide an interesting precedent for future action in exceptional circumstances by the ombudsman enterprise. An LGO was tasked at the request of the SPSO to conduct an external review of how the SPSO had conducted a particular investigation. The conclusions of the review (SPSO 2009a, Annex 1) were so strong and so critical of the office that the ombudsman then felt compelled to submit the subsequent report to the Scottish Parliament.[59] However, one is left to speculate whether such a robust form of watchdog self-reflection is likely to be deployed in circumstances other than

57 The terms of the reference of the independent assessor are available at: <http://www.financial-ombudsman.org.uk/about/IA_terms_reference.htm> (accessed 4 May 2010). In 2008-09, the independent assessor had 265 cases referred to him, of which he upheld 83 cases either wholly or in part and made recommendations for financial compensation in 78 of these. See FOS (2009, 97).

58 The FOS had a total income of £65.8 million in year ended 31 March 2009 (FOS 2009, 66).

59 (SPSO 2009a) was laid before the Scottish Parliament on 5 October 2009 under the Scottish Public Services Ombudsman Act 2002, s.17(4). See also Chapter 4, p. 106, and n.38.

where a new post-holder decides to set up the review of an investigation that took place during the tenure of their predecessor.

The sharpened accountability provided by these forms of external review are limited, however, because the ombudsman will normally retain control in relation to the appointment of, terms of reference, appointment and access to the reviewer.

Judicialized Reviews

Where the administrative review options discussed above have been exhausted, the remaining form of redress is often no more than judicial review. There are strong reasons why a fully fledged judicialized review or appeal process is inappropriate for an ombudsman scheme, but arguments in favour cannot be dismissed lightly. Ultimately, the ombudsman technique relies upon a high degree of faith being placed in the skill and judgment of the office-holder who is endowed with significant discretionary powers, yet there are fewer compensatory procedures to offset the risks associated with such a concentration of power than in the standard judicial process. The ombudsman process does not allow for the cross-examination of arguments by either side to the dispute, and relies upon an interpretation of maladministration that is not supported by precedent and is therefore relatively uncertain. It is generally accepted that the ombudsman process, by itself, does not meet the standards of an independent and open tribunal required for the adjudication of civil rights under Article 6 of the European Convention on Human Rights (ECHR).[60] Such weaknesses, coupled with the reasonable claim that the ombudsman is as capable of making an error as anyone else, provide the basis for an argument that ombudsman decisions should be reviewable to an independent superior body.

The issue goes to the heart of the justification for the distinction between appeal and complaint mechanisms in the administrative justice system. According to this distinction, when a complaint involves a right to a clear legal entitlement, as Article 6 ECHR implies, there is an extremely strong argument that, if necessary, access should be made available to a court or independent tribunal. Adapting the standard legal process, complete with rights of representation and an appeal mechanism, such a tribunal should be capable of determining whether or not the right concerned has been properly acknowledged by the public authority complained against. This logic mirrors the introduction of a whole series of statutory appeal mechanisms in the UK over the last century in those areas where Parliament has chosen to establish tribunals to adjudicate over certain specified areas of the administrative state.

However, there is much case law now to suggest that public law disputes are not necessarily subject to the full procedural ramifications of Article 6, as would be applied to breaches of criminal law or adjudications of private rights.[61] A key

60 *Silver v United Kingdom* (1983) 5 EHRR 347.

61 For an analysis, see *Tomlinson and others (FC) v Birmingham City Council* SC [2010] UKSC 8.

reason for this is that not all public law disputes concern the determination of an identifiable legal right and instead frequently involve the application of significant administrative discretion. In such circumstances, the jurisprudence in this area implies that if a non-judicial complaints procedure is used, the ability to judicially review the decision of the complaints procedure will be a sufficient safeguard.[62]

Set against this broader policy context, the arguments for a fully judicialized review or appeal mechanism in the ombudsman system look weak, particularly as these would undermine the ombudsman technique. For example, a court or tribunal procedure that could reconsider all aspects of the original decision made by the ombudsman, including any factual determinations, would look rather odd. Such a process would enable the complainant to pursue their grievance against the public body in a legal forum in circumstances where Parliament had in effect identified the ombudsman as the appropriate dispute resolution body precisely because it had specifically chosen not to establish a court or tribunal route. An alternative model would be to create a fully structured version of the SPSO precedent of external review (SPSO 2009a) by another ombudsman body as discussed above. However, there is little evidence to support the creation of further ombudsman machinery of this nature and such a development might raise further difficult questions, not least of which would be the issue of connecting our currently asymmetrical ombudsman community in the UK in this way and the question of clarity of redress routes for complainants. In practice, ombudsmen in most systems already sit at the apex of the dispute resolution process outside the court and tribunal systems. Thus they receive complaints after other bodies and various forms of internal dispute resolution mechanisms at lower levels have failed to find in favour of the complainant. In effect this means that ombudsmen are the senior review mechanism and are legitimately constituted as such because, unlike most lower-level complaint-handlers, they are fully independent of the public authority complained against. Establishing a fully external review process would risk further elongating the process and undermining the authority of the ombudsman. The additional costs and delays for complainants of such an approach would be difficult to justify. While the opportunity to challenge a decision of a dispute resolution body is a manifestation of a fair legal system, equally in any administrative justice system there is a public value in achieving finality. The default mechanism in most common law systems of judicial review challenge is considered the appropriate mechanism in this context.

Judicial Review of the Ombudsman's Decision

Ombudsmen in common law jurisdictions are generally amenable to judicial review by either the complainant or the public body involved and so are

62 *Bryan v the United Kingdom* (1995) 21 EHRR 342.

legally accountable for their decisions.[63] This capacity for judicial review is not universally agreed upon within the ombudsman community, because of a concern that granting the courts the power to overrule the decisions of the ombudsman undermines its authority (Harden 2000, 221-2). However, the converse argument which has been accepted in the jurisdictions examined in this study is that judicial review allows for the rule of law to be upheld while presenting the courts with only limited opportunity to question the merits of ombudsman decision-making. Given the potential impact[64] of the discretionary power of ombudsmen and the importance of establishing the accountability of the office, granting the courts the power to judicially review the ombudsman's exercise of its powers carries with it an appropriately small risk. In order to preserve the integrity and autonomy of the scheme, however, it is important that the extent of the court's ability to review ombudsman decisions is limited. One commentator has suggested that the court should only intervene 'when an ombudsman has misinterpreted the law or has made a decision on the facts which is manifestly unfair or unreasonable' (James 1997, 184). Others have expressed strong concern that the judiciary lacks constitutional respect for alternative dispute resolution mechanisms (Jones 1988; Noble 2001). Indeed, over the years there have been some unfortunate rulings on ombudsman decisions (Birkinshaw 2010, 361-3). In the UK, a prime example is the case of the *Balchin* family, who successfully judicially reviewed three separate reports of the PO on three separate occasions before finally receiving a joint report of the LGO and the PO in their favour which recommended substantial financial redress (PHSO 2005b, 5).[65] Put favourably, the affair did reveal some flaws in the ombudsman system at that time in that the PO had not initially felt confident enough in his legislation to conduct a joint investigation with the LGO. However, the decision has been rightly subjected to much academic critique on the basis that, notwithstanding the sympathy for the complainants in the case, the degree of scrutiny on the part of the courts was excessive (Endicott 2009, 488-92). Of most concern, the rulings of the judges in the three cases, albeit using the grounds

63 For example, in the UK it was held in *R v Parliamentary Commissioner for Administration, ex parte Dyer* [1994] 1 All ER 37, that, inter alia, the Parliamentary Commissioner's decisions were susceptible to judicial review. This position is broadly mirrored in other jurisdictions, see for example in Australia, *Botany Council v The Ombudsman* (1995) 37 NSWLR 357; and in Canada, *Re Ombudsman Act* (1970) 72 WWR 176; *Re British Columbia Development Corp. v. Friedmann* (1984), 14 DLR (4th) 129.

64 An alternative argument is that as the ombudsmen do not have the legal capacity to alter an individual's rights, in either a judicial or administrative capacity, there is no reason to put in place a process for appeal or judicial review (Endicott 2009, 488). In the view of the authors, this presents an excessively narrow view of the role of judicial review and underestimates the impact of the ombudsman's work.

65 *R v Parliamentary Commissioner for Administration, ex p Balchin* [1997] JPL 917; *R v Parliamentary Commissioner for Administration, ex p Balchin (No 2)* (2000) 79 P&CR 157; *R v Parliamentary Commissioner for Administration, ex p Balchin (No 3)* [2002] EWHC 1876.

of relevant considerations and reasons, went to the heart of the ombudsman's discretionary interpretation of the maladministration test.

Yet although the courts have occasionally appeared to stretch their powers of scrutiny a little too far, recent case law on the public sector ombudsmen demonstrates a healthy recognition of the ombudsman's sphere of influence.[66] Most importantly, in contradistinction to the *Balchin* cases, there are a series of judicial statements to the effect that 'the Ombudsman and not the court is the arbiter of what constitutes maladministration'.[67] Generally, in the few cases that an ombudsman has lost in the courts, the ruling has been based on a failure of the ombudsman to interpret statutory law correctly. For instance, in *Argyll*[68] the SPSO's finding that the local authority involved had not met its obligations under section 1 of the Community Care and Health (Scotland) Act 2002 was the basis for its finding of maladministration. The Court of Session disagreed with the SPSO's interpretation of the Act and accordingly quashed her report. In a case involving the Health Service Ombudsman (HSO), the Court of Appeal ruled that the ombudsman had misinterpreted her powers under the Health Services Commissioners (Amendment) Act 1996 by extending her investigation beyond the terms of the original complaint and, as a result, the court quashed her report.[69] The judgments in these cases involved the direct interpretation of statute and are thus closely aligned to the court's legitimate sphere of activity in judicial review. Crucially, they do not represent a misunderstanding of the ombudsman's powers to interpret and apply the test of maladministration.

Arguably the courts have sometimes been too willing to impose procedural constraints on the ombudsman derived from the 'adversarial template', which are inappropriate for the ombudsman model (Harlow and Rawlings 2009, 482).[70] In analysing the ombudsman's statutory powers, the courts have sometimes applied questionable interpretations to the ombudsman's discretion to conduct

---

66 E.g. *R v Local Commissioner for Administration, ex parte Liverpool City Council* [2001] 1 All ER 462; *Stephen Atwood v The Health Service Commissioner* [2008] EWHC 2315 (Admin); *Bradley and others v Secretary of State for Work and Pensions Appeal* [2008] EWCA Civ 36, [2009] QB 114. In *Bradley* it was held, *inter alia*, that it had been irrational for the Secretary of State to reject the ombudsman's finding of maladministration. This case has been applied in *R (on the application of Equitable Members Action Group) v HM Treasury and others* [2009] EWHC 2495 (Admin).

67 *R (Doy) v Local Commissioner for Administration* [2001] EWHC Admin 361, 16. See also *R v Parliamentary Commissioner for Administration, ex p Dyer* [1994] 1 WLR 621.

68 *Argyll and Bute Council, Re Judicial Review of a Decision of the Scottish Public Services Ombudsman* [2007] CSOH 168.

69 *Cavanagh and others v Health Services Commissioner* [2005] EWCA Civ 1578.

70 Harlow and Rawlings (2009) cite *R v Local Commissioner for Administration, ex p. Bradford MCC* [1979] QB 287. *R v Local Commissioner for Administration, ex p. Eastleigh Borough Council* [1988] QB 855 and *R v Commissioner for Local Administration, ex parte Croydon London BC* [1989] 1 All ER 1033 in support of this critique.

investigations, but the most recent case on the issue has demonstrated a willingness to recognise that there are limits to the application of standards of procedural fairness to the ombudsman's work.[71] Judicial deference towards the ombudsmen is reflected in the recent success rate for leave applications for judicial review against ombudsmen in the UK. The PHSO reported that of seven applications six had failed to obtain permission to proceed, while a further one remained to be decided (PHSO 2009, 39). In the same year, the LGO reported for 2008-09 that of nine actions brought none had been granted permission, albeit four were outstanding at that time (LGO 2009, 23). A similar trend can be identified from previous years. Such figures are indicative of a very low turnover of cases against the ombudsman actually reaching the Administrative Court.

Judicial review remains an option by which the ombudsman's decision's can be scrutinized, but it is not an appeal process and has a low success rate. The law in other countries has developed in a similar manner.[72] Judicial review provides some accountability of individual decisions but there is a more general deterrent impact implied by the possibility of judicial review challenge. Indications of a potential judicial review challenge place very real pressure on ombudsmen and their staff to double check the legality of their actions. But where ombudsmen operate within the law, judicial intervention is unlikely to reach the discretionary interpretations ombudsmen deploy, and it rarely provides analysis of the ombudsman's contribution to promoting good administration.

Corporate Governance

Strong corporate governance arrangements within an organization provide two important services relevant to this chapter. Firstly, such arrangements better enable ombudsmen to demonstrate independence and autonomy. Secondly, while internal scrutiny mechanisms cannot be relied upon by themselves to satisfy wider public demands for the accountability, they do provide a measure of effective oversight.

Many offices today have very clear lines of internal accountability, although some ombudsman bodies' expectations of corporate governance may be shaped by their relatively small size. Thus, for instance, all of the major UK ombudsman offices have audit committees, which are chaired by an external independent person and, with the exception of the NIO office, have at least 50 per cent independent membership. The PHSO has taken this model slightly further and established in addition an advisory board to act as a 'critical friend', providing particular advice on the 'purpose, vision and values [of the organization]; strategic direction, and planning; accountability to stakeholders, including stewardship of public funds; and

71 *Kay v Health Service Commissioner* [2009] EWCA Civ 732.

72 See for example in Australia, *Botany Council v The Ombudsman* (1995) 37 NSWLR 357; and in Canada, *Re Ombudsman Act* (1970) 72 WWR 176; *Re British Columbia Development Corp. v. Friedmann* (1984), 14 DLR (4th) 129.

internal control and risk management arrangements' (PHSO 2010).[73] The importance of such arrangements lies in the ongoing nature of such scrutiny and its capacity to provide prospective as well as retrospective guidance to the ombudsman.

The most obvious external evidence of the ombudsman's corporate governance arrangements is the production of an annual report and, with most offices, three to five-year strategic or corporate plans complete with annual updated business plans. The means by which these documents feed into the external process of scrutiny forms a vital part of the technique employed by ombudsman schemes to establish accountability.

Reports

The statutory requirement to submit an annual report is the normal minimum accountability mechanism for ombudsmen (see Appendix 2). The usual format is that there is a review of the year, with some statistics on the number of complaints/inquiries with various outcomes and examples from reported cases. There will be material on staffing/organization/governance and usually some degree of financial reporting. The content and manner of presentation in an annual report may be affected by other reports which an ombudsman produces and styles will differ considerably depending on the nature of the office's jurisdiction. Most ombudsman schemes do make available a significant amount of basic information regarding the operation of the office. In keeping with the New Public Management (NPM) reforms referred to in Chapter 3,[74] the annual and other reports demonstrate much evidence of a developed performance-target/transparency public services culture.

The annual reports of the LGO, for example, formerly listed all investigation reports, giving the body investigated, the topic and the outcome. Annual reports today, however, tend to be more focused, thematic and accessible, and details on individual investigations are now generally posted separately on the LGO's website, along with significant other items of information, such as the annual reviews of each local authority, regular customer survey reports and the minutes of their monthly meetings. As with most UK ombudsmen, the LGO produces three-year corporate plans and an annual business plan. These set goals and targets, and performance against these targets is measured. Measuring the work of the ombudsman against a range of standards is extremely beneficial and does contribute towards openness and transparency, and helps inform the process of scrutiny.

To an extent, the increasingly strategic features of annual reports demonstrate greater confidence by the ombudsman enterprise to reflect upon their practice, analyse the challenges presented and advocate future organizational aspirations. In terms of

73 Dr Tony Wright was elected to Parliament in 1992 and became chair of the Public Administration Select Committee in 1999. He stood down as an MP prior to the May 2010 general election and was appointed by Ann Abraham (PHSO) as a member of the Advisory Board to commence from 1 June 2010 (PHSO press release,10/09, 13 May 2010).

74 See pp. 76-7.

the typology of administrative justice presented in Chapter 3 (Figure 3.1), the annual reports reflect the ways in which ombudsman authorities construct their own visions of how their 'putting it right' statutory remit relates to the administration 'getting it right', and how these activities are located in the wider 'setting it right' framework. The annual and other reports provide the raw information which contributes to the accountability of ombudsmen bodies, but they also provide the opportunity for the ombudsmen themselves to proactively identify and define their roles and relationships. There is an inherent tension here between these two functions. Where the ombudsman office places inappropriate emphasis on the latter there is a danger that the required accuracy and transparency of the former are compromised.

Scrutiny through Parliamentary Committees

The capacity for Parliament to scrutinize the work of the ombudsman is one of the most important reasons for linking the ombudsman to Parliament. Such oversight is ordinarily conducted through a select committee, with one of two dominant solutions being adopted: either a specific committee is established which has the ombudsman within its remit; or one or more parliamentary committees engage with ombudsman issues in an irregular fashion, largely driven by events (see Appendix 6).

A practical issue facing all Parliaments is that time, capacity and resource are limited. In the past, the UK Parliament had a permanent committee in place to review only the work of the ombudsmen.[75] The more common solution now is to have a committee oversee the work of a range of watchdog bodies; another is to have a committee covering linked administration-related topics, as with the New Zealand two-committee solution referred to earlier in this chapter[76] or the Public Administration Select Committee (PASC) in the Westminster Parliament.

Not all parliamentary arrangements formally dedicate the work of one committee to overseeing the ombudsman. In the absence of formal arrangements, however, sometimes a practice or convention can evolve whereby one committee tends to consider the ombudsman's annual report. The Scottish Parliament provides an example of this practice, where the local government committee examines the SPSO's annual report, an option at least consistent with the fact that complaints against local government produce the SPSO's largest caseload.

Not all ombudsmen in the common law world have a regular relationship with any one parliamentary committee. In such circumstances an ombudsman is required to report to Parliament, with further scrutiny left largely to the household exigencies of the House and select committees. For example, the Welsh Assembly's Standing

75 The PHSO formerly had its own dedicated committee from 1967 until 1997 when the Parliamentary Commissioner for Administration Select Committee and Public Service Select Committee were merged to form the Public Administration Select Committee (PASC) of the House of Commons.

76 See pp. 163-4 above.

Orders prescribe that the PSOW's annual report is considered in a plenary session.[77] Any subsequent review of the PSOW's work is undertaken on an *ad hoc* basis.

One justification for not creating a mandatory link between the ombudsman and a specific select committee is that this arrangement encourages the ombudsman to be seen as a resource to be used by the whole House. Any committee could, as part of any investigation it is undertaking, request an appearance. In Scotland, the SPSO annually gives evidence to the local government committee, but has also appeared before other committees to brief them.[78]

Linking an ombudsman with a dedicated committee does not necessarily preclude working additionally with other committees but without a formal attachment to a specified committee oversight of the ombudsman is likely to suffer. For instance, since devolution in both Northern Ireland and Wales, there have been very few committee hearings or investigations which have actually scrutinized the reports and work of the NIO or PSOW respectively.[79] A further drawback is that Parliament will be less able or willing to respond to requests for support in the ombudsman's dealings with the executive, thus weakening the ombudsman's authority. A clear example of the problems associated with operating without the active support of an elected body is the LGO in England.

The peculiar problem of the LGO in England is that local government jurisdiction is not within the direct responsibility of Parliament. By contrast, many other ombudsmen schemes outside England include it alongside central/state government departments and agencies. The accepted orthodoxy relating to the LGO scheme in England was that local government had its own elected representatives, and therefore it would be constitutionally inappropriate for the Westminster Parliament to oversee the LGO. This was reflected at the time when the LGOs in England and Wales were created by having representative bodies to oversee their work, receive reports and consider budgets. This solution was almost universally considered to be unsuccessful (Kirkham 2005a, 389) and the representative bodies were abolished in 1989.[80] The LGO has given evidence to a

77 Welsh Assembly, Standing Order 7.61 (National Assembly for Wales 2010).

78 For example, the evidence given by Professor Alice Brown (the first SPSO) to the Scottish Parliament's Justice Committee on the Scottish Human Rights Commissioner Bill (SPSO 2005a). The SPSO has given evidence to the Scottish Parliament on a regular basis compared to other ombudsmen, though in her valedictory evidence to Parliament she expressed the opinion that 'Parliament has not engaged with us as positively and effectively as it could have' (Brown 2009a, col. 1697).

79 In Northern Ireland committees have only rarely picked up on the work of the ombudsman, although see COFMDFM (2010). In Wales, the ombudsman appeared before the Local Government and Public Services Committee to comment on the first six months of the office (LGPSC 2006, 23-7). The PSOW does attend the Finance Committee annually but these sessions do not scrutinize the office's reports.

80 Local Government Act 1974, s.24, as repealed by the Local Government and Housing Act 1989, s.25(1).

select committee on a few occasions,[81] but alternative arrangements to replace the representative body have not materialized. It is probably no coincidence that of all the ombudsman schemes in Ireland, the UK, Australia and New Zealand, the LGO scheme in England is the only one that has ever experienced a significant problem in achieving the implementation of its recommendations.[82] Recent annual reports of the LGO now note a much improved success rate but such rejections of LGO recommendations still occur regularly and attract much criticism from dissatisfied users of the service.[83]

Arguably, an active oversight of the LGO in England by Parliament would be a positive step forward. The LGOs themselves accept that such a source of accountability would help, and successfully lobbied for a legislative amendment which places a duty on them to submit their annual report to Parliament.[84] This arrangement, though, does little to advance the goal of accountability in the absence of active scrutiny on the part of Parliament. The argument that the autonomy of local government might be compromised by granting Parliament oversight responsibility has always lacked real substance.[85] Other than individual investigations being reviewed by Parliament, it is difficult to identify the constitutional risk at stake. Parliamentary intervention in specific ombudsman investigations could be prohibited in legislation,[86] and it could also be confirmed in statute that the purpose of undertaking general reviews of the reports of the LGO would be to scrutinize the operational effectiveness of the LGO, not local authorities.

Assessing Parliamentary Scrutiny

A basic task for all select committees in fulfilling the scrutiny function is to review the annual reports of the ombudsman, a process which varies in extent and intensity across the different ombudsman schemes. This will ordinarily involve a session in which the ombudsman attends and answers questions, having previously been given the opportunity to submit written evidence and/or provide written responses

81 For example, the then chairman of the Commission for Local Administration in England, Edward Osmotherly, gave evidence to PASC during its Review of Public Sector Ombudsmen in England (PASC 2000). In 2005, all three LGOs gave evidence to the Office of the Deputy Prime Minister: Housing, Planning, Local Government and the Regions Committee on the Role and Effectiveness of the Local Government Ombudsmen for England: see ODPM Select Committee (2005, ev 1, 29).

82 See Chapter 4, p. 119, n.92.

83 See Chapter 1, p. 5 n.5

84 Local Government Act 1974, s.23A(3A), inserted by the Local Government and Public Involvement in Health Act 2007, s.170(1), (5).

85 '[T]he benefits in terms of improving the accountability of the office of the LGO, and enhancing its aura of independence from local government, outweigh the need to uphold the autonomy of local government' (Kirkham 2005a, 390).

86 For example, as in the Ombudsman Act 1972 (South Australia), s.31(2).

to pre-hearing requests of the committee. On occasion, a second attendance of the ombudsman will also be required at a different time of the year to facilitate a wider review of the office.[87] At a minimum the purpose of such sessions is to challenge the information in the report, the general performance of the ombudsman and to request more information if necessary. Even where the level of scrutiny in such sessions is weak, formally requiring ombudsmen to attend Parliament creates a pressure on ombudsmen which serves to focus decision-making. The Welsh solution of debating the ombudsman's annual report in a plenary session of the Assembly[88] has the obvious advantage of engaging the whole Assembly in the review process; but it does not enable cross-examination of the ombudsman and arguably lacks the more detailed, analytical scrutiny typically associated with the work of select committees.

Where committees do conduct a review process, the minimum standard is to see whether they are timely and 'apparently satisfactory'[89] according to such standards of readability, consistency, quality and quantity of information, and relevance to past agreed and stated objectives (e.g. Department of the Prime Minister and Cabinet 2009, 3). More profoundly, parliamentary scrutiny requires an evaluation of whether the ombudsman is achieving its performance standards, delivering an acceptable service and whether there are any underlying issues which need to be addressed. The parliamentary forum, unlike the courts, can consider the wider range of roles that the ombudsman can provide and can advise the ombudsman as to what roles it would like it to perform, emphasize or draw back from. No report or opinion offered by the committee binds the ombudsman, but clearly the public process of responding to parliamentary interrogation provides the ombudsman with the opportunity to focus on the task of justifying and explaining operational activities and the strategic choices available.

However, the breadth and depth of parliamentary scrutiny is dependent upon the time allocated to it along with the intellectual, financial and administrative resources of parliamentarians (Norton 2004, 796-8). Given the range of other competing objectives facing Parliament, even where a committee is assigned the specific responsibility to oversee the work of the ombudsman, it cannot be guaranteed that the members will have the requisite degree of knowledge to undertake properly the scrutiny function.

As identified earlier, there has never been a consistent practice of overseeing the work of the LGO in England in Parliament. The last occasion that the select committee responsible for local government has undertaken a review of the LGO was in 2005 (ODPM Select Committee 2005). The exact motivation for conducting this review was unclear, although it was undertaken during a period in which the prospect of major reform to the ombudsman system in England had been raised

87 For example, in Queensland, Australia.

88 Welsh Assembly, Standing Order Standing Order 7.61: see National Assembly for Wales (2010).

89 E.g. Australian Senate's Finance and Public Administration Committee, Senate Standing Order 25(20)(a-g).

by the Collcutt Review (Collcutt and Hourihan 2000)[90] and a number of criticisms about the ombudsman had been received from complainants. The committee held a one-off evidence session and its report consisted mainly of the oral and written evidence, together with a single recommendation.[91] It is unclear exactly what was achieved by this process. No firm conclusions were drawn by the committee as to the operational performance of the LGO and the evidence session itself was riddled with questions which revealed a lack of knowledge amongst the members of the committee about the LGO scheme. This does raise concerns about the ability of informal arrangements to scrutinize the work of ombudsmen effectively.[92]

Connecting the ombudsman to a specific committee does at least provide the framework within which a long-term programme of scrutiny and build-up of expertise can be developed. A particularly effective example of scrutiny is provided by PASC in its scrutiny of the PHSO. In several guises there has been a dedicated select committee scrutinizing the work of the PO and HSO for over 40 years. This longevity has contributed to the effectiveness of the PO and HSO ombudsman schemes. An annual meeting to consider the annual report had been the usual practice for the PHSO and PASC, but in recent years there have been more frequent appearances before the committee. It is largely through these extra appearances and the reports that tend to accompany them that Parliament makes the best use of the wider knowledge and analysis that can be obtained from the work of the ombudsman.

The most dramatic examples of PASC using ombudsman reports to scrutinize government decisions have been where a 'special report' has been laid before Parliament in response to a departmental failure to accept a PHSO's report.[93] Parliament's consideration of these reports demonstrates its ability simultaneously to support the work of the ombudsman and scrutinize it. Thus the input of PASC in favour of the PHSO is not made as a result of a passive acceptance of the ombudsman's argument, but is a position reached by the committee after its own inquiry and deliberation.

> We cannot (and would not expect to) replicate the Ombudsman's investigations, and we are confident in the evidence she assembles, which is also revealed to the Government. This does not mean that we automatically accept her findings without making our own assessment of the Ombudsman's report, the

---

90 See Chapter 3, pp. 82-3.

91 The committee recommended that the Office of the Deputy Prime Minister (ODPM) publish a clear summary of what progress has been made in addressing the recommendations contained in the LGO's review report of its legislation (ODPM Select Committee 2005, 3).

92 This weakness has been noted in the Victorian state Parliament in Australia, where it has been recommended that a specific select committee be established to scrutinize the reports of the ombudsman (PAEC 2006, 75-7).

93 Parliamentary Commissioner Act 1967, s.10(3).

> Government's response and the other evidence available. Our approach is to test the Ombudsman's findings thoroughly. (PASC 2006, 26, para. 61)

This practice illustrates a more far-reaching accountability point, that the 'special report' framework invites PASC to operate as a further review mechanism. As we have seen,[94] the judicial consideration of the substantive merits of ombudsman determinations is in opposition to the ombudsman model. However, the special report process allows a Parliamentary Select Committee to cast a merits-based opinion on both the findings and the recommendations of the PHSO. This also provides the public authority under investigation with an opportunity to defend its position. PASC operates in effect as a safeguard against an overactive ombudsman coming to unacceptable interpretations of its powers. Given that only six special reports have ever been issued in just over 40 years of the office of the PO,[95] and on all occasions the relevant committee has sided with the ombudsman, the utility of the process in terms of promoting accountability is arguable. But in the UK parliamentary system the committee is almost always weighted in favour of the government in terms of membership. Hence ombudsmen will not issue special reports lightly and will always work very hard to ensure that their arguments are factually accurate and logically sustainable. The true impact of the section 10(3) special report goes further than the individual occasions that have been considered this way. The ombudsmen's knowledge that potentially they will have to defend their reports in a detailed committee investigation provides a real safeguard against coming to any ill-defended judgments in writing such reports.

Similar procedures to deal with reports that have been rejected by the public authority are available in other ombudsman schemes, such as the PSOW and the SPSO.[96] The strength of these relatively new arrangements has yet to be fully tested. Outside the PO and HSO Parliamentary Ombudsman schemes in the UK, the level of real scrutiny undertaken by Parliament is mixed. Indeed, even with the PO and HSO schemes there is a sense that the ombudsman has to work hard to obtain the attention of the select committee.

Parliamentary scrutiny normally operates more as a form of latent background pressure than an active interrogator. Parliamentary time should be organized to ensure that a select committee is given the specific minimum responsibility to receive and consider evidence from the ombudsman annually. The fact that a number of the smaller jurisdictions reviewed in this study achieve this standard, either through a general officers of Parliament committee or a subject committee, demonstrates that this can be done. But current practice suggests that the increasing competition for parliamentary time and the level of relevant expertise, interest and knowledge possessed by parliamentarians remain restraints on the scrutiny

94 See pp. 173-7 above.

95 PO (1978, 1995); PHSO (2005a, 2006a, 2009b, 2009d).

96 Respectively, the Public Services Ombudsman (Wales) Act 2005, ss.22-4, and the Scottish Public Services Ombudsman Act 2002, s.16.

process. Rather than assuming that Parliament can perform the accountability function by itself, therefore, other potential solutions should be looked at.

Reviews

One approach that has been used sporadically in the past is to subject ombudsman offices to an external review, with the final report then considered by Parliament and/or the executive. The terms of reference tend to go much further than the standard parliamentary review by requiring a more comprehensive assessment of the ombudsman service. Such wide-ranging reviews have, on occasion, been conducted by Parliaments (e.g. Supported Bodies Committee 2009), but due to the scale of the project are rare even within the larger ombudsman schemes.

There are a couple of examples of regular reviews which are specified in legislation, for example Queensland's five-year strategic review.[97] The government, through the Governor, appoints the reviewer and determines the terms of reference, and the parliamentary committee is consulted on these issues. The report is then submitted to Parliament for its consideration. A further example is contained in the LGO scheme. Here the LGO conducts a three-year review of the relevant legislation[98] and its operation, which is reported to the most relevant government department (e.g. LGO 2009a). The review is not autonomous, however, and is very limited in its remit.

With most ombudsman schemes, however, external reviews are commissioned on an *ad hoc* basis as required. In Scotland and Wales, the respective governments commissioned reviews following the introduction of devolution. This development provided an opportunity to reconsider existing arrangements and led to the rationalization of ombudsman schemes in both countries.[99] In 2000 the Cabinet Office undertook a review of the public sector ombudsmen in England, following the requests of the PHSO and LGO presented to ministers in October 1998 (Collcutt and Hourihan 2000, Annex A). Similarly the NIO sought the review commissioned by the Office of the First Minister and Deputy First Minister (OFMDFM 2004). In 2006 concerns in Scotland about the accountability and governance of parliamentary officers and about the burden of external scrutiny through regulation, audit, inspection and complaint-handling led to a series of reviews which directly and indirectly commented on the work of the ombudsman (Finance Committee 2006; Crerar 2007; Sinclair 2008; Supported Bodies Committee 2009; Mullen 2009). The LGO was also subject to two external reviews in the 1990s (DoE 1995; DoE 1996).[100]

97 Ombudsman Act 2001 (Queensland), ss.82-5.

98 Local Government Act 1974, Part III.

99 See Chapter 3, pp. 83-4.

100 Such *ad hoc* reviews occur in Australia as well, e.g. the Victorian Ombudsman was reviewed by PricewaterhouseCoopers in 2002 (PAEC 2006, 79).

Although there have been uncertainties surrounding external review processes relating to their cost, funding responsibility and the appointment process of the reviewer, such reviews have helped in raising the profile of the ombudsman and the quality of debate. Review teams will generally have more time and intellectual resources to provide more thorough analysis than parliamentary committees. In the Queensland model, for instance, the five-yearly review has added substantially to the quality of Parliament's subsequent investigation of the ombudsman through the select committee process (LCARC 2006). In addition, although neither the LGO reviews in the 1990s nor the Colcutt Review in 2000 have been implemented in full, both helped foster debate on the ombudsman and led to a measure of reform.

Given the practical difficulties of parliamentary scrutiny discussed above, the judicious use of external review to help inform and invigorate parliamentary examination could be an extremely useful combination. Making this a *statutory* requirement to occur within a set time period, as in the Queensland model, would be particularly useful for those schemes that do not at present enjoy a strong or reliable relationship with Parliament.

In the UK, for instance, with ombudsmen being appointed for a fixed term, there is an argument for requiring a review at the midway point of every period of tenure. This would enable a real check to be made on progress against performance targets as outlined in a prior strategic plan produced by the ombudsman and ideally vetted by Parliament.

Oversight by Experts

There is an argument that for the proper scrutiny of unelected accountability institutions we need to look for internally developed modes of accountability (Vibert 2007). For instance, the legal system in the UK contains methodical in-built mechanisms for verifying the quality of judicial decision-making, such as a transparent appeal process and the use of legal method based on internally developed tests, the application of which is capable of outside scrutiny. By such techniques the legal profession itself maintains quality control of the use of judicial power, reducing any need for conspicuous oversight by Parliament or the executive. It cannot be argued, however, that the ombudsman community is currently capable of developing the same degree of internally generated professional oversight. For instance, there is no agreed career route that an individual must follow before being appointed to the post of ombudsman; nor are ombudsman staff currently expected to take any particular professional qualifications.[101] At present, therefore, the framework does not exist within the ombudsman enterprise to provide full assurance of the work of the ombudsmen. However, ombudsman associations such as the BIOA have established

101 Accreditation is currently being explored by the BIOA (2010, 7), while in a direct response to the lack of organized external training for ombudsman staff the Ontario Ombudsman office has recently launched a training programme on investigatory skills (Jones 2009).

significant standards of membership and protected ombudsmen's independent status in addition to their contribution in fostering debate and exchanging ideas.

A further source of expertise that could, and indeed should, become a source of considered oversight is the constitutional body set up to oversee the administrative justice sector in the UK – the Administrative Justice and Tribunals Council (AJTC), further explored in Chapter 7 – and the Administrative Review Council in Australia. If the AJTC can indeed become the 'hub of the wheel' of the wider administrative justice system,[102] it will be in a favoured position to consider and oversee the way in which the ombudsman enterprise is located within that system. The extent to which the AJTC can monitor the work of the PHSO, however, is compromised by that post-holder's membership of the council.

Other Sources of Accountability

Not only are ombudsmen subject to financial audit, as with most public bodies, they are also ordinarily subject to freedom of information legislation. This legislation has helped encourage the added transparency ombudsmen demonstrate today through their websites in particular. Freedom of information legislation also means that ombudsman investigations can potentially be opened up and the documents which were used to inform their investigations subject to wider scrutiny.

Conclusion

What are we to make of the existing accountability arrangements that should secure the legitimacy of the ombudsman enterprise? Despite some residuary concerns, a key component to the preservation of the constitutional status, independence and accountability of the ombudsman is making appropriate use of Parliament. Public sector ombudsman schemes that are not set up this way can struggle to obtain the external verification of their work required to offset the criticisms that they are unaccountable and biased. In this respect, the officer of Parliament model is a sound one for the ombudsman institution. Importantly, the Parliamentary Ombudsman model is not one of subservience; it is instead a sophisticated evolution of the classic tripartite separation of powers formation of the liberal democratic constitution which safeguards the ombudsman's autonomy and includes some essential conditions about the ombudsman's appointment and freedom to operate.

A clear advantage of the Parliamentary Ombudsman model is that Parliaments can provide ombudsman schemes with the most powerful form of accountability. The difficulty with this solution, however, lies in the willingness or capacity of Parliaments to perform this role and the somewhat contradictory need for Parliament to provide support to the ombudsman in its dealings with the executive. The ideal

102 See Chapter 3, pp. 78-9. This may not be possible if the AJTC is abolished, as was announced just as this book was finalised. See Preface, p. xiii, and also pp. 237-8.

is for a specific parliamentary committee to have a dedicated role in scrutinizing the work of the ombudsman and other appropriate accountability institutions. A joint committee of both Houses (e.g. the Constitutional Committee) or some other arrangement is required to preclude government domination of such a committee. There are additional benefits in establishing a separate process to deal with the sponsorship issues of the office. Evidence from around the world also suggests that compensating provisions need to be in place to ensure that the committee retains suitable expertise to undertake effective scrutiny. A particular danger here is that the Parliament/ombudsman relationship is overly dependent on the personalities involved, in particular the chair of the relevant select committee (Barbour 2005, 6).

It is unlikely that all legislatures will be able to adapt their arrangements and practices to guarantee the mixture of regular 'light touch' and periodic in-depth review required to call the ombudsman to account in full. Given the concerns surrounding the active engagement of many democratic assemblies with their ombudsmen, other mechanisms are vital to legitimate the ombudsman enterprise: for example, the procedures for dealing with disputes involving the ombudsman's findings and recommendations – namely judicial review, internal reviews and, where such mechanisms are in place, external reviews and parliamentary reviews of ombudsman reports that a public authority refuses to implement in full. Within the environment of unelected institutions other compensating accountability provisions deserve consideration as part of the overall approach. Thus the requirement for ombudsmen to operate within externally verified freedom of information and audit regimes, as well as its own professionally imposed set of standards, adds a significant layer of assurance. Regular independent reviews of the ombudsmen should also help to address the constraints of Parliament, and arguably the process by which such reviews are staged needs to be placed on a statutory footing.

Differences in design and effective implementation mean that ensuring the accountability of the ombudsman is a continuing concern. Subject to certain exceptions, the accountability arrangements for the various public sector ombudsmen that operate in the UK, Ireland, Australia and New Zealand achieve most minimum standards on accountability; but further improvements could be made. Given that the role of the ombudsman is to address grievances, contribute to the improvement of public services and generally add to the transparency of government, this is an ironic conclusion. Yet as much as anything else it is a conclusion that is indicative of the current state of constitutional development, one that is still learning to come to terms with its evolution from a traditional focus on parliamentary democracy to one much better equipped to take advantage of and control the input of unelected accountability institutions.

Chapter 7
Relationships, Networks and the Administrative Justice System

Introduction

The concept of 'setting it right', as developed in Chapter 3,[1] requires more of ombudsmen than they are rendered accountable for their actions. Properly established, the ombudsman enterprise operates within a wider constitutional and administrative justice framework. Thus, even though the ombudsman design encompasses certain fundamental specialities that mark out a distinct territory within which it is required to operate, there are a series of inevitable overlaps between its functions and those of other institutions. A fully effective system, in both constitutional and administrative justice terms, will be one that manages, rationalizes and understands those overlaps in a way that optimizes capacity and keeps duplication of effort to a minimum. To achieve this result, ombudsmen must be enabled to maintain a series of relationships with other parts of the constitutional order. Analysing this issue is the focus of this chapter.

The chapter explores four key sets of relationships that the ombudsman is required to foster, those with: complainants; the broader administrative justice system; other accountability institutions; and last, but most definitely not least, the leading players in the constitutional system – the executive, Parliament and the courts.

Setting it Right for Complainants

Steering a Route through the Modern Administrative Justice System

Above everything else, the key rationale for the ombudsman is to provide a meaningful service to complainants. This understanding is reflected in a recurring theme of this book: the increasing importance attached to focusing on the needs and interests of the individual complainant within not just the ombudsman community, but the administrative justice system as a whole. This trend is evident in the theoretical and policy-making debates surrounding administrative justice (see Chapter 3) and the approach of the ombudsman community towards complaint-handling (see Chapter 4). Yet there is much research to suggest that the goals

1 See pp. 55-7, 70-6 and Figure 3.1.

aspired to are a long way from being fully realized (e.g. NAO 2005; Dunleavy *et al* 2010).

The issue of the complainant's ability to access the administrative justice system and navigate their way around it in order to obtain the appropriate resolution of their grievance is very much complicated by the different redress mechanisms available. The resultant complex administrative justice map owes more to *ad hoc* development than systemic thinking and has been subject to strong criticism. The basic distinction between appeals and complaints, for example, is arguably one which bears little resemblance to the thinking and desires of aggrieved citizens who will generally want their matter reconsidered in all respects (Dunleavy *et al* 2010, 424-9). But the existence of this distinction is not accidental; it is based on a number of sound reasons. The administrative state is reliant upon enormous reserves of discretionary decision-making power properly held by and/or accountable to elected representatives, not judicial fora. Whilst it may be appropriate on occasion to shape that discretion by way of prescribed rules capable of judicial application in statutory appeal routes, this will not always be the most sensible way to construct government.[2] If all discretionary executive decision-making was subject to possible substitution by a grievance panel this would undermine the basic constitutional model of democratic decision-making power. By contrast, the theoretical strength of judicial review and the ombudsman technique is that they respect the discretionary executive authority of public bodies by creating clear boundaries on the legitimate oversight role of dispute resolution in those areas where executive discretion is required. Save *in extremis*, it is not the role of either High Court judges or the ombudsman to step into the shoes of the decision-maker: intervention has to be justified on the grounds of some form of procedural error or misinterpretation of powers. Complaints systems generally are based upon the same premise.

A further generic influence setting the scene in the administrative justice system is the modern policy to resolve grievances at a level near the cause of the dispute. This trend pre-dates[3] *Transforming Public Services* (DCA 2004), but within that White Paper we see perhaps the strongest political indication yet of the emphasis to be placed on the users of the administrative justice system and the refocusing of administrative justice efforts. The philosophy underpinning that report is encapsulated by the idea of proportionate dispute resolution (PDR). The aims of PDR are to produce a clearer legal framework and to enable the administration to make better decisions with clearer explanations. The public's understanding of their rights and responsibilities, and signposting to appropriate

2 'Elimination of all discretionary power is both impossible and undesirable … The need is to eliminate unnecessary discretionary power and to discover more successful ways to confine, to structure and to check necessary discretionary power' (Davis 1971, 42).

3 For example, see Lord Woolf's recommendations that the civil justice system needed to be more responsive to the needs of litigants in terms of judicial case management of appropriate procedures (LCD 1995; LCD 1996).

sources of advice, should also be improved. In particular the aim is to facilitate early and appropriate advice and assistance where needed, so that problems can be resolved preventively rather than escalating into formal proceedings. The core aim of PDR is to promote the 'development of a range of tailored dispute resolution services' to resolve disputes fairly and efficiently without recourse to the formality of courts and tribunals; the latter being freed up to focus on those cases where formal hearings are necessary (DCA 2004, para. 2.3).

This staged approach can be summarized as seeking to *prevent*, *reduce* and *resolve* disputes, in which resolution should take the form of the method best suited to deal with the characteristics of the dispute, or 'fitting the forum to the fuss'.[4] Moreover, the presumption is that a hearing, whether before a court or tribunal, would be the method of last resort unless it was especially appropriate. This logic points towards a variety of redress mechanisms at different levels of the administrative justice system.

Finally, to add to the complexity of the situation, against the apparently inexorable trend towards complaints systems that are claimed to be more user-friendly there remains the traditional fairness demand for appeal and review mechanisms capable of rectifying errors within the administrative justice system (Le Sueur 2007).

All of these underlying pressures on the administrative justice system are defensible but the result is a complex network of redress mechanisms. Two questions arise: firstly, the ability of users to access and comprehend the system; secondly, the capacity of the system to deal with the overlaps between the different players in the administrative justice system.

Promoting User Access and Comprehension of the Administrative Justice System

In terms of promoting PDR, progress within the UK administrative justice system has so far been uncertain and indeed an Administrative Justice and Tribunals Council (AJTC) survey indicated some professional scepticism about its scope (Thompson 2010, 508). The idea of PDR has been elaborated upon further in the Law Commission's report on housing disputes (Law Commission 2008b). In particular, in dealing with advice and assistance, the concept of 'triage plus' was developed. It consists of three elements:

1. signposting: initial diagnosis and referral;
2. intelligence-gathering and oversight;
3. feedback (Law Commission 2008a, para 3.1).

These elements are all clearly recognizable aspects of the practice of ombudsmen as presented in this monograph, and correspond broadly to the *reduce* and *resolve* elements of PDR. As argued in Chapter 5, the oversight and feedback services

4 See Chapter 3, p. 78, n.23.

are strong suits of the ombudsman, especially when compared to other parts of the administrative justice system. Ombudsmen have expanded their activity through wider dissemination and a more structured approach towards reporting generalizable lessons about particular service areas or issues, or more general administrative good practice guidance. Feedback is, therefore, an important part of what ombudsmen do, and indeed in the housing context the Law Commission noted that the Local Government Ombudsman (LGO) places considerable importance on feeding back on housing complaints to local authorities (Law Commission 2008b, para. 3.75).

The signposting service aspect of the triage plus model, however, raises a more difficult challenge for the ombudsman enterprise. An initial diagnosis of the complainant's grievance is required in order to redirect, or push, the cases through the assessment process to determine if it is within jurisdiction and susceptible to the ombudsman's methods of resolution. As identified in Chapter 4 though, this is not straightforward work for the ombudsmen because complainants often mistakenly approach the ombudsmen through a lack of understanding of their remit. From the ombudsman's perspective, there is a positive aspect to this situation for, as the Law Commission suggests, the advisory role performed by a body in the triage plus model allows that body to 'educate and inform the wider community about the range of ways disputes in the housing sector can be resolved' (Law Commission 2008b, para. 3.16). In addition, ombudsmen should have a more strategic view of the system informed by the breadth of their remit. Their casework is also a source of more detailed information about the actual operation of a reasonable sample of cases, providing contact with the full range of grievance resolvers. Aspects of this are clearly to the fore in the intelligence-gathering and oversight stage, enabling the identification of systemic problems and action to reduce and to prevent their recurrence. As was shown in Chapter 5, this has become a key part of the ombudsman's work.

In terms of actually signposting complaints and advising individual complainants, the ombudsman has many advantages. The flexible quality of the ombudsman enterprise allows the acceptance of complaints that have not previously been dealt with by the internal/agency complaint mechanism, but generally it operates a policy of insisting upon the completion of an internal complaint first. Moreover, even when the complaint is accepted, the ombudsman can choose to apply varying degrees of investigatory detail and formality (even formal hearings) depending on the nature of the dispute (see Appendices 2 and 3). However, as was identified in Chapter 4, there are limitations to what the ombudsmen can achieve without the support of the wider administrative justice system. In particular, a key concern is the volume of complaints received which an ombudsman office is sometimes ill-equipped to deal with, as well as the unrealistic expectations of some complainants. The establishment of an advisory service function in ombudsman offices has been prompted to address these demands, but it should be questioned how far this role can be undertaken by ombudsmen.

Adler (2008, 314-16) notes that while Lord Woolf's approach to PDR in his *Access to Justice* reports (LCD 1995; 1996) offers a 'top-down' approach, leaving procedural judges to allocate cases, and *Transforming Public Services* (DCA 2004) offers a 'bottom-up' approach focusing on the preferences of the user, the Law Commission's approach appears to have found a 'third way'.

> The great virtue of 'triage plus' is that it creates the possibility of *informed choice*. It accepts that people may not know what is in their own best interests, or in the interests of society as a whole, but does not make the mistake of concluding that someone else, some 'expert', should take the decision for them. The role of the expert is seen to be that of providing information and advice, and of discussing the pros and cons of alternative courses of action, so that the person who has experienced the problem can make an informed decision about which course of action (if any) to pursue. (Adler 2008, 315)

Arguably, the signposting element of triage plus might be better organized primarily by elements within the administrative justice system other than ombudsman offices. There is a need for a suitable service to be available whereby citizens could enter the system better prepared to understand and evaluate all the options available to them. There are several examples of good practice in various sectors. For example, the Legal Services Commission provides a General Quality Mark standard for organizations providing advice and/or outline options for members of the public.[5]

The overall development of the administrative justice system, including ombudsmen, will depend greatly on the success or otherwise of PDR and an appropriate model of triage plus. At present, these organizing concepts have some grounding in the real world, but there is much more that could be done to realize the potential efficiencies and benefits that will accrue for users of the system. The contribution that can be made by the ombudsman enterprise is significant, but necessarily limited, within the framework of the administrative justice system[6] as a whole.

Setting the Administrative Justice System Right

The breadth of relationships that the ombudsmen are required to maintain in the administrative justice system derives from the scope of the maladministration/ injustice test which they apply and the related discretionary override that the ombudsmen possess over the bar to accepting a complaint which has an alternative

---

5 The Legal Services Commission General Quality Mark standard has two levels that can be applied for: 'General Help' and 'General Help with Casework'. See the Legal Services Commission website, at: <http://www.legalservices.gov.uk/civil/qm/general_help.asp#aboutthe> (accessed 9 June 2010).

6 The UK is not alone in exploring new ways to improve the complainant's access to the administrative justice system. A similar debate on PDR and triage plus is currently occurring in Australia. See Commonwealth Attorney General's Department (2009) and Creyke and Groves (2010).

remedy.[7] As a result, the ombudsmen may, as a matter of discretion, accept a wide variety of cases as admissible. Operating this discretionary power means that ombudsmen have become knowledgeable about other remedies, which facilitates their diagnosis and signposting decisions on whether there is a remedy and who might provide it and, if there is a choice, to offer advice on the possible outcomes. Thus the ombudsmen may be said to be the buckle in the belt of redress in the administrative justice system as, potentially, they can connect different types of grievance with different remedies and their providers. Accordingly, the links between the ombudsmen and other institutions in the administrative justice system need to be maintained and facilitated by legislative and other arrangements.

Internal Agency Complaint Procedures

The public sector ombudsmen are for many users the final stage in the complaints ladder which begins with the first-instance decision-making department or agency itself and then may escalate either directly or, after an intermediate stage, to an ombudsman. The presumption is that citizens will not seek the ombudsman's help until they have first raised their grievance with the public body that caused it. This is a presumption built into the legislation of ombudsman schemes and is expressed in the idea of PDR. The establishment of fully fledged internal redress mechanisms within public sector organizations, however, is a relatively recent phenomenon prompted by the Citizen's Charter initiatives in the early 1990s: see Prime Minister (1991; 1998). In particular, the continuing legacy created by this era is the expectation that every public body has its own structured complaints procedure and customer service standards. Such a process has been further encouraged by successive government initiatives to establish 'accredited' service standards. Currently, the 'Customer Service Excellent Standard' is an accreditation which public bodies can be awarded if they meet certain criteria; one sub-criterion sets standards for dealing with complaints and using them to improve service (COI 2008, 22-3).

In the UK the end result is that agency complaints procedures have now been established on a more systematic basis over the last three decades. A clear consensus has emerged on good practice in complaint-handling, to which the ombudsmen have contributed their own guidance.[8] Ombudsmen have built on this initiative and, as identified in Chapter 4, the modern evolution of the ombudsman enterprise has been reliant on effective internal redress mechanisms. As a consequence, workloads of the ombudsmen have been manageable and resources have been freed from complaint-handling tasks to diversify into other areas (see Chapter 5).

But this trend, whilst in principle highly understandable and beneficial to all parties, is not without its problems. From the ombudsman's perspective two

7 E.g. Parliamentary Commissioner Act 1967, s.5(2); and Local Government Act 1974, s.26(6).

8 See Chapter 2, p. 31 and Chapter 5, p. 143.

residual concerns need addressing. Firstly, questions remain whether a sufficient volume of complaints are reaching the ombudsman; they appear to be less than in other jurisdictions (Gay 2008, 6). If they are not, then there must be a concern as to whether justice is being delivered at the internal/agency level and whether sufficient knowledge is reaching the ombudsman to inform their systemic work. The answer here is the ombudsman's discretionary power.

The second concern is the quality of the internal complaints mechanisms. Here there is evidence that these procedures are not working as satisfactorily as they might. The arrangements for dealing with health care complaints in England provide a good example of some of the issues that can arise, albeit that health care is possibly a more sensitive area than most public sector activity. Patients usually place a great deal of trust in health care professionals and may be unwilling to complain for a variety of reasons.[9]

National Health Service (NHS) complaints in England have been through three cycles of reform within the last 15 years,[10] the major aim of the latest reform being to have a single complaints system across health and social care in order to resolve complaints locally. In this sequence of reforms it can be seen that some matters are continually highlighted but insufficient progress has been made on them, with more attention being devoted to structures and to processes rather than to complainants, outcomes and cultural change within the NHS trusts. The 2001 review found that complainants did not find the second stage in their journey to be independent or impartial given that it was conducted by the trust itself, and there were also strong reservations about the impartiality of the first, local resolution stage too. Complainants reported that they were not being taken seriously, that the views of the NHS staff were often preferred to their accounts. Overall, there was variable practice in both stages and lessons were not being learnt sufficiently.

The Health Service Ombudsman (HSO) report on the NHS complaints system highlighted that the procedure was still fragmentary, lacked focus and the range of remedies offered was restricted and there was a lack of leadership to drive through the required cultural change (HSO 2005a). The third cycle of reform in England was also concerned with major structural change by seeking to bring together health and social care complaints and to have a single regulator, the Care

9 They may not wish to jeopardize a continuing relationship and suffer what they perceive as adverse repercussions. Some general practices have been known to remove complainants from their lists as a punitive reaction: see Wallace and Mulcahy (1999, 19).

10 The first was UK-wide and implemented in 1996 following a review of NHS complaints processes. The second initiative was put into practice in 2004 following an official NHS review published in 2001 (Department of Health 2001). By this time health care was a devolved responsibility so the NHS in England, Scotland, Wales and Northern Ireland were responding separately and differently to the 2001 review of the 1996 arrangements. The third iteration of reform in this sequence in England commenced in 2009.

Quality Commission (CQC).[11] The CQC would not continue with the complaints review role that one of the predecessor bodies had. Both health and social care complaints would now have two stages, first local resolution and then the relevant ombudsman – HSO for health and LGO for social care.

There is a need for health care complainants in England to have improved awareness of, and support for, complaining. The complainants suffer from imbalances in power and information; not all complaint-handlers are as well trained as they should be; and the organizational culture tends to be defensive rather than welcoming the learning and improvement that they can provide.

These points are also to be found in other complaints processes for other public services: see Gulland (2010). They also demonstrate the need for external, independent review of complaints, though there is a set-off between the expedition that can be achieved via first local resolution against the dilution of the independent element. Nevertheless, the problems associated with lack of independence can be reversed where an agency is committed to learning lessons and seeking improvement. Where the 'complainant journey' moves from the internal/agency level to a (second-tier) ombudsman independence is gained, but at the expense of further delay and the possibility of complainant fatigue and withdrawal from the process.

Given that scenario it must be questioned whether an intermediate stage (e.g. the Adjudicator or Independent Case Examiner)[12] is desirable. After many years of experimentation, the judgment has been made with the health care complaints system in England, Scotland and Northern Ireland (and proposed in Wales) that it is not. On the other hand, in tax and social security the expectation is that dissatisfied complainants will not normally leapfrog the Adjudicator or the Independent Case Examiner respectively to reach the Parliamentary Ombudsman (PO). Despite this, social security and tax are two areas which regularly top the PO's workload.[13]

Generalist or Specialist Ombudsmen?

Alongside working out the relationship of ombudsmen to the varied complaint structure at the internal/agency level, there is also the question of the basic design of ombudsman bodies. Broadly, it can be said that in Australia, Canada and the devolved countries of the UK, a geographical spread of homogenous ombudsman schemes, capable of handling different complaints from a whole spectrum of

11 Replacing the Healthcare Commission (HC) and the Commission for Social Care Inspection (CSCI).

12 See pp. 236-7.

13 For example, in 2008-09 there were 2,692 complaints received about the Department for Work and Pensions (DWP) and 2,159 complaints about HM Revenue and Customs (HMRC) out of the five 'top' departments' total complaints received of 6,780, i.e. representing around 40 per cent (DWP) and 32 per cent (HMRC) of the total complaints received about these five departments (PHSO 2009, 56, Fig. 12).

government activity, has evolved. Chapter 2 described this development in Scotland, Wales and Northern Ireland.

The major arguments for generalist ombudsmen are that from the user perspective this arrangement is clearer and more accessible. From an executive government perspective, they may be much more cost-effective, easier to oversee and assist government claims that they are achieving 'joined-up government'. From the perspective of the ombudsman organization itself, the inclusion of a general range of sectoral areas within its jurisdiction provides opportunities to achieve a wider skill-set and learning about public administration, and consequently to enhance its claim to be an authoritative source of public sector improvement.

However, particularly in England, there has been a trend towards specialist ombudsmen being established. The reasons are sometimes defensive, particularly in relation to the creation of police, prisons and armed forces ombudsman offices. These are all challenging policy areas, raising a range of criminal justice, civil liberties and security issues. The creation of police ombudsmen has met with serious difficulties in establishing a fully independent status.[14]

In large part the resistance of the police themselves led to a determined policy that it would be inappropriate for complete independence in handling complaints against the police.[15] Eventually the police accepted that without independence the arrangements for dealing with complaints against the police lacked legitimacy and public confidence, and so it was in the police's interest as well as the public's for complaint-handling to be independent.[16] But noticeably there was no serious consideration of bringing this responsibility within the sphere of the PO. This sectoral solution had been preceded by the introduction of the *fully* independent Police Ombudsman for Northern Ireland (PONI).[17] The particular circumstances of the civil unrest, in which the former Royal Ulster Constabulary had been perceived as a protector of the unionist community and an infringer of the rights of the nationalist community, meant this particular public service was an ultra-sensitive one in which anything less than full independence was no longer a viable political option.

The situation with regard to prisons in England and Wales is even more confusing. Here the external reviewer of complaints has unfortunately been

14 In 2004, in England and Wales, the Independent Police Complaints Commission (IPCC) replaced the Police Complaints Authority, which had itself been established in 1983 to introduce a measure of independent oversight for the most serious complaints.

15 See generally, Home Affairs Select Committee (1998).

16 The possible tipping point for having an independent system was concern over the police investigation into the death in London of Stephen Lawrence, which raised issues of institutional racism in the police force. One of the conclusions of the subsequent *Stephen Lawrence Inquiry* was 'that a strong element of independent investigation [of complaints] must be considered' (Macpherson 1999, para. 46.35).

17 See Police (Northern Ireland) Act 1998, ss.50-65. Only in Northern Ireland are all investigations carried out by independent staff.

labelled the Prisons and Probation Ombudsman (PPO), a matter about which some members of the ombudsman community have been unhappy because this officer is not independent of the department that operates the prison service.[18] The merits of a decision taken by a minister in relation to a prisoner will be outside the PPO's jurisdiction unless the minister specifically authorizes a PPO investigation. The remit includes both the procedures and merits of (non-ministerial) decisions and is wider than maladministration or service failure in relation to management, supervision, care and treatment, as well as the special role of investigating deaths in custody in order to comply with obligations arising under article 2 of the European Convention on Human Rights (ECHR) – the right to life. In addition to prisoners in prisons managed by the Prison Service or contracted out, those who are supervised under probation and detainees in immigration removal centres are also eligible to have their complaints reviewed by the PPO if they are dissatisfied with the outcome of the local resolution stage in the complaints procedure. There have been various attempts to put the non-statutory PPO and the Northern Ireland Prisoner Ombudsman (NIPrO) onto a statutory basis.[19] The complexities in this area are compounded by the fact that prisoners could complain to the PO about the way the PPO and NIPrO dealt with their complaints. Similar considerations apply to the armed forces. It took a scandal about the bullying of young recruits in one base – *The Deepcut Review*: see Blake (2006) – to lead to the appointment of the Services Complaints Commissioner (SCC),[20] again only qualifying for 'associate membership' under the BIOA's independence criteria and having a limited jurisdiction.[21]

The '*ad hocery*' of ombudsman and quasi-ombudsman creation is redolent of the piecemeal development of tribunals which eventually acted as a persuasive driver underlying the rationalization of the tribunal system that was introduced

---

18 The PPO has only been given 'associate membership' of the British and Irish Ombudsman Association (BIOA) under their membership criteria: see Chapter 2, p. 50.

19 The last attempt was in 2007-08 but the proposals were withdrawn from the Criminal Justice and Immigration Bill during its committee stage in the House of Lords following the concerns which the two office-holders and the PO had about the proposed governance and accountability arrangements and the effect on their independence: see *Hansard*, HL Debs, vol. 698 cols 953-60, 5 February 2008. The NIPrO resigned over the affair.

20 Armed Forces Act 2006, s.366. The SCC has a website at: <http://armedforcescomplaints.independent.gov.uk/> (accessed 10 June 2010). The SCC came into effect on 1 January 2008 with a statutory role limited to two functions.

21 The SCC may act as an alternative point of contact for those alleging discrimination, harassment, bullying or bias, referring complaints to the relevant officer in the chain of command under the Armed Forces Act 2006, s.388. There is also an annual reporting duty (s.389) to the Secretary of State on the efficiency, effectiveness and fairness of the operation of the services complaints system and its own referral role; and the report must be laid before Parliament but parts of it may be redacted on the grounds of harming national security interests or jeopardizing the safety of any person.

following the Leggatt review of tribunals (Leggatt 2001) and later the Tribunals, Courts and Enforcement Act 2007. There are similar debates about the respective merits and drawbacks of generalist versus specialist justice in the tribunal context (Buck, Bonner and Sainsbury 2005, 21-3, 220-26). It may take an equally robust review of the ombudsmen and other complaint-handlers (see Chapter 8) to reset, in an appropriate way, the desired balance between the general and specialist features of complaint architecture.

Tribunals

There is a general expectation that if a complainant has a right to take a case before a tribunal or other statutory appeals process, then instead of pursuing a complaint to an ombudsman, the tribunal route should be chosen. This best connects to parliamentary intention in setting up appeal mechanisms in specific areas of government activity. Moreover, tribunals conform to an extent to the goals of PDR. They are inexpensive to operate and are designed to be informal and to enable a user to present their appeal without the need for a representative, whether legal or otherwise.

Given this presumption the crossover between the tribunal system and the ombudsmen presents few problems. There will of course be exceptions, such as where there are service issues that deserve fuller investigation or where there has been a breakdown in trust between the agency and the complainant which suggests use of the appeals procedure would not be appropriate. To deal with such instances, the ombudsman's statutory discretion, discussed below, is sufficient although in Australia some tribunals and ombudsman schemes have developed an interesting practice of establishing a joint protocol on referring cases between each other.[22]

Exchanging Cases with the Courts

The overlap in the workload of the ombudsman and the courts provides a neat illustration of the difficulties in constructing a coherent administrative justice system. As identified in Chapter 2,[23] both institutions contribute to the aim of resolving disputes about good administration. Clearly, their respective jurisdictions are not identical, but due to the expansion of the grounds of judicial review over the years and the pliable nature of the maladministration test, there will be many occasions when in principle an aggrieved party will have a theoretical claim in either dispute resolution mechanism. This raises a series of

---

22 See the State Administrative Tribunal Act (Western Australia) 2004, s.168. See also, Queensland Civil and Administrative Tribunal Act (Queensland) 2009, s.227.

23 See pp. 35-8.

problems about the allocation of grievances between the respective fora (e.g. Kirkham 2006).[24]

To deal with this problem there are already procedures in place. For instance, in England and Wales the Pre-Action Protocol implies that the Administrative Court retains the discretion to refuse permission if it deems an alternative remedy, such as the ombudsman, a preferable redress route for the claimant.[25] Likewise, despite the wording of ombudsman legislation apparently favouring dispute resolution through the courts if that route is available, in practice ombudsmen retain significant discretion to override this statutory bar, an understanding that has received judicial approval (*R v Commissioner for Local Administration ex parte Liverpool City Council* [2001] 1 All ER 462).[26] The generic reason for exercising such discretion is if it would be unreasonable in all the circumstances, including the complainant's potential redress needs and personal situation, to expect the complainant to take the legal route. This line of reasoning generally facilitates a flexible, common sense approach to the distribution of cases between the ombudsman and the courts. There will, though, sometimes be good reasons why the ombudsman should not exercise this discretion, such as if the dispute hinges on a contested point of law.

There are, however, some residuary problems with the current arrangements. An important one is that the shorter time limit for judicial review (three months) when compared to the ombudsman (ordinarily 12 months) creates a perverse incentive to pursue judicial review. This can cause problems in that the ombudsman can later choose to reject a complaint on the basis that an alternative remedy has been pursued (Law Commission 2008, para. 5.64). The general policy in administrative justice is to discourage 'forum shopping' but the existence of the different procedural time limits for bringing a complaint suggests that this is one area where the ombudsmen should be left to exercise their discretion in deciding whether to accept complaints previously considered for judicial review (Law Commission 2008, paras 5.60-67). Moreover, sometimes there may be good reasons to allow action in both the courts and with the ombudsman. For example, where a decision has been quashed in judicial review then it may be right to allow compensation for past losses to be sought in a parallel complaint to the ombudsman. Views vary on the current situation. The Pre-Action Protocol, for instance, in its advice to claimants states that '[p]arties may wish to note that the Ombudsmen are not

24 The relationship between the ombudsmen and the courts has recently been looked at by the Law Commission (2008; 2010) for England and Wales as part of its study of redress against public bodies.

25 See the Ministry of Justice website for the text of the *Pre-Action Protocol for Judicial Review* at: http://www.justice.gov.uk/civil/procrules_fin/contents/protocols/prot_jrv.htm (accessed 11 June 2010).

26 A slightly contradictory case is *R v Local Commissioner for Administration ex parte Croydon London BC* [1989] 1 All ER 1033, but this case can be distinguished on the facts.

able to look into a complaint once court action has been commenced'.[27] Yet the 'statutory bar' is not that clear and it is arguable that the legislative reference to a 'remedy' only excludes full remedies.[28]

As will be seen in Chapter 8, we believe that a strong step in the right direction in maintaining a sensible management of the overlap between the courts and the ombudsman would be the implementation of the recommendations that the Law Commission have made.[29] The Law Commission suggests recommendations targeted at both sides of the overlap. Thus the time limit barrier for ADR could be mitigated by 'providing the courts with a power to stay proceedings specifically for the purpose of referring a matter to an ombudsman' (Law Commission 2008, para. 5.36). Legal proceedings could only then be continued after exhaustion of the ombudsman process.[30] At the same time, the statutory bar in the ombudsman legislation should be rewritten to reflect better the PDR expectation that today lies behind the exercise of the ombudsman's discretion (Law Commission 2008, para 5.55-75).[31] Finally, the Law Commission has proposed that the ombudsmen should be enabled to transfer a case to the courts. The reasoning for this is that there may be some cases, not thought to be many, in which the investigation of maladministration depends upon the determination of a contentious or unresolved point of law which only arises midway through the investigation (Law Commission 2008, paras 5.41-2). This recommendation is qualified by the advice that '[the] reference procedure should be invoked only where the complaint is essentially about maladministration but cannot be progressed without prior resolution of a legal issue' (Law Commission 2008, para. 5.46). A further disincentive against excessive use of the procedure would presumably be that it would involve additional court costs for both the ombudsman and the public body involved, and possibly for the complainant.[32]

---

27 *Pre-Action Protocol for Judicial Review*, para. 3.2.

28 E.g. '[T]he Commissioner shall not conduct an investigation under this Act … any action in respect of which the person aggrieved has or had a remedy by way of proceedings in any court of law' (Parliamentary Commissioner Act 1967, s.5(2)(b)).

29 See p. 235.

30 There is a possibility that such an arrangement would be in breach of Article 6 ECHR. However, probably the better view is that it would operate as a precondition on the right to access to a court and not an ouster of it (Law Commission 2010, para. 5.35). See also *Golder v United Kingdom* (1975) 1 EHRR 524; *Ashingdane v United Kingdom* (1985) EHRR 528 and also the reiteration of the principle by the House of Lords in *Seal v Chief Constable of South Wales* [2007] UKHL 21; [2007] 1 WLR 1910.

31 There has been a recent attempt to amend the statutory bar in ombudsman legislation, but it was rejected by government. See Vera Baird QC MP, the Solicitor General, *Hansard* (HC) 27 March 2007, Tribunal, Courts and Enforcement Bill Committee, 7th sitting, col. 246.

32 Due to the cost issue, in the Law Commission's (2010, para. 5.89) report *Administrative Redress* it has accepted that more work will need to be undertaken before this proposal is finalized.

System Coordination?

Due to the *ad hoc* way in which the administrative justice system in the UK has evolved each of the elements has its own accountability and governance arrangements. There is, therefore, no single overall 'setting it right' framework for the administrative justice system. Yet there is now a body which does have a remit (in Great Britain) to keep the administrative justice system under review – the Administrative Justice and Tribunals Council (AJTC), of which the PO is an *ex officio* member.[33] This review function can play an important part in promoting the setting it right aspect of the administrative justice system, particularly in relation to tribunals and inquiries where the AJTC retains the duty of its predecessor, the Council on Tribunals, to keep under review and report on the constitution and working of listed tribunals and statutory inquiries.[34] The wider remit of the AJTC is to:

- keep under review the administrative justice system, that is the putting it right and getting it right elements of the statutory definition or, in its own words, 'from the initial decision affecting the citizen to the final outcome of any complaint or appeal';
- consider ways to make the system accessible, fair and efficient, to advise on the development of the system;
- make proposals for change to the Lord Chancellor, Scottish and Welsh ministers and the Senior President of Tribunals;
- make proposals for research into the system.[35]

The interaction between the AJTC and the different governments around the country is likely to vary depending on the devolved arrangements in place. Likewise, while the AJTC and its committees' reports are laid before the different Parliaments and Assemblies in Great Britain, as with the ombudsman's reports, the degree to which they are scrutinized and influence policy will depend a lot on the parliamentary arrangements for reviewing them. It is too early in the AJTC's life to come to a conclusion on such arrangements yet, or on its other efforts to contribute to policy development, such as submitting responses to consultations.

The early signs of the intent of the AJTC are positive (e.g. see AJTC 2010; 2010a)[36] and chime with many of the points made in this monograph. For instance in its *Action Plan 2010-11* the AJTC has earmarked cross-cutting projects on:

a. the development of principles for administrative justice and assessment framework to be used for self-assessment by bodies;

33 The PO is also an *ex officio* member of the AJTC's Scottish and Welsh Committees along with, respectively, the SPSO and PSOW: see TCEA 2007, Sched. 7, paras 4 and 7.

34 TCEA 2007, Sched. 7, paras 14-15.

35 TCEA 2007, Sched. 7, para. 13(1).

36 But see Preface, p. xiii above and pp. 237-8 below.

b. getting it right first time, in which the benefits to users, decision-makers and tax-payers will be demonstrated and examples of good practice identified for dissemination;
c. PDR, in which after a review of national and international literature and meetings with practitioners, proposals will be made for its development and use in the UK's administrative justice system;
d. technology, and how the use of information and communications technology can facilitate the administrative justice system, disseminate good practice and enhance access by appellants (AJTC 2010a).

Inevitably, however, there are fundamental question marks about the administrative justice system and its scope that will be beyond the AJTC alone to resolve. For instance, as identified in earlier chapters,[37] the interaction between the public and private sectors has become ever more difficult to comprehend under traditional public law approaches. In one of the key areas where this is a relevant problem for the public sector ombudsmen, private adult social care, this issue has been resolved through a specific legislative amendment to the jurisdiction of the LGO.[38] Yet there remains some confusion about the legitimate reach of the administrative justice system when it comes to dealing with the apparently 'public function' work undertaken in the private sector.[39] This issue has led to several calls for a much broader approach to be taken to the issue reaching outside public law jurisprudence (Oliver 2010), and including ostensibly 'private' law ombudsmen within debates on and the oversight arrangements of the administrative justice system (Brooker 2008; Merricks 2010).

Providing Assurance: Partners in Resolution

The modern ombudsman operates in a complex regulatory environment within which there are significant numbers of other accountability institutions that oversee the work of the public sector. By way of example, the Crerar Review of the arrangements in Scotland took evidence from 36 separate external scrutiny organizations (Crerar 2007, 10). All such accountability institutions will have their own specialities and be established for distinct core purposes. Nevertheless, even in

37 See Chapter 1, pp. 6-7 and Chapter 4, pp. 107-108.

38 Health Act 2009, s.35 and Sch. 5.

39 The current leading case is *YL v Birmingham City Council* [2007] UKHL 27; [2008] 1 A.C. 95. By a 3:2 majority the House of Lords held that a company running a residential care home was not a body carrying out functions of a public nature in relation to those residents whose fees were paid for by a local council under the National Assistance Act 1948. On the particular facts of the case, this decision has since been reversed by s.145 of the Health and Social Care Act 2008 but the reasoning of the House of Lords' majority still applies to the interpretation of public functions.

the best designed constitutional system there will be overlaps in the workload and interests of the various institutions. To complicate the matter further, governments will also have an interest in furthering public service delivery and striving for 'joined-up government', and will have their own units in place to further such goals.[40] For instance, at Westminster the Cabinet Office has a primary role to support the Prime Minister and Cabinet in the organization and coordination of government business, including public services reform. In the devolved administrations public service reform tends to be shared between the departments of the First Ministers and Finance.[41]

The relationship that the ombudsman has with government will be discussed shortly, but key overlaps with the ombudsman's work include those with auditors, regulators and inspectorates. Auditors, whether in the UK[42] or abroad, were originally established to conduct financial audits of the regularity and propriety of the annual accounts of governmental and public bodies. This still constitutes a significant amount of their work, but to this role has been added value for money or performance auditing.[43] Such audits do not permit direct questioning of government policy itself but they are concerned with policy *implementation*, a distinction that is not always easy to identify.

Performance auditing reports are mostly studies of services or agencies but some are cross-cutting.[44] As such, some of this work has the potential to cross over into the ombudsman's work in conducting systemic investigations, as covered in Chapter 5. Likewise, the Audit Commission's powers of producing reports on the performance of local authorities were widened beyond the economy, efficiency and effectiveness of the use of resources, to the risks of their failing to perform their functions adequately or at all, and on their ability to secure improvement.[45] In the furtherance of this aspect of their work, auditors will publish case studies of

---

40 Although thinking about coordination in government is not new, it is thought this expression derived from the establishment of the Social Exclusion Unit by the first New Labour administration in 1997 (Bognador 2005, 2).

41 In Wales there is a Department for Public Service Improvement: see <http://wales.gov.uk/about/civilservice/departments/pslgd/psi/?lang=en> (accessed 9 June 2010). In Northern Ireland there has been a focus on structural reform under the Review of Public Administration programme: see <http://www.rpani.gov.uk/> (accessed 9 June 2010).

42 See the Local Government Finance Act 1982, s.26, which authorized the (newly created) Audit Commission to conduct studies, and Part II of the National Audit Act 1983, which did the same for the similarly newly established National Audit Office (NAO).

43 In 2009-10 the NAO audited expenditure and revenue amounting to some £950 billion across 475 government departmental and agency accounts. In the same year it published 63 major 'value for money' reports commenting on specific government projects and programmes and making recommendations for improvement (NAO 2010, 16-17).

44 For example, the NAO's report *Helping Government Learn* examined 11 case examples of learning, including 'learning from complaints' (NAO 2009, 23-5).

45 See Audit Commission Act 1998, s.47, inserted by the Local Government and Public Involvement in Health Act 2007, s.157.

good practice. Here the potential for overlap with the systemic and promotion of good administration aspects of the ombudsman's work is strong. A clear example of this overlap can be seen in the use the Audit Commission makes of the LGO's work in assessing the performance of councils.[46]

In the modern regulatory environment, however, performance assessment has not been left to auditors alone. Various public services are subject to regulation and/or inspection to ensure that they meet standards of provision and service. For example, health and social care is a territory most frequently investigated by ombudsmen, but it is subject to a number of other regulatory and inspectoral scrutiny bodies, and this sector has devolved counterparts.

Clearly there is a distinction to be made between the work of the ombudsman and other accountability institutions. Thus the contribution of the ombudsmen in the UK tends to be more episodic, incident-based and reactive. But taken together, the role of external scrutiny can be described as one of providing 'independent assurance that services are well-managed, safe and fit for purpose and that public money is being used properly' (Crerar 2007, 1). Within that concept the ombudsman, particularly in its systemic work, fits extremely well, with their particular emphasis on promoting good administration and what might be termed equity for the service users. For instance, ombudsman investigations in the past have identified gaps in intra- and inter-agency arrangements and other failures of not taking a user-focused approach. Moreover, as explored in Chapter 5, there are occasions when a special report is more akin to a performance audit; for example the PO's report and follow-up of *Tax Credits* (PHSO 2005c; 2007d).

Coordinating the Work of Integrity Bodies

Even in an era when the range of so-called quangos are under review and efforts are being put into rationalizing the overall scrutiny network, a variety of accountability institutions are likely to remain and their work will on occasion overlap.[47] In this context, the process of 'setting it right' means that it is important that ombudsmen maintain suitable connections with other accountability institutions working to promote what might generically be termed 'institutional integrity'. Although it is hard to substantiate empirically, ombudsmen are more likely to achieve efficient accountability gains where they work in effective partnerships with other bodies. In addition it is plausible that these partnerships themselves provide a degree of oversight and scrutiny of each other's work.

Evidently, there has always been an *ad hoc* awareness of links between different integrity bodies to avoid duplication of work. In health and social care, for instance, the ombudsmen may come across information in their investigations which they

46 This assessment has changed from a comprehensive performance assessment to a comprehensive area assessment done in conjunction with other inspection bodies.

47 For a review of the current debates on the issue of the perceived proliferation of scrutiny bodies, see Levitt *et al* (2010, ch. 1).

ought to raise with a relevant regulator. To do so it is important that ombudsman legislation specifies that this is a legal exception to the general confidentiality obligations imposed on ombudsmen. On occasion, coordinated work between different bodies has led to impressive joint pieces of work. An example is the pair of reports produced by the PHSO and the NAO on an *ex gratia* compensation scheme for fishermen caught up in the so-called 'Cod Wars' between Iceland and the UK in the 1970s (PHSO 2007c; NAO 2007). The legitimate interests of both agencies in this affair were clear, yet the agencies demonstrated a successful degree of coordination in their investigations that avoided excessive overlap and maximized the impact of their work.

There are risks in relying upon only intermittent awareness of overlaps between integrity bodies; some issues may be missed entirely or there is an inappropriate duplication of effort by multiple agencies. To minimize such risks and improve messages of good practice, it is unsurprising that experiments have been put in place from time to time to harness joint ideas. In local government there can be informal arrangements or formal protocols with regulatory bodies in housing and the ethical standards bodies. Comprehensive Area Assessment ('Oneplace'[48]) allows people to see the value of bringing together inspection data from the Audit Commission, the Care Quality Commission and the Police, Prisons and Probation inspectorates. The 'Improvement Network' is an initiative, sponsored by the Audit Commission, the Chartered Institute of Public Finance and Accountancy (CIPFA) and others, to provide successful partnership working in local areas and cross-sectoral improvement.[49]

In Australia, this process has gone a stage further with some interesting new examples of the formalization of such relationships. For example, in Western Australia an Integrity Coordinating Group has been established, consisting of the Auditor-General, Ombudsman, Crime and Corruption Commission and the Office of Public Sector Standards. The group meets quarterly, produces reports and stages joint events to promote and monitor integrity issues and inspire cooperation by public sector organizations.[50]

Perhaps the most advanced model yet is the Integrity Commission of Tasmania,[51] expected to start operations on 1 October 2010.[52] The commission will coordinate and investigate the resolution of 'integrity' complaints against public authorities and officials and promote standards of integrity and education. Clearly, the work

48 See: <www.audit-commission.gov.uk/localgov/audit/caa/pages/default.aspx> (accessed 29 August 2010).

49 See the Improvement Network website: <http://www.improvementnetwork.gov.uk/imp/core/page.do?pageId=1> (accessed 10 June 2010).

50 See the Western Australia Integrity Coordinating Group website: <http://www.opssc.wa.gov.au/ICG/About_Us/> (accessed 10 May 2010).

51 See the Integrity Commission Act (Tasmania) 2009.

52 See: <http://www.justice.tas.gov.au/corporateinfo/projects/integrity_commission> (accessed 10 June 2010).

of the Integrity Commission is sufficiently broad that its operations will risk overlapping with the work of other bodies, such as the ombudsman. To get around this problem, the Board of the Integrity Commission will include the membership of both the Auditor-General and the ombudsman.[53] A Parliamentary Select Committee specifically designed to oversee the Integrity Commission will also be established to lend this body additional constitutional *gravitas*. The work of the new Joint Standing Committee on Integrity will include reviewing the reports and work of named integrity institutions, including the ombudsman.[54] While it might be argued that this network of institutions is unnecessarily dense, it does create a clear chain of oversight through which Parliament can put pressure on government efforts to promote integrity and respect the work of integrity institutions. At the same time, of course, it is to be presumed that the various integrity institutions themselves will be required to demonstrate the overall coherence of their work, account for their actions and evidence any benefits that have accrued from information sharing arrangements.

Partners in the Constitutional Order

The final sets of relationships that it is important to consider are those between the ombudsman and the traditional tripartite institutions of the constitution: Parliament, the executive and the courts. The effectiveness of the ombudsman enterprise is dependent to a large degree on the tangible respect of these key institutions, even where the ombudsman is formally confirmed in the constitution. Remarkably perhaps, the decision-making of the ombudsman has hardly ever led to what might be termed 'conflict' and the ombudsman's will has almost always prevailed. Of course, it could be argued that this result has been achieved through timidity; in other words, that the ombudsman institution generally has had a minimal impact, to the extent that the executive has only rarely felt sufficiently indisposed to reject the ombudsman's findings. Throughout the ombudsman's history just this accusation has been made on a regular basis (e.g. Lewis and Birkinshaw 1993, ch.7). Yet such a conclusion does not easily chime with the recent trend in the ombudsman enterprise towards increased systemic activity as noted in Chapter 5 and although the ombudsman's complaint-handling function is small in terms of numbers, this work can be highly significant in terms of its wider impact (e.g. HSO 2003). A more valid conclusion, therefore, is that the executive has learned to live with the ombudsman. As ombudsman legislation implies, public bodies have the last word following an ombudsman report. But the general policy of the executive is to respect the decision-making of the ombudsman (e.g. Cabinet Office 1997; PHSO 2009c). Likewise, as will be described here, the courts have made it more difficult

53 Integrity Commission Act (Tasmania) 2009, s.14(1)(b) and (c).

54 *Ibid*, s.24.

for public bodies to dismiss ombudsman reports and Parliament has on occasion acted to support the ombudsman in its disputes with the government.

Working with Government

One of the most important links that an ombudsman needs to build and maintain is with the organizations it investigates. The importance of this link is doubly important for a parliamentary ombudsman when it comes to central government, both because it is the work of the various branches of central government that the ombudsman investigates and because the government is responsible for driving forward any legislative amendments and policy shifts that may impact on the ombudsman's work.

Given the ombudsman's lack of enforcement powers it is essential that the ombudsman establishes and maintains a healthy working relationship with public bodies. The traditional approach, based on cooperation and 'moral suasion' (Marin 2009), has been described by the Ontario Ombudsman, André Marin, as relying upon three broad tactics: (i) the publication of an annual report, which 'is somewhat like a report card on government' (*ibid.*, para. 7); (ii) by formulating recommendations in individual cases which can involve '[e]ach side giv[ing] a bit and tak[ing] a bit in the interest of compromise and achieving consensus' (*ibid.*, para. 6); and (iii) informal networking.

> [O]n an ongoing basis, we establish our general credibility with government through informal networking. We exchange information with government about our work. We establish strategic contacts in positions of power that we can rely on to move issues forward. We meet key stakeholders to educate them about our processes. All the while, we are seeking to reassure government that we are all part of the same mission: Improving public policy. We want to demystify our work and create an atmosphere of mutual trust and understanding. (*Ibid.*, para. 5)

Marin's argument is that solely focusing on this approach towards the public bodies an ombudsman investigates is misguided and leads to just the sort of ineffectual institution decried by the critics of the ombudsman. This analysis is not an opinion shared by all ombudsmen; indeed what is clear from the operation of most ombudsman schemes is that a primary function of the ombudsman is to put in significant work behind the scenes building support to secure results. Part of this work is the provision of basic information. Even within the higher echelons of government some past ombudsman reports reveal that behind the government's response there has been a disappointing level of ignorance of the working method of the ombudsman.[55] Coupled with this, it probably still remains

55 E.g. witness the saga of the *Debt of Honour* report (PHSO 2005a; Kirkham 2006).

the case that government thinking is too often dominated by legalistic advice, apparently unappreciative of the demands engrained within the maladministration concept (PHSO 2009d). The active promotion by ombudsmen of standards of good administration within government circles, therefore, is of much importance.

There is some evidence that this sort of advice is actively sought by the government. Dunleavy *et al* (2010) found in their research that civil servants feared a critical judgment of the ombudsman more than a negative finding in the courts, precisely because it represented a critique of their capacity to make good administrative decisions. This sense of critical judgment of the conduct of officials is an inherent part of the work of the ombudsman and, as defended in Chapter 2, rightly so. Yet to get around the extra pressures and misunderstandings that this may cause civil servants, the education and training of officials is important. Along just these lines, in a recent piece of research commissioned by the PHSO, it was found that officials were responding to such pressures by seeking more regular access with the ombudsman's office (IFF Research 2010), a version of events which represents an interesting twist on the more traditional model outlined by Marin above. As was described in Chapter 5, ombudsmen around the world have responded by running training sessions for administrative bodies.

From both sides, therefore, there is interest in refining a professional working relationship. There are also signs in some schemes that the framework within which this relationship operates is being set in a more formal setting. A prototype for the government/ombudsman relationship can be seen in the requirement for the Commission on Local Administration to conduct a triennial review of the work of the LGO and submit it to the relevant government department for consideration.[56] A more recently formalized example is provided by the jointly signed *Statement of Responsibilities* drawn up between the PHSO, the Cabinet Office, the Treasury, the Department of Health and the Ministry of Justice (PHSO 2009c). Although it is a non-legally binding explanatory document, it supports the ongoing gradual constitutional entrenchment of the ombudsman office. It contains clear commitments to the maintenance of the ombudsman scheme by the government. The *Statement* itself is to be reviewed on a biennial basis and the Cabinet Office undertakes to take forward an Order in Council annually to update the jurisdiction of the PHSO (PHSO 2009c, paras 2 and 8). The *Statement* outlines the respective responsibilities for the various signatories to the document. In doing so, the Cabinet Office is given a list of policy and liaison responsibilities that illustrate the need to maintain a coherent institutional framework within which the ombudsman must operate. These include:

- providing guidance to government departments on working with the PHSO and setting up new ombudsman schemes;
- ensuring that the PHSO is consulted on any aspects of policy development that impact on the office's jurisdiction or powers;

56 See p. 185.

- ensuring that the statutory provisions of the PHSO are correct, comprehensive and fit for purpose;
- ensuring that there is a departmental contact to provide the PHSO with prompt and comprehensive responses to requests for information and documents;
- staging a meeting between the Cabinet Office and the PHSO at least every two months;
- ensuring that a named Permanent Secretary is designated as the 'Ombudsman Champion' (PHSO 2009c, para. 8).

A similar relationship is defined with the Department of Health and Ministry of Justice, with intriguingly specific reference made within the *Statement* to the need for an effective working relationship with the PHSO 'because of the Ombudsman's constitutional position and her role in the wider administrative justice landscape, for which [the Ministry for Justice] has specific responsibilities' (PHSO 2009c, para. 11).

Parliament

The fundamental importance of Parliament's role in helping to secure the independent status of the ombudsman and calling the office to account was analysed in Chapter 6. What remains to be looked at is Parliament's additional role in supporting the ombudsman in its work. This is important in three interlinking respects. Firstly, the relationship that the ombudsman has with its accompanying legislature can provide a revealing insight into the boundary line between the legitimate work of the ombudsman and the political sphere. As the current PHSO has written:

> there is [a] contested area of policy direction and of when remedying maladministration has inescapable policy implications. I have already cited the example of the tax credits system. The point at which an Ombudsman report necessarily strays into territory that is rightly that of the Executive is indeterminate and quite possibly indeterminable. To avoid the risk of ever encroaching at the edges would, at least on one account, be seriously to diminish the effectiveness of the Ombudsman. (Abraham 2008, 1)

Strong parliamentary oversight and, if necessary, support of the ombudsman reduces the risk of ombudsmen straying too far into constitutionally inappropriate territory, while at the same time providing the ombudsman with the confidence to continue probing at maladministration close to the core of government policy-making.

Secondly, Parliament can provide the ombudsman with the opportunity to gain a wider and more influential public hearing than is normally available to the office. For instance, in 2010 the Office of the First Minister and Deputy

First Minister (OFMDFM) Committee twice invited the Assembly Ombudsman for Northern Ireland (AONI) to give evidence. In particular, the second hearing (OFMDFM Committee 2010) enabled the ombudsman to raise in public the need for the reform of his office along the lines recommended some years previously in a commissioned review (OFMDFM 2004). Such opportunities help to secure the constitutional strength of the office.

Thirdly, the crux of Parliament's role comes in the support it provides the ombudsman on those occasions when, in the first instance, the executive chooses to resist the recommendations of the ombudsman. The need for such demonstrations of support has been rare in most ombudsman schemes. This lack of apparent need for Parliament to play an active role in support of the ombudsman, particularly in Australia where ombudsmen have been so active, adds to the sense of the strength and autonomy of the ombudsman enterprise. But in the UK, the work of the Public Administration Select Committee (PASC) in support of the PHSO has been hugely influential in establishing the credibility of the ombudsman enterprise, so much so that in more than one recent lecture the current ombudsman expressed concern about the uncertainty that would surround the office when a new committee and new chair were appointed following the 2010 election (e.g. Abraham 2009a; 2009c).

Despite being non-typical, the interaction between the PHSO and PASC reveals the fascinating dynamic that exists between the traditional tripartite institutions of the constitution and other accountability institutions, and illustrates the three aspects of Parliament's supporting role as identified above. As described in Chapter 6,[57] the PO has two methods by which to alert Parliament of investigations that have given rise to significant issues in their dealings with the executive: the submission of an additional report and a special report.[58] These powers are mirrored in the legislation of the HSO.[59] There are a variety of reasons why the ombudsmen may want to use this power to submit a report, but a leading one is that the office is experiencing difficulties in persuading the government to accept various features of its work. In other words, the informal processes through which the ombudsman/government relationship is ordinarily managed have broken down.

Compliance with the ombudsmen's recommendations is extremely good.[60] In the 43 years of the PO there have been a total of six reports[61] made to Parliament under section 10(3). These six cases are summarized in Appendix 7. Alongside these six reports, there have been at least three additional reports that have involved serious and lengthy disagreement between the PO and government and led to a

57 See pp. 185-7.

58 Parliamentary Comissioner for Administration Act 1967, ss.10(4) and 10(3).

59 Health Services Commissioner Act 1993, s.14.

60 See p. 118.

61 PO (1978; 1995), PHSO (2005a; 2006a; 2008a; 2009d).

parliamentary response.[62] All are worthy of in-depth analysis of the kind that space prohibits here (e.g. Gregory and Drewry 1991; James and Longley 1996; Kirkham 2006; Kirkham, Thompson, Buck 2008; Harlow and Rawlings 2009, 554-62). But taken together they reveal an interesting pattern.

Unsurprisingly, the six PO special reports and the three additional reports share strong common features. Most importantly, they all demonstrate very clearly that ombudsman investigations can and do impinge on sensitive areas of government decision-making. In these investigations the PO has periodically attempted to resolve a dispute in a subject matter that has far-reaching implications for government policy and has caused widespread grievance. Thus all nine reports identified above have:

(i) concerned decisions made by government that impacted on significant numbers of people;[63]
(ii) included a finding that the government's approach to establishing a compensation scheme constituted maladministration;
(iii) in effect recommended that the government commit large sums of money to making additional compensation available;
(iv) tackled head-on the government's concern that acceptance of the ombudsman's recommendations might set a difficult precedent for the future.

A further similarity is that the nature and/or difficulties in demonstrating causation between loss and departmental action have on occasion been an issue (Gregory and Drewry 1991). In particular, the difficult question has arisen as to whether the government should be deemed liable in the compensatory sense for failures of regulation over highly complex areas of private sector activity. It has been argued that this form of government decision-making is very different from those areas where public authority implements actions which have a direct effect on individuals. In other words, because the government is not the 'primary wrongdoer' (Harlow and Rawlings 2009, 562) there is an argument that resultant instances of maladministration should be treated differently by the ombudsman. A key reason for taking such an approach might be to reduce the risks of the ombudsman being drawn into areas of complex regulatory decision-making which the office lacks the expertise and competence to investigate (*ibid*). But there is nothing in the legislation to rule out the investigation of maladministration in regulatory areas of government practice, and it is not entirely clear that the nature of the issues involved are so very different in the application of standards of good administration than

62 See the Third Report of the PCA, Sachsenhausen (HC 54 of 1967-68); Fifth Report of the PCA, Court Line (HC 498 of 1974-75); and Barlow Clowes (HC 76 of 1989-90).

63 The smallest affected groups are in Sachsenhausen (HC 54 of 1967-68) and Cold Comfort (PHSO 2009d), which involved 12 and 24 people respectively. In all the other reports the numbers of people involved measured in the hundreds and thousands.

other areas of government practice. What is different is the scale and consequent political nature of the dispute.

There is not the room in this work to resolve this particular debate; albeit the growth of the ombudsman's systemic investigatory work in other countries identified in Chapter 5 suggests that the ombudsman is precisely the sort of independent and permanently established accountability/integrity institution that should be called upon to investigate controversial government actions that appear to involve maladministration. What does need to be explored further here though is the means by which disputes are resolved on those occasions when the ordinary informal framework of consultation and persuasion breaks down. Resolving such disputes is made all the more complicated because, in most instances where they have occurred, the issue will have arrived at the ombudsman's door having already been considered either by the courts[64] or some form of inquiry,[65] and in some instances both.[66] The solution in most parliamentary ombudsman schemes is for differences between the ombudsman and the executive to be aired before Parliament.[67] Given the proximity of such disputes to the political sphere of responsibility, such a resolution process is entirely appropriate. Any process that gave the courts the final word could have the effect of reducing cooperation during ombudsman investigations and increasing the likelihood of entrenched positions being taken (Kirkham, Thompson and Buck 2008). This would not only affect the resolution role of the ombudsman method/enterprise but also its efforts to improve administration.

In this respect the work of PASC and its predecessor, the Select Committee on the Parliamentary Commissioner for Administration, in response to the section 10(3) reports listed in Appendix 7 have represented refreshingly constructive examples of parliamentary practice. Inquiries have been conducted which have involved taking evidence from the PO, officials and sometimes ministers, as well as external experts and complainants. In each instance the committee has produced a report that has supported the PO, but only after an in-depth investigation has been undertaken that at least countenanced the possibility of disagreeing with aspects of the PO's report.[68] The select committee has not slavishly supported its PO; rather

64 See *Debt of Honour* and *Association of British Civilian Internees: Far East Region v Secretary of State for Defence* [2003] EWCA Civ 472; [2003] QB 1397.

65 E.g. *Barlow Clowes* and the Le Quesne Inquiry, *Financial Regulation Review*, Summer 1988.

66 E.g. *Equitable Life* and the Penrose Inquiry, *Report of the Equitable Life Inquiry*, HC 290 2003/04 and *Equitable Life Assurance Society v Hyman* [2002] 1 AC 408.

67 See pp. 183-5.

68 SCPCA 1978 *Land Compensation Act 1973* HC 591 of 1977-78; SCPCA 1995 *The Channel Tunnel Rail Link and Exceptional Hardship* HC 270 of 1994-95; PASC *A Debt of Honour* HC 735 of 2005-06; PASC (2006); PASC, *Justice Delayed: The Ombudsman's Report on Equitable Life* (HC 41 of 2008-09). In *Cold Comfort* the matter was resolved following PASC's evidence session with the Permanent Secretary and exchanges of letters with the minister.

they have considered each case for themselves and on the evidence come to a view. Despite having a government majority the committee has not operated along party lines, which is appropriate given its constitutional role. In some instances the committee has returned to the issue at a later date[69] and debates have been forced on the floor of the House by way of an Estimates Day adjournment debate.[70]

An assessment of the parliamentary procedure to resolve ombudsman/government disputes would suggest that it has been successful in upholding the credibility of the ombudsman, in that every case (eventually) has led to an outcome with which the PO is satisfied. This assessment needs to be qualified by the existence of additional activities that have often surrounded the resolution of such disputes. Significant lobbying of government and MPs often takes place alongside parliamentary consideration of ombudsman reports and sometimes parallel legal actions have placed further pressure on the government to seek a resolution.[71] This spread of activity makes it extremely difficult to ascertain where ultimate credit should lie for the achievement of a resolution.

In the bigger context though, the section 10(3) procedure could also be considered successful in that it remains a very rarely used weapon of the ombudsman. The section 10(3) process in effect represents the cutting edge of ombudsman practice and acts as a barometer for the health of the institution. Overuse of the process could indicate an ombudsman scheme under pressure and no longer being given the respect of government. This has at points been a concern. Indeed, of late there has been a small but symbolically significant increase in non-compliance with the PO's reports, with four out of the six section 10(3) reports issued made between 2005 and 2009. Following the government's initial rejection of one of these reports PASC responded vigorously.

> We share the Ombudsman's concern that the Government has been far too ready to dismiss her findings of maladministration. Our investigations have shown that these findings were sound. It would be extremely damaging if Government became accustomed simply to reject findings of maladministration, especially if an investigation by this Committee proved there was indeed a case to answer. It would raise fundamental constitutional issues about the position of the Ombudsman and the relationship between Parliament and the Executive.[72]

Yet the impressive return of the PO in resolving disputes, albeit with the help of a variety of mechanisms, suggests that an appropriate balance has been struck

---

69 E.g. PASC *Justice Denied? The Government's Response to the Ombudsman's Report on Equitable Life* (HC 219 of 2008-09).

70 *Hansard*, HC vol. 454, cols 512-47 (7 December 2006).

71 E.g. *Elias v Secretary of State for Defence* [2005] EWHC 1435 (Admin); [2005] IRLR, *Robins and others v Secretary of State for Work and Pensions* Case C-278/05 and *R (Equitable Members Action Group) v HM Treasury* [2009] EWHC 2495 (Admin).

72 PASC (2006, para. 78).

between the government and the ombudsman, and that Parliament has succeeded in operating as an arena within which such disputes can be slowly resolved through dialogue and time. As will be discussed in the next section, though, of late this may have only occurred thanks to the intervention of the courts.

To make this process even more powerful, PASC (2009a, 5) has advised that when the PHSO issues a special report 'a [parliamentary] mechanism is needed to ensure a debate and decision on how to respond', in particular one that does not rely on the goodwill of the government. It recommended that in the long term the Procedure Committee should examine ways in which such a debate could be triggered under Standing Orders, but as an interim measure 'that the Government commits to providing a three-hour debate, in government time and on a substantive motion, on any future report by the Ombudsman concluding that injustice has gone unremedied and laid under section 10(3) of the Parliamentary Commissioner Act 1967' (PASC 2009a, 5). However, the government has rejected this suggestion (PASC 2010, 3).[73]

One final consideration is whether an equivalent to the section 10(3) process could be used to bolster the work of the LGO. After all, both the Scottish Public Services Ombudsman (SPSO) and the Public Services Ombudsman for Wales (PSOW) can make such reports about local authority issues to their respective Parliament and Assembly. Would it be so constitutionally inappropriate for the LGO to be able to make such a report to Westminster and thus require locally elected representatives and their officials to justify before a nationally elected Parliament their decision to reject the recommendations of a nationally appointed ombudsman? It would certainly be a controversial power for Parliament to possess, yet under such a process a Parliamentary Select Committee would have no power to force a local authority to implement an ombudsman's report, but would be able to subject it to enhanced public scrutiny. We would submit that this is a preferable solution to allowing the courts to intervene.[74]

This latter conclusion is drawn because, implicit in the ombudsman model that we have described in this monograph, is the understanding that even after the input of Parliament, a public authority should retain the power to make the final decision as to the way forward and this can include rejecting the ombudsman's recommendations. Recent years have revealed, however, that there is an additional route by which an impasse between the ombudsman and a public authority can be challenged.

73 In addition to this recommendation, PASC has also suggested the abolition of the 'MP filter'. At the same time, the government once again rejected the abolition of the MP filter: see PASC (2009a; 2010).

74 The legal solution has been much debated in the past: see Himsworth (1985) and Widdicombe (1986).

The Courts

The courts can directly influence ombudsman investigations in three ways. Firstly, as discussed in Chapter 6, the courts in common law countries have taken the view that ombudsman reports are reviewable but at the same time have generally shown a healthy degree of respect towards their decision-making.[75] Secondly, on occasion parallel judicial proceedings can heavily influence the government's response to an ombudsman investigation.[76] Thirdly, as demonstrated in two recent cases,[77] the courts can rule upon the legality of the government's response to an ombudsman report. It is this last form of judicial intervention that needs to be explored here as it has profound implications for the ombudsman's constitutional status.

The capacity of the court to rule upon the legality of the government's response to an ombudsman report was confirmed in *Bradley*. This case concerned the government's negative response to the PO's *Occupational Pensions* report, which led to a parliamentary enquiry under the section 10(3) process discussed in the previous section. A virtually identical case followed in *R (Equitable Members Action Group) v HM Treasury* [2009] EWHC 2495 (Admin) (*EMAG*), which concerned the government's rejection of the *Equitable Life* report. In both instances the government had rejected both findings and recommendations of the PO. The court made no ruling with regard to the government's decision to reject the *recommendations* of the PO, but in both cases the court ruled that the government had acted irrationally in rejecting the PO's *findings* in that it had failed to demonstrate 'cogent reasons' for its response.[78] The end result in both cases was that the government had to reconsider its position and eventually this process, together with continued parliamentary scrutiny of the matter and other influences, led to the government implementing, at least partially, the recommendations of the PO.

The significance of the *Bradley* ruling is that it provides further evidence of the enhanced status of the modern ombudsman enterprise within the constitution. By requiring public bodies to provide cogent reasons for rejecting the PO's findings it confirms in law that the ombudsman is the authoritative voice in determining the application of the maladministration/injustice test to public sector activity. Public bodies cannot simply choose to agree to disagree with the ombudsman or to express a bona fide difference of opinion.[79] Admittedly, the impact of the *Bradley* ruling is that dense ombudsman/executive disputes will be given an added level of complexity, and the freedom to act of both the executive and Parliament will be

---

75 See pp. 174-7.

76 E.g. *Elias v Secretary of State for Defence* [2005] EWHC 1435 (Admin); [2005] IRLR 788.

77 *R (on the application of Bradley and others) v Secretary of State for Work and Pensions* [2008] EWCA Civ 36, [2008] 3 All ER 1116 and *R (Equitable Members Action Group) v HM Treasury* [2009] EWHC 2495 (EMAG).

78 *Bradley* at [126]; *EMAG* at [112].

79 *Bradley* at [72].

compromised to a degree (Varuhas 2009, 112-14). But whilst the *Bradley* ruling strengthens the impact of the ombudsman's findings, it does this without altering either the executive's ultimate legal discretion to act (or not act) in response to an ombudsman's findings or remove Parliament's ability to influence the outcome. It is submitted here that this is an entirely appropriate rebalancing of the constitutional balance of power in the twenty-first century.

The decision in *Bradley* has, however, been subject to academic critique (e.g. Varuhas 2009; Endicott 2009), broadly along the lines that it represents an affront to Parliament's authority and that it invites the judiciary to subject government decision-making to a degree of inquisition that is inappropriate for the judicial review process.

The first argument rests on a particular view of the constitution and the lack of reference given to the legal authority of ombudsman reports in ombudsman legislation, in particular the Parliamentary Commissioner Act 1967. By contrast, the Act does refer specifically to the section 10(3) process, with the implication that the resolution of PO/government disputes should be a purely political matter (e.g. Endicott 2009, 484-5). But the Act is over 40 years old and was written in an era which pre-dates modern judicial review. Moreover, in the intervening years it has become painfully obvious to most political scientists that Parliament is ill-equipped to call the executive to account by itself, notwithstanding the attractive simplicity of the traditional separation of powers version of the constitution. The *Bradley* ruling is a powerful and necessary recognition of the reliance the modern constitution places on a series of accountability institutions, not just the ombudsman. Were it possible, and indeed legal, for the government to be able to ignore the PO's findings on the sole ground that it had a rational reason for coming to an alternative viewpoint, then potentially the government could treat the PO's report with no respect and subsequently bulldoze its way past the Parliamentary Select Committee process confident in its parliamentary majority. In effect, before the court's intervention, there was a real danger that this was precisely what was happening with both the *Occupational Pensions* and *Equitable Life* reports referred to above. To combat this potential outcome, what the *Bradley* ruling does is make the government work harder in defending its position when it presents its case to Parliament, while at the same time placing further pressure on the ombudsman to ensure that its findings cannot be easily dismissed by way of rational argument.

Significantly, the *Bradley* ruling does not grant the court the final say on the matter of either the findings or the recommendations in an ombudsman report; it only implies that the government should not be able to act as if it were the final arbiter on the facts of the dispute and the findings of the ombudsman. Indeed, the ruling does not even imply that the government cannot disagree with the findings of the ombudsman. It only requires that if the government chooses to disagree with the ombudsman it needs to provide 'cogent reasons' that directly address those findings, rather than simply expressing an alternative point of view. In this respect, it is noticeable that in both *Bradley* and *EMAG* the court found that a fundamental flaw in the government's response was a tendency to misinterpret the position of the PO and consequently avoid addressing the true findings made.[80]

The consequence of the *Bradley* ruling is that where the government fails to demonstrate cogency in its response, the matter is returned to the political arena for resolution within which the government retains full control of the eventual outcome. The added burden for the government is that at this stage it is required to confront the ombudsman's report directly and rationally and, if it opts to do so, find alternative reasons for rejecting the PO's recommendations. The PO has stated on a number of occasions that this is a perfectly acceptable approach for the government to take as there may be strong political grounds for rejecting an ombudsman's recommendations, including the costs of implementation (PASC 2006, para. 69).[81]

The second major critique of the *Bradley* ruling is that it allows for an improper degree of judicial scrutiny of government decision-making, which goes against the underlying role of the courts. Further, it has been argued that judicial review should only be available to an individual where other suitable remedies are unavailable. According to this logic, being as the complainants that brought the case had access to the PO, and the PO had access to the section 10(3) process and Parliament, the *Bradley* ruling represents an improper extension of the court's remit (Endicott 2009, 485-7). Given the inherent discretion possessed by the Administrative Court in choosing which cases to accept for review, and indeed the court's decision to review decisions of the ombudsman,[82] the latter point rests upon a particular conception of judicial review that does not appear to have the full support of current case law. It does though map directly onto a traditional understanding of the law/politics divide implicit in the separation of powers model, which grants accountability institutions such as the ombudsman only a subsidiary role belonging to the political branch of the constitution. Given that our research has identified that in practice the ombudsman operates in a significantly more autonomous manner than traditional theory allows, this is not an account of the modern constitution that we can subscribe to. The fascinating outcome of *Bradley* is that it would appear that neither does the Court of Appeal.

The critique that the courts in *Bradley* and *EMAG* were required to undertake rigorous examination of the merits of the government response to the PO's reports, and that this represents an unwanted extension of the test of irrationality, is a powerful one (Endicott 2009, 495-6). Yet, even here, it is submitted that this does not represent an illegitimate evolution of the judicial review process. Although the *Bradley* ruling applied a more powerful variant of the normal irrationality

80 *Bradley* at [108]; *EMAG* at [108]-[112].

81 There was, however, an *obiter* statement in *Bradley* that the LGO's finding by contrast would be considered binding. See further, Law Commissioner (2010a, paras 6.61-62).

82 *R v Parliamentary Commissioner for Administration, ex parte Dyer* [1994] All ER 375; *R v Local Commissioner for Administration for the North and East of England, ex parte Bradford County Council* [1979] QB 287.

test, this is justified by the constitutional status of the ombudsman. This was not an instance of a public body choosing to differ in its opinion upon advice that it had received, or a public body failing to take fully take into account a relevant consideration. The ombudsman is a leading player in the administrative justice system, specifically charged by Parliament with providing an independent determination on matters of maladministration. As such the ombudsmen have been described by the Law Commission as 'a system of justice in their own right' (Law Commission 2010, para. 5.25). What the government did with the *Occupational Pensions* and *Equitable Life* reports was to fail to address directly the authoritative finding of this system of justice; such an activity can certainly be considered as an abuse of power worthy of judicial scrutiny.

There are legitimate fears that the addition of the *Bradley* course of action to the ombudsman process could lead to added legalization of the ombudsman process and further slow down the process of resolution (Varuhas 2009, 113-14). It is submitted here that this is highly unlikely to occur, and if it did, then it would be evidence of a much deeper underlying problem in the ombudsman system. Ombudsman/executive disputes should, if necessary, be resolved by the ordinary political process. The *Bradley* ruling only really applies in situations where the government uses disingenuous tactics to avoid the full reasoning behind an ombudsman finding or Parliament fails in its role in effectively scrutinizing the ombudsman's conclusions. If this was occurring on such a regular basis that considerable numbers of applications were being made to court based on *Bradley*, then this would indicate either that the PO was consistently overstepping the mark in its investigations, or that the government no longer respected the institution. Both scenarios would call for a radical rethink of the ombudsman enterprise and powerful intervention on the part of Parliament.

Conclusion

This chapter has explored the need for the ombudsmen to work with others to enhance its potential to achieve its core objectives. Perhaps the most obvious set of relationships for the ombudsmen to pursue are those with other institutions in the administrative justice system. Yet the term 'system' is more of an aspiration than a description. The different partners do not yet cooperate with everyone, nor to the fullest extent. There is not even an organized and coherent access point to the system for its users. The idea of a system and a holistic, integrated approach to administrative justice is new and yet to take root. The AJTC may understand these issues and has a clear remit to push for improvements, but the body is relatively new and has limited resources. It is likely, therefore, that the ombudsmen will be required to pursue a range of approaches to enhance its relationships with other aspects of the administrative justice system.

Of all the relationships reviewed in this chapter, it is perhaps the connection of the ombudsman with the traditional institutions of the tripartite separation of powers that represents the most challenging development. The development of additional layers of scrutiny by which governmental decisions can be scrutinized represents a fascinating evolution of the modern constitution, whereby the different branches appear to engage in an ongoing dialogue about the efficacy of a particular set of decisions. Lying behind the critique of the *Bradley* ruling is the sense that an ostensibly political process that takes place in the parliamentary branch of the constitution is being infiltrated illegitimately by the courts. Such a conclusion, however, is at odds with the argument being presented in this book, that in fact the ombudsman stands alone in the constitution and that its position deserves respect and support. It is not an agent of Parliament; it is an autonomous institution, albeit one whose work heavily intertwines with both the operation of the traditional three branches of the constitution and the more recently introduced accountability agents in a series of simultaneous relationships. This is the way of the modern constitution. It is impossible and unrealistic to chart a way back to the relatively simple world of the past in which accountability actions could be labelled as either political or legal; moreover, nor should one want to. As the concept of good administration demonstrates, there are constitutional issues that are not easily resolvable through the traditional mechanisms.

This chapter has explored the importance of the ombudsman creating a series of strong, workable relationships with other institutions in the constitution, and in particular the administrative justice system, in order to provide the optimum scenario for the efficient and effective delivery of its core roles. In the final chapter we take some of these findings a stage further to make recommendations about how the overall system can be improved.

PART IV
Conclusion

Chapter 8
The Twenty-First Century Ombudsman Enterprise

Introduction

Of the many underlying aims that motivated the writing of this monograph, a primary goal was to update the rather tired analysis of the ombudsman that too often appears in standard textbooks. Much of what is written still owes more to past commentaries on the institution as an overly formal, inefficient 'Rolls-Royce' complaint-handler operating at the margins of dispute resolution than current reality. By contrast, our research has uncovered a potentially dynamic and flexible institution, better equipped to tackle the needs of the modern administrative justice system and facilitate the goals of proportionate dispute resolution than the other options available. In this chapter, we summarize our findings and understanding of the ombudsman enterprise at the beginning of the twenty-first century. It is an overview that we hope will establish the template for future research in this area.

But in this concluding chapter we go a stage further. Although the research has been informed by developments in ombudsman practice around the world, it is targeted in the first instance at a UK audience. In this respect, as much as we have found evidence of much good practice, there are a number of reforms that would further improve the ombudsman model. This chapter details some of our leading recommendations before some concluding remarks summarizing the trajectory and implications of the ombudsman enterprise from the margins to a central position within the constitutional order.

The Ombudsman Enterprise and the Constitutional Order

One of the leading themes of this monograph has been to argue that our concept of the 'ombudsman enterprise'[1] should be mainstreamed within the constitutional order. Previously public and scholarly attention to the role and impact of ombudsmen has been marginal and marginalized. We have argued that ombudsman institutions in liberal democracies do not fit well within traditional Diceyan constitutional analysis. Ombudsman offices are better understood as 'integrity' bodies, operating alongside a series of other institutions that promote integrity and accountability in

1 See pp. 1-9.

the constitutional order.[2] Collectively, the scale and impact of the work performed by such bodies challenges the separation of powers orthodoxy of legislature, executive and judiciary, arguably through the addition of an integrity branch of the constitution. We found much evidence to support this position, not only from the scholarly literature (e.g. Brown and Head 2005; Spigelman 2004; Sampford *et al* 2005; Head *et al* 2008; Stuhmcke 2008a), but also from our interviews with ombudsman office-holders and others in the UK, Ireland, Australia and New Zealand. Recent court rulings in the UK have provided further evidence to support this constitutional development.

The utility of the ombudsman idea has also been demonstrated by its increasing global take-up and its ability to reach across the public/private divide, developments that should be matched by a reappraisal of the wider contribution that ombudsmen can make towards reforming the constitutional order. One explanation for its increasing popularity and endurance as an institution has been that the ombudsman model is relatively flexible and adapts successfully in diverse nation states. Characteristically, its flexibility has been sustained in many cases by quite robust, proactive and even experimental management, thus justifying the 'enterprise' title deployed in our book.

We have argued that the key to understanding the ombudsman's potential contribution to constitutional arrangements is an appreciation of the underlying *values* that the ombudsman upholds. A prime example of such values can be found in the wider concept of 'good administration' which includes not only substantive legal and procedural rules, but also, in the words of the European Ombudsman, a set of non-legal standards, a 'life beyond legality' (Diamandouros 2007, para. 4), or not only 'lawfulness' but 'proper conduct' (Brenninkmeijer 2006, 3). The ombudsman offices can provide an important constitutional service in terms of promoting this notion of good administration. Of necessity there remains an opaque division of labour between the courts and ombudsmen in promoting good administration, reflecting the strengths and weaknesses of their respective core techniques of adversarialism and investigation. Judicial review proceedings have generally been quite limited in interrogating evidential matters, while one of the paradigm features of the ombudsman institution is the wide-ranging power of investigation.

The Ombudsman Enterprise and Administrative Justice

We have further argued that an understanding of the place of the ombudsman enterprise within the overall constitutional order necessarily requires an appreciation of the way in which it fits within the 'administrative justice system'. The narrative given about the policy developments in the UK relating to this

---

2 See pp. 15-29.

system[3] shows that although the holistic notion of such a system exists from at least the time of the publication of *Transforming Public Services* (DCA 2004), the reality of a more recognizable system remains to date an aspiration – one which ideally the Administrative Justice and Tribunal Council (AJTC) would contribute to in the future. We examined both the descriptive and normative concepts of administrative justice and concluded that a tripartite definition was appropriate, as follows:

1. all initial decision-making by public bodies impacting on citizens – this will include the relevant statutory regimes and the procedures used to make such decisions ('getting it right');
2. all redress mechanisms available in relation to the initial decision-making ('putting it right');
3. the network of governance and accountability relationships surrounding the public bodies tasked with decision-making impacting upon citizens and those tasked with providing remedies ('setting it right').

The notions of 'getting it right' and 'putting it right' are well established in contemporary scholarship on administrative justice;[4] and the 'setting it right' category appears to us to be a convenient way to characterize the wider constitutional and socio-political environments which will inevitably condition 'getting/putting it right' activity.

Building on this understanding through a review of theories of administrative justice, we have offered our own typology of administrative justice that seeks to combine our functional and institutional definition of administrative justice with existing explanatory typologies.[5] This analysis has enabled us to offer an illustration of how our typology might look as applied to specific administrative justice systems,[6] the point being that our typology should facilitate the critical exposure of a number of interacting analytical layers at work within the administrative justice system.

The relationships between concepts, theories and policy developments relating to administrative justice have also been given further focus. For example, the developments in public expectations and public management culture (e.g. the charter initiatives, New Public Management (NPM) and 'digital-era governance') have clearly required transformations in the policy direction of key parts of the system. Policy in this area has attempted to identify and support the consumer or 'user's' viewpoint, if necessary demolishing existing hierarchies in order to

3 See pp. 76-80.

4 See also the definition of 'administrative justice system' in relation to the AJTC's functions: TCEA 2007, Sched. 7, para. 13(4), discussed at pp. 59-60.

5 See Chapter 3, Figure 3.1.

6 See Chapter 3 for references to the theorists' works and see also Figures 3.1 and 3.3.

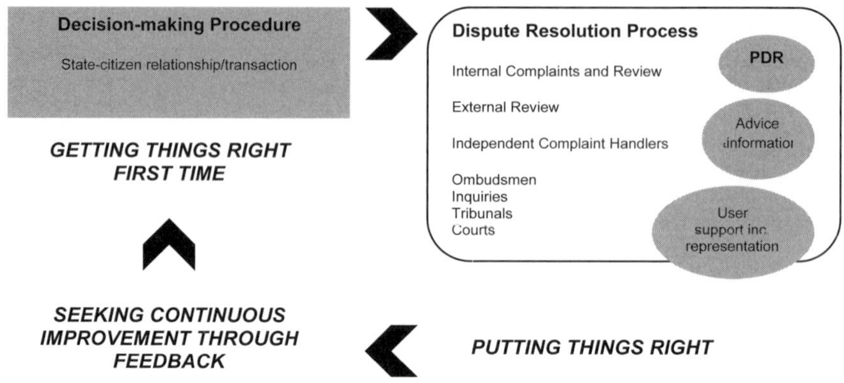

Figure 8.1 Dynamic model for 'getting things right first time'
Source: AJTC (2009, 8).

achieve this; the transformation of the tribunals systems is a case in point. Not unconnected to this 'bottom-up' version of system-building, there has also emerged a broad consensus in the policy communities to pursue 'appropriate' or 'proportionate' dispute resolution (PDR). Given the historic flexibility of the ombudsman enterprise referred to above, and as evidenced by their increasing strengths in building customer service values, it is likely that ombudsman offices are now particularly well placed to deliver PDR solutions that governments will require, particularly in a period of austerity. We would advise though that the ombudsman will work best if properly integrated into a suitably coordinated administrative justice system.

Getting it Right

The antidote to the almost exclusive concern of administrative law scholarship with *remedies* has been the emergence of administrative justice theory which, at least initially, provided an equally exclusive focus on the mass of *first-instance decision-making* performed by public service organizations. The ombudsman enterprise, though primarily like the courts and tribunals and other independent complaint-handlers in the business of 'putting it right', has also made a significant contribution to 'getting it right'. Put another way, the ombudsman's role is not only to provide individual resolution of disputes, but also to disseminate collective lessons of improvement for administrative bodies in order that they 'get it right' first time in their routine decision-making that affects the citizen. The figure above from an AJTC scoping paper illustrates the relevant interactions relevant to the wider landscape of administrative justice (Figure 8.1).

We have examined the various and sometimes innovative ways via outreach activity in which such lessons are drawn out from the basis of individual complaint-handling.[7] This side of the ombudsman's work has been transformed by the tendency in recent years for the public agencies investigated to have their own internal complaint mechanism. One consequence of this development in public administration has been the general result that the ombudsman is now acting as a second-tier complaint-handler. This has in turn produced ideal conditions in which ombudsmen have developed further their expertise as producers of authoritative advice on complaint-handling; the appearance of the Parliamentary and Health Service Ombudsman's *Principles of Good Administration* (PHSO 2007a) is a good example of this. We think it is likely that this development should be further intensified by reform initiatives, already on public agendas in Scotland and Wales, that will place ombudsman offices more formally in the role of a 'design authority' that will oversee the full range of internal complaint-handling within public agencies.[8]

One of the most striking features identified in our research and by other commentators is the extent to which the ombudsman enterprise has made efforts to encourage the public bodies it investigates to develop good administrative practice. There is plenty of evidence of ombudsman offices expanding and enhancing their investigatory skill sets in order to deliver the message of good administration so that public services are more likely to 'get it right' first time. We have examined some of the ways in which ombudsman offices publicized and reflected upon their investigatory practice, for example, by 'annual letters', regular case digests and commentaries. The ombudsman office-holders we interviewed in the course of our research were well aware of the potential opportunities to draw out lessons from their individual dispute resolution work and feed these back to achieve systemic improvements in public services. This was achieved principally by conducting major investigations into a recurrent theme of concern. On occasion two or more ombudsman offices combined their efforts and resulting reports to address particular issues (e.g. PSOW and LGO 2006; HSO and LGO 2008; 2009). Such investigations often benefited from a larger pool of information from which wider conclusions could legitimately be inferred. This iterative process of investigation, recommendation and later follow-up can clearly act as an effective early warning system of the existence of systemic flaws in administrative systems. However, the 'follow-up' element of this process is not always undertaken, with the consequence that the institutional learning of an ombudsman organization may be lost. The legal frameworks usually permit discretionary special and further reports to be made, often to a Parliament (see Appendix 4). The ensuing public debates following such reports have frequently made a real impact; the *Long-Term Care* (HSO 2004), *Debt of Honour* (PHSO 2005a), *Tax Credits* (PHSO 2005c; 2007d) and *Occupational Pensions* (PHSO 2006a) reports are prime examples. On occasion the impact takes some time to be achieved. At the time of completing our

7 See pp. 125-41.

8 See Sinclair (2008, 4) and p. 145, n.53, for developments in Scotland and Wales respectively.

manuscript of this monograph, the PHSO's work on *Equitable Life* (PHSO 2008a; 2009b) was acknowledged in the form of an Equitable Life Payments Scheme Bill, announced in the coalition government's first Queen's Speech in May 2010, which will apparently set up a 'fair and transparent' compensation fund for Equitable Life policy-holders who have suffered from the 'serial regulatory failure' identified by the Parliamentary Ombudsman (PO).[9] On occasion, such reports have had a far-reaching and pervasive influence on administration, for example, the major investigation into immigration cases conducted by the Australian Commonwealth Ombudsman (CO 2007a). Some work has been carried out in an attempt to develop a convincing methodology by which the impact and cost-effectiveness of such big investigations can be calibrated (e.g. Stuhmcke 2006), and this is likely to need further development for the future.

Related to this important aspect of ombudsmanry is the existence of an 'own-initiative' power of investigation in many jurisdictions we considered (see Appendix 2). This power is usually triggered by existing individual complaint-handling work and generally the authority to conduct such investigations is only limited broadly by the remit of the complaints received. However, we also considered cases where own-initiative powers were used without reference to individual complaints, for example, in one case being triggered by 'media and academic sources' (QO 2008a, x). There appears to be an increasing amount of evidence that such own-initiative powers can provide a more targeted and proactive investigation than more orthodox forms of systemic inquiry, and there were some good examples of best practice, for example, the approach of the Special Ombudsman Response Team (SORT) in Ontario (Ontario Ombudsman 2009, 33). Increasingly we found evidence of the ombudsman enterprise developing a research base, knowledge management systems and training to support themed, systemic and own-initiative work.

In keeping with some commentators' observations that the ombudsman model has evolved from 'fire-fighting'/'resolution' and 'fire-watching'/'improvement' to 'fire-prevention' (Snell 2007), we also observed an enthusiasm, more so in Australia than the UK, for 'compliance auditing', i.e. the monitoring of various bodies' conformity with legal and other standards. The promotion of good administration by such means of audit and inspection has good prospects, in our view, of strengthening the ombudsman enterprise's ability to make a significant contribution to the integrity of the constitutional order. However, it is equally true that care and sensitivity needs to be taken in identifying suitable ombudsman schemes with which to introduce such new techniques. Given the very different spread of regulatory bodies that exist in the UK, it is possible that not all of the

---

9 See 'Parliamentary Ombudsman welcomes Equitable Life Bill', *PHSO News Release*, 25 May 2010. Available at: <http://www.ombudsman.org.uk/about-us/media-centre/press-releases/2010/parliamentary-ombudsman-welcomes-equitable-life-bill> (accessed 1 June 2010).

ombudsman techniques adopted elsewhere will be easily transplanted into the UK ombudsman community.

Putting it Right

Within the ambit of our tripartite definition, the ombudsman enterprise is (like the courts and tribunals) pre-eminently involved in the task of 'putting it right' for individual complainants. This corresponds to the primary 'resolution' or 'redress' role referred to in existing ombudsman scholarship (Heede 2000).

The task of 'putting it right' requires the provision of a service that will uphold standards of customer care. Some of the past delays in processing ombudsman complaints (see PO 1998, para. 1.10) are surely unacceptable and will tend to undermine fatally the legitimacy of the ombudsman's core activity. In that respect, although there have been efforts to upgrade customer care and service, there are always likely to be further improvements that could be made especially as the ombudsman should be an exemplar of complaint-handling practice if the office is to retain any legitimacy. Regular customer satisfaction surveys are useful sources of information, but there is a need for some objective verification of them in terms of methodology and interpretation if they are not to be captured by ombudsman offices as a ready means to provide supportive headlines in their annual reports. Furthermore, it should not be forgotten that a significant disadvantage of the investigatory technique is the risk that complainants experience a loss of ownership of the process.[10] One under-researched area we have identified is the extent to which closure for complainants is achieved by ombudsman services.[11] The quality and direction of such customer service is likely to be dependent on the leadership given within the ombudsman community, but also will be significantly influenced by the location of ombudsmen within the wider administrative justice system.

There have been some persistent concerns over the level of the public's awareness about the existence and nature of the ombudsman's services,[12] reflecting a wider confusion about the possible routes of appeal and complaint that are available. This issue will need to be addressed as part of a more proactive style of ombudsmanry and as part of public legal education about rights and remedies which we would support.

A key feature of the ombudsman enterprise is its flexibility and generally this has been supported by a legal framework that allows significant areas of discretionary decision-making, such as the acceptance of complaints within jurisdiction, the conduct of the investigation process and other matters. The maladministration test and its equivalents have in the past been seen as restrictive but our research has indicated that the existing legal threshold tests are now used fairly flexibly to

10 See p. 5 at n.5 for the website addresses of 'ombudsmanwatch' organizations.

11 See pp. 120-21.

12 See pp. 94-8.

encompass both unlawfulness and a broader notion of improper conduct. There has also been a noticeable development in recent years for ombudsman offices to integrate the human rights agenda within their operations and culture (O'Reilly 2007; O'Brien 2009a). The remedies that ombudsmen recommend are generally a practically oriented package of measures, including the much underrated 'apology' and financial compensation. As we have seen, the latter can be substantial.

Setting it Right

A key theme of this monograph has been that we need to understand fully the network of accountability and governance relationships surrounding ombudsman bodies that arise from the wider environments of the administrative justice system and the overall constitutional order. The 'setting it right' element of our definition of administrative justice requires a system that manages, rationalizes and understands those relationships. As with the need to sensibly coordinate the operation of the administrative justice system, this implies that there is a need for ombudsmen to explore ways of interconnecting their work where appropriate with other accountability bodies such as auditors, if only to ensure that duplications of work are avoided. We concluded that the ombudsman enterprise relies upon three key institutional features: statutory and parliamentary support, independence and accountability.[13] All three will need to be addressed in any future design and management of an ombudsman scheme.

Our analysis of the link that many of the ombudsman offices have with a Parliament or other democratic assembly has shown how important that linkage can be, in particular when executive government is minded to reject the ombudsman's recommendations. It appears that the 'officer of Parliament' model of the ombudsman is essentially an unstable one requiring careful management.[14] There are some contradictions with parliamentary involvement in the work of the ombudsman; a select committee or similar will need to be close enough to the ombudsman to scrutinize its work, but sufficiently distant to respect the ombudsman's use of discretion. But while such parliamentary committees are constituted with a government majority there will continue to be tensions in its role, particularly in circumstances where severe criticisms are made by the ombudsman which reflect on that government's policy. However, the history of the Local Government Ombudsman (LGO) demonstrates that an absence of a satisfactory relationship with an elected body will undermine the legitimacy of the organization and ultimately may contribute towards a comparatively poor record of implementation of recommendations.

It is important too that the independence of ombudsman office-holders is maintained. The general move away from lifetime security of tenure towards fixed-

13 See generally, Chapter 6.

14 See pp. 158-60.

term appointments does not in our view undermine that objective, at least where the fixed term is an appreciable number of years. Parliamentary committee oversight needs to involve at least a working distinction between its *sponsorship* (e.g. budget, resources, appointment) and *scrutiny* (e.g. reports, policies, administration), a point well demonstrated by the 'two-committee model' from New Zealand. We also consider the recent interest in the UK to hold pre-appointment hearings for office-holders (Ministry of Justice 2007, paras. 76-9) to be a useful innovation.

In terms of accountability, the presentation of annual reports to Parliament and the accountability to a parliamentary committee provide default checks on the proper use of public funds. Annual reports have developed into more focused, themed and accessible documents, though their innovation from year to year also tends to disrupt methodologies for collecting and collating data, which makes year-on-year comparisons problematic. Ombudsman offices have tried to develop stronger corporate governance arrangements, for example, by setting up audit committees and issuing regular business plans. The PHSO has set up an advisory board as a 'critical friend' (PHSO 2010, 2-3). In addition, we found that increasingly ombudsman offices are developing internal reviews in relation both to their own decisions on complaints and about the service standards provided. However, the additional assurance of any external review seems beyond all but the largest ombudsman organizations – such as the Financial Ombudsman Service (FOS), which has contracted out this function. The provision of a further complaint route to another ombudsman also appears to be an approach that would inappropriately elongate the complaint process and lose the current advantage of relative expedition without any perceivable gain. It may be that this type of external review (of decisions) should be used sparingly and in exceptional cases, such as the complaint referred by the Scottish Public Services Ombudsman to an LGO (SPSO 2009a). Judicial review remains an important though limited default mechanism to ensure that the ombudsman enterprise remains within the bounds of 'legality, but it has far less to contribute to the additional territory of 'proper conduct' occupied by the ombudsman. The analysis of the recent case law[15] shows that where ombudsmen operate within the law there has developed a reasonable measure of deference to the ombudsmen's various discretionary powers. Judicial reviews are not likely to reach into these important discretionary areas; nor are they likely to provide much analysis of the ombudsman's contribution to good administration. Ideally, we conclude that the combination of regular, light-touch oversight by an informed parliamentary committee along with a comprehensive and in-depth periodic review, perhaps set at the mid-point of an ombudsman's fixed term of seven years' appointment, would provide an effective model of review and reflection.

---

15 See pp. 106-14.

Recommendations

In this last section we make certain recommendations about the future of the ombudsman enterprise in the UK and how it might be best nurtured within the wider administrative justice and constitutional environments. Although the design of UK ombudsmen offices has not been modified significantly since the PO was introduced in 1967, and has broadly withstood the test of time due to flexibility in both remit and operation, we believe it is now time for a thorough reappraisal to take place.

Leggatt-style Review of Ombudsmen Services

It is of the greatest importance, particularly in a period following the global recession of 2007-10, that public services are organized efficiently and are cost-effective. The pervasive cuts in public expenditure announced by the coalition administration on taking office in May 2010 will prompt close scrutiny of the public sector generally. Over the decade since the last review of (English-only) ombudsmen (Collcutt and Hourihan 2000) the landscape of administrative justice in the UK has changed significantly. There has been a significant development in the growth of internal complaint mechanisms within central and local government departments which has assisted the shift of principal ombudsman organizations into a second-tier complaint role. The various devolved solutions to the ombudsman technique have posed another set of challenges. There have also been huge changes in the policy direction and institutional structure in other parts of the administrative justice system reflected in the aspirations of *Transforming Public Services* (DCA 2004) and the establishment of a rationalized Tribunals Service and two-tier tribunals structure. This monograph has argued that these and other developments have played their part in moving the ombudsman enterprise into the centre of our constitutional arrangements.

Consequently, we recommend that a comprehensive reappraisal and review of ombudsmen and complaints schemes, along the lines of the Leggatt Review of tribunals (Leggatt 2001), is justified and should be established forthwith.[16] The overall remit would be to consider the role of ombudsman and other complaint services with a view to achieving a better fit within the wider administrative justice system. One of the issues on which we urge particular consideration is jurisdiction. One of the problems, particularly for the PHSO is the complexity of the arrangements of bodies within remit. Our preference would be for a legislative approach which stipulates public bodies as being within jurisdiction unless specifically excluded. The items explained below should also be within the remit of the proposed review.

---

16 The PHSO has also noted the likely need for such a review (Abraham 2008, 10; 2009c, 8).

Structural Reform: The Wiring Diagram

The issue which requires immediate attention in such a review is a fresh look at the rationalization of ombudsman offices that has been achieved to an extent in Scotland, Wales and Northern Ireland, compared to the asymmetry of ombudsman organization in England. There is a need for the construction of a new wiring diagram of ombudsman services in the UK. This would include considering the merits of an English Public Services Ombudsman responsible for health services and local government.[17] There also needs to be further consideration of the number of specialist ombudsmen and their relationships with each other. Different approaches may be needed in different parts of the UK. The population size of England might mean that police and prison complaints could not be as easily absorbed within a 'one-stop shop' as might be possible in Scotland, Northern Ireland and in the Australian states. Consideration should also be given to ensuring that the normal standards of independence for ombudsmen are applied throughout public services and that the title 'ombudsman' is protected accordingly.[18] The rationalization that has been achieved in the devolved territories should be further supported. The proposals in the review of the Northern Ireland ombudsman services in 2004 remain unimplemented: for example, the proposal, which we support, to merge the offices of the Assembly Ombudsman for Northern Ireland (AONI) with the Northern Ireland Commissioner for Complaints (NICC) to form a Northern Ireland Public Services Ombudsman. We are acutely aware that the consideration of such structural reforms must have regard to the larger administrative justice and constitutional frameworks which are also in a process of change and development. It is important therefore that our proposed review also takes into account the relationships that ombudsmen have with other 'integrity' institutions; in particular, we suggest that close scrutiny of the existing and potential interaction and collaboration with auditor bodies would be beneficial.

Removal of 'MP Filter'

The PO should have the 'MP filter' removed. It is an unnecessary barrier which we note both the PO and the select committee overseeing the PO have deplored, joining a number of authoritative statements to similar effect over at least the past decade (e.g. Collcutt and Hourihan 2000, paras 3.17-3.54; Law Commission 2008, paras 5.76-5.88; PASC 2009, Ev.12). The government's case for not including it

---

17 See Elliot (2006, 101), who supports this approach. Although we do not agree with the proposal, consideration should also be given to establishing *regional* ombudsmen in England (Dunleavy *et al* 2010).

18 As we have seen prisons ombudsmen occupy an unusual place, neither a fully independent specialist ombudsman nor the normal external review between the local resolution stage and the final stage of a public service ombudsman.

in the Regulatory Reform Order (RRO) of 2007[19] was that primary legislation was the appropriate way to implement such a reform, a far from compelling argument given the scope which RROs were intended to have in relation to statutes. In the Law Commission's recent consultation on this question, of 32 consultees, 31 were in favour of abolishing the MP filter and 16 favoured the 'dual track' option, i.e. keeping the current statutory provision but also allowing direct access to the PO (Law Commission 2010, paras 5.34, 5.38). The AONI has a similar 'Member of the Legislative Assembly (Northern Ireland) filter' which should also be removed.

Enhanced Legal Powers of Resolution

The UK ombudsman offices should have their legal powers of resolution enhanced, in line with the model provided by the Public Services Ombudsman for Wales (PSOW),[20] so that they are authorized to take any action deemed appropriate to resolve a complaint within jurisdiction; and this power may be exercised in addition to or instead of conducting an investigation. The RRO of 2007 only authorizes mediation in an investigation, although the proposal in the consultation paper for the RRO was wider (Cabinet Office 2005, paras 50-56). Further thought needs to be paid to the use of mediation by ombudsman services, in order that it can be applied proportionately, cost-effectively and without prejudice to complainants' rights to pursue their complaint in appropriate cases to a formal report stage. Legal powers also need adjusting so that *all* ombudsman offices have a legislative mandate to allow oral, in addition to written, complaints (see Appendix 1). A further legislative adjustment that will assist complainants' access to ombudsman services is to subject public bodies within the ombudsman's jurisdiction to a general legal duty[21] to inform members of the public of their legal right to complain to the ombudsman.

Enhanced Legal Powers of Improvement

We also consider that the ombudsmen's role in improvement can be enhanced by the addition of certain legal powers. In particular, we are persuaded that conferring an 'own-initiative' power of investigation would be beneficial. We were particularly struck by the fact that the Australasian ombudsmen simply cannot conceive of not having such a power. The LGO has a half-way house position which came into effect in 2008, stipulating that where matters come to the attention of the LGO in the course of an investigation, they may be taken up if it appears that a member of the public may have suffered injustice (see Appendix 2). The drawback is that it is reactive, whereas we suggest that it should be proactive, and that additionally implies there should be an adequate research capacity to analyse and to guide the

19 SI 1889/2007. See the discussion of the RRO at pp. 82-3.

20 Public Services Ombudsman (Wales) Act 2005, s.3.

21 See SPSO Act 2002, s.22 and PSOW Act 2005, s.33.

application and use of own-initiative investigation. We suggest that a full own-initiative power, allied with better coordination and cooperation with auditors and other integrity bodies, would assist ombudsman bodies further to play to their existing public service strengths. The enhanced learning that would result from a greater collaboration between these integrity bodies could be a more reliable basis to trigger such investigations, inspections or audits as appropriate.

As we have seen, the non-binding nature of ombudsman recommendations is a defining feature of the ombudsman enterprise. However, this does not mean that public bodies should not be placed under more structured arrangements to respond to such recommendations. We suggest a legislative provision that required public bodies to provide the ombudsman with evidence that their recommendations had been implemented (or alternatively to produce an argued explanation for non-implementation) would send out the right message and further inform the process of ombudsman follow-up. We also suggest the express addition, in existing legislation where necessary, of jurisdictional coverage where there is 'service failure', a point entirely consistent with the movement towards systemic investigation in ombudsman activity.

Implementation of the Law Commission's July 2008 Proposal

We would support the four proposals put out by the Law Commission for consultation in 2008 which have been revisited in a recent consultation (Law Commission 2008; 2010; 2010a):

- (i) the courts should have a specific power to stay proceedings when a case would be more appropriately dealt with by an ombudsman's investigation;
- (ii) the removal of the existing MP filter and its replacement with the dual track option (see above);
- (iii) the repeal of the current statutory bars which qualify the jurisdiction of the ombudsman to accept complaints that could be pursued in the courts, and its replacement with a legislative provision permitting ombudsman investigation where, in all the circumstances of the case, it was in the 'interests of justice' to investigate the claim;
- (iv) the ombudsmen be given the power to refer questions of law to a court (see Appendix 1).

The Law Commission's (2010a) review of these particular questions will be a useful contribution to, but not a substitute for, the more comprehensive Leggatt-style review of ombudsmen that we are proposing.[22]

22 The Law Commission's (2010a) consultation paper also makes suggestions regarding the appointment of the Parliamentary Ombudsman, harmonising the publication of reports into three types, the resolution of complaints (drawing on the Welsh provisions)

Access to Administrative Justice: Supporting Triage

Access, information, advice and support for members of the public are of fundamental importance both to the wider administrative justice system and its component parts, including the ombudsmen. The gathering evidence that the public do not understand the distinction between a complaint and an appeal (NAO 2005, 15; Dunleavy *et al* 2010, 445) needs to be robustly addressed. The distinction is not unimportant but it should not be a barrier to access to justice for an aggrieved person. We recommend that, within the remit of our proposed review, there is a clear steer towards the further consideration of triage and PDR as organizing concepts for the construction of first-contact advice and guidance sites within the administrative justice system. In principle, we support the suggestion that, instead of separate points of contact for complaints and appeals, there should be one door for each public body (Mullen 2009, para. 8.12), and the more radical proposal to create a 'common access point nationwide for all non-emergency public services', i.e. a Public Services Direct (PASC 2008, para. 42), also needs to be examined. There may however be circumstances where conjoining complaint and appeal-handling guidance is not possible, in which case we agree with the suggestion of the Public Administration Select Committee (PASC) that 'the distinction should be made as clear as possible and the person guided through the system' (PASC 2008, paras 19-22). There also needs to be care taken to avoid public confusion between advice, guidance and support services and the remedial complaint and appeal mechanisms available.[23] Finally, attention must also be given to the existing communication and information technology (IT) infrastructures and how these can be appropriately upgraded to facilitate the greater collaboration and shared learning that we envisage developing within and between integrity bodies.

Standardizing Complaints Procedures

We suggest that consideration be given to standardizing the internal complaints procedures of public services and the complaints procedures used by ombudsmen. We further advise that consideration be given to removing entirely the intermediate complaint bodies that have developed in certain sectors: for example, the Adjudicator's Office,[24] which examines complaints principally

---

and requiring the Local Government and Housing Ombudsmen to publish all of their reports to Parliament.

23 For example, confusion may arise in relation to National Health Service (NHS) trusts where they have Patient Advice and Liaison Services to provide quick advice and trouble-shooting services, but these are separate from the statutory Complaints Officer. See also Dunleavy *et al* (2010).

24 See the Adjudicator's Office website at: <http://www.adjudicatorsoffice.gov.uk/index.htm> (accessed 3 June 2010). The Adjudicator also examines complaints about the

about HM Revenue and Customs (HMRC), and the Independent Case Examiner,[25] who examines certain areas of complaint within the Department for Work and Pensions (DWP). We believe that this additional tier of complaint-handling simply adds an unnecessary obstacle in the duration of the 'complainant's journey'. We are not persuaded that the arguments are credibly made out for such intermediate complaint-handlers, for example, on the basis of their larger numbers (PASC 2008, para. 64). In our view, the existence of these intermediate bodies better demonstrates the need for government departments such as the HMRC and DWP to improve their own complaint-handling capacity rather than, in effect, delegating their internal complaint function to be dealt with by such bodies. Local internal complaint resolution is justified on the basis of speed and organizational learning and improvement, but if the complainant is dissatisfied with that then they should have access to a truly independent ombudsman.

Accountability and Oversight

Connected to our consideration of structural reforms and the construction of an appropriate 'wiring diagram' (see above), it is important that serious consideration is given by the UK's Parliaments and Assemblies to their arrangements for overseeing ombudsmen and the administrative justice system as a whole. In particular, we recommend that the English LGOs should have an adequate accountability framework and come under the remit of PASC. We recommend that the accountability and assurance of the ombudsman enterprise provided by the relevant link to an elected parliamentary or other body needs to combine regular committee review with a comprehensive in-depth review at the mid-point of an ombudsman office-holder's fixed-term appointment.[26] It is important too that the advice about complaint-handling and good administration, such as the *Principles* from the PHSO's office, is incorporated into the existing local government *Comprehensive Area Assessment*[27] and the central government *Capability Review Programme*.[28]

Office of the Public Guardian and The Insolvency Service.

25 See the Independent Case Examiner's website at: <http://www.ind-case-exam.org.uk/index.asp> (accessed 3 June 2010). The Independent Case Examiner also deals with complaints about the Child Maintenance and Enforcement Division (Northern Ireland) and the Northern Ireland Social Security Agency.

26 See pp. 230-31.

27 See: <http://www.idea.gov.uk/idk/core/page.do?pageId=8811984> (accessed 3 June 2010).

28 See: <http://www.civilservice.gov.uk/about/improving/capability/index.aspx> (accessed 3 June 2010).

Administrative Justice and Tribunals Council (AJTC)[29]

This body, unlike its predecessor, has a statutory remit to oversee the whole of the administrative justice system, including ombudsman organizations. Its position as the independent 'hub of the wheel' of the administrative justice system suggests that it must be a major stakeholder in the Leggatt-style review that we have proposed. Indeed, we believe that it is best placed to consult and advise government on the terms of reference for such a review and the options for appointment of the panel to undertake it.

In addition, there are a number of tasks that we believe the AJTC, in partnership with auditing and other bodies, could appropriately explore in the future: for example, the prospects for developing a standard methodology to compare costs of complaint resolution services; developing a more objective methodology to guide the construction of annual reporting; the facilitation of research capacity in particular for the smaller ombudsman offices that do not have the resources to sustain a dedicated research capacity by themselves; and the provision of objective verification of customer satisfaction survey work. We have observed[30] that the AJTC's broad remit implies selectivity and setting priorities for its work, but we believe that a significant input into the Leggatt-style review we have proposed would be consistent in particular with the cross-cutting areas of activity that the AJTC has already identified (AJTC 2010; 2010a). In addition, we consider that it would be desirable to have a concrete right to administrative justice in any future British Bill of Rights.[31] Again, the AJTC is in pole position to prepare the groundwork for the inclusion of this right.

Supporting Human Rights

We also support the general developments we have identified in this monograph for ombudsman organizations to integrate the human rights agenda within their processes and culture. As we have seen,[32] breaches of human rights, considered 'fundamental to the concept of good public administration' (SPSO 2005, col. 2521), can inform findings of maladministration where a public authority has failed to give due consideration to human rights legislation (O'Reilly 2007;

---

29 At the time of correcting proofs there were leaks of an intention to abolish 177 Quangos, including the AJTC: see <http://www.guardian.co.uk/news/datablog/2010/sep/24/quango-list-cuts> (accessed 28 September 2010). See further, the comments in the Preface, at p. xiv.

30 See pp. 78-9, 202-203.

31 The coalition government elected in May 2010 planned to 'establish a Commission to investigate the creation of a British Bill of Rights that incorporates and builds on all our obligations under the European Convention on Human Rights' (Cabinet Office 2010, 11).

32 See pp. 37-8, 87 and 108-112 for the relevance of human rights to the ombudsman enterprise.

Abraham 2008c; O'Brien 2009).[33] We do not believe that it is necessary to clarify this development in legislation.

Concluding Remarks

This monograph has set out a vision of a proactive ombudsman enterprise at the centre of our constitutional arrangements, performing key 'integrity' functions within a balanced 'setting it right' environment which optimizes its operations within the context of a wider administrative justice system. The social and economic value of the ombudsman enterprise can only be maximized by achieving greater clarity and understanding of the ways in which it might optimize its operation within the wider administrative justice system. The establishment of systemic investigation, 'own-investigation' initiatives and expansion into compliance auditing and inspection are paradigm indicators of the way in which the ombudsman enterprise has evolved into a far more strategic site of administrative and constitutional activity than has been recognized hitherto.

We believe this wider role for the ombudsman will achieve constitutional permanence, but recognize that significant challenges lie ahead for the ombudsman. Demonstrating impact and effectiveness, retaining strong links with Parliament and dealing with changing styles of governance, such as the use of the private sector to deliver public functions, are all ongoing battles that current and future ombudsmen will have to fight. Nor can the public sector ombudsmen ignore the developments occurring with private sector ombudsmen, including the different ideas that sometimes stem from that sector and the challenges of subjecting them to suitable oversight. However, current intellectual developments in administrative justice, and the recognition of PDR as a core goal of the system, mean that the ombudsman is very much an idea whose time has come. There is much more work, particularly empirical research, that needs to be done to demonstrate the effectiveness of the ombudsman enterprise and to scrutinize and understand its operations. These qualifications aside, we hope that the work in this monograph will assist in the important task of achieving greater public recognition and clarity about the valuable role performed by the ombudsman enterprise.

33 See also *Six Lives* (HSO and LGO 2009, 20-21) and *Injustice in Residential Care* (HSO and LGO 2008, 6-8), where the relevance of human rights standards are expressly stated.

Appendices

Appendix 1 UK, Irish and Australasian ombudsmen: who can complain and how

Office[1]	Principal Act	Who may complain	Oral/ Written	Open/ Filter	Time limit	Refer to court?[2]
PHSO	Parliamentary Commissioner Act 1967, Health Commissioners Act 1993	Person aggrieved not governmental representative	Written only; PO also oral for HSO	MP filter for PO Open for HSO	12 months but discretion to ignore	No
LGO	Local Government Act 1974	Person aggrieved, representative	Written but discretion	Open	12 months but discretion to ignore	No
SPSO	Scottish Public Services Ombudsman Act 2002	Person aggrieved/ authorized request from body	Written but discretion	Open	12 months; 3 years health providers	No
PSOW	Public Services Ombudsman (Wales) Act 2005	Person aggrieved/ authorized Referred by body	Written but discretion	Open	12 months for complaint and referral	No
NIO	Ombudsman, Commissioner for Complaints (Northern Ireland) Orders 1996	Person aggrieved not governmental representative	Written	MLA filter for NIAO Open for NICC	12 months	No
Ire	Ombudsman Act 1980	Person not a governmental body	Written	Open	12 months	No
Cth	Ombudsman Act 1976	Not specified	Oral or written	Open	12 months	Yes
ACT	Ombudsman Act 1989	Not specified	Oral or written	Open	12 months	Yes
NSW	Ombudsman Act 1974	Any person or body	Written but discretion for oral	Open	Discretion to ignore where conduct at too remote a time	Yes

Appendix 1 (continued)

NT	Ombudsman Act 2009	Person aggrieved or representative, third party, parliamentary reference	Oral or written	Open	12 months but discretion to ignore	Yes
Qld	Ombudsman Act 2001	Person, body apparently affected, parliamentary reference	Oral or written	Open	12 months but discretion to ignore	Yes
SA	Ombudsman Act 1972	Person, body, representative, parliamentary reference	Oral or written	Open	12 months but discretion to ignore	Yes
Tas	Ombudsman Act 1978	Person, body aggrieved, representative, governor, Parliament	Oral or written	Open	24 months but discretion to ignore	Yes
Vic	Ombudsman Act 1993	Aggrieved person body/ representative, parliamentary reference	Written	Open	12 months but discretion to ignore	Yes
WA	Parliamentary Commissioner Act 1971	Aggrieved person/body, representative, parliamentary reference	Oral or written	Open	12 months but discretion to ignore	Yes
NZ	Ombudsmen Act 1975	Aggrieved person, representative, PM, parliamentary reference	Oral or written	Open	12 months but discretion to ignore	No

Notes: [1] See Table of Abbreviations, p. ix-x; [2] 'Refer to court' indicates whether there is a specific power authorizing reference to a court to determine whether the ombudsman has jurisdiction: wider in Cth and ACT. This can be made by the ombudsman or the authority/ interested party (ombudsman only in Queensland). Judicial review could be sought on this point in the UK and Ireland.

Appendix 2 UK, Irish and Australasian ombudsmen: summary of investigatory process

Office*	Process	Preliminary investigation	Own motion	Resolution
PHSO	Private, as thinks appropriate	Screening	No	Mediation in an investigation
LGO	Private, as thinks appropriate	Screening	May take up if issue comes to attention in investigation before complainant had notice and likely injustice suffered	Mediation in an investigation
SPSO	Private, as thinks fit	Screening	No	Power to take any action to resolve
PSOW	Private, as thinks appropriate,	Screening	No	Power to take any action to resolve
NIO	Private, as thinks appropriate	Screening	No	Power to effect a settlement (NICC)
Ire	Private, as thinks appropriate	Specific preliminary power	Specific power	No specific power
Cth	Private, as thinks fit	Specific preliminary power	Specific power	No specific power but may discontinue
ACT	Private, as thinks fit	Specific preliminary power	Specific power	No specific power but may discontinue
NSW	Private	Specific preliminary power	Specific power	Power to conciliate
NT	Private, as thinks appropriate	Specific preliminary power to investigate if within remit, and to decide to investigate	Specific power	Power to conciliate/mediate own motion or on request

Appendix 2 (continued)

Office*	Process	Preliminary investigation	Own motion	Resolution
Qld	Private, as thinks appropriate	Specific preliminary power	Specific power	No specific power but may discontinue
SA	Private	Specific preliminary power	Specific power	Power to conciliate
Tas	Private, as thinks appropriate	Specific power	Specific power	Power to conciliate
Vic	Private, as thinks fit	Inquiry to decide if investigation or informal resolution	Specific power	
WA	Private, as thinks fit	Screening	Specific power	Power to investigate informally if possible expeditious resolution
NZ	Private, as thinks fit	Screening	Specific power	No specific power but may discontinue

Notes: *See also Appendix 1, col. 2, which lists the principal Acts in each jurisdiction; In the Australasian and Republic of Ireland jurisdictions, there are specific preliminary powers to conduct investigations to determine whether an investigation is to be carried out. In the UK jurisdictions, however, there is the screening process to determine whether within jurisdiction and whether an investigation will be conducted.

Appendix 3 UK, Irish and Australasian ombudsmen: summary of evidence-gathering powers

Office*	Interviews	Papers	Entry powers	Obstruction	Exempted
PHSO	Can be under oath HSO can decide if legal representation	Specific power	Not specified	May certify a case to be dealt with by a court as contempt	Cabinet items if a certificate (PO); prejudice to state safety (HSO)
LGO	High Court powers for witnesses, can permit legal or other representation	Specific power	Not specified	May certify to High Court to treat as contempt	
SPSO	Can be under oath, can permit legal representation	Specific power	Not specified	Can be dealt with by a court as contempt	Scottish Cabinet items if certificate
PSOW	Can be under oath, can permit legal representation	Specific power	Not specified	Can be dealt with by a court as contempt	
NIO	Can be under oath, can permit legal representation	Specific power	Not specified	Can be dealt with by a court as contempt	NI Executive items if certificate
Ire	Can be under oath, can permit legal representation	Specific power	Not specified	Not to obstruct if it could be contempt	Prejudice to the public interest if certificate
Cth	Can be under oath	Specific power	Specific power	Apply to Federal Court, must inform minister first	Contrary to public interest if certificate
ACT	Can be under oath	Specific power	Specific power	Apply to Supreme Court, must inform minister first	Contrary to public interest if certificate
NSW	Power to hold inquiry	Specific power	Specific power	Ombudsman can apply to Supreme Court for an injunction to restrain action affecting a (proposed) investigation	Cabinet items if certificate
NT	Hearing, can be under oath, can permit legal representation	Specific power	Specific power	Can issue order to stop action prejudicial to investigation unjustified non-compliance reported to Assembly	

Appendix 3 (continued)

Office*	Interviews	Papers	Entry powers	Obstruction	Exempted
Qld	Can be under oath	Specific power	Specific power	A magistrate's court on ombudsman's request can issue a subpoena or arrest warrant; ombudsman can certify contempt to Supreme Court	Cabinet items if certificate
SA	Royal Commission powers can permit legal representation	Specific power	Specific power	Obstruction offence	Cabinet items if certificate
Tas	Can permit legal representation	Specific power	Specific power	Obstruction offence	
Vic	Powers of commissioner under Evidence Act	Specific power	Specific power	Obstruction offence	Ministerial Parliamentary Committee deliberations
WA	Informal, power of Royal Commission; can permit legal representation	Specific power	Specific power	Obstruction offence	Cabinet items if certificate
NZ	Can be under oath	Specific power	Specific power	Obstruction offence	Cabinet, security, defence international relations if certificate

Note: *See also Appendix 1, col. 2, which lists the principal Acts in each jurisdiction

Appendix 4 UK, Irish and Australasian ombudsmen: summary of report publications

Office*	Recipients	Published	Non-compliance	Other special report
PHSO	MP, Principal Office (PO); complainant, service provider (HSO)	Investigation reports are not published but may be summarized in reports to Parliament	Report to Parliament	Yes
LGO	Complainant, authority	Investigation report published, to be available for inspection. If satisfied with action to be taken may send reasons on why not preparing a report; may require report not to be published or made available for inspection	3-month period in which to consider report and response, if non-compliance LGO can require authority to publish a press notice of steps outlined in an LGO further report which have not been taken in response to recommendations, and the authority can give its reasons for non-compliance	Advice and guidance on good administrative practice
SPSO	Complainant, authority, Scottish ministers	Investigation report laid before Parliament	Special report, also to Parliament, may be publicized	On exercise of functions
PSOW	Complainant, authority, others affected First Minister (FM)	May decide to publish investigation report or may decide not to if happy with proposed remedial action and not in public interest to publish	Special report to complainant, body and others at discretion	On functions (extraordinary)
NIO	AONI-MLA authority; NICC-complainant authority	Investigation reports are not published but may be summarized in reports to Assembly	Report to Assembly – AONI; complainant can go to county court – NICC	Other matters as sees fit
Ire	Authority, others considered appropriate; complainant gets the recommendations and outcome	Investigation report not published	Report to Parliament	On functions
Cth	Complainant, authority; and minister if adverse	Investigation report not published	Report to PM and also to Parliament	On exercise of powers and functions

Appendix 4 (continued)

Office*	Recipients	Published	Non-compliance	Other special report
ACT	Complainant, authority; and minister if adverse	Investigation report not published	Report to Chief Minister and Assembly	On exercise of powers and functions
NSW	Authority, may be given to complainant, to minister if adverse	Investigation report may be recommended for publication	Report to Parliament and minister, who must report to Parliament	On discharge of functions
NT	Complainant, authority, minister if adverse	Investigation report not published	Original report to minister; may take further for tabling in Assembly	Own initiative on functions or case to minister for tabling
Qld	Complainant informed of outcome; department and minister	Investigation report not published	Original report to Premier, original and further to Speaker for tabling	To Speaker for tabling on performance of functions
SA	Complainant informed of outcome, authority, responsible minister	Investigation report may be published	Report to Premier and to Speaker for tabling	
Tas	Complainant informed of outcome, authority, responsible minister	Investigation report not published	Report to Premier, minister and Parliament	Performance of functions and special to public
Vic	Complainant informed of outcome, authority, responsible minister	Investigation report not published	Report to governor/mayor; also may be sent to Parliament	Performance of functions
WA	Complainant informed of outcome, authority, responsible minister	Investigation report not published	Report to Premier; also to Parliament	Exercise of functions
NZ	Complainant informed of outcome, authority, responsible minister	Require body to publish summary	Report to PM; also to Parliament	Exercise of functions

Note: *See also Appendix 1, col. 2, which lists the principal Acts in each jurisdiction.

Appendix 5 UK, Irish and Australasian ombudsmen: summary of appointment and governance arrangements

Office*	Appointment	Term	Removal	Pay	Budget
PHSO	HM Queen, PM recommends, consults; Leader of Opposition and Select Ctte chair	Single term of up to 7 years	HM Queen on address from both Houses	Act links to Permanent Secretary; practice links to judicial	Negotiates 3-year settlement with Treasury
LGO	HM Queen, recommended by minister, after consultation	Single term of up to 7 years	HM Queen for incapacity or misbehaviour	Determined by minister, linked to judicial scales	Negotiates with dept (DCLG) gets top slice of RSG
SPSO	HM Queen, nominated by Parliament	Up to 5 years, reappointable usually once; retiring age 65	HM Queen on address with 2/3 of all MSPs	Determined by SPCB	Through SPCB
PSOW	HM Queen, nominated by Assembly	Single term of 7 years	HM Queen on address with 2/3 of all AMs	Determined by Assembly, linked to judicial scales	Assembly's Finance Ctte considers, consults and may amend
NIO	HM Queen, recommended by FM and DFM	Until retiring age of 65	HM Queen on address from Assembly	Determined by FM and DFM, linked to judicial scales	Negotiates with Dept of Finance, has separate vote
Ire	President, on resolutions	6 years, reappointable; retiring age 67	President following resolutions by both Houses	Legislatively linked to High Court judge	Negotiates with Dept of Finance
Cth	Governor General, no address	Up to 7 years, reappointable; retiring age 65	Governor General on address; may suspend then statement and vote	Remuneration tribunal	Dept of Prime Minister and Cabinet
ACT	See for Cth as the Cth post-holder acts under Memorandum of Understanding				
NSW	Governor, Premier consults Parliamentary Ctte, which can veto	Up to 7 years, reappointable; retiring age 65	Governor on addresses, no suspension	Statutory Officers Remuneration Tribunal	Treasury, Cabinet, Parliament

Appendix 5 (continued)

Office*	Appointment	Term	Removal	Pay	Budget
NT	Administrator	Single term of 7 years	Administrator for certain things, and after suspension by the Assembly	Determined by the Administrator	Chief Minister
Qld	Governor, minister must hold (a) public process and (b) consult Parl Ctte on process and appointee	Up to 5 years, reappointable but not if total exceeds 10 years	Governor on address can remove/suspend; Premier must consult Parl Ctte over motion	Determined by Governor, linked to CEO of State Dept	Premier is the responsible minister
SA	Governor, on resolutions; Parl Ctee conducts	Until retiring age of 65	Governor on address can remove and suspend	Determined by Governor on recommendation of Remuneration Tribunal	Negotiation with Attorney General
Tas	Governor	Up to 5 years, reappointable; retiring age 65	Governor on address can suspend and remove	Determined by Governor	Separate item in Consolidated Fund
Vic	Governor	Single term of 10 years	Governor on addresses, may suspend, then statement and vote	Determined by Governor	Dept of Premier and Cabinet
WA	Governor	5-year term; Act is silent on reappointment, some have been reappointed	Governor on address can remove and suspend, can suspend but statement	Determined by Governor, Salaries and Allowances Tribunal	Parliament
NZ	Governor-General on resolution; Parl Ctte conducts	5 year term, reappointable; retiring age 72	Governor on address can remove and suspend	Determined by Remuneration Authority	Separate vote recommended by Parl Ctte

Note: *See also Appendix 1, col. 2, which lists the principal Acts in each jurisdiction.

Appendix 6 UK, Irish and Australasian ombudsmen: summary of parliamentary accountability, reporting and review arrangements

Office*	Annual report to	Specific committee	Convention or practice	No committee	Regular review
PHSO	Parliament	(House of Commons) Public Administration			No
LGO	Parliament			√	Internal 3 years
SPSO	Parliament		Local Govt ctee deals with Ann Rep		No
PSOW	Assembly		Plenary debate on Add Rep	√	No
NIO	Assembly	Consultation paper issue, late 2010		√	No
Ire	Parliament			√	No
Cth	PM, Parliament		Annual report considered by (Senate) Finance and Public Administration		No
ACT	AG, Assembly			√	No
NSW	Speakers, Parliament	(Joint) Office of the Ombudsman and Police Integrity Commission			No
NT	Chief Minister, Assembly			√	No
Qld	Speaker, Parliament	Law, Justice and Safety†			External strategic, 5 years
SA	Speakers, Parliament	(Joint) Statutory Officers			No
Tas	Speakers, Parliament	Joint Integrity Ctte in 2009 Act, not yet established			No
Vic	Speakers, Parliament			√	No
WA	Speakers, Parliament	(Legislative Council) Public Administration			No
NZ	Speaker, Parliament	Officers of Parliament			No

Note: * See also Appendix 1, col. 2, which lists the principal Acts in each jurisdiction. † Until May 2009 known as Legal, Constitutional and Administrative Review Committee.

Appendix 7 Parliamentary Ombudsman's section 10(3) reports

Name/Issue/Year/Dept	Disputed PO Findings and/or Recommendations	Governmental Objections	Select Committee View	Outcome/Reason
Rochester Way, Road Administration of compensation, 1978 Dept of Transport	Defective arrangements for publicizing details of compensation scheme led to applications being rejected as out of time	To make *ex gratia* payments would override the will of Parliament	The commitment to inform people about the compensation scheme was not met	Amendments made to the legislation authorizing payments for late claims
Channel Tunnel Rail Link, Planning blight, 1994, Dept of Transport	There was exceptional uncertainty about an unusual project which gave rise to general blight but this caused exceptional hardship for some people	The project, the uncertainty and the hardship were not so exceptional as to override policy of not compensating for general blight	Dept had not considered identifying those who were inequitably affected by rigid adherence to the letter of law	Ombudsman satisfied as government indicated it was prepared to discuss terms of compensation but nothing done until change of government in 1997
Wartime Detainees, Administration of compensation, 2005, Ministry of Defence	Both the scheme's terms and its announcement were unclear; new criterion not reviewed to check for equal treatment; no information provided to applicants on clarification of criteria; no review undertaken	Challenged PO's decision to investigate new 'bloodlink' criterion given an unsuccessful judicial review; complainant's case should not have been accepted	In preparing for select committee appearance, new evidence found suggesting unequal treatment; committee hoped MoD would pay	Ombudsman satisfied following the subsequent ministerial statement
Occupational Pensions, Compensation for poor regulation, 2006, Dept for Work and Pensions, Treasury, National Insurance Contributions Office (HMRC), Occupational Pensions Regulatory Authority	Misleading information on degree of protection; maladministration in not following advice on disclosing risks; maladmin in changing Minimum Funding Requirement and so contributed to losses in winding-up process	Rejected findings which were not substantiated; leaflets not comprehensive guide and no causal link to loss in the winding-up of companies	Agreed that maladmin had occurred, govt should engage properly with PO's recommendations rather than assuming too large a burden on the public purse	Ombudsman satisfied as Government Actuary Department (GAD) review found ways to improve Financial Assistance Scheme

Equitable Life, Compensation for poor regulation, 2009, HM Treasury	PO found a total of 10 instances of maladmin by DTI, GAD, FSA and recommended apology and compensation scheme. In s.10(3) report the terms of reference for the judge's advice will restrict those eligible for compensation and the likely amount will not be adequate	Accepted most findings, not accepting proposed compensation but asking judge to advise on a narrower *ex gratia* scheme for those who had suffered disproportionate impact	Select Committee supported PO's initial report before govt response report; their reaction to it made before s.10(3) report; disliked disproportionate impact test, not simple or quick	Ombudsman satisfied as following 2010 election new coalition government proposed better terms
Single Payments Scheme and Rural Land Register, 2009, Department for Environment, Food and Rural Affairs (Defra)	Maladmin by not determining issues in stipulated period; did not react appropriately following indications of problems which led to delay and these two cases were representative, so apply recommendations to 22 others similarly placed	Dept concerned that indications on targets for decisions had become legitimate expectations; compensation had been paid, which was adequate and to provide the recommended compensation for other cases was a distraction	Following its evidence session with Permanent Secretary, the chair wrote to minister advising the dept had misunderstood basis for PO's decisions on targets; compensation for other 22 cases within Treasury guidance	Ombudsman satisfied as minister completely accepted recommendations following Select Committee chair's letter

Note: * See also Appendix 1, col. 2, which lists the principal Acts in each jurisdiction.

Bibliography

Abraham, A. (2003), *The Work of the Ombudsman*, HC 506-I, session 2002-03, Minutes of Evidence for Thursday 6 March 2003, Ann Abraham, Parliamentary Commissioner for Administration and Health Service Commissioner for England, Memorandum (OW 1) (London: The Stationery Office).

Abraham, A. (2006), 'The Ombudsman, the Constitution and Public Services: A Crisis or an Opportunity?' (seminar), Constitution Unit, University College London, 4 December 2006. Available at: <http://www.ombudsman.org.uk/about-us/media-centre/ombudsmans-speeches/archive/sp2006-03> (accessed 10 June 2010).

Abraham, A. (2007), 'Launch of the Administrative Justice and Tribunals Council' (speech), Parliamentary and Health Service Ombudsman, 20 November 2007. Available at: <http://www.ombudsman.org.uk/about-us/media-centre/ombudsmans-speeches/archive/sp2007-04> (accessed 8 March 2010).

Abraham, A. (2007a), 'Rethinking Good Administration in the European Union' (speech), Parliamentary and Health Service Ombudsman, 6th Seminar of National Ombudsmen of EU Member States and Candidate Countries, *Remedies, Redress and Solutions: What Do Ombudsmen Have To Offer?* October 2007. Available at: <http://www.ombudsman.org.uk/about-us/media-centre/ombudsmans-speeches/archive/sp2007-03> (accessed 12 March 2010).

Abraham, A. (2008), 'The Ombudsman and "Paths to Justice": A Just Alternative or Just An Alternative?', *Public Law* Spr, 1-10.

Abraham, A. (2008a), 'The Ombudsman as Part of the UK Constitution: A Contested Role?', *Parliamentary Affairs* 61:1, 206-15.

Abraham, A. (2008b), 'The Ombudsman and Individual Rights', *Parliamentary Affairs* 61:2, 370-79.

Abraham, A. (2008c), 'The Ombudsman and the Executive: The Road to Accountability', *Parliamentary Affairs* 61:3, 535-44.

Abraham, A. (2008d), 'The Future in International Perspective: The Ombudsman as Agent of Rights, Justice and Democracy', *Parliamentary Affairs* 61:4, 681-93.

Abraham, A. (2009), 'The PHSO and Alternative Dispute Resolution' (speech), Parliamentary and Health Service Ombudsman, University College London Seminar, 27 February 2009. Formerly available on PHSO website (accessed 11 March 2010). A copy is now available on request from the authors.

Abraham, A. (2009a), 'The Ombudsman and the Constitution', Gabriele Ganz Lecture, Parliamentary and Health Service Ombudsman, Southampton

University, 22 October 2009. Available at: <www.ombudsman.org.uk/documents/Gabriele-Ganz-lecture.doc> (accessed 11 March 2010).

Abraham, A. (2009b), 'Ombudsman and Government in "a New Era of Responsibility"', Brasenose Lecture, Parliamentary and Health Service Ombudsman, 12 February 2009. Formerly available on PHSO website (accessed 23 May 2010). A copy is now available on request from the authors.

Abraham, A. (2009c), Future Challenges for the Ombudsman' (speech), Parliamentary and Health Service Ombudsman, Northern Ireland ombudsman 40th anniversary event, November 2009. Available at: <http://www.bioa.org.uk/docs/NIO-AnnAbraham.pdf> (accessed 9 June 2010).

Ackerman, B. (2000), 'The New Separation of Powers', *Harvard Law Review* 113:3, 633-729.

Adler, M. (2003), 'A Socio-legal Approach to Administrative Justice', *Law and Policy* 25:4, 323-52.

Adler, M. (2006), 'Fairness in Context', *Journal of Law and Society* 33:4, 615-38.

Adler, M. (2006a), 'Tribunal Reform: Proportionate Dispute Resolution and the Pursuit of Administrative Justice', *Modern Law Review* 69:6, 958–85.

Adler, M. (2008), 'The Idea of Proportionality in Dispute Resolution', *Journal of Social Welfare and Family Law* 30:4, 309-21.

Adler, M. (ed.) (2010), *Administrative Justice in Context* (Oxford and Portland, OR: Hart Publishing).

Adler, M. and Bradley, A. (1975), *Justice, Discretion and Poverty* (Abingdon: Professional Books).

Adler, M. and Bradley, A. (2001), 'The Case for Systematic Reform and the Establishment of a Unified Administrative Tribunal', in Partington (ed.), pp. 1-30.

AJTC (2009), *The Developing Administrative Justice Landscape* (London: Administrative Justice and Tribunals Council). Available at: <http://www.ajtc.gov.uk/adjust/articles/landscape_paper.pdf> (accessed 20 May 2010).

AJTC (2010), *Strategic Plan 2010-13* (London: Administrative Justice and Tribunals Council).

AJTC (2010a), *Action Plan 2010-11* (London: Administrative Justice and Tribunals Council).

Allison, J. (1994), 'The Procedural Reason for Judicial Restraint', *Public Law* Aut, 452-73.

Anderman, S.D. (1962), 'The Swedish Justitieombudsman', *American Journal of Comparative Law* 11:2, 225-38.

ANZOA (2010), *Essential Criteria for Describing a Body as an Ombudsman*, policy statement endorsed in February 2010 by the Members of the Australian and New Zealand Ombudsman Association (ANZOA). Available at: <http://www.anzoa.com.au/ANZOA%20Policy%20Statement_Ombudsman_Essential%20Criteria_Feb2010.pdf> (accessed 3 May 2010).

Austrian Ombudsman Board (2008), *Annual Report of the Austrian Ombudsman Board to the National Council and the Federal Council 2008*. International abridged version (Vienna: Austrian Ombudsman Board).

Ayeni, V.O. (2000), 'The Ombudsman Around the World: Essential Elements, Evolution and Contemporary Issues', in Ayeni, Reif and Thomas (eds), 1-28.

Ayeni, V.O., Reif, L. and Thomas, H. (eds) (2000), *Strengthening Ombudsman and Human Rights Institutions in Commonwealth Small and Island States: The Caribbean Experience* (London: Commonwealth Secretariat).

Baldwin, R. and Cave, M. (1999), *Understanding Regulation: Theory, Strategy, and Practice* (Oxford: Oxford University Press).

Barber, N. (2001), 'Prelude to the Separation of Powers', *Cambridge Law Journal* 60:1, 59-88.

Barbour, B. (2005), 'Parliamentary Oversight from the Ombudsman Perspective', New South Wales Ombudsman's presentation to the Australasian Study of Parliament Group Annual Conference, 7 October 2005. Available at: <http://www.aspg.org.au/pdf/sydney2005/ASPG%202005%2004%20Barbour.pdf> (accessed 28 April 2010).

Barry, R. and Robinson, Z. (2008), 'An Overview of Northern Ireland's Constitutional Watchdogs', in Gay and Winetrobe (eds), pp. 59-70.

BCO (2007), *Winning Fair and Square: A Report on the British Columbia Lottery Corporation's Prize Payout Process*, Special Report No.31 to the Legislative Assembly, May 2007 (British Columbia: Office of the Ombudsman).

Beatson, J., Matthews, M. and Elliott, M. (eds) (2005), *Administrative Law: Text Cases and Materials*, 3rd edition (Oxford: Oxford University Press).

Beattie, A. (2006), 'Officers of Parliament: The New Zealand Model', *Australasian Parliamentary Review* 21:1, 143-56.

Bevan, D. (2007), 'The Use of Investigative Planning in Complex Investigations' (seminar notes) Queensland Ombudsman, Thirtieth Anniversary of Commonwealth Ombudsman, Canberra, 9 August 2007. Available at: <http://www.ombudsman.gov.au/docs/30th-anniversary-seminar/seminar_notes_David_Bevan.pdf> (accessed 22 May 2010).

Bevan, D. (2008), 'Systemic Investigations' (unpublished presentation), Queensland Ombudsman, Meeting of the Australasia and Pacific Region, International Ombudsman Institute, Melbourne, 28 March 2008.

Beyleveld, D. and Brownsword, R. (1983), 'Law as a Moral Judgement vs. Law as the Rules of the Powerful', *American Journal of Jurisprudence* 28, 79-117.

Bingham, R. (2009), 'Speech Notes of Richard Bingham, State Ombudsman', Local Government Association of South Australia, Annual General Meeting, 30 October 2009. Available at: <http://www.ombudsman.sa.gov.au/publications/LGAAGM.pdf> (accessed 28 August 2010).

Bingham, T. (2007), 'The Rule of Law', *Cambridge Law Journal* 66:1, 67-85.

BIOA (2007), *Guide to Principles of Good Complaint Handling: Firm on Principles, Flexible on Process* (Twickenham: British and Irish Ombudsman Association).

BIOA (2010), *Annual Report 2009-2010* (Twickenham: British and Irish Ombudsman Association).

Birkinshaw, P. (1994), *Grievances, Remedies and the State*, 2nd edition (London: Sweet & Maxwell).

Birkinshaw, P. (2010), 'Grievances, Remedies and the State: Revisited and Re-appraised', in Adler (ed.), pp. 353-82.

Black, J. (2008), 'Constructing and Contesting Legitimacy and Accountability in Polycentric Regulatory Regimes', *Regulation and Governance* 2:2, 137-64.

Blake, N. (2006), *The Deepcut Review: A Review of the Circumstances Surrounding the Deaths of Four Soldiers at Princess Royal Barracks, Deepcut between 1995 and 2002*, HC 795, session 2005-06 (London: The Stationery Office).

Bland, H. (1973), *Committee on Administrative Discretions*, a report by Sir Henry Bland, Parliamentary Paper No. 53 (Canberra: Australian Government Publishing Service).

Bognador, V. (ed.) (2005), *Joined-up Government* (Oxford: Oxford University Press/British Academy).

Bondy, V. and Sunkin, M. (2009), 'Settlement in Judicial Review Proceedings', *Public Law* Apr, 237-59.

Bonner, P. (2003), 'Ombudsmen and the Development of Public Law', *European Public Law* 9:2, 237-67.

Bovens, M., Schillemans, T. and Hart, P.T. (2008), 'Does Accountability Work? An Assessment Tool', *Public Administration* 86:1, 225-42.

Bradley, A.W. (1995), 'Administrative Justice: A Developing Human Right?', *European Public Law* 1:3, 347-69.

Brenninkmeijer, A. (2006), *Fair Governance: A Question of Lawfulness and Proper Conduct* (edited version of the Van Slingelandt lecture), the National Ombudsman of the Netherlands, Dutch Association for Public Administration, 21 November 2006. Available at: <http://www.ioi-europe.org/goodadministration/Nederlands.pdf> (accessed 23 February 2010).

Brooker, S. (2008), *Lessons from Ombudsmania* (London: National Consumer Council).

Brown, A. (2009), 'The Impact of the Ombudsman in Scotland: What Makes the Difference?', in Passemiers et. al (eds), 203-16.

Brown, A. (2009a), 'Scottish Public Services Ombudsman Annual Report: Evidence from Professor Alice Brown on the 2007-08 Annual Report and Work of the SPSO', SP OR LG&C 11 February 2009, cols 1696-706.

Brown, A.J. and Head, B. (2005), 'Assessing Integrity Systems: Introduction to the Symposium', *Australian Journal of Public Administration* 64:2, 42-7.

Buchanan, R. (2008), 'Commonwealth Experience II – Officers of Parliament in Australia and New Zealand: Building a Working Model', in Gay and Winetrobe (eds), pp. 81-92.

Buck, T. (1998), 'Judicial Review and the Discretionary Social Fund: The Impact on a Respondent Organization', in Buck (ed.), *Judicial Review and Social Welfare* (London and Washington: Pinter), pp. 115-42.

Buck, T. (2001), 'A Model of Independent Review?', in Partington (ed.), pp. 127-40.

Buck, T., Bonner, D. and Sainsbury, R. (2005), *Making Social Security Law: The Role and Work of the Social Security and Child Support Commissioners* (Aldershot: Ashgate).

Buckley, M. (2002), 'Evidence to the Public Administration Select Committee'. Memorandum by the Parliamentary Commissioner for Administration (OM 5), HC 563-ii, session 2001-2002, 14 June 2002 (London: The Stationery Office).

Bull, D. (1980), 'The Anti-discretion Movement in Britain: Fact or Phantom?', *Journal of Social Welfare Law* 2:2, 65-83.

Cabinet Office (1997), *The Ombudsman in Your Files*, last revision Jan 1997 (London: Cabinet Office). Available at: <http://www.cabinetoffice.gov.uk/media/cabinetoffice/propriety_and_ethics/assets/ombudsman_1.pdf> (accessed 11 June 2010).

Cabinet Office (2003), *Government Response to the Public Administration Select Committee's Third Report of Session 2002-03 'Ombudsman Issues' [HC 448]*, Cm 5890, July 2003 (London: The Stationery Office).

Cabinet Office (2005), *Reform of Public Sector Ombudsmen Services in England*, consultation paper, August 2005 (London: Cabinet Office).

Cabinet Office (2010), *The Coalition: Our Programme for Government*, May 2010 (London: Cabinet Office).

Caiden, G.E. (ed.) (1983), *International Handbook of the Ombudsman: Volume 1 Evolution and Present Function* (Westport, CT: Greenwood Press).

CAIPE (2005), *A New Process for Funding Officers of Parliament*, House of Commons Standing Committee on Access to Information, Privacy and Ethics, May 2005 (Canada: House of Commons).

Cameron, A. (2001), 'The Ombudsmen: Time For a Jurisdictional Expansion: The Case for Extending the Jurisdiction of the Statutory Ombudsmen to Cover the Exercise of Public Power in the Private Sector', *Victoria University of Wellington Law Review* 32:2, 549-72.

Cane, P. (2004), *Administrative Law*, 4th edition (Oxford: Oxford University Press).

Cane, P. (2009), *Administrative Adjudication and Administrative Tribunals* (Oxford: Hart Publishing).

Cane, P. (ed.) (2010), *The Hart–Fuller Debate in the Twenty-First Century: 50 Years On* (Oxford: Hart Publishing).

Canon, B.C. (2004), 'Studying Bureaucratic Implementation of Judicial Policies in the United States: Conceptual and Methodological Approaches', in Hertogh and Halliday (eds), pp. 76-100.

Carnwath, R. (2009), *Seniot President of Tribunals Third Implementation Review*, July 2009 (London: Tribunals Service).

Carolan, E. (2009), *The New Separation of Powers: A Theory for the Modern State* (Oxford: Oxford University Press).

CHSSPS (2008), 'Northern Ireland Ombudsman's Report on a Complaint against Belfast City Hospital', Committee for Health, Social Services and Public Safety, 18 September 2008 (Belfast: Northern Ireland Assembly).

CLA (2009), *Customer Satisfaction Study*, Memorandum for the March meeting of the Commission for Local Administration, CLA 1700, 24 March 2009. (London: Commission for Local Administration). Available at: <http://www.lgo.org.uk/GetAsset.aspx?id=fAAxADAAMAAwAHwAfABGAGEAbABzAGUAfAB8ADAAfAA1> (accessed 20 April 2010).

Clarke, J., Newman, J. and McDermont, M. (2010), 'Delivering Choice and Administering Justice: Contested Logics of Public Services', in Adler (ed.), pp. 25-46.

Clothier, C. (1996), 'Fact-finding in Inquiries – The PCA's Perspective', *Public Law* Aut, 384-90.

CO (2004), *Annual Report 2003-2004*, Commonwealth Ombudsman of Australia (Canberra: Commonwealth Ombudsman).

CO (2005), *Annual Report 2004-2005*, Commonwealth Ombudsman of Australia (Canberra: Commonwealth Ombudsman).

CO (2006), *Annual Report 2005-2006*, Commonwealth Ombudsman of Australia (Canberra: Commonwealth Ombudsman).

CO (2007), *Annual Report 2006-2007*, Commonwealth Ombudsman of Australia (Canberra: Commonwealth Ombudsman).

CO (2007a), *Lessons for Public Administration: Ombudsman Investigation of Referred Immigration Cases*, Report No 11/2007 (Canberra: Commonwealth Ombudsman).

CO (2007b), *The Automated Assistance in Administrative Decision-Making: Better Practice Guide*, February 2007 (Canberra: Australian Government/Commonwealth Ombudsman).

CO (2008), *Annual Report 2007-2008*, Commonwealth Ombudsman of Australia (Canberra: Commonwealth Ombudsman).

CO (2009), *Annual Report 2008-2009*, Commonwealth Ombudsman of Australia (Canberra: Commonwealth Ombudsman).

CO (2009a), *Better Practice Guide to Complaint Handling*, Commonwealth Ombudsman, Better Practice Guide 1, April 2009 (Canberra: Commonwealth Ombudsman).

COFMDFM (2010), *Assembly Ombudsman for Northern Ireland and Northern Ireland Commissioner for Complaints*, Committee for the Office of the First Minister and Deputy First Minister, 21 April 2010.

Cohen, J.R. (2002), 'Legislating Apology: The Pros and Cons', *University of Cincinnati Law Review* 70:3, 819-72.

Cohler, A.M., Miller, B.C. and Stone, H.S. (eds) (1989), *The Spirit of the Laws*, annotated edition (Cambridge: Cambridge University Press) [originally published in 1748 anonymously as *De l'Esprit des Lois*].

COI (2008), *Customer Service Excellence: The Government Standard* (London: Central Office of Information).

Collcutt, P. and Hourihan, M. (2000), *Review of the Public Sector Ombudsmen in England: A Report by the Cabinet Office*, April 2000 (the 'Collcutt Review') (London: Cabinet Office).

Committee on Administrative Discretions (1973), *Final Report of the Committee on Administrative Discretions* (the 'Bland Committee report'), Parliamentary Paper No. 316 (Canberra: Australian Government Publishing Service).

Committee on Standards in Public Life (2005), *Getting the Balance Right: Implementing Standards of Conduct in Public Life, Tenth Report of the Committee on Standards in Public Life*, Cm 6407, January 2005 (London: The Stationery Office).

Commonwealth Attorney-General's Department (2009), *A Strategic Framework for Access to Justice in the Federal Civil Justice System: A Guide for Future Action*, 23 September 2009 (Canberra: Attorney-General's Department).

Craig, P. (2008), *Administrative Law*, 6th edition (London: Sweet & Maxwell).

Craigforth Consultancy and Research (2009), *SPSO Complainant Survey and Analysis 2008-09*, August 2009 (Edinburgh: Craigforth Consultancy and Research).

Crerar, L. (2007), *Report of the Independent Review of Regulation, Audit, Inspection and Complaints Handling of Public Services in Scotland*, September 2007 (the 'Crerar Review') (Edinburgh: Scottish Government). Available at: <http://www.scotland.gov.uk/Publications/2007/09/25120506/0> (accessed 20 February 2010).

Creyke, R. (2010), 'Administrative Justice in Australia', in Adler (ed.), pp. 271-300.

Creyke, R. and Groves, M. (2010), 'Administrative Law Evolution: An Academic Perspective', *Administrative Review* 59, 20-29.

Creyke, R. and McMillan J. (eds) (1998), *The Kerr Vision of Australian Administrative Law – at the Twenty-Five Year Mark*, Centre for International and Public Law, ANU (Canberra: Australian National University).

Creyke, R. and McMillan, J. (eds) (2000), *Administrative Justice: The Core and the Fringe: Papers Presented at the 1999 National Administrative Law Forum* (Canberra: Australian Institute of Administrative Law).

CRG (1996), *Report of the Constitution Review Group* (Dublin: Stationery Office).

Davis, K.C. (1971), *Discretionary Justice: A Preliminary Inquiry* (Chicago: University of Illinois Press).

DCA (2004), *Transforming Public Services: Complaints, Redress and Tribunals*, Cm 6243, White Paper, Department for Constitutional Affairs (London: The Stationery Office).

DCA (2007), *Tribunals, Courts and Enforcement Bill: Detailed Policy Statement on Delegated Powers*, March 2007 (London: Department for Constitutional Affairs).

De Smith, S.A. (1962), 'Anglo-Saxon Ombudsman', *Political Quarterly* 33:1, 9.

Department of Health (2001), *Reforming the NHS Complaints Procedure – A Listening Document*, September 2001 (London: Department of Health).

Department of Immigration and Citizenship (2007), 'Palmer Report: Two Years of Progress – The Secretary's Introduction', Information Sheet 1, June 2007. Available at: <http://www.immi.gov.au/media/publications/palmer-progress/_pdf/introduction.pdf> (accessed 22 May 2010).

Department of the Prime Minister and Cabinet (2009), *Requirements for Annual Reports for Departments, Executive Agencies and FMA Act Bodies*, approved by the Joint Committee of Public Accounts and Audit under subsections 63(2) and 70(2) of the Public Service Act 1999, 17 June 2009, Australian Government. Available at: <http://www.dpmc.gov.au/guidelines/index.cfm> (accessed 28 May 2010).

Diamandouros, P.N. (2005), 'The Role of the Ombudsman in Strengthening Accountability and the Rule Of Law' (speech), European Ombudsman, Constitution Unit, University College London, 29 November 2005. Available at: <http://www.ombudsman.europa.eu/speeches/en/2005-11-29.htm> (accessed 27 February 2010).

Diamandouros, P.N. (2007), 'Legality and Good Administration: Is There a Difference?' (speech), European Ombudsman, Sixth Seminar of National Ombudsmen of EU Member States and Candidate Countries on 'Rethinking Good Administration in the European Union', Strasbourg, 15 October 2007. Available at: <http://www.ombudsman.europa.eu/speeches/en/2007-10-15.htm> (accessed 26 February 2010).

Dicey, A.V. (1885), *Introduction to the Study of the Law of the Constitution* (London: Macmillan and Co. Ltd). An online version is available at: <http://www.constitution.org/cmt/avd/law_con.htm> (accessed 24 February 2010).

DoE (1995), *Report of the Financial Management and Policy Review of the Commission for Local Administration in England – Stage One: Prior Options Review*, Sir Geoffrey Chipperfield Review, November 1995 (London: Department of Environment).

DoE (1996), *Report of the Financial Management and Policy Review of the Commissioner for Local Administration in England: Stage Two*, August 1996. (London: Department of Environment).

Douglas, M. (1970), *Natural Symbols: Explorations in Cosmology* (London: Barrie & Rockliff, The Cresset Press).

Douglas, M. (1982), 'Introduction to Group-Grid Analysis', in Douglas (ed.), *Essays in the Sociology of Perception* (London: Routledge and Kegan Paul).

Dowdle, M. (ed.) (2006), *Public Accountability: Designs, Dilemmas and Experiences* (Cambridge: Cambridge University Press).

Doyle, M., Ritters, K. and Brooker, S. (2004), *Seeking Resolution: The Availability and Usage of Consumer-to-Business Alternative Dispute Resolution in the UK* (London: National Consumer Council).

Drewry, G. (1997), 'The Ombudsman Parochial Stopgap or Global Panacea?', in Leyland and Woods (eds), pp. 83-106.

Drewry, G. (2005), 'Citizen's Charters: Service Quality Chameleons', *Public Management Review* 7:3, 321-40.

Drewry, G. and Harlow, C. (1990), 'A Cutting Edge? The Parliamentary Commissioner and MPs', *Modern Law Review* 53:6, 745-69.

Dunleavy, P., Bastow, S., Tinkler, J., Goldchluck, S. and Towers, E. (2010), 'Joining up Citizen Redress in UK Central Government', in Adler (ed.), pp. 421-56.

Dunleavy, P., Margetts, H., Bastow, S. and Tinkler, J. (2006), 'New Public Management is Dead – Long Live Digital-era Governance', *Journal of Public Administration Research and Theory* 16:3, 467-94.

Ekins, R. (2003), 'Judicial Supremacy and the Rule of Law', *Law Quarterly Review* 119:Jan, 127-52.

Elliott, M. (2006), 'Asymmetric Devolution and Ombudsman Reform in England', *Public Law* Spr, 84-105.

Endicott, T. (2009), *Administrative Law*, 1st edition (Oxford: Oxford University Press).

European Ombudsman (2008), *Annual Report 2007*, The European Ombudsman (Strasbourg: European Communities).

European Ombudsman (2009), *Annual Report 2008*, The European Ombudsman (Strasbourg: European Communities).

Feldman, D. (2010), 'Changes in Human Rights', in Adler (ed.), pp. 97-126.

Finance Committee (2006), *Accountability and Governance*, Finance Committee 7th report, 2006, The New Scottish Parliament Building (SPP 631), 15 September 2006.

Finn, C. (ed.) (2000), *Sunrise or Sunset? Administrative Law in the New Millennium: Papers Presented at the 2000 National Administrative Law Forum* (Canberra: Australian Institute of Administrative Law).

Fordham, M. (2003), 'Reparation For Maladministration: Public Law's Final Frontier', *Judicial Review* 8:2, 104-8.

Fordham, M. (2009), 'Monetary Awards in Judicial Review', *Public Law* Spr, 1-4.

Franks Committee (1957), *Report of the Committee of Administrative Tribunals and Enquiries* (chairman, Rt Hon. Sir Oliver Franks), Cmnd 218 (London: HMSO).

French, D. and Kirkham, R. (2010), 'Complaint and Grievance Mechanisms in International Dispute Settlement', in French, Saul and White (eds), pp. 57-86.

French, D., Saul, M. and White, N. (eds) (2010), *International Law and Dispute Settlement: New Problems and Techniques* (Oxford: Hart Publishing).

FOS (2009), *Annual Review: FY 2008-2009* (London: Financial Ombudsman Service Ltd).

FOS (2010), *Annual Review: FY 2009-2010* (London: Financial Ombudsman Service Ltd).

Fuller, L. (1957-58), 'Positivism and Fidelity to Law: A Reply to Professor Hart', *Harvard Law Review* 71:4, 630-72.

Fuller, L. (1978), 'The Forms and Limits of Adjudication', *Harvard Law Review* 92:2, 353-409.

Galligan, D.J. (1996), *Due Process and Fair Procedures: A Study of Administrative Procedures* (Oxford: Clarendon Press).

Gamble, A. and Thomas, T. (2010), 'The Changing Context of Governance: Implications for Administration and Justice', in Adler (ed.), pp. 3-24.

Gay, O. (2008), *The Ombudsman – The Developing Role in the UK*, House of Commons Library, SN/PC/04832, Parliament and Constitution Centre, 20 October 2008 (London: House of Commons).

Gay, O. and Winetrobe, B. (2003), *Officers of Parliament – Transforming the Role*, The Constitution Unit (London: University College London).

Gay, O. and Winetrobe, B. (eds) (2008), *Parliament's Watchdogs: At the Crossroads*, UK Study of Parliament Group. The Constitution Unit (London: University College London).

Giddings, P. (2008), 'The Parliamentary Ombudsman: a Classical Watchdog', in Gay and Winetrobe (eds), pp. 93-104.

Gilad, S. (2008), 'Accountability or Expectations Management: The Role of the Ombudsman in Financial Regulation', *Law and Policy* 30:2, 227-53.

Gill, C. (2009), 'What is the Impact of the Scottish Public Services Ombudsman on the Routine Administrative Decision-making of Local Authority Housing Administrators?' (unpublished masters thesis), School of Social and Political Science, University of Edinburgh, August 2009.

Goldman, L. (ed.) (2008), *Alexander Hamilton, James Madison, John Jay: The Federalist Papers* (Oxford: Oxford University Press).

Goldring, J. (1985), 'The Ombudsman and the New Administrative Law', *Canberra Bulletin of Public Administration* 12:4, 286-97.

Gottehrer, D.M. and Hostina, M. (1998), *Essential Characteristics of a Classical Ombudsman*. Available at: <http://www.usombudsman.org/documents/PDF/References/Essential.pdf> (accessed 16 April 2010).

Gregory, R. and Drewry, G. (1991). 'Barlow Clowes and the Ombudsman Part II', *Public Law* Aut, 408-42.

Gregory, R. and Giddings, P. (2002), *The Ombudsman, the Citizen and Parliament* (London: Politico's Publishing).

Gregory, R. and Giddings, P. (2002a), *The Ombudsman and Parliament: A History of the Parliamentary and Health Service Ombudsman* (London: Politico's Publishing).

Gregory, R. and Giddings, P. (eds) (2000), *Righting Wrongs: The Ombudsman in Six Continents* (Amsterdam: IOS Press).

Griffith, G. (2005), *Parliament and Accountability: The Role of Parliamentary Oversight Committees*, New South Wales Library Research Service, Briefing Paper No. 12/05 (Sydney: New South Wales Parliamentary Library).

Groves, M. (2002), 'Ombudsmen's Jurisdiction in Prisons', *Monash University Law Review* 28:2, 181-205.

Groves, M. and Lee, H.P. (eds) (2007), *Australian Administrative Law* (Cambridge: Cambridge University Press).

Gulland, J. (2009), 'Independence in Complaints Procedures: Lessons From Community Care', *Journal of Social Welfare and Family Law* 31:1, 59-72.

Gulland, J. (2010), 'Current Developments in the UK: Complaints Procedures and Ombudsmen', in Adler (ed.), pp. 457-82.

Halford, J. (2009), 'It's Public Law, But Not As We Know It: Understanding and Making Effective Use of the Ombudsman Schemes', *Judicial Review* 14:1, 81-102.

Halliday, S. (2004), *Judicial Review and Compliance with Administrative Law* (Oxford: Hart Publishing).

Halliday, S. and Scott, C. (2010), 'A Cultural Analysis of Administrative Justice', in Adler (ed.), pp. 183-202.

Hansard Society (2001), *The Challenge of Parliament: Making Government Accountable* (London: Vacher Dod Publishing).

Harden, I. (2000), 'When Europeans Complain: The Work of the European Ombudsman', *Cambridge Yearbook of European Legal Studies*, vol. 3, pp. 199-237.

Harlow, C. (1978), 'Ombudsmen in Search of a Role', *Modern Law Review* 41:4, 446-54.

Harlow, C. (2010), 'Rationalising Administrative Compensation', *Public Law* Apr, 321-39.

Harlow, C. and Rawlings, R. (1997), *Law and Administration*, 2nd edition (London: Butterworths).

Harlow, C. and Rawlings, R. (2009), *Law and Administration*, 3rd edition (Cambridge: Cambridge University Press).

Harris, M. and Partington, M. (eds) (1999), *Administrative Justice in the 21st Century* (Oxford: Hart Publishing).

Hart, H.L.A. (1958), 'Positivism and the Separation of Law and Morals', *Harvard Law Review* 71:4, 593-629.

Hawkins, K. (ed.) (1995), *The Uses of Discretion* (Oxford: Clarendon Press).

Head, B., Brown, A.J. and Connors, C. (2008), *Promoting Integrity: Evaluating and Improving Public Institutions* (Farnham: Ashgate).

Heede, K. (2000), *European Ombudsman: Redress and Control at Union Level* (London: Kluwer Law International).

Henrichsen, C. (2010), 'Administrative Justice in a Scandinavian Legal Context: From a Liberal and a Social State to a Market State or a Milieu State', in Adler (ed.), pp. 321-50.

Hertogh, M.L.M. (2001), 'Coercion, Cooperation, and Control: Understanding The Policy Impact of Administrative Courts and The Netherlands', *Law and Policy* 23:1, 47-67.

Hertogh, M.L.M. (2010), 'Through the Eyes of Bureaucrats: How Front-Line Officials Understand Administrative Justice', in Adler (ed.), pp. 203-26.

Hertogh, M.L.M. and Halliday, S. (eds) (2004), *Judicial Review and Bureaucratic Impact: International and Interdisciplinary Perspectives* (Cambridge: Cambridge University Press).

Hewart, G. (1937), *Not Without Prejudice* (London: Century Hutchinson Ltd).

Himsworth, C. (ed.) (1985), *Judicial Teeth for Local Ombudsmen?* (Edinburgh: Department of Constitutional and Administrative Law, University of Edinburgh).

Hirschman, A.O. (1970), *Exit, Voice and Loyalty: Responses to Decline in Firms, Organizations and States* (Cambridge, MA: Harvard University Press).

Home Affairs Select Committee (1998), *Police Disciplinary and Complaints Procedure*, HC 258-I, session 1997-98, 15 January 1998 (London: The Stationery Office).

Hood, C. (1991), 'A Public Management for All Seasons?', *Public Administration* 69:1, 3-19.

Hood, C. (1995), 'The "New Public Management" in the 1980s: variations on a theme', *Accounting, Organizations and Society* 20:2/3, 93-109.

Hood, C. (1998), *The Art of the State: Culture, Rhetoric and Public Management* (Oxford: Oxford University Press).

Hopkins, A. (2005), *A Fair Complaint?: The Case for an Integrated Public Services Ombudsman* (London: National Consumer Council).

Hossain, K., Besselink, L.F.M., Selassie, H.S.G. and Völker, E. (eds) (2000), *Human Rights Commissions and Ombudsman Offices: National Experiences Throughout the World* (The Hague: Kluwer Law International).

Housing Ombudsman (2009), *Annual Report and Accounts 2009*, Housing Ombudsman Service (London: Independent Housing Ombudsman Ltd).

HSO (1999), *Investigation of Complaint about Treatment by Deputising Doctors and Monitoring of a GP Deputising Service*, HC 341, session 1998-99 (London: The Stationery Office).

HSO (1999a), *Investigations about Aspects of the NHS Complaints Procedure*, HC 410, session 1998-99 (London: The Stationery Office).

HSO (2003), *NHS Funding for Long-Term Care*, Second Report, HC 399, session 2002-03 (London: The Stationery Office).

HSO (2004), *NHS Funding for Long-Term Care: Follow-up Report*, HC 144, session 2004-05 (London: The Stationery Office).

HSO (2005), *Consent in Cardiac Surgery: A Good Practice Guide to Agreeing and Recording Consent*, Health Services Ombudsman and the Society of Cardiothoracic Surgeons of Great Britain and Northern Ireland (London: Parliamentary and Health Services Ombudsman).

HSO (2005a), *Making Things Better? A Report on Reform of the NHS Complaints Procedure in England*, HC 413, session 2004-05 (London: The Stationery Office).

HSO and LGO (2008), *Injustice in Residential Care: A Joint Report by the Local Government Ombudsman and the Health Service Ombudsman for England*, HC 421, session 2007-08 (London: The Stationery Office).

HSO and LGO (2009), *Six Lives: The Provision of Public Services to People with Learning Disabilities*, Part One, Overview and Summary Investigation

Reports, HC 203-I, session 2008-09, 23 March 2009. (London: The Stationery Office).

Hurtubise-Loranger, E. (2008), 'Commonwealth Experiences I – Federal Accountability and Beyond in Canada', in Gay and Winetrobe (eds), pp. 71-80.

Hyson, S. (ed.) (2009), *Provincial and Territorial Ombudsman Offices in Canada* (Toronto: Institute of Public Administration of Canada).

IFF Research (2010), *Impact Study: Presentation of Findings* (London: PHSO).

Innerarity, D. (2006), *La démocratie sans l'État – Essai sur le gouvernement des sociétés complexes* (Paris: Climats).

IO (2008), *Annual report 2007-2008*, Irish Ombudsman (Dublin: Office of the Ombudsman).

IO (2009), *Annual report 2008-2009*, Irish Ombudsman (Dublin: Office of the Ombudsman).

IPPR (1991), *The Constitution of the United Kingdom* (London: Institute for Public Policy Research).

Ipsos MORI (2007), 'Customer Satisfaction Survey for the Local Government Ombudsman July–August 2007', February 2008.

James, R. (1997), *Private Ombudsmen and Public Law* (Aldershot: Ashgate).

James, R. and Longley, D. (1996), 'The Channel Tunnel rail link, the ombudsman and the Select Committee', *Public Law* Spr, 38-45.

Joint Committee on Human Rights (2008), *A Bill of Rights for the UK?* HL 165-II; HC 150-II, session 2007-08, 10 August 2008 (London: The Stationery Office).

Jones, G. (2009), *Conducting Administrative Oversight and Ombudsman Investigations* (Aurora, Ontario: Canada Law Books).

Jones, M(elinda) (1999), 'Administrative Justice: Some Preliminary Thoughts on a (Post) Modern Theoretical Perspective', National Administrative Law Forum conference paper, in Creyke and McMillan (eds) (2000), pp. 40-55.

Jones, M(ichael) (1988), 'The Local Ombudsmen and Judicial Review', *Public Law* Wnt, 608-22.

Jowell, J. (2007), 'The Rule of Law and its Underlying Values', in Jowell and Oliver (eds), pp. 5-24.

Jowell, J. and Oliver, D. (eds) (2007), *The Changing Constitution*, 6th edition (Oxford: Oxford University Press).

Justice (1977), *Our Fettered Ombudsman: A Report*, David Widdicombe QC (chair) (London: Justice).

Justice-All Souls (1988), *Administrative Justice: Some Necessary Reforms: A Report of a JUSTICE-All Souls Committee* (Oxford: Clarendon Press).

Kagan, R.A. (2010), 'The Organisation of Administrative Justice Systems: The Role of Political Mistrust', in Adler (ed.), pp. 161-82.

Kairys, D. (2003), 'Searching for the Rule of Law', *Suffolk University Law Review* 36:2, 307-29.

Kerr, J.R. (1971), *Commonwealth Administrative Review Committee Report*, Hon. Mr Justice J.R. Kerr, Parliamentary Paper No. 144 of 1972 (Canberra: Australian Government Publishing Service).

Kerrison, S. and Pollock, A. (2001), 'Complaints as Accountability? The Case of Health Care in the United Kingdom', *Public Law* Spr, 115-33.

King, A. (2007), *The British Constitution* (Oxford: Oxford University Press).

King, J.A. (2007a), 'Accountability: The Value of Courts in the Light of the Alternatives', Social Science Research Network (SSRN) paper (18 June 2007). Available at SSRN: <http://ssrn.com/abstract=1027626> (accessed 1 March 2010).

King, J.A. (2007b), 'The Justiciability of Resource Allocation', *Modern Law Review* 70:2, 197-224.

King, J.A. (2008a), 'The Pervasiveness of Polycentricity', *Public Law* Spr, 101-24.

King, J.A. (2008b), 'Institutional Approaches to Judicial Restraint', *Oxford Journal of Legal Studies* 28:3, 409-441.

Kirkham, R. (2003), 'Why Ombudsmen are Important: Helping Long-term Patients', *Journal of Social Welfare and Family Law* 25:3, 267-75.

Kirkham, R. (2005), 'A Complainant's View of the Local Government Ombudsman', *Journal of Social Welfare and Family Law* 27:3/4, 383-94.

Kirkham, R. (2005a), 'Auditing by Stealth? Special Reports and the Ombudsman', *Public Law* Wnt, 740-48.

Kirkham, R. (2006), 'Challenging the Authority of the Ombudsman: The Parliamentary Ombudsman's Special Report on Wartime Detainees', *Modern Law Review* 69:5, 792-818.

Kirkham, R. (2007), *The Parliamentary Ombudsman: Withstanding the Test of Time*, HC 421, session 2006-2007, Parliamentary and Health Service Ombudsman (London: The Stationery Office).

Kirkham, R. (2008), 'Explaining the Lack of Enforcement Power Possessed by the Ombudsman' (ombudsman section), *Journal of Social Welfare and Family Law* 30:3, 253–63.

Kirkham, R. (2009), 'The Constitutional Role of the Ombudsman', *International Ombudsman Yearbook*, vol. 13 (The Hague: Kluwer Law International).

Kirkham, R., Thompson, B. and Buck, T. (2008), 'When Putting Things Right Goes Wrong: Enforcing the Recommendations of the Ombudsman', *Public Law* Aut, 510-30.

Kirkham, R., Thompson, B. and Buck, T. (2009), 'Putting the Ombudsman into Constitutional Context', *Parliamentary Affairs* 62:4, 600-617.

Kucsko-Stadlmayer, G. (ed.) (2008), *European Ombudsman-Institutions* (Vienna: SpringerWienNew York).

Langford, M. (ed.) (2009), *Social Rights Jurisprudence: Emerging Trends in Comparative and International Law* (Cambridge: Cambridge University Press).

Lapsley, I. and Lonsdale, J. (2010), 'The Audit Society: Helping to Develop or Undermine Trust in Government?', in Adler (ed.), pp. 73-96.

Law Commission (2008), *Administrative Redress: Public Bodies and the Citizen*, Consultation Paper No. 187, 17 June 2008 (London: Law Commission).

Law Commission (2008a), *Administrative Redress: Public Bodies and the Citizen*, Summary of Consultation Paper No. 187 (July 2008). (London: Law Commission).

Law Commission (2008b), *Housing: Proportionate Dispute Resolution* (Cm 7377), Law Com No. 309 (May 2008) (London: Law Commission).

Law Commission (2010), *Administrative Redress: Public Bodies and the Citizen*, HC 6, Law Com No. 322 (25 May 2010) (London: The Stationery Office).

Law Commission (2010a), Public Services Ombudsmen, Consultation Paper No. 196, 2 September 2010 (London: The Stationery Office).

Lazare, A. (2004), *On Apology* (New York: Oxford University Press).

LCARC (2006), *Report on the Review of the Strategic Management Review Report – Office of the Ombudsman, April 2006; Report on the 2005-06 Annual Report of the Office of the Ombudsman*, Report No. 57 (2005-06), Legal, Constitutional and Administrative Review Committee (Brisbane: Queensland Parliament).

LCD (1995), *Access to Justice: Interim Report* (London: The Stationery Office).

LCD (1996), *Access to Justice*, July 1996 (London: The Stationery Office).

LCD (2000), *Review of the Crown Office List*, Sir Jeffrey Bowman's report to the Lord Chancellor's Department (London: Lord Chancellor's Department).

Le Sueur, A. (2007), 'Courts, Tribunals, Ombudsmen, ADR: Administrative Justice, Constitutionalism and Informality', in Jowell and Oliver (eds), pp. 317-38.

Leggatt, A. (2001), *Tribunals for Users – One System, One Service: Report of the Review of Tribunals* (March 2001) (the 'Leggatt Review') (London: The Stationery Office).

Levitt, R., Martin, S, Nutley, S. and Solesbury, W. (2010), *Evidence for Accountability: Using Evidence in the Audit, Inspection and Scrutiny of UK Government* (London: Nuffield Foundation). Available at: <http://www.nuffieldfoundation.org/fileLibrary/pdf/Evidence_for_accountability_web_PDF.pdf> (accessed 11 June 2010).

Lewis, N.D. (1993), 'World Ombudsman Community: Aspects and Prospects', *Indian Journal of Public Administration* 39:4, 663-676.

Lewis, N.D. and Birkinshaw, P. (1993), *When Citizens Complain: Reforming Justice and Administration* (Buckingham: Open University Press).

Lewis, N.D. and James, R. (2000), 'Joined-up Justice: Review of the Public Sector Ombudsman in England', *The International Ombudsman Yearbook*, vol. 4, 109-40.

Leyland, P. and Woods, T. (eds) (1997), *Administrative Law Facing the Future: Old Constraints and New Horizons* (London: Blackstone Press).

LGO (2001), *Good Administrative Practice* (London: Local Government Ombudsman).

LGO (2005), *Remedies: Guidance on Good Practice* (London: Local Government Ombudsman).

LGO (2007), *Local Government Ombudsman Annual Report 2006/07* (London: Commission for Local Administration in England).

LGO (2007a), *Local Government Ombudsmen Annual Report 2006/07: Supplement to the Annual Review* (London: Commission for Local Administration in England).

LGO (2007b), *Guidance Note on 'Unreasonably Persistent' Complainants and 'Unreasonable Complainant Behaviour'*, January 2007/revised January 2009 (London: Commission for Local Administration in England).

LGO (2008), *Local Government Ombudsman Annual Report 2007/08* (London: Commission for Local Administration in England).

LGO (2008a), 'Trafford Metropolitan Borough Council' (05/C/11921) (London: Commission for Local Administration in England).

LGO (2009), *Local Government Ombudsman Annual Report 2008-2009* (London: Commission for Local Administration in England).

LGO (2009a), *Running a Complaints System: Guidance on Good Practice* (London: Commission for Local Administration in England).

LGO (2009b), *Triennial Review of the Operation of Part III of the Local Government Act 1974* (London: Commission for Local Administration in England).

LGPSC (2006), 'The Public Services Ombudsman for Wales: The First Six Months', Local Government and Public Services Committee, LGPS(2)-12-06(p5), 21 September 2006 (Cardiff: The National Assembly for Wales).

Liaison Committee (2008), *Pre-Appointment Hearings by Select Committees*, HC 384, session 2007-08, House of Commons Liaison Committee, 5 March 2008 (London: The Stationery Office).

Lipsky, M. (1980), *Street-level Bureaucracy: Dilemmas of the Individual in Public Services* (New York: Russell Sage Foundation).

Llewellyn, K. (1940), 'The Normative, the Legal and the Law Jobs: The Problem of Juristic Method', *Yale Law Journal* 49:8, 1355-400.

Longley, D. and James, R. (1995), 'Judicial Review and Tragic Choices: Ex Parte B', *Public Law*, Aut, 367-73.

Loughlin, M. (2003), *The Idea of Public Law* (Oxford: Oxford University Press).

Loughlin, M. and Walker, N. (eds) (2006), *The Paradox of Constitutionalism: Constituent Power and Constitutional Reform* (Oxford: Oxford University Press).

Lunn, J. (2009), *Ex-gratia Payment for Far East POWs and Civilian Internees*, House of Commons Library, SN/IA/3887, International Affairs and Defence Section, 27 March 2009 (London: House of Commons).

Macpherson, W. (1999), *The Stephen Lawrence Inquiry*, Report of an Inquiry by Sir William Macpherson of Cluny, Cm 4262-I, February 1999 (London: The Stationery Office).

Maer, L. (2008), *Parliamentary Involvement in Public Appointments*, House of Commons Library, SN/PC/4382, Parliament and Constitution Centre, 6 June 2008 (London: House of Commons).

Maer, L. (2009), *Proposals for a Petitions Committee for the House of Commons*, House of Commons Library, SN/PC/5203, Parliament and Constitution Centre, 22 December 2009 (London: House of Commons).

Margetts, H. and Partington, M. (2010), 'Developments in E-government' in Adler, M. (ed.), pp. 47-72.

Marin, A. (2009), 'Leveraging Moral Suasion through SORT Investigations' (speech), Ombudsman of Ontario, IXth International Ombudsman Institute World Conference Swedish Parliamentary Ombudsman Bicentennial Stockholm, June 10, 2009. Available at: <http://www.ombudsman.on.ca/en/media/speeches/2009/leveraging-moral-suasion---stockholm-conf-jun-10-09.aspx> (accessed 18 May 2010).

Marshall, G. (1973), 'Maladministration', *Public Law* 32-44.

Mashaw, J.L. (1974), 'The Management Side of Due Process: Some Theoretical and Litigation Notes on the Assurance of Accuracy, Fairness and Timeliness in the Adjudication of Social Welfare Claims', *Cornell Law Review* 59:5, 772–824.

Mashaw, J.L. (1981), 'Administrative Due Process: The Quest for a Dignitary Theory', *Boston University Law Review* 61:3, 885-931.

Mashaw, J.L. (1983), *Bureaucratic Justice: Managing Social Security Disability Claims* (New Haven and London: Yale University Press).

Mashaw, J.L. (2006), 'Accountability and Institutional Design: Some Thoughts on the Grammar of Governance', in Dowdle (ed.), pp. 115-56.

McMillan, J. (2005), 'The Ombudsman and the Rule of Law', *Australian Institute for Administrative Law Forum* 44, 1-16.

McMillan, J. (2005a), 'The Ombudsman, Immigration and Beyond' (unpublished paper) Commonwealth Ombudsman, IPAA Seminar, Canberra, 25 October 2005. Available at: <http://ombudsman.gov.au/docs/speeches/IPAA-Immigration-and-beyond_25oct2005.pdf> (accessed 6 March 2010).

McMillan, J. (2009), 'Future Directions 2009: The Ombudsmen', Paper to Australian Institute of Administrative Law National Administrative Law Forum Commonwealth Ombudsman, Canberra, 7 August 2009. [This paper has been published in (2010) 63 *AIAL Forum*.]

McMurtie, S. (1997), 'The Waiting Game: the Parliamentary Commissioner's Response to Delay in Administrative Procedures', *Public Law* Spr, 159-73.

Mendes, J. (2009), 'Good Administration in EU Law and the European Code of Good Administrative Behaviour', *EU Working Papers Law 2009/09* (Florence: European University Institute).

Merricks, W. (2007), 'The Financial Ombudsman Service: Not Just an Alternative to Court', *Journal of Financial Regulation and Compliance* 15:2, 135-42.

Merricks, W. (2010), 'Where and How Should the Private Sector Ombudsman Be Seen in the Administrative Justice Landscape?', in Adler (ed.), pp. 249-68.

Millett, P.J. (2002), 'The Right to Good Administration', *Public Law* Sum, 309-22.

Ministry of Justice (2007), *The Governance of Britain*, Cm 7170, July 2007 (London: The Stationery Office).

Ministry of Justice (2009), *Rights and Responsibilities: Developing Our Constitutional Framework*, Cm 7577, March 2009 (London: The Stationery Office).

Ministry of Justice (2009a), *Government's Response to Law Commission Consultation Paper – Administrative Redress: Public Bodies and the Citizen*, 3 June 2009 (personal communication to authors from the Law Commission).

Ministry of Justice (2009b), *Government Response to Law Commission's Report on Housing*, 16 July 2009.

Ministry of Justice (2010), *Judicial and Court Statistics 2008*, Cm 7697, session 2008-09, Ministry of Justice (London: The Stationery Office).

Mitchell, J.D.B. (1965), 'The Irrelevance of the Ombudsman Proposals', in Rowat (ed.), pp. 273-81.

MORI (2003), *Ombudsmen Awareness Survey 2003*, Survey of the General Public and Advisory Bodies, Study Conducted for the PHSO and LGOs, May-July 2003. Summary and full reports available at: <http://www.lgo.org.uk/about-us/surveys/public-awareness-survey-2003/> (accessed 22 March 2010).

Mulcahy, L. (1999), 'Sliding Scales of Justice at the End of the Century', in Harris and Partington (eds), pp. 66-82.

Mulgan, R. (2003), *Holding Power to Account: Accountability in Modern Democracies* (Basingstoke: Palgrave Macmillan).

Mullen, T. (2009), *Administrative Justice in Scotland – The Way Forward*, The Final Report of the Administrative Justice Steering Group, June 2009 (Glasgow: Consumer Focus Scotland).

Mullen, T. (2010), 'A Holistic Approach to Administrative Justice?', in Adler (ed.), pp. 383-420.

Murkens, J.E.K. (2009), 'The Quest for Constitutionalism in UK Public Law Discourse', *Oxford Journal of Legal Studies* 29:3, 427–55.

NAO (2001), *Joining Up to Improve Public Services*, Report by the Comptroller and Auditor General, HC 383, session 2001-02, 7 December 2001 (London: The Stationery Office).

NAO (2005), *Citizen Redress: What Citizens Can Do If Things Go Wrong With Public Services*, Report by the Comptroller and Auditor General, HC 21, session 2004-05, 9 March 2005 (London: The Stationery Office).

NAO (2007), *The Compensation Scheme for Former Icelandic Water Trawlermen*, Report by the Comptroller and Auditor General, HC 530, session 2006-07, 29 June 2007 (London: The Stationery Office).

NAO (2009), *Helping Government Learn*, Report by the Comptroller and Auditor General, HC 129, session 2008-09, 27 February 2009 (London: the Stationery Office).

NAO (2010), *Annual Report 2010* (London: National Audit Office).

National Assembly for Wales (2010), *Standing Orders of the National Assembly for Wales*, February 2010 (Cardiff: National Assembly for Wales Commission).

National Ombudsmen of EU Member States (2007), *Rethinking Good Administration in the European Union*, Sixth Seminar of the National

Ombudsmen of EU Member States and Candidate Countries, Strasbourg, 14-16 October 2007 (Luxembourg: Office for Official Publications of the European Communities).

NIO (2007), *Annual Report of the Assembly Ombudsman for Northern Ireland and the Northern Ireland Commissioner for Complaints 2006-2007*, NIA 37/06-07 (Belfast: Office of the Northern Ireland Ombudsman).

NIO (2007a), *Corporate Plan 2007-10: Incorporating the 2007-2008 Business Plan* (Belfast: Office of the Northern Ireland Ombudsman).

NIO (2008), *Annual Report of the Assembly Ombudsman for Northern Ireland and the Northern Ireland Commissioner for Complaints 2007-08*, NIA 182/07-08 (Belfast: Office of the Northern Ireland Ombudsman).

NIO (2009), *Annual Report of the Assembly Ombudsman for Northern Ireland and the Northern Ireland Commissioner for Complaints 2008-09*, NIA 108/08-09 (Belfast: Office of the Northern Ireland Ombudsman).

Noble, R. (2001), 'Keeping Ombudsmen in their Place: The Courts and the Pensions Ombudsman', *Public Law* Sum, 308-28.

Norton, P. (2004), 'Regulating the Regulatory State', *Parliamentary Affairs* 57:4, 785-99.

NSWO (2001), *Annual Report 2000-01* (Sydney: New South Wales Ombudsman).

NSWO (2002), *Annual Report 2001-02* (Sydney: New South Wales Ombudsman).

NSWO (2004), *Investigating Complaints: A Manual for Investigators* (Sydney: New South Wales Ombudsman).

NSWO (2006), *Annual Report 2005-06* (Sydney: New South Wales Ombudsman).

NSWO (2008), *Annual Report 2007-08* (Sydney: New South Wales Ombudsman).

NSWO (2009), *Annual Report 2008-09* (Sydney: New South Wales Ombudsman).

NSWO (2009a), *The Rights Stuff: Tips for Making Complaints and Solving Problems – A Toolkit for Consumers of Community Services in NSW* (Sydney: New South Wales Ombudsman).

NSWO (2009b), *Apologies: A Practical Guide*, 2nd edition (Sydney: New South Wales Ombudsman).

NSWO (2009c), *Australian Ombudsman: Unreasonable Complainant Conduct Project Report Guide* (Sydney: New South Wales Ombudsman).

NSWO (2009d), *Managing Unreasonable Complainant Conduct Practice Manual* (Sydney: New South Wales Ombudsman).

NTO (2009), *31st Annual Report 2008-2009*, Ombudsman for the Northern Territory of Australia (Darwin: Ombudsman for the Northern Territory of Australia).

Nuffield Foundation (2008), *Administrative Justice: Choice of Redress Mechanisms*, Briefing Note No. 3 (London: Nuffield Foundation). Available at: <http://www.nuffieldfoundation.org/go/grants/accesstojustice/page_480.html> (accessed 11 March 2010).

NZO (2002), *Annual Report 2001-02* (Wellington: New Zealand Ombudsman).

NZO (2005), *Annual Report 2004-05* (Wellington: New Zealand Ombudsman).

NZO (2007), *Annual Report 2006-07* (Wellington: New Zealand Ombudsman).

NZO (2008), *Annual Report 2007-08* (Wellington: New Zealand Ombudsman).

NZO (2009), *Annual Report 2008-09* (Wellington: New Zealand Ombudsman).

O'Brien, N. (2009), 'Ombudsmen and Social Rights Adjudication', *Public Law* Sum, 466-78.

O'Brien, N. (2009a), 'Ombudsmen, Equality and Human Rights – Challenges and Opportunities' (conference paper), Equality, Human Rights and Good Relations: Evidence Based interventions and Policy Making Conference, the Foresight Centre, University of Liverpool, 21 May 2009.

O'Donnell, D. (2007), 'Lessons from the Public and Private Ombudsman Divide' (seminar notes), Commonwealth Ombudsman 30th Anniversary Seminar, August 2007. Available at: <http://www.ombudsman.gov.au/docs/30th-anniversary-seminar/seminar_notes_Deidre_ODonnell.pdf> (accessed 5 May 2010).

O'Donnell, G. (1999), 'Horizontal Accountability and New Democracies', in Schedler, Diamond and Platner (eds), pp. 29-51.

O'Reilly, E. (2007), 'Human Rights and the Ombudsman', Lecture of the Ombudsman of Ireland at the 2007 Biennial Conference of the British and Irish Ombudsman, 27 April 2007 (University of Warwick: British and Irish Ombudsman Association). Available at: <http://www.bioa.org.uk/docs/HumanRightsOmbudsmanEmilyOReilly.pdf> (accessed 18 September 2009).

O'Reilly, E. (2009), 'Watching the Watchdog', in Passemiers *et al* (eds), pp. 287-97.

O'Reilly, E. (2009a), 'The Relationship between the Ombudsman and the Media' (speech), Irish Ombudsman, International Symposium of Namur, 23 November 2009. Available at: <http://www.ombudsman.gov.ie/en/SpeechesandArticles/Ombudsmansspeeches/Name,11171,en.htm> (accessed 14 April 2010).

O'Reilly, E. (2009b), 'The Role of the Ombudsman in an Economic Downturn' (speech), Irish Ombudsman and Information Commissioner, 40th Anniversary of the Northern Ireland Ombudsman's Office, 25 November 2009. Available at: <http://www.ombudsman.gov.ie/en/SpeechesandArticles/Ombudsmansspeeches/Name,11173,en.htm> (accessed 28 May 2010).

OBC (2006), *The Power of an Apology: Removing the Legal Barriers*, Special Report No. 27, February 2006 to the Legislative Assembly of British Columbia (Victoria: Ombudsman British Columbia).

ODPM Select Committee (2005), *The Role and Effectiveness of the Local Government Ombudsmen for England*, HC 458, session 2004-05 (London: The Stationery Office).

OFMDFM (2004), *Review of the Offices of the Assembly Ombudsman for Northern Ireland and the Northern Ireland Commissioner for Complaints*, March 2004, Final report (Belfast: Deloitte MCS Limited). Available at: <http://www.ni-ombudsman.org.uk/pubs/Review%20of%20the%20Office%20Part%201.pdf> (accessed 19 March 2010).

Oliver, D. (2010), 'Towards the Horizontal Effect of Administrative Justice Principles', in Adler (ed.), pp. 229-48.

Ombudsman for Bermuda (2007), *A Tale of 2 Hospitals: Who Gets the Benefit of the Doubt?* The Ombudsman for Bermuda's own motion systemic investigation into allegations of discrimination involving medical professionals at King Edward VII Memorial Hospital, November 2007 (Hamilton, Bermuda: Office of the Bermuda Ombudsman).

Ombudsman for Bermuda (2009), *Annual Report* 2008-09 (Hamilton: Bermuda).

Ontario Ombudsman (2009), *Annual Report of the Ontario Ombudsman 2008-2009* (Ontario: Office of the Ontario Ombudsman).

OPC (2002), *Report on Procedures for the Appointment of an Officer of Parliament*, Officers of Parliament Committee, I.15A, Forty-Seventh Parliament, Rt Hon. Jonathan Hunt (chair) (Wellington, New Zealand: House of Representatives).

OPC (2009), 'Inquiry into the Appointment of an Ombudsman', Report of the Officers of Parliament Committee, 17 December 2009 (Wellington, New Zealand: House of Representatives).

ORC International (2008), 'Scottish Public Services Ombudsman: Complainant Satisfaction Survey 2007' (London: ORC International). Available at: <http://www.scottishombudsmanwatch.org/files/SPSO_07_satisfaction_survey__21_February_2008.pdf> (accessed 20 May 2010).

OV (2008), *Annual Report 2007-08* (Melbourne: Ombudsman Victoria).

OV (2009), *Annual Report 2008-09* (Melbourne: Ombudsman Victoria).

Owen, S. (1990), 'The Expanding Role of the Ombudsman in the Administrative State', *University of Toronto Law Journal* 40:3, 670-86.

Pacquet, G. (2009), 'The Judgment of Wider Courts: Ombudspersons as Producers of Governance', *Optimum Online: The Journal of Public Sector Management* 39:3, 5-20.

PAEC (2006), *Report on a Legislative Framework for Independent Officers of Parliament*, Public Accounts and Estimates Committee, 67th report, No. 130, session 2003-06 (Melbourne: Parliament of Victoria).

Page, A. (1999), 'The Citizen's Charter and Administrative Justice', in Harris and Partington (eds), pp. 85-98.

Partington, M. (ed.) (2001), *The Leggatt Review of Tribunals: Academic Seminar Papers*, Bristol Centre for the Study of Administrative Justice, Working Paper Series No. 3 (Bristol: Bristol Centre for the Study of Administrative Justice).

Partington, M. and Kirton-Darling, E. (2006), *Feedback*, Research Issues Paper 1, Administrative Justice and Tribunals Council (London: Administrative Justice and Tribunals Council).

PASC (2000), *Review of Public Sector Ombudsman in England: Report, Proceedings of the Committee and the Minutes of Evidence*, HC 612, session 1999-2000, Public Administration Select Committee, 8 August 2000 (London: The Stationery Office).

PASC (2003), *Ombudsman Issues*, HC 448, session 2002-03, February 2003 (London: The Stationery Office).

PASC (2005), 'Ombudsman Issues and Tax Credits', Oral Evidence given by Ann Abraham, Parliamentary and Health Service Ombudsman, HC 577-i, session 2005-06, 20 October 2005 (London: The Stationery Office).

PASC (2006), *The Ombudsman in Question: The Ombudsman's Report on Pensions and its Constitutional Consequences*, HC 1081, session 2005-06 (London: The Stationery Office).

PASC (2007), 'Work of the Ombudsman', Oral Evidence given by Ann Abraham, Parliamentary and Health Service Ombudsman, HC 1086-I, session 2007-08, 18 October 2007 (London: The Stationery Office).

PASC (2007a), *Ethics and Standards: The Regulation of Conduct in Public Life*, HC 121-I, session 2006-07 (London: The Stationery Office).

PASC (2008), *When Citizens Complain*, HC 409, session 2007-08 (London: The Stationery Office).

PASC (2008a), 'Public Services: Putting People First', Oral Evidence given by Ann Abraham, Parliamentary and Health Service Ombudsman, HC 408, session 2007-08, 18 January 2007 (London: The Stationery Office).

PASC (2008b), 'The Work of the Ombudsman' Oral Evidence given by Ann Abraham, Parliamentary and Health Service Ombudsman, HC 1144-i, session 2007-08, 30 October 2008 (London: The Stationery Office).

PASC (2008c), *Parliament and Public Appointments: Pre-appointment Hearings by Select Committees*, Public Administration Select Committee, HC 152, session 2007-08, 16 January 2008 (London: The Stationery Office).

PASC (2009), 'Work of the Ombudsman in 2008-09', Oral and Written Evidence of Ann Abraham, Parliamentary Ombudsman, HC 122, session 2009-10 (London: The Stationery Office).

PASC (2009a), *Parliament and the Ombudsman*, HC 107, session 2009-10, 9 December 2009 (London: The Stationery Office).

PASC (2010), *Parliament and the Ombudsman: Further Report – With the Government's Response to the Committee's Fourth Report*, HC 471, session 2009-10, 10 March 2010 (London: The Stationery Office).

Passemiers, R., Reynaert H. and Steyvers, K. (2009), *The Impact of Ombudsmen* (Bruges: Vanden Broele Publishers).

PB Statement (2009), *Portfolio Budget Statements 2009–10*, Budget Related Paper No. 1.15a, Prime Minister and Cabinet Portfolio (Canberra: Commonwealth of Australia). Available at: <http://www.dpmc.gov.au/accountability/budget/2009-10/pbs/pbs_2009-10.pdf> (accessed 23 April 2010).

PCAC (1993), *The Powers, Work and Jurisdiction of the Ombudsman*, Select Committee on the Parliamentary Commissioner for Administration, HC 33, session 1993-94 (London: HMSO).

Pearce, D. (1993), 'The Ombudsman: Review and Preview: The Importance of Being Different', *The Ombudsman Journal* 11, 13-36.

Pearce, D. (1998), 'The Commonwealth Ombudsman: The Right Office in the Wrong Place', in Creyke and McMillan (eds), pp. 54-72.

Pearce, D. (2005), 'The Jurisdiction of Australian Government Ombudsmen', in Groves, M. (ed.), *Law and Government in Australia: Essays in Honour of Enid Campbell* (Annandale NSW: Federation Press), pp. 110-38.

Pearson, L., Harlow, C. and Taggart, M. (eds) (2008), *Administrative Law in a Changing State: Essays in Honour of Mark Aronson* (Oxford: Hart Publishing).

PHSO (2005), *Annual Report of the Parliamentary and Health Service Ombudsman: A Year of Progress*, HC 348, session 2004-05, 20 July 2005 (London: The Stationery Office).

PHSO (2005a), *'A Debt of Honour': The Ex Gratia Scheme for British Groups Interned by the Japanese during the Second World War*. 4th Report of the Parliamentary and Health Service Ombudsman, HC 324, session 2004-05, 12 July 2005 (London: The Stationery Office).

PHSO (2005b), *Redress in the Round: Remedying Maladministration in Central and Local Government*, HC 475, session 2005-06, 11 October 2005 (London: The Stationery Office).

PHSO (2005c), *Tax Credits: Putting Things Right*, HC 124, session 2005-06, 21 June 2005 (London: The Stationery Office).

PHSO (2006), *Annual Report of the Parliamentary and Health Service Ombudsman: Making a Difference*, HC 1363, session 2005-06, 12 July 2006 (London: The Stationery Office).

PHSO (2006a), *Trusting in the Pensions Promise: Government Bodies and the Security of Final Salary Occupational Pensions*, HC 984, session 2005-06 (London: The Stationery Office).

PHSO (2007), *Annual Report of the Parliamentary and Health Service Ombudsman: Putting Principles into Practice*, HC 838, session 2006-07, 18 July 2007 (London: The Stationery Office).

PHSO (2007a), *Principles of Good Administration* (London: The Stationery Office).

PHSO (2007b), *Principles of Good Administration: Response to Consultation*, 27 March 2007 (London: Parliamentary and Health Service Ombudsman).

PHSO (2007c), *Put Together in Haste: 'Cod Wars' Trawlermen's Compensation Scheme*, Second Report of the Parliamentary and Health Service Ombudsman, HC 313, session 2006-07, 21 February 2007 (London: The Stationery Office).

PHSO (2007d), *Tax Credits: Getting it Wrong?*, HC 1010, session 2006-07, 8 October 2007 (London: The Stationery Office).

PHSO (2008), *Annual Report of the Parliamentary and Health Service Ombudsman 2007-2008*: *Bringing Wider Public Benefit from Individual Complaints*, HC 1040, 6 October 2008 (London: The Stationery Office).

PHSO (2008a), *Equitable Life: A Decade of Regulatory Failure, Part Five – Guide to the Main Report and Summary of Findings and Recommendations*, HC 815-v, session 2007-08 (London: The Stationery Office).

PHSO (2009), *Every Complaint Matters*: *Annual Report 2008-2009*, Parliamentary and Health Service Ombudsman, HC 786, 15 July 2009 (London: The Stationery Office).

PHSO (2009a), *Three Year Strategic Plan 2009–12*, 15 July 2009 (London: Parliamentary and Health Service Ombudsman). Available at: <http://www.ombudsman.org.uk/__data/assets/pdf_file/0020/3539/Three-Year-Strategic-Plan-2009-12.pdf> (accessed 30 August 2010).

PHSO (2009b), *Injustice Unremedied: The Government's Response on Equitable Life*, HC 435, session 2008-09 (London: The Stationery Office).

PHSO (2009c), 'Statement of Responsibilities between the Parliamentary and Health Service Ombudsman and the Cabinet Office', HM Treasury, Department of Health and Ministry of Justice, August 2009. Available at: <http://www.ombudsman.org.uk/__data/assets/pdf_file/0016/3409/Statement-of-responsibility-August-2009.pdf> (accessed 4 June 2010).

PHSO (2009d), *Cold Comfort: The Administration of the 2005 Single Payment Scheme by the Rural Payments Agency*, HC 81, session 2009-10, 15 December 2009 (London: The Stationery Office).

PHSO (2010), *Making an Impact*: *Annual Report 2009-2010*, Parliamentary and Health Service Ombudsman, HC 274, 14 July 2010 (London: The Stationery Office).

PHSO (2010a), 'Governance Statement' March 2010. Available at: <http://www.ombudsman.org.uk/about-us/our-role/governance/governance-statement> (accessed 30 August 2010).

Platt, L., Sunkin, M. and Calvo, K. (2010), 'Judicial Review Litigation as an Incentive to Change in Local Authority Public Services in England and Wales' (in Incentives and Public Service Performance: A Special Issue), *Journal of Public Administration Research and Theory* 20:Supplement 2, 243-60.

PO (1967), *Aircraft Noise*, HC 47, Second Report of the Parliamentary Commissioner for Administration, session 1967-68, 14 December 1967 (London: HMSO).

PO (1967a), *Sachsenhausen*, HC 54, Third Report of the Parliamentary Commissioner for Administration, session 1967-68, 20 December 1967 (London: HMSO).

PO (1978), *Rochester Way, Bexley – Refusal to Meet Late Claims for Compensation*, HC 598, session 1977-78, 25 July 1978 (London: HMSO).

PO (1993), *Compensation to Farmers for Slaughtered Poultry*, HC 519, session 1992-93 (London: HMSO).

PO (1995), *The Channel Tunnel Rail Link and Blight: Complaints against the Department of Transport*, HC 193, session 1994-95, 8 February 1995 (London: The Stationery Office).

PO (1998), *Annual Report 1997-98*, HC 845, session 1997-98 (London: The Stationery Office).

PO (2004), *Annual Report of the Parliamentary Ombudsman 2003-04*, HC 702, session 2003-04 (London: The Stationery Office).

PO (2004a), *A Further Investigation of the Prudential Regulation of Equitable Life?* Parliamentary Commissioner for Administration, HC 910, session 2003-04 (London: The Stationery Office).

PONI (2008), *Annual Report: April 2007-2008* (Belfast: Police Ombudsman for Northern Ireland).

PONI (2009), *Public Awareness of the System for Complaints Against the Police in Northern Ireland*, Police Ombudsman for Northern Ireland (Research and Performance Directorate) (Belfast: Police Ombudsman for Northern Ireland). Available at: <http://www.policeombudsman.org/Publicationsuploads/omnibus%20report%202009.doc> (accessed 22 March 2010).

Posnett, J., Jowett, S., Barnett, P. and Land, T. (2001), *NHS Complaints Procedure National Evaluation*, Health Economics Consortium/NFO System Three Social Research (London: Department of Health).

PPO (2008), *Report for the Prisons and Probation Ombudsman on the Relevance and Effectiveness of Their Current Publicity Materials*, Prisons and Probation Ombudsman. Available at: <http://www.ppo.gov.uk/docs/Report-on-effectiveness-of-PPO-Publicity-Materials.pdf> (accessed 14 April 2010).

PPO (2009), *Annual Report 2008-09*, Prisons and Probation Ombudsman for England and Wales, Cm 7661 (London: The Stationery Office).

Prime Minister (1991), *The Citizen's Charter: Raising the Standard* (Cm 1599), July 1991 (London: HMSO).

Prime Minister (1999), *Modernising Government* (Cm 4310), March 1999 (London: The Stationery Office).

Prime Minister (2009), *Building Britain's Future* (Cm 7654), June 2009 (London: The Stationery Office).

PSOW (2006), *Guidance to Local Authorities on Complaints Handling*, Public Services Ombudsman for Wales, September 2006 (Pencoed: Public Services Ombudsman for Wales). Available at: <http://www.ombudsman-wales.org.uk/uploads/publications/196.pdf> (accessed 22 March 2010).

PSOW (2006a), 'Special Report under Section 22 of the Public Services Ombudsman (Wales) Act 2005 into Two Complaints of Maladministration Made Against Gwynedd Council', 16 November 2006. Available at: <http://www.ombudsman-wales.org.uk/uploads/publications/214.pdf> (accessed 21 May 2010).

PSOW (2006b), *Housing Allocations and Homelessness*, a special report by the Local Government Ombudsman for Wales (Pencoed: Public Services Ombudsman for Wales).

PSOW (2009), *Annual Report of the Public Services Ombudsman for Wales: 2008-2009* (Pencoed: Public Services Ombudsman for Wales).

PSOW and LGO (2006), *Memorial Safety in Local Authority Cemeteries*, Joint Special Report of the Public Services Ombudsman for Wales and Local Government Ombudsman for England, March 2006. Available at: <http://www.ombudsman-wales.org.uk/uploads/publications/138.pdf> (accessed 23 May 2010).

QO (2002), *Annual Report 2001-02* (Brisbane: Queensland Ombudsman).
QO (2003), *Annual Report 2002-03* (Brisbane: Queensland Ombudsman).
QO (2005), *Annual Report 2004-05* (Brisbane: Queensland Ombudsman).
QO (2007), *Annual Report 2006-07* (Brisbane: Queensland Ombudsman).
QO (2008a), *The Regulation of Mine Safety in Queensland: A Review of the Queensland Mines Inspectorate*, June 2008 (Brisbane: Queensland Ombudsman).
QO (2009), *Annual Report 2008-09* (Brisbane: Queensland Ombudsman). Available at: <http://www.ombudsman.qld.gov.au/PublicationsandReports/AnnualReport/AnnualReport200809/tabid/374/Default.aspx> (accessed 14 April 2010).
QO (2009a), *Tips and Traps for Regulators*, 2nd edition, October 2009 (Brisbane: Queensland Ombudsman).
Ranjan, Jha, R. (1990), *Lokayukta: The Indian Ombudsman* (Varanasi: Rishi Publications).
Rautio, I. (2002), 'The Ombudsman's Work in Safeguarding Fundamental Economic, Social and Cultural Rights in Finland' (speech), Deputy Parliamentary Ombudsman, Finland, 18 April 2002. Available at: <http://www.oikeusasiamies.fi/Resource.phx/eoa/english/publications/speeches.htx> (accessed 22 March 2010).
Rawlings, R. (1990), 'The MP's Complaints Service', *Modern Law Review* 53:1, 22-42 (part 1); 53:2, 149-69 (part 2).
Rawls, J. (1999), *A Theory of Justice*, revised edition (Oxford: Oxford University Press).
Regulatory Reform Committee (2007), *Proposal for the Regulatory Reform (Collaboration etc between Ombudsmen) Order 2007*, HC 383, session 2006–07 (London: The Stationery Office).
Reif, L.C. (2004), *The Ombudsman, Good Governance and the International Human Rights System* (Leiden: Martinus Nijhoff).
Richardson, G. (2004), 'Impact Studies in the UK', in Hertogh and Halliday (eds), pp. 103-28.
Robbennolt, J.K. (2006), 'Apologies and Settlement Levers', *Journal of Empirical Legal Studies* 3:2, 333-73.
Roberts, S. and Palmer, M. (2005), *Dispute Processes: ADR and the Primary Forms of Decision-Making* (Cambridge: Cambridge University Press).
Rowat, D.C. (1967), 'Recent Developments in Ombudsmanship: A Review Article', *Canadian Public Administration* 10:1, 35-46.
Rowat, D.C. (1985), *The Ombudsman Plan: The Worldwide Spread of an Idea*, 2nd edition (Lanham, MD: University Press of America).
Rowat, D.C. (2007), 'The American Distortion of the Ombudsman Concept and its Influence on Canada', *Canadian Administration* 50:1, 42-52.
Rowat, D.C. (ed.) (1965), *The Ombudsman: Citizen's Defender* (London: George Allen and Unwin).

Sainsbury, R. (2008), 'Administrative Justice, Discretion and the "Welfare to Work" Project', *Journal of Social Welfare and Family Law* 30:4, 323-38.

Sampford, C.J., Smith, R. and Brown, A.J. (2005), 'From Greek Temple to Bird's Nest: Towards a Theory of Coherence and Mutual Accountability for National Integrity Systems', *Australian Journal of Public Administration* 64:2, 96-108.

Sander, F. and Goldberg, S. (1994), 'Fitting the Forum to the Fuss: A User Friendly Guide to Selecting ADR Procedure', *Negotiation Journal* 10:1, 49-68.

SAO (2002), *Annual Report 2002-2003*, Southern Australian Ombudsman (Adelaide: State Ombudsman).

SAO (2009), *Annual Report 2008-2009*, Southern Australian Ombudsman (Adelaide: State Ombudsman).

Schedler, A., Diamond, L. and Platner, M.F. (eds) (1999), *The Self-Restraining State: Power and Accountability in New Democracies* (Boulder, CO: Lynne Rienner Publishers).

Scott, C. (2000), 'Accountability in the Regulatory State', *Journal of Law and Society* 27:1, 38-60.

Select Committee on PCA (1968), *Second Report of the Select Committee for the Parliamentary Commissioner for Administration*, HC 350, session 1967-68 (London: The Stationery Office).

Select Committee on PCA (1986), *Second Report of the Select Committee for the Parliamentary Commissioner for Administration*, HC 312, session 1985-86, 25 March 1986 (London: HMSO).

Select Committee on PCA (1993), 'The Powers, Work and Jurisdiction of the Ombudsman', Parliamentary Commissioner for Administration, HC 33, session 1993-94 (London: The Stationery Office).

Select Committee on the Constitution (2004), *The Regulatory State: Ensuring Its Accountability*, HL 68-I, session 2003-04 (London: The Stationery Office).

Seneviratne, M. (2000), '"Joining up" the Ombudsmen: The Review of the Public Sector Ombudsmen in England', *Public Law* Wnt, 582-91.

Seneviratne, M. (2002), *Ombudsmen: Public Services and Administrative Justice* (London: Butterworths).

Shergold, P. (2007), '"At Least Every Three Decades": Acknowledging the Beneficial Role of the Commonwealth Ombudsman' (seminar notes), Dr Peter Shergold, Secretary, Department of the Prime Minister and Cabinet, 30th Anniversary of the Commonwealth Ombudsman, Canberra, 8 August 2007. Available at: <http://www.ombudsman.gov.au/docs/30th-anniversary-seminar/seminar_notes_Peter_Shergold.pdf> (accessed 23 May 2010).

Sinclair, D. (2008), *Report to Ministers*, Fit For Purpose Complaints System Action Group, Douglas Sinclair (chair) review, July 2008. Available at: <http://www.scotland.gov.uk/Topics/Government/PublicServiceReform/IndependentReviewofReg/ActionGroups/ReporttoMinisters> (accessed 19 March 2010).

Skinner, S. and Hyman, C. (2006), 'The Ombudsman Offices in Denmark and British Columbia, Canada: A Comparative Study', *International Ombudsman Yearbook*, vol. 10 (The Hague: Kluwer Law International).

Snell, R. (2000), 'Towards an Understanding of a Constitutional Misfit: Four Snapshots of the Ombudsman Enigma', in Finn (ed.), pp. 188-205.

Snell, R. (2007), 'Australian Ombudsman: A Continual Work in Progress', in Groves and Lee (eds), pp. 100-115.

Speaker's Committee (2008), 'Appointment of the Chairman of the Electoral Commission', HC 961, session 2007-08 (London: The Stationery Office).

Spigelman, J.J. (2004), 'The Integrity Branch of Government', *Australian Law Journal* 78:11, 724-37.

Spigelman, J.J. (2005), 'Judicial Review and the Integrity Branch of Government' (speech), Chief Justice of New South Wales, World Jurist Association Congress, Shanghai, 8 September 2005. Available at: <http://www.lawlink.nsw.gov.au/lawlink/supreme_court/ll_sc.nsf/pages/SCO_spigelman080905> (accessed 26 February 2010).

SPSO (2005), *Annual Report 2004-05* (Edinburgh: Scottish Public Services Ombudsman).

SPSO (2005a), *Evidence to the Scottish Parliament Justice 1 Committee on the Scottish Human Rights Commissioner Bill*, Professor Alice Brown, Scottish Public Services Ombudsman, SP OR J1 21 December 2005, cols 2521-36.

SPSO (2006), *SPSO Guidance on Apology*, SPSO Advice leaflet 2 (Edinburgh: Scottish Public Services Ombudsman).

SPSO (2007), *Annual Report 2006-07* (Edinburgh: Scottish Public Services Ombudsman).

SPSO (2007a), *Better Complaints Handling: A Response to the Crerar Report*, 18 December 2007 (Edinburgh: Scottish Public Services Ombudsman).

SPSO (2007b), 'Research into Complaints that Come to the SPSO Too Early i.e. Before the Complaints Process of the Body Concerned has been Completed ("Premature" Complaints)', March 2007 (Edinburgh: Scottish Public Services Ombudsman).

SPSO (2008), *Annual Report 2007-08* (Edinburgh: Scottish Public Services Ombudsman).

SPSO (2009), *Annual Report 2008-09* (Edinburgh: Scottish Public Services Ombudsman).

SPSO (2009a), 'An "Other" Report by the Scottish Public Services Ombudsman about a Report on the Handling of a Complaint (200502514) by the SPSO', Jerry White's report and Jim Martin's response. Available at: <http://www.spso.org.uk/webfm_send/2351> (accessed 25 April 2010).

SPSO (2009b), *Unacceptable Actions Policy*, revised March 2009 (Edinburgh: Scottish Public Services Ombudsman).

SSO (2009), *Standing Orders and Other Orders of the Senate*, June 2009 (Canberra: Commonwealth of Australia).

Straw, J. (2009), 'Constitutional Change and the Future of Parliamentary Democracy', The Right Honourable Jack Straw MP, Lord Chancellor and Secretary of State for Justice, Magna Carta Institute Lecture, Brunel University, 23 November 2009. Available at: <http://www.brunel.ac.uk/about/acad/magnacarta/activitiesandevents> (accessed 27 February 2010), or <http://www.justice.gov.uk/news/speech241109a.htm> (accessed 4 June 2010).

Stuhmcke, A.G. (2006), 'Evaluating Ombudsman: A Case Study in Developing a Quantitative Methodology to Measure the Performance of the Ombudsman', *The International Ombudsman Yearbook*, vol. 10, 23-82.

Stuhmcke, A.G. (2008), 'Changing Relations Between Government and Citizen: Administrative Law and the Work of the Australian Commonwealth Ombudsman', *Australian Journal of Public Administration* 67:3, 321-39.

Stuhmcke, A.G. (2008a), 'Ombudsmen and Integrity Review', in Pearson, Harlow and Taggart (eds), pp. 349-76.

Sunkin, M., Calvo, K., Platt, L. and Landman, T. (2007), 'Mapping the Impact of Judicial Review on the Quality of Local Authority Services in England and Wales', *Public Law* Aut, 545-67.

Supported Bodies Committee (2009), *Review of Scottish Parliamentary Corporate Body*, Supported Bodies Committee, 1st Report, The New Scottish Parliament Building (SPP 266), 21 May 2009.

Thomas, A. (2008), 'Parliamentary Officers in Wales: Evolving Roles', in Gay and Winetrobe (eds), pp. 47-57.

Thompson, B. (1999), 'Towards the Millennium: Towards Integration?', in Harris and Partington (eds), pp. 463-81.

Thompson, B. (2001), 'Integrated Ombudsmanry: Joined-up to a Point', *Modern Law Review* 64:3, 439-58.

Thompson, B. (2010), 'Current Developments in the UK: System Building – From Tribunals to Administrative Justice', in Adler (ed.), pp. 483-515.

Thompson, B., Buck, T. and Kirkham, R. (2008), *Public Services Ombudsmen and Administrative Justice: Models, Roles, Methods and Relationships*: Full Research Report, ESRC End of Award Report, RES-000-22-2133 (Swindon: ESRC).

Thomson, M., Ellis, R. Wildavsky, A. and Wildavsky, M. (1990), *Cultural Theory* (Boulder, CO: Westview Press Inc.).

Titmuss, R.M. (1971), 'Welfare "Rights", Law and Discretion', *Political Quarterly* 42:1, 113-32.

TO (2007), *Ombudsman Tasmania: Annual Report 2006-07* (Hobart: Office of the Tasmanian Ombudsman).

TO (2008), *Ombudsman Tasmania: Annual Report 2007-08* (Hobart: Office of the Tasmanian Ombudsman).

TO (2009), *Ombudsman Tasmania: Annual Report 2008-09* (Hobart: Office of the Tasmanian Ombudsman).

Tollenar, A. and de Ridder, K. (2010), 'Administrative Justice from a Continental European Perspective', in Adler (ed.), pp. 301-20.

TSol (2006), *Judge Over Your Shoulder*, 4th edition, January 2006 (London: Treasury Solicitors Department).

Turpin, C. and Tomkins, A. (2007), *British Government and the Constitution*, 6th edition (Cambridge: Cambridge University Press).

UK Border Agency (2009), *Immigration Appeals – Response to Consultation: Fair Decisions; Faster Justice* (London: UK Border Agency/Tribunals Service).

Van Roosbroek, S. and Van de Walle, S. (2008), 'The Relationship Between Ombudsman, Government, and Citizens: A Survey Analysis', *Negotiation Journal* 24:3, 287-302.

Varney, D. (2006), *Service Transformation: A Better Service for Citizens and Businesses, a Better Deal for the Taxpayer*, HM Treasury, December 2006 (London: The Stationery Office).

Varuhas, J. (2009), 'Governmental Rejections of Ombudsman Findings: What Role for the Courts?' *Modern Law Review* 72:1, 102-15.

Verkuil, P. (1975), 'The Ombudsman and the Limits of the Adversary System', *Columbia Law Review* 75:4, 845-61.

Vibert, F (2007), *The Rise of the Unelected: Democracy and the New Separation of Powers* (Cambridge: Cambridge University Press).

Vile, M.J.C. (1967), *Constitutionalism and the Separation of Powers* (Oxford: Oxford University Press).

Vines, P. (2008), 'Apologies and Civil Liability in the UK: A View from Elsewhere', *Edinburgh Law Review* 12:2, 200-230.

VO (2009), 'Formal Investigations and Section 14 of the Ombudsman Act', *Fact sheet 13* (Melbourne: Victorian Ombudsman).

VO (2010), *Ombudsman's Recommendations: Report on their Implementation*, Victorian Ombudsman, P.P. No. 279, session 2006-10, February 2010 (Melbourne: Victorian Ombudsman).

Wade, H.W.R. and Forsyth, C.F. (2009), *Administrative Law*, 10th edition (Oxford: Oxford University Press).

Waldron, J. (2006), 'The Core of the Case Against Judicial Review', *Yale Law Journal* 115:6, 1346-406.

Waldron, J. (2008), 'The Concept and the Rule of Law', *Georgia Law Review* 43:1, 1-62.

Wales Audit Office (2009), *Services for Children and Young People with Emotional and Mental Health Needs* (Cardiff: Auditor General for Wales).

Wallace, H. and Mulcahy, L. (1999), 'Cause for Complaint: An Evaluation of the Effectiveness of the NHS Complaints Procedure', September 1999 (London: Public Law Project).

WAO (2005), *Annual Report 2004-05* (Perth: Western Australian Ombudsman).

WAO (2008), *Annual Report 2007-08* (Perth: Western Australian Ombudsman).

WAO (2009), *Annual Report 2008-09* (Perth: Western Australian Ombudsman).

Watkins, D.J. (2006), *Report to the Ministry of Defence on Investigation into Civilian Eligibility Criteria for Ex Gratia Payments to Former Far East*

Prisoners of War, 7 July 2006. Formerly available on PHSO website (accessed 10 March 2010). A copy is now available on request from the authors.

White, C. (1994), 'Enforcing the Decisions of the Ombudsmen: The Northern Ireland Local Government Ombudsman's Experience', *Northern Ireland Law Quarterly* 45, 395-402.

White, J. (2005), 'Special Reports: A New Way of Getting the Message Across', *The Ombudsman*: *Newsletter of the British and Irish Ombudsman Association*, issue 25, January 2005, p. 14. Available at: <http://www.bioa.org.uk/theombudsman/25.pdf> (accessed 4 June 2010).

White, J. (2007), 'Social Welfare and Family Law Issues and the Local Government Ombudsman for England', *Journal of Social Welfare and Family Law* 29:1, 77-86.

Whyatt, J. (1961), *The Citizen and the Administration: The Redress of Grievances*. A Report by Justice, Sir J. Whyatt (chair) (London: Stevens).

Widdicombe, D. (1986), *Report of the Committee on the Conduct of Local Authority Business*, Cmnd 9797 (London: HMSO).

Winetrobe, B.K. (2008), 'Scotland's Parliamentary Commissioners: An Unplanned Experiment', in Gay and Winetrobe (eds), pp. 33-45.

Winetrobe, B.K. (2008a), 'Conclusion – Parliamentary Watchdogs: Time for Decision', in Gay and Winetrobe (eds), pp. 115-21.

WPC (2010), *Decision Making and Appeals in the Benefits System*, HC 313 (incorporating HC 1030-i and ii, session 2008-09), session 2009-10, Work and Pensions Select Committee (London: The Stationery Office).

WPC (2010a), *Decision Making and Appeals in the Benefits System: Government Response*, HC 533, session 2009-10, Work and Pensions Select Committee (London: The Stationery Office).

Index